LETTERS OF
SYLVIA TOWNSEND WARNER

LETTERS

SYLVIA
TOWNSEND WARNER

Edited by
WILLIAM MAXWELL

1982
CHATTO & WINDUS
LONDON

Published by
Chatto & Windus Ltd
40 William IV Street
London WC2N 4DF

*

Clarke, Irwin and Co Ltd
Toronto

British Library Cataloguing
in Publication Data

Warner, Sylvia Townsend
Letters of Sylvia Townsend Warner
1. Warner, Sylvia Townsend—Biography
I. Title   II. Maxwell, William
828'.91209   PR6045.A812
ISBN 0-7011-2603-5

Printed by
Clark Constable Ltd
Edinburgh

CONTENTS

frontispiece   Sylvia Townsend Warner
(reproduced by permission of the Dorset
Natural History and Archaeological Society,
the Dorset County Museum, Dorchester.)

Introduction   *page* vii

A Note on the Editing   xviii

Letters   I

Index   307

INTRODUCTION

If story-telling had not appealed to her more, Sylvia Townsend Warner might have been a formidable historian. She had a secure sense of what it was like to live in other times than her own. Chaucer's England, France during the Revolution of 1848, 17th-century Spain, Polynesia during the reign of Queen Victoria. She also knew—and not merely from her reading—what it was like outside the comfortable and cultivated social class she was born into. She had a connoisseur's eye for the bogus, and a hatred of the assumptions of privilege. Her heart was with the hunted, always. An American woman who was being shown around her garden, unfamiliar with *Bellis perennis*, asked if it hurt English daisies if you walked on them, and her reply was 'It doesn't do anything good to be stepped on.' Along with an extraordinary fancy she had a deep understanding of human behaviour, so that nothing, no feeling, seemed to lie beyond the reach of her imagination. Her finest short story is about a love affair between a brother and sister. She considered the innocent and the guilty with the same judicial and ironic detachment. Her literary style is rather formal but not Mandarin. She had the true novelist's awareness of the wheel (the image is hers) turning and turning in 'the bright implacable river' of life.

Among her seven novels, I have a particular fondness for *Mr Fortune's Maggot, Summer Will Show, After the Death of Don Juan, The Corner That Held Them,* and *The Flint Anchor.* Though various accidents and impressions contributed to their conception, the effect in every case is of an inevitability that makes assessment seem pointless; there is nothing like them nor, I think, ever will be. She also published eight collections of short fiction and four volumes of poetry. The early poems are compact and narrative, showing an influence of Crabbe and Thomas Hardy, the later ones abstract and philosophical. At the age of seventy she was prevailed upon to do a life of T. H. White. The result stands with the few perfect biographies. In her eighties she had a sudden late flowering and wrote some twenty stories about elfin kingdoms and their heartless inhabitants — stories that are of great beauty and that have such an appearance of authenticity that they suggest, like William Blake's account of a fairy funeral procession, a first-hand knowledge.

In the midst of an active life Miss Townsend Warner managed to keep a private journal, as yet untranscribed, that runs through forty notebooks. And she wrote letters, thousands of them. The letters from the first half of her life are written, more often than not, on a typewriter. After that they were usually by hand, I think because it was late at night when she sat down to them and Valentine Ackland, the friend she lived with, was often unwell and she did not want to disturb her. At the beginning of the Second World War she wrote: 'If I had known we would be left so long in Norfolk I would not have left my typewriter behind. My handwriting looks as elegant as a vine, but no one can read it; and the thought of being a lost hieroglyphic in one's own lifetime deters one from writing letters.' Her handwriting is not really all that difficult, and nothing deterred her from writing letters for very long. It was not unusual for her to write two or three a day.

The personal correspondence of writers feeds on left-over energy. There is also the element of lavishness, of enjoying the fact that they are throwing away one of their better efforts, for the chances of any given letter's surviving are fifty-fifty, at most. And there is the element of confidence—of the relaxed backhand stroke that can place the ball anywhere in the court that it pleases the writer to have it go. No critic is looking over his shoulder; the writer's reputation is not at stake — not that Sylvia Townsend Warner was much concerned with either. But consider this: 'We were in Sherborne this afternoon, it was raining, and in one of the half-holiday classrooms a boy was practising the trumpet. Other more respectable boys were outside, holding pads and cricketing boots and looking at the sky and waiting for it to clear. Not so he. He was *not* playing cricket, he was enjoying both sacred and profane love, the virtue of practising his trumpet, the pleasure and rapture of playing it. Every note said so. Such flourishes! Such offended blackbird's squawks.'[1] And this: 'I hope you have had the same moonlight nights there have been here: the downs like sleeping deities and a moonlit badger feeding on the lawn.'[2] And this: 'I wish you could see the two cats, drowsing side by side in a Victorian nursing chair, their paws, their ears, their tails complementally adjusted, their blue eyes blinking open on a single thought of when I shall remember it's their suppertime. They might have been composed by Bach for two flutes.'[3] Though they are characteristic of the way her mind worked, sometimes her comparisons are so unexpected that I think even she herself must have been a little surprised by them.

Mr Fortune, the missionary hero of her second novel, who went to the South Sea island of Fanua armed with tinned meats, soup-squares, a chest of tea, soap, a toolbox, a second-hand harmonium, an oil lamp, and a sewing machine to make clothes for his converts, found himself at the end of the first year with only one disciple, and by the end of the following year had lost his own faith. As he is on the point of leaving this paradise he remarks to himself sadly, 'One does not admire things enough: and worst of

1. Letter to Alyse Gregory, 30:vi:1953.
2. Letter to Joy Finzi, 24:ix:1975.
3. Letter to the editor, 6:i:1965.

all one allows whole days to slip by without once pausing to see an object, any object, exactly as it is.' It is possibly the voice of his creator speaking through him, but in its context it is a very sad observation.

Her letters written when she was away from home pick up the place where she is bodily and send it through the mail: 'Everything falls into our laps like ripe plums. We managed to arrive at San Lorenzo fuori le Mura at the same moment as a funeral—with such a hearse, gold angels all over its roof and sitting on either side of the coachman in a glistening black cocked hat and black cloak, and a fat priest in his vestments came out of the first coach like an overgrown dahlia, and roared his way through the service with a speed only to be matched by the speed of the organist, who kept on tripping him over with the first chord of the responses, like a rugby tackle. After that a sexton, equally brisk and efficient, tossed us and two stout travellers from Southern Italy into the confessio and left us to contemplate de Gasperi's coffin. After this riveting introduction we all went for an affable walk in the Campo Verano, where the simpler Southern gentleman was absolutely spellbound by the verisimilitude of a marble mattress (with a dead lady on it), and kept on poking his finger into its dimples with sighs of admiration. I thought the lady very fine, too, especially the lace on her nightgown; but he had eyes only for the mattress.'[1] The moonlit badger feeding on the lawn, the traveller from Southern Italy serve no larger plan or purpose. The boy with the trumpet exists only for that moment. He, in fact, *is* that moment. The experience rises from the page, unrevised, unimprovable. It resembles the play of fountains. Even when she is giving rein to a fancy, the image is exact, the scene recognizable: 'There is a stretch of wooded round-shouldered hills near Leintwardine which seems Arthurian, it is so remote, so solitary, so *forgetful*. You know those landscapes that have forgotten centuries of history and now listen rather inattentively to what the woodpeckers have to say?'[2]

The reader who settles down to a volume of letters is nearly always motivated by curiosity, of a kind that is most agreeably satisfied if one arrives at a more intimate knowledge of the letter-writer as one does with a close friend—by bits and pieces, out of chronological order, as the spirit moves. The reader ought to know a little, however. Sylvia Townsend Warner was born on 6 December 1893, at Harrow-on-the-Hill. Her father, George Townsend Warner, was a Harrow House Master. Her mother, Nora Hudleston, as a child lived in India. According to some notes that were taken down from Miss Townsend Warner's dictation in 1966, her mother fell into labour at the sound of a knell—a Harrow governor had just died—and she was born with a caul, which the midwife claimed and probably sold to a sailor as a protection against death by drowning. The ghost

1. To the editor, 12:x:1955.
2. Letter to the editor, 11:iv:1955.

of her maternal grandmother visited her cradle. Who saw this apparition the notes do not say. She herself as a grown woman not only believed in ghosts but (in a letter that has managed to make itself invisible to me) described how she saw them, on two different occasions — the daughter of the house, who had died a year or two before her visit, and an old man who had taken his own life.

One of her earliest memories was of a sudden storm in June. Hailstones shattered the window in her nursery, glass fell across the tea table, and her father rushed in with an eiderdown and wrapped her in it and carried her to safety.

She grew up in two societies, School and Town. Her father lived by the school rhythm—up by bell at 6.45. On hot summer evenings the sound from the cricket fields of the bat striking the ball, in winter the 'melancholy moo-ing' of the crowd watching a football match. She was an only child.

Her mother taught her to read, partly from the Bible. When she was about seven she was sent to kindergarten. Without any malicious intentions she mimicked the mistresses and disrupted discipline and her parents were asked to remove her from the school. Foreseeing that this would happen again and again, her father decided that she should be educated at home. Her mother gave her lessons for two hours every morning in her workroom at the top of the house. At the bottom of the house there was another room that survives in *A Spirit Rises*. The framework of this story is a conversation, at a party, between the middle-aged daughter of a dead schoolmaster and one of his favourite pupils. 'She saw once again the long room, running the whole width of the house. At one end was the fireplace, with St Jerome above it, his bald, studious head eternally bent, his small lion for ever waiting for a word of recognition. At the other end of the room was the carpenter's bench, with its array of tools, and near by it the rocking horse. The rocking horse was ten hands high and a dapple grey, with tail and flowing mane of silvery horse-hair. The saddle and harness, scuffed with usage, were of crimson leather, and it was mounted on rockers, painted green . . . The room was a half basement . . . dusky, shabby, smelling of books, wood shavings, tobacco, and sometimes glue. Its windows looked out on a steeply rising bank where ferns and irises grew and autumn scattered fallen leaves from a Virginia creeper. The bookshelves lining the walls gave it an additional sombreness, and as there were heaps of books on the floor . . . one had to pick one's steps . . . She had no consciousness of those pupils arriving to supplant her. Perhaps they had not even begun to arrive, for at that time her father was a young man, a junior master at the foot of the ladder. Certainly at that time he had more leisure. The sounds of carpentering ascended through the house; he fitted new limbs to her wooden dolls and showed her how to bore holes with a gimlet. He strolled into the garden, snuffing the sweetbriar or hunting for slugs among the auriculas; he was chief mourner at many tad-pole funerals. When her mother was out for the afternoon, he would fetch her down to have tea with him — in summer under the hawthorn where you could hear people walking and talking in the road behind the tall wooden paling, in winter below St Jerome, where the fire and the reading lamp changed the rest of the room into a cave. After tea, she would stay on till her bedtime, pulling out from the lower shelves books she couldn't read and methodically replacing them while he wrote at his desk, a cat dripping from his knee, or sat on the dapple-grey horse, reading and gently rocking.'

When she was eight she went with her parents to Ireland to stay with her grandmother's younger sister, who was married to Ponsonby Moore, later Earl of Drogheda. Her great-aunt drank water from a jewelled chalice and was a friend of Hugh Lane and Lady Gregory. The house, Moore Abbey in County Kildare, had a splendid avenue of yews, a wonderful Georgian doll's house, and a sedan chair that the child spent hours sitting in. It also had a notorious poltergeist that on occasion made such an uproar no one in the place could sleep. 'It was eventually let,'—I am quoting from the notes—'or sold, to Count John McCormack, the singer, who had it exorcised—but for all that it was burnt to the ground.'

Like Virginia Woolf, she had the run of her father's library; she found and read half-way through *Vanity Fair* before she was ten.[1] Also Mackay's *Popular Delusions*. And she remembered sitting on the stairs repeating the spells for raising the devil, from the chapter on witchcraft, to her black cat and 'feeling a black hope that they would work'.

The nursemaids of her childhood were succeeded by a French governess, whom she did not like very much, and her father taught her history informally on holidays in Cornwall or on the Continent. He was an inspiring teacher, and in time, like the woman in the story, she was all too aware of 'those special pupils who came thronging between her and her birthright, whose voices rose and fell behind the study door, who learned, who profited, who demanded, who endeared themselves by their demands, who were arrayed for the ball while she, her father's Cinderella, went barefoot like the cobbler's child in the adage.'

She came of age thinking she was committed to music, and would have gone to Vienna to study composing with Arnold Schönberg if the outbreak of the First World War had not prevented it. Instead she went to work in a munitions factory. Her first published writing was an article about this experience.

Her father died in 1916 at the age of fifty-one. Her mother was an immensely capable, witty, autocratic woman and not easy to live with. Both were strongminded. Rather than stay in Devonshire and quarrel with her mother she went to live in London, on an extremely small allowance.

Through her friendship with the music master at Harrow, Dr Percy Buck (knighted in 1936), she was drawn into the field of musicology. In a

1. It was the book she was reading at the time of her death.

letter that was intended to be used as source material for a publisher's blurb, she wrote: 'For the last six years I have been romantically engaged in tracing scoring and collating Masses, Motets and so on by the Henrician and Elizabethan composers, which only exist in contemporary Mss part-books. It is the rediscovery of a lost epoch: for in the XVI cent. England was more celebrated for its music than even for literature or piracy, and it (the music) was completely forgotten. Names of composers, if required: John Taverner, Thomas Tallis, William Byrd, Orlando Gibbons.'[1] In a letter written fifty years later she recalled this experience. 'The discrepancies between the earlier (Elfin) stories and those which I wrote later are like nothing but *The Gospels*, or Taverner's *Missa Salve Intemerata* which bore four conscientious scholarly Tudor Church Music Editors[2] into regular nervous breakdowns once a week. There we sat round a table, saying But if; or with a gleam of hope, But why not? And the tugs on the river hooted, clearer & clearer, as the traffic quieted, till the Almoner's house in the Charterhouse (where we sat) became almost as hushed as when it was part of the real Charterhouse, in the clayey Moorish fields.'[3] The fruit of their combined labours, *Tudor Church Music*,[4] is a monumental effort of English musical scholarship that ranks with the *Paléographie Musicale* and the *Bach-Gesellschaft*.

She was as steeped in poetry as she was in music. In 1953 she wrote to an American acquaintance, 'Do you remember the quack doctor in Crabbe, who treated the young man for syphilis, and said so consolingly

> "Just take the boluses from time to time,
> And hold but moderate intercourse with crime."

Crabbe is a poet I delight in. No one has such a repertory of aunts, no one has a better control of humdrum, nor a bleaker gaunter way of ascending to his high spots. Long ago, when I was first living in London, poor, hungry and sensual, I walked out on a late summer morning to buy a loaf at the breadshop, and paused twice on the way back, first to buy half a pound of those very small tomatoes that are clipped off the vines to encourage the growth of large tomatoes, and then to buy, from the sixpenny tray outside the second-hand bookshop, a battered volume of Crabbe's poems in an embossed Victorian binding. And I can still remember the intense happiness of that morning, reading more and more Crabbe, and eating more and more bread, and all the tomatoes—with everything that I should have been doing, and even the things I ought not to have done and which would have been my natural occupation, all forgotten and amnestied. I read him *as*

1. To Charles Prentice, 6:xi:1925.
2. Dr Buck, Dr E. H. Fellowes, STW, and the Reverend A. Ramsbotham.
3. To the editor, 25:i:1976.
4. Oxford University Press, for the Carnegie Trust, 10 vols. 1922-29.

though I were writing him; there is no comparable excitement to that. And never again have there been such tomatoes, or such heavenly dry bread.'[1]

Among her friends in London were a certain number of bright young men whom she had known as little boys at Harrow. One of them, the sculptor Stephen Tomlin, carried her off to David Garnett's literary bookshop at 19 Taviston Street and introduced them. In *The Familiar Faces* Garnett has left a vivid portrait of her as a young woman: 'Sylvia is dark, lean and eager with rather frizzy hair. She wears spectacles and her face is constantly lighting up with amusement and intelligence and the desire to interrupt what I am saying and to cap it with something much wittier of her own. I sometimes speak slowly, waiting for the right word to come to me and when I am talking to Sylvia it very rarely does come, for she cannot restrain herself from snatching my uncompleted sentence out of my mouth and giving it a much better ending. She quivers with eagerness as though I were really going to say something good and then dashes in and transforms my sentence and my meaning into a brilliance that I should have been the last person to have thought of. In her company I soon come to think I am witty, though vicariously witty, it is true.

'The first time that we met Sylvia spoke of the beauty of the Essex marshes and I suggested that we should visit them together on the following Sunday. It was a grey wintry morning and we spent most of it in the unwarmed carriage of a very slow train and later splashing through the mud while I listened, and Sylvia gave an extraordinary display of verbal fireworks. Ideas, epigrams and paradoxes raced through her mind and poured from her mouth as though she were delirious. Meanwhile we plodded under a grey sky across grey fields towards an invisible grey horizon. Finally we reached a bank of *zostera* and mud and the limits of the Thames estuary at high tide. Sylvia was right, the grey marshes had a melancholy eerie beauty that was all their own.' In the late afternoon, after a long day's tramp through the mud, they climbed half-frozen into another empty badly-lit railway carriage and were carried back to London. Too exhausted to talk, she was 'the quiet intimate companion who sat beside me in the cold train with her clothes and even her face spattered with mud from the Dengie Flats.'

She gave him one of her poems to read and he sent it on immediately to Charles Prentice at Chatto and Windus, who asked to see more, and published them. He then asked if she had ever thought of writing a novel and she showed him *Lolly Willowes*, which he also published, with considerable success.

Stephen Tomlin saw to it that she met Theodore and Violet Powys, whose acquaintance he had made on a walking trip in Dorset, and they became her friends as well. The Powyses lived in the village of East Chaldon,

1. To Mrs Hoskins, 13:i:1953.

about a mile from the sea between Lulworth and Weymouth. On her visits to them she kept hearing of a young woman in the village who lived alone and who exchanged books with Theodore. She had been married at twenty and the marriage had been annulled. She wore trousers, which were not commonly found on women at that period. Not in Dorset, anyway. And she wrote poetry. Sylvia Townsend Warner's first meeting with Valentine Ackland was not a success. She felt afterwards that she had seemed aggressively witty and over-talkative, and she noticed that the younger woman was avoiding her. A year or so later Valentine Ackland wrote to her, asking if she would like to borrow her cottage for the summer, an offer she was unable to accept, but word of it got round, and the farmer who owned the cottage, assuming it was being sublet and probably for a vast sum, turned his tenant out of it at a week's notice. Feeling responsible, Miss Townsend Warner bought another cottage, with the idea that Valentine Ackland would live there. Shyness prevented her from being altogether clear about her intention. In the course of making this rather cramped and neglected place habitable they uncovered a depth of feeling for each other that bound them together for the rest of their lives. They lived in one place and another and finally settled permanently in a house by the River Frome, a short walk from the village of Maiden Newton, in Dorset.

When they were separated for any reason they usually wrote at the beginning and end of every day, and these letters, love letters, largely through happenstance were preserved. After Valentine Ackland's death Miss Townsend Warner put them in the proper sequence and had them transcribed and wrote an introduction and connecting narratives, all with the idea that they should some day be published. She also put certain restrictions on their publication, which her executors are honouring. I have therefore not included any of them in this volume.

Profoundly affected by what was going on in Germany at the time and believing that there was a very real danger of the madness spreading to England, STW and Valentine Ackland concluded that the only adequate defence against fascism was communism. In 1935 they applied for membership in the Communist Party of Great Britain and were accepted. The letters of this period sometimes have the irritating tone of the newly converted. In at least two of the novels *Summer Will Show* (1936) and *After the Death of Don Juan* (1938) a political element is obvious. It doesn't take the form of propaganda; STW was never not a literary artist.

In the summer of 1939 the two women attended a writers' conference in New York City, and they came home in October to an England at war. It is, needless to say, a matter of chance which letters survive to fall into the hands of an editor, but I have been struck by the fact that the letters written after STW's return from America no longer have the same political fervour. Or indeed mention the Party at all. The fact that they were living deep in the country, with no petrol and restrictions on travel, does not seem, in itself, enough to account for this. On the other hand, during the 1940s STW was writing for Edgell Rickword's *Left Review* and *Our Time*, and for *Theatre Today* — all Party-oriented publications.

After Valentine Ackland's death, in going through her things, STW came upon and subsequently offered to the poet Arnold Rattenbury a motor-horn which they had used to take with them when they went to public demonstrations, to honk at policemen with.

An American friend, the poet Jean Starr Untermeyer, said again and again that she ought to submit something to *The New Yorker*.

At last, in order to prove that *The New Yorker* would not publish her— for she was somewhat irritated by this nagging—she did submit something, a hilarious piece called *My Mother Won the War*. The battleground in question was local, a Red Cross committee where two equally high-handed women could not agree as to whether the soldiers' pyjama trousers should have a button on them. It appeared in the issue of 30 May 1936. Over the next four decades *The New Yorker* published one hundred and forty-four stories by her, and nine poems. If this isn't a record it is close to it.

When Mrs E. B. White, her first editor, left New York to live in Maine, I inherited Miss Townsend Warner. I had been reading her with delight since I was in college. I met her for the first time when she came to *The New Yorker* office in the fall of 1939. She was dressed in black. Her voice had a slightly husky intimate quality. Her conversation was so enchanting it made my head swim. I did not want to let her out of my sight. Ever. The dimensions of the Second World War were not yet clear, but there wasn't much to be optimistic about, even so. The Embassy was encouraging British citizens who happened to be abroad at that moment to stay there, rather than return home and become another mouth to feed. I begged her to remain in the United States, where bombs were unlikely to fall and we could continue our conversation. I didn't persuade her, but the conversation did continue, in letters back and forth and on the margins of galley proofs. Viz: '. . . On galley seven I have substituted clattered for *flounced* for the noise that Rosalind made with the bucket. If you have a bucket handy, and some nice echoing floor, and snatch the bucket up and put it down again rather violently in much the same place that you took it from, that will be what I choose to call flouncing with a bucket; and anyone who has taken part in church decorations, especially at Easter when tempers are at their worst, will recognize the action.'

When the American novelist Anne Parrish died in 1956, Miss Townsend Warner wrote to the executors, asking that her letters be returned to her. I assume that they were but do not know it to be a fact. They were not found among her papers and it is quite likely that she asked for them in order to destroy them. I do not think it occurred to her that her correspondence might some day be collected and published until she had finished transcribing and editing the letters to and from Valentine Ackland. In a letter written after I had agreed to be her literary executor, she said, 'I will try to clear things away, or mark them for destruction. The people who were attached to me might, however, like a collected volume of my letters. I love reading Letters myself, and I can imagine enjoying my own.' I suspected that she wanted me to do this and was too delicate to say so. So I asked her, and she admitted that it was the case. She gave me a list of half a dozen correspondents, told me that it was important to select freely, and warned me against leaning over backward when it came to publishing her letters to me. There we left it.

In the pursuit of her correspondence I have now and then been blocked by chance, by the destruction of an old house during the Nazi bombing, or by the death of the person she was in the habit of writing to. For example, Robin Perry, of the Belfast *Telegraph*, about whom I have been able to learn nothing whatever except that he is no longer living. I have, even so, managed to get my hands on a considerable quantity. Some were in the Beinecke Library at Yale, others in the Library of Congress, the Berg Collection, and the Humanities Research Center in Austen, Texas. The preponderance were and still are in the hands of the people to whom they were written. They were very kind about trusting me with them. I have no doubt that a diligent search would unearth a great many more.

Her letters to people she saw frequently and was in very close touch with are, on the whole, less interesting (that is to say, they are like anyone's letters) than the letters to people who lived at a distance from her. Marchette and Joy Chute saw her in all over a period of about six days. Anne Parrish and Paul Nordoff not very many times. George Plank only once. Leonard Bacon she never met; only his daughter, who carried on where he left off. With all of these there was a flood of correspondence lasting for years and in most cases terminated only by their deaths.

The letters offer a running report on her life—on the weather, the annual arrival of gypsies, flowers blooming in the garden, Rembrandts at the National Gallery, *The Turn of the Screw* as an opera, a drinking old lady, Proust's shortcomings as a literary critic, the fountains of the Villa d'Este, the creatures of the river, often in flood, that flowed past her house, the pleasures of travel, politics, a dream of King Arthur and Merlin, remedies and recipes, Rupert Brooke at the Café Royal, the ingratitude and bad manners of the birds, a seance with the celebrated Screaming Skull, a Victorian merry-go-round signed and dated by the maker, a crèche animé in Provence, the physical benefits of singing, Goethe's Conversations with Eckermann, the mysterious being that walks overhead when she is downstairs and on the ground floor when she is upstairs, the Spanish Civil War, Blake's verbs, cold houses, thunderstorms, the Cuban Missile Crisis, swans, the parish magazine, divorce, what Edward Thomas was like, the inequity of the human condition, an impending guest, a bad fall, a sick animal, a perverse moorhen, and so on. To index the letters is pointless; everything is as interesting as everything else and it would be like indexing life itself. Better to think of her as she once described herself—Frau Noah leaning out of a window with a coffee cup in her hand admiring last night's flood and seeing everything exactly as it is.

A NOTE ON THE EDITING

The customary dating of STW's letters changed over the years; periods became colons, Arabic numerals sometimes replaced Roman. I have left it as she had it, grateful that she was so scrupulous about dating them. The undated letters are few and fairly easy to place. Once she and Valentine Ackland settled permanently at Frome Vauchurch there seemed no reason to print the address from which a letter was written unless she was away from home.

Titles of books, operas, plays, etc. are sometimes underlined in the letters and sometimes not. I have italicized them throughout for the sake of consistency. Words inserted by me to fill a gap of some kind are bracketed. Since she herself seldom used dots to indicate a pause or a shift of subject, I have used three dots, unbracketed, to indicate an omission of the beginning of a letter, of the end of a paragraph or of the beginning of the paragraph that follows. Where a whole paragraph or more has been omitted, I have used a space to indicate this. I have not used three dots to indicate that there is more than the last sentence; too many dots becomes an offence to the eye.

The letters have a characteristic form that I don't suppose she was aware of. They tend to begin with thanks for a gift or for a photograph clipped from a newspaper and sent to amuse her; or with a statement of what she has just been doing, or what the weather has been doing. Or they pick up where the letter she is answering left off. When she reached for a way to round off her letter it was usually something to do with her cats (those comedians) that served this purpose. It can be taken for granted that the beginning and close of the letter, which I have more often than not omitted to save space, are both affectionate.

This book is being published in two countries from the same plates and what is common knowledge in one isn't, sometimes, in the other. I apologize, therefore, for any footnotes that may strike the reader as egregious.

STW was under the impression that she was a good speller, and in fact she was, but she habitually spelled *t'other 'tother* and when in doubt did not always bother to reach for a dictionary or an atlas, or stop to put in accents of French words. With the reader's comfort in mind, I have corrected what is obviously unintended. I perhaps should not have. In writing for *The New Yorker* she accepted the in some respects rather quirky style of that magazine, and when she didn't like an editorial suggestion, instead of insisting on having the sentence the way she wrote it (as she might well have; no editorial change was ever forced upon her), she made some substitution that had nothing to do with the editor's suggestion and by some sleight-of-hand robbed it of any point.

'One thing,' she wrote to Carol Walton,[1] who was typing the manuscript of her life of T. H. White: 'When it comes to the USA edition . . . I shall be awkward . . . USA publishers have a habit of what they call "editing in accordance with American procedure". This means they rearrange one's paragraphs, alter one's punctuation, and generally bedevil the text. *I will not be edited* . . . They can spell colour, color if they will die otherwise; but no further . . . In other respects I will be tractable as a lamb. I promise this with a clear conscience, having been knocked head over heels by a vast pet lamb that came bounding down a Northumberland hillside at me: two tons of affectionate curiosity.'

I have tried not to bedevil the text.

ACKNOWLEDGEMENTS

I wish to thank, before all others, Janet Machen for the extraordinary lengths she went to in securing for me the complete correspondence with David Garnett.

My indebtedness to Graham C. Greene of Jonathan Cape Ltd. for photocopies of the entire correspondence concerning the T. H. White biography, to Norah Smallwood for more than fifty years of letters to and from Chatto & Windus, and to Marshall Best for giving me access to the files of The Viking Press, is very great indeed. Also to Donald Gallup of the Beinecke Library at Yale for a huge number of photocopies of letters to George Plank and for turning up, on his own, uncatalogued letters to Leonard Bacon, and to David E. Schoonover for permission to use them; to Ellen S. Dunlap of the Humanities Research Center, The University of Texas at Austin for special courtesies and for lending me photocopies, again very numerous, of letters to Nancy Cunard, Alyse Gregory, and others; to Dr Lola Szladits and Brian McInerney of the Berg Collection of the New York Public Library for material not ordinarily accessible; to Paul J. Heffron of the Library of Congress for letters to and from Ben Huebsch; to Rosemary Manning for searching out in the files of the Powys Society important letters to Alyse Gregory; to the University of Sussex Library for letters to Leonard Woolf, and to the University of Reading Library for letters to Helen Thomas.

I am grateful to the very many persons who have entrusted me with original letters or had photocopies made for me; to all those who have answered my letters of enquiry; and to those I have turned to for particular help and advice — most importantly, Joy and Marchette Chute, Steven Clark, Hugh Ford, Mavis Gallant, Leo Lerman, Julius Lipton, Hilary Machen, William Meredith, Sabina Nordoff, George D. Painter, Susanna Pinney, Martin R. Pollock, Arnold Rattenbury, Helen Stark, Francis Steegmuller, Charles Verrill, Charles Warner, and Ursula Vaughan Williams.

I do not know how to thank Celia Owens, whose editorial assistance and passionate interest were invaluable; or Elizabeth Cullinan, who transcribed more than two decades of longhand letters to me and would not accept any remuneration.

1921

Little Zeal.[2]
South Brent. Devon

. . . No words can describe the furry succulence of the chows; nor the ecstatic flat-headedness of their welcome to me. They wound round my knees like sea-weed, and kissed my hands with the tips of small cold bleue de plombage tongues. There are also for my delight a baker's dozen of coal-black ducks, arching their preened slick necks like serpents, and waddling about the garden like a Nonconformist congress all in dark grey galoshes. I have christened them all. Swedenborg, Mr Toplady, Joanna Southcott, Wesley and Whitfield, the Rev Chalmers, Frances Ridley Havorgal, Madame de Guyon, and Miss Maude Royden. But it is not the slightest use, because they are all so exactly alike that we can't tell t'other from which, not even Mr Cadwallader Jones, who begot them.

1. Woman of letters, author of, principally, several books on Victorian customs and manners; married to the composer and BBC conductor, Mark Lubbock.
2. Her mother's house.

1924

To David Garnett[1] *10:ix:1924*   *Idbury Manor. Kingham.*
                                          Oxfordshire

My dear David,

You must have thought me very ungrateful in not writing before to thank you for taking so much trouble about my poems. My time has been taken up with visitors. I will certainly send them to Ch and Windus—the poems: the visitors went this afternoon. Need I send them immediately? I should like to sleep a little longer on some that I brought down here. How shall I please you in return? I think I can do it rather prettily.

The visitors were my charwoman and her two little girls. When I had lit my wood fire these sat down on the rug and said: Now tell stories. It came into my head to put you to the test, so I told them the story of *Lady into Fox*. They sat listening like two owlets; and each evening they demanded that I should tell it again. On the last evening they had it almost by heart, and I suppose that, back in the Portobello Road, they will tell it to their friends. So it is quite probable that you will turn into folklore.

. . . If you have begun bargaining with your house, you will certainly get it . . . I am so glad that it is in Huntingdonshire . . . There is an extraordinary charm about that landscape of large fields and hedgerows dotted with clumsy elms, especially on some rather undistinguished evening when the sun has gone down without making a fuss about it. A cloudy sky goes best, one with a good deal of detail, as though it were a blurred reflection of the landscape. Large untilled skies, and gallivanting cumulus should be kept for chalk downs. And I always like any place where there are quantities of hares, small soggy copses, Dutch barns looking like Cannon Street Station, and a number of useless ponds.

Some time you can tell me if it is really like this. I have always imagined it so.

1. (1892-1981), C.B.E. Novelist, memoirist, editor, and at that time a partner in the Nonesuch Press and the Soho bookshop of Birrell and Garnett.

To Charles Prentice[1] 4:xi:1924   121 *Inverness Terrace.*
                                                     [London] W.2.

Dear Mr Prentice,

    Mr Garnett tells me that he has spoken to you about my poems, and that you have been kind enough to say that you would like to look at them. I am very grateful to you both.

    I should like to dispose you in their favour so I will tell you that Theodore Powys[2] thinks well of them.

To David Garnett [undated]   121 *Inverness Terrace* W.2.

. . . I went to see Mr Prentice.[3] It was rather painful to begin with. I arrived feeling very sick and highly-strung because a bus had leapt at me sideways and only missed me by about four and a half inches . . . I was shown into a small room and presently a stranger came in and looked at me without a word. I transferred a great many bus tickets from my right hand to my left and we shook hands and sat down. After a very long pause I said: Are you Mr Prentice? And he said: yes. And after another *long* pause we both began to speak at once. It was like a nightmare, or a religious ceremony. But he said such praising things about my poems that I soon felt quite at home with him. He said that they were a great surprise to him. Of course you had spoken very highly of them—my dear, you *have* done it handsomely— and that he had a great opinion of your judgement and all that, still—um— he himself didn't think it would be a real rabbit or words to that effect. And he said that it was unusual to find a woman writing so objectively. And that I had such variety (this amazed me). And that my carriage chaste with slender waist would leave a swan repining. In fact he said so many pleasant things that I can't help repeating them.

    Can't you get a wheelbarrow on credit, a squeaky one? You should always wear the same suit if you want the ducks to trust you. They can't bear black clothes or people in mackintoshes. My step-father has quantities and when they saw him in white flannels they fled into a thicket. You used to wear a snuff-coloured suit with checks and rather a tight waist. I should

1. Head of Chatto and Windus, and a master of typography. He retired in the late 1930s and at the beginning of the War he returned to help out and left again after six months. Like Proust's M. Swann, he had become entangled with a woman who was not in his style and whom he could not marry. He died in 1949.
2. T. F. Powys (1875-1953), novelist, brother of John Cowper Powys and Llewelyn Powys.
3. See Introduction, p. xiii.

think they would take kindly to that. I love hearing about Hilton Hall.[1]
If you ever feel you must boast about it to someone, remember me.

To David Garnett *28:xi:1924*   *121, Inverness Terrace*

. . . Theo is much excited about Hilton Hall, and asked if it is in the fens.
While I was there I read *Mockery Gap*,[2] which may come out in 1927. I
think it is the best thing he has done. There are an enormous number of
characters including an ape and the Dorset Archaeological Society. The
action is like the best twelve-part counterpoint, a counterpoint in which
each part had a separate fugal subject which it develops quite independently
of its share in the development of the whole. And the whole affair is as
abstract as music. It has no relation to life except to the life of Theo's mind.
The writing is very rapid, aloof and flippant, and entirely without transitions.
It has nothing to do with any book since 1500. It is like a gothic scene of
the last Judgement executed by a Chinese mind.

Chaldon[3] was looking very beautiful and resigned. The undercliff was
covered with Lords-and-Ladies, a devilish orange on the black shale. I
scrambled down and wished I hadn't, for it frightened me.

Mr Jones the clergyman recently told his congregation that *The Song of
Songs* was written by Solomon to his first wife. There is a new lych-gate at
Winfrith which is promised to last for three hundred years and appears to be
constructed of biscuit.

1. The handsome old house David Garnett had just bought, in the village of
   Hilton, seven miles from Huntington.
2. A novel by T. F. Powys.
3. The village in Dorset where T. F. Powys lived.

To Charles Prentice *25:ii:1925*   121 *Inverness Terrace*
                                          W.2.

Dear Mr Prentice,

Here is my story about a witch[1], that you were kind enough to say you would like to read. If you like it well enough to think it worth publishing I shall be extremely pleased. If you don't, I shan't be much surprised.

To David Garnett *14:iv:1925*   121 *Inverness Terrace*
      '*near Whiteleys*' if you like: personally I prefer '*far from Gamages.*' More refined. [*London*] *W*.2.

My dear David,

Your letter was a great disappointment to me. I made sure it was to say that you had a daughter. I am growing quite tired of looking in the *Times*. I'm sure she should have come by now. It is all very well to tell me that your ducks lay 8 eggs a day. I cannot take that as extenuating circumstances.

I am not (now) going to be cremated. I am going to be buried with as much solemnity and as little privacy as possible in Kensal Green. I went there the other day, all the blackbirds and thrushes were singing and there were the mausoleums like peers and peeresses opening Parliament, or Indian elephants and potentates at the Durbar, or the gateposts along Eton Avenue.— But nothing can convey how enormous, how ornate and how expensive they are. Angels, sphynxes, obelisks, soup-tureens, pilons, trogloditic dwellings, gothic thingumjigs, Aberdeen granite poured out like water, animated busts, mosaic texts, tessellated sentiments, central heating, magnificent lounges, palms in abundance, three hundred and seventy-nine bathrooms, Church of England service — Hallelujah! And all for nothing. And all to oneself. Not a single mourner. Not a dry eye to be seen anywhere. Nothing except the neighbouring gas-works, looking like more mausoleums.

You see how eloquent it makes me. I don't know what you might tell the American consumer about Theo. You might tell 'em that when he was a boy and lived at Montecute rectory he used to catch snakes, and loose them down the stairs when his sisters were coming up. Snakes *and* ladders, that ought to fetch a refined progressive pure-souled People, I should think.

Darling Theo! I can't think of anything else that isn't libellous. I have

1. *Lolly Willowes.*

5

been remembering him as I sit here, and it is as though he had come into the room with a cold face, as though the moonlight were still shining on it, behaving with a rather guilty politeness, and propping up his stick with immense caution.

'Well, Theo, did you have a nice walk, with nothing frightening?'

'Well my dear, I *did* hear a curious noise in the hedge. At first I said to myself it was nothing but a rat, but then I remembered *Who made that rat.*'

Theo is more afraid, more tunnelled and worked with fears than anyone else I know, even than myself. That is why he is always considering death. He turns to death with relief, for it is so certain, so reliable, so safe. It is the judgement of a child to compare him with Donne and Webster, as all those intellectual idiots do, for *they* could not keep away from the thought of death, it was like pressing the sore tooth to them, but with Theo it is the only tooth that will not fail him. His despair of the universe is an intellectual thing, he knows there is nothing good, nothing true, nothing kind, that until he is dead he is at the mercy of life, and that at any moment from behind some impassive mask we choose to call blessed, a blue sky, a primrose, a child, a nicely-fried egg, life, not death, will look out with its face of idiot despair, idiot cruelty.

To CHARLES PRENTICE *2:v:1925*   121 *Inverness Terrace W*.2

Dear Mr Prentice,

I hope you have not been thinking me rude. I have been in Dorset and only came back last night to find your kind present . . .

I have been staying with Theo. Chaldon Herring was out of its wits over the wedding of the post-mistress's son and the road-man's daughter, a large smooth creature like a bedroom ewer. Such a to-do as never was, the lane strewn with confetti and dead primroses, and a case of whisky, three casks of beer and forty pounds of butter consumed at the wedding feast!

I am longing to see my *Espalier*.[1] I have no suggestions to offer about where to send copies for review: David ought to do his best for it somewhere, alas! I have no other influential friends.

To DAVID GARNETT *16:vi:1925*   121, *Inverness Terrace.*
                                  [*London*] *W*.2.

My dear David,

I have been meaning for some time to write and thank you for your pretty flatteries. Indeed I am not likely to feel bored with your good opinions

1. Her first book of poems.

. . . So if you should happen to think of any more, pray do not hesitate to send them—or better still to say them. For I should love to see you again; and when I hear that you have been in London I take it rather ill that you have not been to see me.

I have been reading *Eckermann's Conversations with Goethe* with much delight. Do you know what the Chinese novel can be that he read and compared to Richardson? It has young ladies in it seated on cane chairs, which (Goethe says) calls up ideas of great elegance and lightness.

It must be very different to *Mrs Dalloway*. What do you think of that? While I read it I felt like Joseph resisting Potiphar's wife . . .

I met her the other day. She is so charming that I had the greatest pleasure in stifling my scruples and telling her how much I admired it.

Give my love to Ray.[1] She wrote me such a charming account of the new baby that I felt perfectly converted to his sex.

To DAVID GARNETT *6:x:1925*   121 *Inverness Terrace*

. . . I have just come back from Oxfordshire. Tangley Hall was looking as charming as ever. They have a fine flock of white Aylesbury ducks there, and the garden was full of golden-rod and smoky-looking Michaelmas daisy. About a mile from Tangley there is a deserted farm called The Warren. I came on it quite by accident for it lies in a little dell among woods, far from the road and the field-path to it is vanishing from disuse. I found a way in and walked over the house as much as I dared for the staircase is broken away and all the timber eaten with dry rot. The parlour windows are grown over with nettles and gooseberry run wild, and growing up through the broken stone floor is a flourishing elder-bush, singularly bright green from its indoor life. The doors and chimney-pieces are carved with names and dates, mostly 18th cent.

I was very pleased with my find, and when I had done with the polite part of the house I turned to the back-kitchens and wash-houses. These were even more dilapidated and darkened, and I was just thinking that I had had enough of them when I saw an archway leading into a sort of cellar with a barrel roof. I went in looking at the roof and nearly fell into a well. It was so dark and smooth and plumb with the floor that it looked like a slate. It then seemed to me that this deserted house I had been pitying so was uncommonly disappointed that I hadn't gone a step further into its trap. It had been waiting so long for something to happen; and a drowned lady would have been a pleasant secret to hint of to the woods on a winter's night.

1. His wife.

Afterwards I met a man who told me that the well was the finest and coldest spring in the district, and that three children had died of diphtheria at that farm in one week.

I wish you would come to see me. I am trying to write another story. The prologue is the best thing I have ever done, and the rest is like a dead codfish wrapped up in verbiage. I am blasted with discouragement, couldn't you come and flatter me a little?

Give my love to Ray. The woodcut of Tulip[1] is beautiful. I only wish there had been more.

I hope you are all well and happy.

To David Garnett *11:xi:1925*   121, *Inverness Terrace*
                                       [*London*] *W*.2.

Dearest David,

Your letter has given me a great deal of silent joy. It has given me the assurance I wanted, and if it comes from you I can believe it. Other people who have seen *Lolly* have told me that it was charming, that it was distinguished, and my mother said that it was almost as good as Galsworthy. And my heart sank lower and lower.

1. The African princess who is the melancholy heroine of *The Sailor's Return*.

To David Garnett *20:ii:1926*   121, *Inverness Terrace*
                                     [*London*] *W*.2.

My dear David,

I owe you such a pleasant afternoon that I must write and thank you for it. It was your good idea that a copy of Lolly should go to Miss Murray (Witch-cult in Western Europe).

She liked my witch though she was doubtful about my devil, and wrote to me a very pleasant letter to say so. Now I have just come back from lunching with her.

She is most fit and right; short and majestic, a Queen Victoria with the profile of Louis Quatorze and small fierce fat white hands. I wish I were in her coven, perhaps I shall be. Round her neck she wears a broad black velvet band probably for a good reason. She said things that would make the hairs of your head stand bolt upright.

To David Garnett *4:viii:1926*   *Little Zeal South Brent.*

I am also in need of your skill as a zoologist. In my earthquake I killed a parrot (the bough of a falling tree broke it: Victor said this was improbable and should have a footnote to say that it was subsequently ascertained that the parrot died a natural death; however it happened to the raven in Selbourne) and dislodged a hive of wild bees. But does one say hive for the wild bees, or is there a wilder word?

Indeed I will hold your hand, provided you will hold mine too. My missionary[2] is an impossible length, fatally sodomitic, alternately monotous and melodramatic, his only success is an aigre-doux quality which will infuriate any reader after the third page. I love him with a dreadful uneasy passion which in itself denotes him a cripple.

1. Victor Butler, only son of Sir Harcourt Butler, Governor of Burma. His lifelong friendship with STW began at Harrow.
2. The central character of her second novel, *Mr Fortune's Maggot.*

A note on *Mr Fortune's Maggot*, written in the mid-1960s, to the editor.

When I first went to live in London, in 1917, in a flat over a furrier's at 127 Queen's Road, Bayswater, I was poor and could not afford a lending library subscription. I had the British Museum by day but I wanted something to read in the evenings. Then I found the Westbourne Grove branch of the Paddington Public Library. It was a very snuffy establishment with a great many biographies of unimportant people and all the books had the same smell (I suppose it was some public disinfectant). One of the books I took out was a volume of letters by a woman missionary in Polynesia. I can't remember the title, or her name, but the book pleased me. It had only the minimum of religion, only elementary scenery and a mass of details of every-day life. The woman wrote out of her own heart—for instance, describing an earthquake she said that the ground trembled like the lid of a boiling kettle.

I suppose it was in 1918 or 1919 that I read it.

I had finished *Lolly Willowes*, and Chatto & Windus had taken it , and I was writing poetry and a few short stories when one early morning I woke up remembering an extremely vivid dream. A man stood alone on an ocean beach, wringing his hands in an intensity of despair; as I saw him in my dream I knew something about him. He was a missionary, he was middle-aged and a deprived character, his name was Hegarty, he was on an island where he had made only one convert and at the moment I saw him he had realised that the convert was no convert at all. I jumped out of bed and began to write this down and even as I wrote a great deal that I knew from the dream began to scatter; but the main facts and the man's loneliness, simplicity and despair and the look of the island all remained as actual as something I had really experienced.

I made a few notes of the development, discarded the name of Hegarty because it might lead me into a comic Irishman, and began to write. The opening, with hardly a word's alteration, is as I wrote it then. This must have been in winter, because I remember Duncan Grant coming to dinner, and we had the gas fire on and ate some kind of stewed game. The moment he had gone I went on writing; and the description of the island, especially its colouring, shows the influence of Duncan's painting, which at that date was particularly brilliant and free.

My remembrance of the book from the Public Library was so vivid and substantial that I never felt a need to consult other books. I could supplement the lady's earthquake by Bea Howe's childish recollection of the Valparaiso earthquake. This gave me the lamp beginning to swing; and the Howes' bulldog who spent the night killing the neighbour's ducks parented my pigs. The missionary lady gave me the lava in the crater flowing towards the south.

The definition of an umbrella arose from a conversation with Victor Butler, in which he said everything was definable in mathematical terms. How would you define an umbrella? I said. Next day I got a postcard beginning, 'An umbrella, Sylvia' etc.[1] Victor also supplied the practical bones of the tree-measuring episode. The parrot lived next door to the cottage at Wayford in Somerset I rented that summer. It sat in a tree and I grew very familiar with its voice and noticed how much quieter unconfined parrots sound.

There must have been some breaks between Duncan coming to dine and listening to the parrot but when I went back to London that autumn I wrote steadily, and with increasing anxiety: not because I had any doubt about the story but because I was so intensely conscious that the shape and balance of the narrative must be exactly right—or the whole thing would fall and break to smithereens and I could never pick it up again. I remember saying to Bea that I felt as if I were in an advanced pregnancy with a Venetian glass child. This was made the more alarming by the way in which things kept on working out right—like the business of Mr Fortune's watch, for instance. I was in a state of semi-hallucination during the last part of the book—writing in manuscript and taking wads of it to be typed at the Westbourne Secretarial College in Queen's Road.

I remember writing the last paragraph, and reading the conclusion and then impulsively writing the envoy, with a feeling of compunction, almost guilt, toward this guiltless man I had created and left in such a fix.

I took two copies, one for England and one for USA, to Chatto and Windus myself. I was afraid to trust them by post. It was a very foggy day and I was nearly run over. I left them with a feeling that my world was nicely and neatly over.

When the book was in proof I went to stay at Hilton Hall with the Garnetts. David took the proofs to read and shut himself up with them. When he came out, having read the book, he began to tell me that he thought it was good. His face swelled and reddened and we both realised that he was in tears.

1. 'An umbrella, Lueli, when in use resembles the — the shell that would be formed by rotating an arc of curve about its axis of symmetry, attached to a cylinder of small radius whose axis is the same as the axis of symmetry of the generating curve of the shell. When not in use it is properly an elongated cone, but it is more usually helicoidal in form.' *Mr Fortune's Maggot*, p. 183.

Little Zeal. South Brent.
Devon.

Dear Mr Huebsch,

I am so glad that you are pleased with *The Fairy*.[2] I have sent on your kind words to the authoress, who is disporting herself in Czecho-Slovakia.

But now I come before you with another plea: a plea so near my heart that I could almost wish that I had not been so lucky the first time, in case my luck should have run out.

Perhaps this feeling is the result of having been brought up on the *Moral Tales* of Miss Edgeworth . . . . "No, Henry," replied his Papa, looking sad. "I will not throw you a life-belt. You have already wished for a Hoop, a Butterfly net, and an Orange, and the indulgence of a Parent has bestowed them. So now, Rash Boy, farewell."

'Henry sank beneath the billows. And that was the end of
THE THREE WISHES.'

Though you may not think it from this opening, I am extremely and entirely serious in my hope that you will publish *Mr Weston's Good Wine*, by T. F. Powys.

Mr Weston is an elderly wine-merchant who with a young assistant called Michael visits a small Dorset village to sell his wine. The wine is the fulfilment of men's different desires; and the best and darkest wine is Death. For Mr Weston is really God. Only one man in the village is spiritually rich enough to purchase the deadly wine; he is the vicar, Mr Grobe. Mr Grobe's motherless daughter is pursued by the farmer's two sons, who believe in the *droit de seigneur*, and in very little else. But she escapes them because in her maiden mind she is determined to marry an angel (so are all young women when first they fall in love). At Mr Weston's bidding she goes to the village green, where, under an oak-tree that has sheltered less innocent loves, she finds Michael and recognizes him for her angel. The tree, old in wickedness, is struck by lightning, and Tamar is carried to heaven by her lover. As for the farmer's sons, they are hunted by the devil in the shape of a lion, whom Mr Weston unlooses from his van.

As you can see, the story contains elements that might be difficult to carry off in a novel, and Mr Knopf, who has previously been Mr Powys's American publisher, has refused to take this book, on the grounds that it is improper and blasphemous, and would render him liable to prosecution. But perhaps Mr Knopf is not a very spiritually-minded man, and has failed to observe that this is not a novel, but an allegory, like *The Pilgrim's Progress*. Moreover, Mr Knopf has not made a success of selling the previous

1. (1876-1964), American publisher. In 1925 he merged his house with the newly-formed Viking Press and continued as editor-in-chief.
2. Bea Howe's *A Fairy Leapt Upon My Knee*.

novels; and this may have prejudiced him unconsciously against this work. You will decide for yourself on this count (that is, if you consider publication, as I most sincerely hope you will do); but in my opinion a story containing such unusual incidents as the devil going about like a roaring lion, and a virgin carried to heaven by an angel is not very likely to be taken as a novel of real life, or judged by the standards of propriety which we apply to realistic fiction.

If you should think it would be as well to safeguard the character of the book by saying: 'An Allegory,' on the title-page, I feel sure that Mr Powys would have no objection. Or if you think my reputation as a spinster-like author would be of any avail as a guarantee that Mr Powys is not an improper writer, I would gladly do an introduction to the American edition. This I could manage the more easily since I know Mr Powys well, and am at this time writing a book about him[1] .. a rather Tristram Shandean biographical portrait that I much hope you will take under your wing, as I think it promises to be good reading.

Mr Powys is not a writer for everybody, but I am sure that he is a writer for posterity: indeed, of living authors I consider him the most notable, both as a thinker and a stylist. *Mr Weston's Good Wine* is the maturest and most profound of his books, and that it should have been sniffed at and turned over as though it were an indecent work is nothing short of an affront to the whole profession of letters.

1. Never finished; some seventy typescript pages were found among her papers.

To David Garnett *15:vi:1928*   15, *Launceston Place,*
                                   Kensington. [*London*] *W*.8.

Dearest Bunny,

Bea has just been telling me that you like my poems, and are pleased with me. Please will you come and tell me all over again?

I am here in the Raymonds'[1] spare bed with a large confused dog-bite in my leg. Such sad scenes by the Round Pond. Sylvia being as brave as death in a pool of blood, surrounded by people saying they never did trust those Alsatians. It was a chow. He did it quite by accident, thinking my leg was William.[2]

I am perfectly well, but mayn't move. Next week I am going out in a bath-chair. I have always longed to do that. Will you ring up and suggest a time?

I have been reading Remizov.[3] I am completely bowled over by him. *The Fifth Pestilence* is like Christ's last view of the world from the Cross with the darkness settling down. No one ever told me about him, and I supposed in my arrogance he was just another of those dreary Russians. Charles says you have met him, and that he is like a monkey. Has he got cold tight-fitting hands?

To David Garnett *12:x:1928*   113 *Inverness Terrance*
                                   [*London*] *W*.2.

. . . I cannot write about Aimée Semple Macpherson.[4] She is beyond my poor powers. I might perhaps snatch the hem of her garment in a very long, richly harmonized, mellifluously orchestrated Symphonic Poem, but she is quite out of reach of any words but her own.

I was perfectly carried away by her, and wished with all my heart that I could be just such another, thrilling the Albert Hall with the story of my life. Charles was not so much impressed. He sat a neat self-contained shape of suspicion, like a Lesser Cat who has been offered a dish of over-sweetened rhubarb.

1. Harold and Vera Raymond. See p. 17.
2. Her chow dog.
3. Aleksey Mikhaylovich Remizov (1877-1957), novelist and story writer.
4. The California revivalist.

I hear of you sometimes from him. It would be nice to hear of you from yourself.

Could you come to dinner one day next week, and see my new abode? And Ray? Couldn't she be in London buying roasting chestnuts and come too?

Love from
Sylvia

I have got two Virgins[1] since you saw me last and a box with twenty-one compartments. And I have finished my next novel.[2] 70,000 words and a love interest.

1. See letter to Paul Nordoff, 13:viii:1940.
2. *The True Heart.*

To Harold Raymond *2:xi:1929* · 113 *Inverness Terrace*

Dear Chatto,

Thanks for your letter. Please arrange with Tauchnitz as you suggest: £25 for their copyright of *Lolly Willowes* for an edition not exceeding 5000, the copyright after the edition is exhausted to remain with me, or lapse into me, or to sink into my bosom, or other Tennysonian words to that effect.

To Harold Raymond[1]   [113 *Inverness Terrace.*
                                      Undated, summer of 1930]

Dear Chatto,

I am just back from the late Miss Green's cottage.[2] It is having a back door put in and a fireplace taken out: the garden is covered with heaps of rubble and wheel-barrows reversed. Even so to the eye of ownership it looks very affable. I hope to get the furniture in next month, and the weeds out in 1945. Both these hopes are probably vain. Charles gave me a saw, and now I feel I never want to use a pen again, I am so much better at sawing.

1. He succeeded Charles Prentice as head of Chatto & Windus. His wife took to calling him 'Chatto' and he became Chatto to his intimates.
2. Which she had just bought: '. . . a small slate-roofed cottage with nothing to be said in its favour except that it was totally unpicturesque and stood by itself'. From an unpublished ms.

1931

To Charles Prentice 5:ix:1931   *Houseboat Memories,*
P.O. Thurne, Flegg Burgh. Norfolk.

Dear Charles,

I think I will send you the enclosed, which arrived yesterday, forwarded from 113.

I do not feel particularly warmly towards Mr Benn, and this proposal is rather sketchy. I am not able to add up so many pennies, but even my business acumen warns me that the difference between 20,000 and 100,00[0]d makes the offer of payment a little difficult to assess. Also, he says nothing of copyright. And I know, since I have heard it from someone he said it to, that his system with the 6d Library has been to throw overboard any volume that was not an immediate success: so if one's story didn't catch, and was scrapped, one would lose copyright (presumably) and not have much to comfort one.

On the other hand these are hard times; and if you have heard this scheme well spoken of, and think I should be a fool to stand out of it, I know you will tell me. I myself, as Queen Victoria would say, do *not* feel inclined.

Meanwhile I am very happy here on a sleek river with a flat marsh landscape all around in which only yachts, windmills and wherries stand perpendicular. Wherries are beyond words lovely—a very broad low build, with one enormous oblong sail, sometimes a black one. The most solemn gait you ever saw.

1932

To Harold Raymond *5:iv:1932*   *The Hill:*[1] *Winterton:*
                                        Norfolk:

Dear Chatto,

I have been a long while in returning the French translation of *Lolly*—Freudian reluctance, and the fact that I have been a-visiting of my mother, and other jauntings to and fro.

It is as thick-ankled as ever; but that is a fault in grain, and no revision could alter it. The revision of details has mended one or two of the worst misapprehensions, and she has removed those painful *excitations*. So now I think it had better be handed back, with those suitable words of tombstone approbation, which you, dear Chatto, will compose for me.

I live in a whirl of birds-nesting—a delightful form of social activity, though later when instead of going round to admire the eggs I find myself going round with *worms* it may prove more taxing. Also I read the local paper. It tells me how a cat at Diss spent a day on a roof-top, couldn't descend, and was aided by the local police-force. 'Once on terra firma, pussy had no difficulty in eluding the Man in Blue.'

Things like these elevate my soul. Also the Tombland's Fair, with a booth labelled Night Life in Paris. Inside, in cages, were two hens, three monkeys, some fancy rats, and a very fine badger. The N. L. was a little magnifying peephole, through which one beheld the Psyche of Sir Lawrence Alma-Tadema.

To Llewelyn Powys[2] [*undated fragment*]

. . . I must go to bed. Valentine[3] is so sleepy that she is reeling round our small room looking such innocence and debauchery it is as though she were drunk for the first time. Her face is pale with sleep, and a lappet of hair dangles forlornly over her left eye, and if she knew I were saying all this she might become indignant. So I must put this, and my love, swiftly into an envelope, lest she pounce.

1. The holiday house built by Valentine Ackland's father and later her mother's year-round home.
2. (1884-1939), nature philosopher and essayist. His home was in the village of East Chaldon in Dorset but he was for long periods of time a patient in Swiss tuberculosis sanitoria.
3. See Introduction, p. xiv.

. . . About your coming here? Will the first week-end in July suit you? It
seems better for us for these reasons; a. the strawberries should be ready.
b. green peas will be more abounding, c. our newly stocked cellar will have
more time to repose itself.

I will arrange with Mrs Way about your room; but not with Mrs Hall;
for we hope to have the pleasure of meeting you ourselves in the little car.

On Wednesday we took Theo to Montacute in it, to see his mother's
grave. We had several picnics en route, and Theo put up a fallen hurdle in a
field, to protect us against a fierce horse and some tempestuous sheep. It
was all a great success.

It is very dry here, and very beautiful. We have several improvements
to show you; and we have got the entry of Mr Goult's chapel, if we want to
go and work exclusively.

Mr Todd has had a stroke, but is better.

I hope it is a judgement on him for dismissing poor old Mr Dove, who
wept to part from his flocks.

TO DAVID GARNETT *22:vi:1932* *East Chaldon. Dorchester*
Dorset.

Dearest David,

I hope with all my heart you have got Scott's Close. In weather like this
one wants to buy every field one sees; and I remember those as very nice
fields, where I once took a walk with Richard,[2] talking about echoes.

Next to that I am delighted that you are going to America, though personally I should be afraid of Virginia—it is, or seems to be, so cultured. I
know all about the morse hanging on the trees. Did I not hear Gamel
Brenan[3] last summer telling old Arthur Machen—whom you met at my
house once, and liked—all about the bilberries of her native clime. They
grow in bahgs, said she. Excuse me, said Arthur, who is a little deaf. Baaahgs,
she repeated. Oh yes, yes, of course.

It was not all that they had hoped, that meeting, because at the onset
Arthur said, I believe I have met you before. In Ealing. He meant no harm,
to his mind Ealing is as remarkable a place as any other. But both Mr and
Mrs Brenan looked a trifle nipped.

1. His father was a clergyman, and Theodore Powys as a boy lived in Montecute
Vicarage.
2. His small son.
3. *Née* Gamel Woolsey, an American poet who married the writer Gerald Brenan.

You will have a lovely time on the boat, eating caviare. If you explain to your waiter, you can have it at every meal. Try it for breakfast. And if you visit Richmond Va. you will be introduced to Miss Ellen Glasgow,[1] a dear old lady with an ear-trumpet and white crochet lapels like a first class smoker. I was told, by some one else from Richmond Va. that until I had met her I could have no idea of the graciousness and culture of the South. And indeed she was a charming old pussy.

I too am absolutely broke. My half year's cheque from Chatto and Windus was Four Pounds Three Shillings and Fivepence. I have just dedicated a story[2] to Charles, to show there's no ill-feeling. It takes place in the Argentine. Thank God I do not know any young man called Brewer, or I should have had to go there. As it is, I have killed a rhea for local colouring, and put in some hens. They are invaluable animals because they can be studied at home, and transplanted almost anywhere.

How far are you from East Dereham, where Cowper died? I am concerned about a man there, called Craske, whose pictures you may have seen at the Warren Galleries, where they were shown about two years ago. He is a fisherman, who was blown up in a mine-sweeper, and made an invalid of; and being slightly blown out of his mind, he began to paint. He is a sort of English Douanier Rousseau, but with an English seriousness, for I always feel with Rousseau, except when he's in the tropics, that if his tongue, just the tip of it, wasn't in his cheek, it ought to have been. Now I hear that Craske has fallen on very bad times, and is ill and miserable. I can't afford to go there myself, and I have been trying to think of some one intelligent in his neighbourhood, who would go, and look at his work, and revive him. It is attention he needs, more than L.S.D.[3]

His address, just in case you or Ray should feel inclined to go there, is 42, Norwich Road, East Dereham. He has a very nice wife called Laura. His tariff, I may mention, is moderate. One guinea for water-colours, thirty shillings for the larger needlework pictures. They are both so respectable and speechless that it is worth knowing this. The pictures really are magnificent, Defoe-like pictures, stuggy, exact, and passionate. What I really should like would be for Ray to go and choose one she likes and let me give it to Hilton as a present for your return from America. I would really like this.

Talking of Defoe, dear Bunny, have you ever read a story called *The Island of Pines*? It is about a ship-wrecked Englishman, who was cast up with three white women and a negress, and by the time he was eighty he had in children, grandchildren and great-grandchildren one thousand, seven hundred, and eighty nine. It is a sort of animated Malthus, I haven't

1. American novelist (1873-1945).
2. *The Salutation*, published in the collection with that title.
3. That is to say, pounds, shillings, and pence.

21

enjoyed anything so much for months. It was written by Henry Neville, an early seventeenth century writer. He only lay with the blackamoor in the dark.

This place is exquisite. The fields, hay-cutting has only just begin, are so full of flowers that in the evenings they smell exactly like the breath of cows. On Tuesday old Mrs Moxon brought us a young owl, which she had caught, with the recommendation that we should kill it and have it stuffed for an ornament. We kept it caged in the woodshed till dusk to save it from being mobbed. When we let it out it gave one shove with its claw, like a fenland skater, leaving a deep scar on Valentine's wrist, and was gone in one swoop, with nothing to tell where it went but a shrill scolding from small birds a-bed.

My love to you both, and my best wishes for America. I shall think of you in your canary coloured spats.

1933

To Oliver Warner[1] *18:ii:1933*   *East Chaldon. Dorchester*
Dorset.

. . . We are awaiting a fall of snow—it snowed a little last night, and Granny
Moxon, going home late from the village, saw our lighted bedroom window,
and shouted up the news—and at this moment Valentine is buying chump
chops from the travelling butcher, in case we are snowed up and have no
food over the week-end. As for the cold—the north-wind is raving, and the
air is bruised and black, and even William has come in and settled down by
the fire for the rest of the day.

To Harold Raymond *18:iii:1933*   *East Chaldon. Dorchester.*
Dorset.

Dear Chatto,
    I have been shamelessly belated in writing to thank you for *The Chazzey
Tragedy*.[2] Local tragedies have rather taken up my mind, for all Beth Car has
been ill, Violet seriously, and what with towing about reviving broths in
covered jugs, fetching nurses at dead of night, holding hands and taking
temperatures, let alone putting in the seeds and the spring vegetables, and
enquiring after the postmistress who has also been at D.'s door, considerably
to the derangement of the general level of village intelligence, since lately
even post-cards have been going about unhonoured and unsung, anything
like writing letters has seemed to be as indefinitely deferred as the end of
this sentence.

To Harold Raymond *17:vi:1933*   *East Chaldon. Dorchester.*
Dorset.

. . . I have just signed a year's lease of a mouldering grange in Norfolk,

1. (1903-76), biographer and naval historian. He was then sharing a house in
   London with STW and was a reader for Chatto & Windus. He later held
   positions of distinction in the Honours and Awards Department of the
   Admiralty and in the Publications Department of the British Council. He was
   married to Elizabeth Warner: see p. 193.
2. By F. J. Prewett.

which I intend to share with Valentine for a year's experiment of rather larger living than we get here.

It is a seventeenth century house, called Frankfort Manor. It has a Dutch gable, a drive, two asparagus beds and a trap for visitors. For having approached, with all suitable enthusiasm, its blonde brick face, and gone in by its reeded and elegant door, they are tossed straight into an intact Edwardian long hall, complete with carved oak staircase and c. 1900 beams. We have already tried it on Valentine's brother-in-law, and it worked like a charm. He burst into inarticulate praise, and went on praising louder and louder as his sensibilities became more and more confused and uneasy.

Otherwise the house is nice and intact, except for a remarkable experiment in dining-room fireplaces, where there is a sort of ground-floor oven beside the hearth, faced with a grille: which I can only explain as a cage for salamanders.

Chaldon has been blackened with frequent funerals. Two members of the Jacobs family died in one week, one here, one at Dorchester; and there was a good deal of family feeling about this, ending with both corpses being buried on the same day, either party of mourners being anxious to bereave the rival graveside of attendance. As for wreaths . . . madonna lilies tossed about like buttercups.

It was a sad quandary for Violet, with a choice of being chief mourner at either funeral. But she chose the better part, that is to say the further funeral, which enabled her to have a car-ride and a little shopping in Dorchester; and came home much refreshed. We have not got the biscuit crumbs and broken blossoms out of the car yet.

The adopted baby is adding its quota to the intellectual life of the village by looking day by day exactly like various members of the Powys family. It has a large choice to draw from, and is going through the repertory with the greatest steadfastness. Any conjectures that this might lead to are forestalled by a variety of scientific explanations: from Theodore and Violet.

Lately it took to flourishing its hands about in the identical gesture of its aunt Katie.[1] Theo, noticing my attentive eye, remarked, first, 'What a quantity of leaves there are this summer, my dear.' Finding this perhaps a trifle abstruse he added. 'Do you notice that little child's hands, my dear? There is a reason for that. Her mother, when she was pregnant, went to a seaside resort and *rowed* a great deal. The doctor said that must have been the cause.' 'Which doctor, Theo?' 'Oh, my dear, the one in the nursing home where the child was born.'

I think perhaps they will both be rather glad than sorry when our eyes remove their gaze to Frankfort Manor.

1. Catherine Edith Philippa Powys, sister of Theodore, Llewelyn, etc. and sometimes referred to in the letters as Philippa.

Dear Llewelyn,

It was a most sharp-edged grief to us, when we were so busy scampering round our new house, saying, 'Llewelyn will appreciate that'—'This must go in the spare room because of Alyse', to hear that your old foe[1] had smitten you with such a shrewd sally.

We both felt guilty that we were not still in East Chaldon. Not so much supposing that we could have done anything to help; but a deeper feeling, that instinct one has to be near a friend in trouble, to stand round and help to make a wall. But our thoughts and strong wishes have walled you round.

This house looks out on a great rampart of trees; all day they are motionless in the strong sun: But at dusk they seem to creep silently across the lawn, until looking from my window I seem to see their enormous foreheads pressed to the pane.

I have never lived with trees before. They take some mastering; but I think I shall be on good terms with them even before I see them naked.

Valentine is intensely happy. She has only one request: for more rats to shoot with her rifle. I could almost wish for more rats too, since to-day, failing other targets, she must needs put three bullets through a fine sleek swelling jargonelle pear, hanging harmlessly on the south wall.

. . . How very delightful, my dear, that you are well enough to write letters, to read Dante, and to despise him. I quite agree with you—a black-hearted, cold-hearted prig . . .

If I had not a cat on my lap I would get up and find for you some very practical remarks of Leigh Hunt's about him. But I have a cat on my lap; for since we came here William fell sick, was doomed by the vet's word to a lingering, though painless; and I could not bear to see him slow and bewildered who had always been so sprightly and confident. So he had morphia first, and then prussic acid, and Valentine dug his grave.

Now it is her innings, and we have already three cats, and the Lord knows how many more may not be added unto us. And what Scotch people call a Rough Cat in the garden. To look at, she is all of a wild cat, with shock fur standing out against all weathers, a short heavy tail, a round face and glaring round eyes. To see her is to be transported to a Brazilian jungle. She moves with a snakelike slouch, a swift grovelling.

1. Pulmonary tuberculosis.

One evening we heard strange sounds in the house, thumps and heavy boundings. It was dark. We carried a lamp and a gun in search of the sounds, could not for a long while track them down, for they would cease and begin again. At last, in the sitting room we saw, crouched in the middle of the room, what seemed to be a massive fur hassock. The hassock rose into the air, and soared out into the garden, not knowing much more when she landed of the nature of glass than when she started, for she went through it like a cannon ball. A leap of ten or twelve feet, a magnificent leap. But we became rather pensive, and now, at nightfall, we shut the doors.

We have dug up all our potatoes, gathered all our nuts, stored our apples and keeping pears. Now to chop and saw wood for the winter, the lantern hanging on a wooden peg, the stable very dusky and enlarged around us, and rustling with rats. It is rainy weather at last, the blackbirds sing almost as though it were February, and this morning when I woke I saw the air between us and the hanging tapestry of trees laced with straight glittering rods of rain, each separate, intentional, like a rain of spears.

I am glad. The rain is settling me in; though sometimes I have such a passionately distinct homesickness for Chaldon that to remain here is almost more than I can bear.

The straw is ricked, and the ricks have corn-babies on them. One at either end, standing up like weathercocks. They are baubles of plaited straw, made in different shapes, sometimes crosses, sometimes sharp stars, sometimes birds with long tails. It is on the first-finished rick they are put—for ornament we were told.

Mushrooms and a bull have appeared simultaneously in the field behind the house. It is a pity that the same day should always quicken both. However, we had mushrooms for lunch.

The other day we went to King's Lynn. It is a most beautiful town, stately and prim, with seagulls crying through it. And on our way back we drove through the outskirting grounds of Sandringham. Sandy roads, very smooth, with clipped green grass margins and well-kept rabbits . . . All the neighbourhood is excessively spruce, covered with model post-offices and tailored hedges. Suddenly, after about a four mile radius, one sees the landscape sinking back into carpet-slippers with a sigh of relief.

We have a library now, all Valentine's books and mine at last assembled and in order. The rest of the house is also furnished, perfectly to our satisfaction; though when I see strangers looking rather wistfully round the very large hall it occurs to me that perhaps one horsehair sofa, two chairs, a bust and two guns is not quite all the furniture they would expect.

But very few strangers come. And so far, all of them are dull. So we hope that a word has gone round about us, and that we shall be avoided as lepers and eccentrics.

I prefer visitors from further away. They arrive with more glory, and, there is a more certain joy at their coming. Now that you can write letters, have slid further from under those Jaws, I begin to allow myself to think how delightful it will be when Alyse and Llewelyn come to stay.

Valentine is rattling in the hall. The rattles are increasing in volume and imperativeness, in a moment I shall have to depose the cat and obey that summons. For we have got to drive over to Winterton, to dine there. And on our journey back we must travel by headlights, the hedges suddenly called up, unreally green, theatrical pasteboard bowers, and swung behind us. Did I ever tell you how when Theodore was taken out by Garrow Tomlin[1] in his car, one hot summer's night, with a great many moths about, plastered dying on the headlights, he said, his only remark after the drive, 'To motor by night must be agony to a moth-collector.'

Now the other cat has climbed up my back and is thoughtfully chewing my ear. I cannot bear it, this is worse than rattlings. *Valentine must be in that cat.*

To LLEWELYN POWYS *7:xii:1933*   *Frankfort Manor. Sloley.*
                                   Norwich.

... I have been re-reading that extraordinary woman's *Diary of Our Life in the Highlands*. Really, Llewelyn, she and her Albert were an amazing pair. They would go off, down an unknown road in the Highlands, in a strange pony-chaise, all by themselves, ford torrents, scramble up mountains, gather ferns and cairngorms and I should think in all probability inaugurate some more heirs to the throne under a pine-wood or on the edge of a precipice, without a care or a scruple. And with their faces still quite filthy, tufts of heather sticking to their clothing, a most unsuitable freedom still gipsyfying their countenances, they would return to be an example of wedded decorum to all the courts and homes of Europe.

1. Brother of STW's friend Stephen Tomlin, the sculptor. He was killed in a flying accident.

To Oliver Warner *26:i:1934*   *Frankfort Manor. Sloley.*
                                                       Norwich

. . . I have almost finished my light-hearted pot-boiler by Franklin Gore-Booth.[1] Some of it strikes me as very funny; and the other night, late, Valentine, who had fallen asleep, was awaked by a burst of wild laughter, and at first supposed I had fallen into hysterics, or that the house had been invaded by fiends. I looked up to find her standing in the door-way, pale but dauntlessly resolved to deal with whatever it was. When I explained that I was amused at my own jokes, she was slightly reproachful.

We have discovered that we are related, very distantly. Need I say that the link is in Scotland? It is so very distant that I don't think we need fear that it will do anything to estrange us.

All our animals are very well, and we have the temporary addition of Valentine's mother's Pekingese. Winterton is at the moment shut up, during a change of servants; so he came to us. When he arrived we had the cats shut up, lest there should be any unpleasantness—not from him, he has always been brow-beaten by Ruth's cats—but from them. Later on we loosed him and them into the garden. It was like stories of Red Indians; for wherever one looked there was a cat, house or wild, stealthily emerging from bushes, or standing at bay with their backs arched like croquet-hoops. His courage was amazing, and the tact with which he appeared to remain unconscious that there was anything in the garden beyond the usual beauties of nature.

To Llewelyn Powys *16:ii:1934*   *Frankfort Manor. Sloley.*
                                                       Norwich.

. . . My God, we are gardening so hard. At this moment the whole of my back is uttering smouldering growls of fatigue. But we are not entirely given up to virtuous acts. We have eaten cold partridge legs out of doors, sitting on a heap of dry rushes on a heath, and watched, very disapprovingly, by two church towers, one to the east and one to the west. It is impossible to frolic anywhere in this country without a church tower on the horizon to eye one. There they rear themselves, like melancholy teeth from an old jaw.

1. See letter of 18:ii:1934, p. 29.

. . . I have finished my light novel and quite exhausted my ribbon. It is a nice piece of work, I am glad I persevered with it. The name of the author is Franklin Gore-Booth; and his anonymity is to be strictly preserved; I mention this, though it is not very likely that you should be meeting many literary news-mongers in the Sudan. The truth is, there are Theo and Llewelyn to the life; and it will make conversation with them easier if they are not obliged to know that I can take them so lightly.

Since I wrote to you last I have been very busy in the orchard—pruning our labyrinthine fruit-trees, and, what is worse, grease-banding them. Oliver, have you ever put on grease-bands? And do you know that they are covered with treacle, and wave madly round one, even when there is not a breath of wind to stir them; and that, wherever they touch, they cleave? Never in my life have I spent such an afternoon; and after it was over, I and the scissors and the string had all to be cast into a bath with strong alkalis and left there till an awful scum slowly detached itself from us, and rose in chemical iridescence to the surface.

To Harold Raymond *9:iii:1934*   *Frankfort Manor. Sloley.*
Norwich.

Dear Chatto,

I am so sorry that I have involved you in the writing of a letter which oppressed you as an unpleasant business;[1] and at the first reading I found myself unable to think of any reply beyond an answering sob that it hurt me as much as it hurt you, so to speak.

But don't let us be hurt, either of us, over what is only a traffic. I have the greatest esteem for my butcher, whose fillet steak is all I could desire; but when I thought there were too many lights (or should I say too much light) in the cats-meat, I told him so without flinching. Nor did he, from what I saw, flinch much either.

I should hate to think I had less philosophy than my butcher has; and I hope you won't feel more regret than I did in expressing my views as housekeeper because you have expressed your views as a publisher. With this lofty example before our eyes let us feel that nothing has happened that we need grieve over.

I must now go and make a mulligatawny. But the shortness of this letter is only amicable, because I wanted to write at once and put you out of any possible doubt as to my wounded feelings. I only regret if you have had to give a wrench to your own.

1. Her 'pot-boiler' was not liked.

To Charles Prentice 15:iii:1934   *Frankfort Manor. Sloley.*
                                       Norwich.

Dear Charles,

Dove and Seagull[1] alighted duly this morning, an agreeable addition to the usual menagerie which appears with early morning tea—three cats and a hybrid Pekingese.

You touch nothing that you do not adorn; even sheets from America. It is an object lesson in what can be done by small adjustments to compare the English and the American copies; and I am thinking of showing the two specimens to my Irene to be a guide and an inspiration to her to apply the same principles in the handling of the spice-box.

To Llewelyn Powys 24:iii:1934   *Frankfort Manor. Sloley.*
                                     Norwich.

. . . Your letter came to me when I was in sad need of a friend's hand. We have been through a week of murrain and pestilence.[2] There is a killing disease here that in six days has slain, to our certain knowledge, over twenty cats and four dogs. Four of our cats, alas, among them, and two of those the house kittens which I had reared up from babyhood. They were extremely dear to us, and it was misery to see them so suddenly blasted and turned from the comely looks and happiness into little bags of bones wrapped in sullied fur. It is a most virulent and mysterious plague, for the vet., even after two post-mortems, cannot account for it. It is not poisoning, it is not any known distemper. The people are waiting most uneasily to see if it spreads to cattle; and even if it does not it is still a calamity; for the rats will be all over us if it is not stayed.

I have given Valentine a small pocket telescope, by which she observes birds and the moon . . . It was a hazardous gift to make, because Valentine's grandfather had, among twenty other expensive and devouring passions, a turn for astronomy and an even more marked turn for telescopes; and I have been waiting for the words, 'Sylvia, we must sell the car and the silver and all we have and buy an astronomer's telescope. And then we will fit it

1. *Whether a Dove or Seagull*, a volume of poetry, half by STW and the other half by Valentine Ackland. 'The authors believe that by issuing their separate work under one cover the element of contrast thus obtained will add to the pleasure of the reader; by withholding individual attributions they hope that the freshness of anonymity will be preserved. The book, therefore, is both an experiment in the presentation of poetry and a protest against the frame of mind, too common, which judges the poem by the poet, rather than the poet by the poem.' Prefatory note.
2. See the Introduction to *The Cat's Cradle Book*.

up on a cement platform in the garden, and build a little shelter, and I will sit there all night, observing the heavens. I shall be perfectly happy, I shall not wish for anything else. We must get it instantly.'

However, so far she seems content with a fifteen diameter magnified moon, and the pleasure of watching the expressions of the hens in the field across the lane.

To Jean Starr Untermeyer[1] 25:vii:1934

> West Chaldon, Dorchester,
> Dorset.

. . . Do you know what you should be singing? You ought to be singing Gluck. I have said so before, I repeat it now. It is the rarest equipment of all, the equipment for Gluck, the tone broad enough and full enough to sit down on, the finesse of the lieder-singer, the enthusiasm sustained enough to wear those splendid folds of music without twitching them or creasing or sullying them, or pinning foolish nosegays to them . . .

If I could sing Gluck, I would do nothing, nothing, NOTHING else, I tell you. I would sing his recitative at meals, and his arias all the rest of the time. And when invited to take the oath in the Dorchester law courts, I would shake my ribs free and begin *Divinités du Styx*.

To Llewelyn Powys 25:ix:1934   *Frankfort Manor. Sloley.*
Norwich.

Dearest Llewelyn,

It is strange being in this house and knowing how soon we shall leave it;[2] and in the middle of practical considerations about china and blankets I

1. (1886-1970), American poet and translator, living in New York City. She was trained as a musician and made her début as a lieder singer in Vienna in 1925.
2. A Chaldon woman licensed by the Dorset County Council to train mentally defective young women for domestic service was believed to be holding them in virtual slavery. Llewelyn Powys drew up a petition for inquiry and collected forty-one signatures in the village, among them those of STW and Valentine Ackland. The petition provided grounds for a libel suit, having threatened the woman's income and livelihood. In the charges only Powys, STW and Valentine Ackland were named, perhaps because they were the only persons among the signatories who had means. The case went against the defence. According to the account in Jean Starr Untermeyer's *Private Collection*, Llewelyn Powys's expenses, with lawyer's fees, came to £573.8s.3d. STW and Valentine Ackland were fined £100 each and costs. As a result they could no longer afford to rent Frankfort Manor, and moved into a neglected cottage in West Chaldon.

turn and stare out of the windows, thinking how much more important it is to carry with me the shape of a tree.

To Oliver Warner *11:xii:1934*   *24, West Chaldon,*
Dorchester, Dorset.

... Our surroundings grow muddier and muddier, the cart track which passes our house is now impassible to us except when I remember to throw the morning ashes into the mud—the green slope which leads to the foot-bridge is now a brown slide; and still the wind blows us more rain. By every reason we ought to be sorrowing; but we continue very happy and comfortable, and so does Victoria Ambrosia,[1] though she leads now a some-what secluded life, since when the weather is rough she stays in her shed. However, what she lacks in variety of scenery she more than makes up in variety of diet. Now that the grass feed is so poor we offer to her fickle palate oats, corn, cake, mangolds, swedes, apples, potatoes, and bread. She is full of vanity and puffed up with feminine changeableness, and what she adored yesterday she won't look at to-day. Valentine waits on her with the utmost tenderness and ingenuity, she might be rearing a very delicate heir to a throne.

I am so sorry about Charles leaving, you will miss him profoundly, I know. I hope that when the firm moves to its new mansion—is this the result, or was it the cause, of Charles's departure?—you will have a nicer room. It is high time you had. What is the new one like? I mean the new young man called Maconochie or something,[2] not the mansion. I could wish he were not a Celt, as he must be from his name, even though I have got it wrong. My private opinion of Celts is that they very rarely have any creative faculty, and even more rarely critical faculty. No race so naturally gifted with improvisation and rhapsody is going to get much further than rhapsody and improvisation. So if he is a bit of an Ossian, I shall not be surprised.

Routledge's Mr Warburg[3] was here the other day. A bit grand and lofty, but I didn't dislike him, and about political questions and social questions I found him very gratifying. He brought a somewhat overwhelming wife who designs mit schoepferisch Genie originelle Huetten—or petticoaten or something of that sort.

---

1. A goat, brought with them from Frankfort Manor.
2. John McDougall, a partner in the firm.
3. Frederic Warburg, who was later one of the two founders of the publishing firm of Secker and Warburg.

Dearest Llewelyn,

I am sending up this number of *The Countryman*—perhaps you take it already—but if you do not, then I think you will like the photographs of birds and bats, and the bat story.

Nice bats, delicate Gothic creatures I could grow very fond of. I had one for a day, once. I found it one morning, crouched up in a corner of my bedroom, huddled against the light. It allowed me to pick it up and admire its fine mackintosh wings and furious fairy face. And since it was a day of ruthless sunlight I put it into a cupboard to meditate in dusk till sundown,

We are all busy discussing the new Brodies. We had Mrs B. to tea. I suppose she is a superior example of the present-day farmer's wife. A sharp town-bred intelligence, sharp enough just to see over the counter and no further; a great deal of assertive ambition and industry; and no heart whatsoever.

'We shall put it all down to grass,' said she grandly. I thought of the whispering barley on the way to Chydyock, and of the silent men working in those fields.

. . . An outrageous wind has blown for days and days, I feel as though at any moment the house might begin to disintegrate like a haystack . . .

Valentine has been having influenza, not badly, compared to what she can do, but still she has spent a niggling week in bed, enlivened by nightmares. She caught it from Theodore, which no doubt added a special twang of pessimism to the variety. He is up and around again, indeed, poor Theodore, he wasn't able to get much down, since he and Violet were both sick at once; and I see him going for his very imprudent walks in the face of the gale, with a look of great caution. I only hope that the look of caution may mislead the elements into thinking that he is too wily for them. As for Llewelyn, he is getting better daily. His kill or cure jaunt did him most decisive good.

Our old Mr Weld, our land-owner, is dead. I am sorry. His legs were so neat, and his back so straight, and the one eye left to him so shrewd and piercing. His legs in particular were a pleasure to me, they were as neat and trim as yours. The village was much impressed because the estate lorry came charging down the lane to fetch the estate workmen who were here on a job, and carry them off to Lulworth for a requiem mass. I do not know if this counted as ordinary work or overtime.

We had lunch at Max Gate the other day. I have always wanted to see the inside of that house, and it is well worth seeing. The present Mrs T.H., very properly, has altered nothing; and it is a perfect specimen of a genteel house of the nineties, I suppose. Walls covered with pictures, sketches, prints, and photographs. A conservatory opening out of the drawing room with budgerigars shrieking in it; and a great deal of dark oak fittings. All the chairs and sofas are as marrowy as they can be, and reflect the greatest credit on T.H. Altogether, it is a nice comfortable house, and I would much rather live in it than in most of my friend's houses which are in so much better taste.

There is a nice Hardyesque garden, too, very green, with a decided flavour of churchyard (though there is a good practical kitchen garden tucked away at the back). There is a long narrow walk, with conifers on either side, which he paced over for hours. It is exactly right, melancholy, respectable (what more respectable than conifers?) grim and genteel. The conifers wag their heads and sigh.

To Julius Lipton[1] *9:vi:1935*   *24 West Chaldon Dorchester Dorset*

. . . A thunderstorm is coming, grumbling up over the hills between us and the sea. Poor Valentine! She hates them. Her eyes go black like a cat's and her hair crackles. Last summer in Norfolk we had a series of very bad thunderstorms. There were trees all round the house, an inflammable thatch roof, and a telephone that used to jangle whenever there was a flash of lightning. There we used to sit, side by side on a black horsehair sofa, each of us soothing a cat, and waiting for the house to be struck.

To Julius Lipton *28:vii:1935*   *24 West Chaldon Dorchester Dorset.*

. . . We have bought a second-hand caravan, about the size of a double bed, and it is perched on the grass beside the house. We sleep out in it, because our rooms are hot and stuffy at night; and if it weren't for the fact that the second-hand air-mattresses leak, and have to be reblown up at intervals of every two hours or so, I could describe it as very restful and refreshing. But if we can mend a mattress sufficiently for it to remain air-tight, you can sleep out in it, if you like the idea; and defy the cows from behind a barbed-wire stockade. At first they thought the caravan had been put there on purpose for them to scratch themselves against, and my god! didn't they scratch. Now the wire keeps them at a distance, so they stand round and utter reproachful sighs.

To Oliver Warner *26:ix:1935*   *24 West Chaldon Dorchester Dorset.*

. . . We saw a great many good things in our tour;[2] lovely moors between Durham and the North Riding, enormous, and solemn, and solitary, hillsides laced with silver water, single farmsteads like fortresses inside their bounding walls. And we also saw Haworth, which surpassed even my appetite for gloomy churchyards. Glutted, is the only word for it. And the

1. Born 1910, poet and political activist, married to Queenie Lipton. He was at that time employed as an underpresser in an East End workshop and lived in Holborn. In 1978 he published a selection of Valentine Ackland's poetry.
2. She and Valentine Ackland drove to Edinburgh with Jean Starr Untermeyer in a hired car.

Black Bull Inn, where Bramwell spent so much time, is exactly like its name, dark-stone and massive, and with a stab of realisation I knew that Anne Brontë felt exactly that way about it, and foiled her horror of the inn with her fear of black bulls.

To Julius Lipton 21:x:1935   24 West Chaldon

. . . last week we made a rapid raid into S. Wales, stayed at Cwmfelinach for a night, and drove around and about . . . At Trelewis (where the people tore up the manager's washing poles complete with line and washing all dangling, and carried the whole affair through the streets like a captured banner) there must have been a good three hundred police in one small valley. Two vast buses, filled to the brim with them like a school treat; scores of them walking up and down in groups of four (One for sorrow, two for mirth, three for a wedding, four for a birth, like magpies); and an even greater quantity of them in hiding on the mountainside, hiding coyly in pairs under trees and behind bushes, like courting couples.

It was very interesting being there, and bitter to think that the stay-in men have been tricked to the top on such bad terms, since now the pits will be closed, and they out of work.

To Julius Lipton 28:xi:1935   24 West Chaldon Dorchester.

We organised a Labour meeting here, in the schools. Such a thing has not happened within the memory of man, and as neither of the other candidates came near us, that was telling too. A labourer in the chair, very good he was, and all of us wetter than we had ever been in our lives before, for that night there was a cloud-burst.

The trouble we were up against was transport. Nothing but our MG. Valentine did over a hundred miles, taking voters in ones, and just when we thought that we had about finished the people we knew, we heard of a whole new settlement, bungalows on the heath near Wool; and they had to be dealt with. The thing that gave us our greatest pleasure was that we prevailed on a local Conservative to spend his evening (usually spent at the inn) in conveying those who were too fat or too rheumatic to get into the MG. He was far too chivalrous, we told him, being a Conservative and everybody knows how chivalrous the Conservatives are, to let a little thing like party stand in his way. He was sour, but gave in.

The thing I enjoyed next was discovering that I can heckle. The last evening before the election we decided to spend an evening off and have a busman's holiday of going to hear Cranbourne, the Government man, speaking at Weymouth. He'd been heckled there before, and we hoped for fun. Fun there was. Not a five minute's quiet throughout the evening; and to my rapture I found that of all things I loved making rude remarks at the top of my voice and that the top of my voice was gratifyingly loud and nasty. I had never even been to a large political meeting before, it is awful to think of all the years this good gift has been slumbering in me.

Those pretty cottages you saw at West Chaldon have just had a foot of filthy water in them, because the farmer didn't clear out that stinking ditch.

To Julius & Queenie Lipton *23:iii:1936*   *24 West Chaldon*
Dorchester Dorset.

Dear Julius, dear Queenie,

Now that I am back in this place I am beginning to think that yesterday was rather exhausting, and that police-charges[1] are not things that one can take as placidly as tea-parties. So this will be a short letter, just to tell tou how very happy we were in your Potemkin,[2] and how very grateful we are for all you did, the bed, and the breakfast, and the good welcome.

I can't tell you what a comfort it was to have you to come to, after that long evening, and the rather dreary tag-end feeling of coming away through the vast complacent unmoved bulk of London, all those upper windows with bourgeois going to bed, all those respectable front-doors safely locked against surprises as against new ideas. After that to come into your place, so alight and full of projects and excitement and determination was like a drink in closing hours.

Let us know if anything crops up in the Westminster Police-Court that isn't reported in the D.W. Embrace that kitten from me, if you can dare its claws.

1. 'Mosley, of the British Union of Fascists, was holding a meeting at the Royal Albert Hall on 22 March 1936, and a large anti-fascist demonstration was directed, by the police, well away from the meeting as a half-mile ban had been imposed. However, the organisers later insisted that they had had permission to hold a meeting at a place called Thurloe Square. According to reporters and other eye-witnesses (including Sylvia and myself), while the Reverend Schiff was in the midst of making a speech the mounted police—who had waited until they were well inside the crowd—made a baton charge, drawing their staves and beating the audience about the heads and shoulders. (My wife was pushed against a wall by a mounted policeman and badly bruised.)' Julius Lipton to the editor, 21 July 1981.
2. 'No 5 Great Ormond Street in Bloomsbury, where the top floor was let out room by room to me and my friends, and which Sylvia, in another letter, called a "rabbit-warren". It was quite normal to offer my bed to out-of-town visitors and for me to find an empty bed elsewhere.' Ibid.

... We have just had a telegram asking us to go to Barcelona to help in the Red Cross bureau there. We have been trying hard to get out to Spain, we are lucky to have this chance. But I am sorry that I can't see you before I start.

Will Chatto and Windus please announce my going to Spain (stressing that it is for the Sp. Government side, I don't want to be confused with Owen O'Duffy's fascist legion!) It should be good advt for the book,[1] and also it may explain my whereabouts for I shan't have time to write to many people saying I am off.

In case I get nipped off by a piece of shell or a bit of gas (I don't think it at all likely) I have left a will of sorts, in which I have named you as an executor. It is in the top drawer of the little tallboy in my pink room down here, and at this moment the top drawer is wedged shut by some accident or other. But if needs be you will get it opened. There is a letter with it of wishes about small bequests and mementoes.

I have received the cheque for £75 from Chatto. Will you please take this as a receipt?

I understand it is very slow work getting letters through, so don't worry if you don't hear anything of me, though I will try to send a picture postcard, if possible of a nice ruined church!

A note on *Summer Will Show* written, like the other, in the 1960s.

It must have been in 1920 or 21, for I was still in my gaunt flat over the furrier in the Bayswater Road and totally engaged in *Tudor Church Music*, that I said to a young man called Robert Firebrace that I had invented a person: an early Victorian young lady of means with a secret passion for pugilism; she attended prize-fights dressed as a man and kept a punching-ball under lock and key in her dressing-room. He asked what she looked like and I replied without hesitation: Smooth fair hair, tall, reserved, very ladylike. She's called Sophia Willoughby.

And there she was and there she stayed. I had no thought of doing anything with her. A year or so later and equally out of the blue I saw Minna telling about the pogrom in a Paris drawing-room and Lamartine leaning against the doorway. And there she stayed. I had written my first three novels and *Opus 7* and *The Salutation* and was living at Frankfort Manor in Norfolk with Valentine when we went to Paris (1932, I think) and in the

---

1. *Summer Will Show.*

rue Mouffetard, outside a grocer's shop, I found that I wanted to write a novel about 1848. And Sophie and Minna started up and rushed into it.

When we got back I sent to the London Library for histories and memoirs, as close to the date as I could find. This was a lesson in history. Legitimists, Orleanists, Republicans all told incompatible versions of the same events, and several times didn't even agree on dates. But their prejudices made them what I needed. It was from one of these that I read how Marie-Amélie urged poor Louis-Philippe to go out and confront the mobs, adding, 'Je vous bénirai du haut du balcon.' I reflected that this nonsense coincided with the Communist Manifesto, and this shaped the argument of the book. I read several guidebooks of that date, too, and discovered Columbin who sold English buns, and the Dames Réunies; and I re-read Berlioz's *Mémoires*, and with an effort put the French novelists out of my mind.

Caspar came out of the Scotch branch of my own family tree. My grandmother remembered his black hand beside her white one when he arrived in Edinburgh as the little boy Uncle Alexander was interested in. She remembered, too, being held over a lime-kiln for whooping-cough.

The character I most enjoyed creating was Léocadie: she was so detestable and so estimable. In the end, I found she was the only person on her side of the fence who had enough stuffing to be set opposite Engels.

I drafted the book in Norfolk, continued it in Dorset, ended it at Lavenham in Suffolk, where I had gone to be alone with it. Once it was begun, I wrote it with great impetus—too much impetus, for there are some howlers. The Sabbath candle should have been lit by Minna's mother, for instance. But mainly I was lucky. If one goes fast enough, one is less likely to trip.

To Julius Lipton 27:x:1936   24 *West Chaldon Dorchester*
                                     Dorset.

Dear Julius,

To deal with the blacker aspects first. That pamphlet. O God of Israel Isaac and Jacob, what the bloody hell did those intellectual dodderers think they were doing?

Gollancz would almost certainly have done it, is there not the Marsdon Press, prepared to do anything and doing quite a lot of mixed stuff anyhow. Is there not Faber, Methuen, Constable, all of them cashing in on the Left. And then they trot off to Chatto and Windus. Jesus! Why not the Society for the Promotion of Christian Knowledge (who have indeed some experience with tracts, whereas Chatto and Windus know about as much about handling tracts and pamphlets as I know about aero-dynamics).

I do not blame you, my Julius, but as for Garman and West I could tread on their faces. They spent five hours here on Sep. 18th, saying how essential it was to get the thing out quickly. Now all those fish that I caught so carefully, Priestley that Great Whale, and Rebecca West and Ethel Mannin (on all of whom I had my eye for improving the Writer's Ass. and on all of whom I impressed the need for promptitude) will have subsided into pets and disillusionment and disgust, and must be written off for any more good we can hope to get out of them.

Here is a clean page, thank the lord I can now write about something pleasant.

We are both so pleased, dear Julius and dear Queenie, to hear about the wedding coming off so soon. We will come if we possibly can. . .

Can Queenie, by any chance, address the enclosed to the widow of that Emmanuel Julius (Party member) who was killed about ten days ago, fighting in Aragon, and reported in the *D. W.*? I met him in Barcelona, and had a conversation with him which it might be some small comfort to her to hear about.

To Elizabeth Wade White[1] *14:xi:1936*   *24 West Chaldon*
                                            Dorchester Dorset
Dearest Elizabeth,

Just the very day before your letter was written with its hope I was neither in Spain nor pining to go there, we got back from Barcelona. And have had fits of pining, on and off, ever since, to be back again, among the friends we made there. We had a job, a three weeks job, on the English Red Cross unit out there, an office-boy sort of job. Heard of it by wire, sprang into the car, and drove across France at a rate which would have been intolerable if we had not been on our way to Spain.

I don't think I have ever met so many congenial people in the whole of my life, liking overleapt any little bounds of language. My substantives were Spanish, my verbs, being picked up locally, were Catalan. I got on beautifully. Barcelona, by the time we saw it, was I suppose the nearest thing I shall ever see to the early days of USSR . . . the very first days, when everything was proceeding on the impulse of that first leap into life. After the military rising, combatted in its first showing by an almost unbelievable mixture, police and middle-class (it happened all of a sudden when the workers were boxed in the factories) after a couple of days fighting, Barcelona was taken over by committees of trades union men, and the worker's militia; in other words, it is a Soviet town.

One sees a lot of committees, one goes to them for anything that is

1. Biographer, living in Middlebury, Connecticut.

wanted, from a permit to an elephant. They sit in the mansions and the offices of the great (which they keep in the tenderest order, I saw one where they were preserving the original aviary, and another was a kind guardian to a flock of goldfish) sentries in wicker easy chairs sit at the door, els boys scouts de Catalonia stand round in order serviceable, and inside is a kind of humane efficiency and good sense such as no one could believe in who had not seen it. Inside also are great crowds, and a quantity of children, for children are everywhere, like bees round a honeysuckle. If one wants to please a child one allows him or her to play with fire-arms. Thanks to the rest of Europe fire-arms are cake and humming-birds. There were not many in Barcelona when we were there, there had been a census a few days earlier, and two-thirds of those available had been sent to Madrid.

There are a great many shells and skulls of churches. It seemed quite natural that churches should have been used as machine-gun nests, I have never seen churches so heavy and hulking and bullying, one can see at a glance that they have always been reactionary fortresses. I did not find a single person of any class who resented their being gutted, though we did find two domestic servants, one old and nasty, one young, charming, and unable to read or write, who felt a certain uneasiness about it, as though God might yet pop out of those ruined choirs and grab them by the scruff. The not being able to read or write is the crux. A people naturally intellectual, and with a long standard of culture, have thrown off the taskmasters who enforced ignorance on them.

And you cannot imagine, after this mealy-mouthed country, the pleasure of seeing an office with a large painted sign, Organisation for the Persecution of Fascists. Anarchists, of course. That beautiful directness is typical of anarchism, a most engaging type of thought, though I do not want to be an anarchist myself. The world is not yet worthy of it, but it ought to be the political theory of heaven.

P.S. It is only the papers which call the Spanish Communists. They are nearly all anarchists: all one to a journalist, but this does answer your doubt as to the applicability of Communism to Spain.

To Oliver Warner *3:xii:1936*   *24 West Chaldon Dorchester Dorset.*

Dearest Oliver,

It is extremely kind of Mr Pennington, and I feel very much honoured by his suggestion; but the baseness of my nature is such, that though I would love to come to a dinner I would not love to speak . . . certainly not be principal speaker. I might screw a few graceful words out of myself, but I could never be a chief speaker.

I am so sorry. I must seem both ungrateful and pusillanimous. Indeed, I daresay I am pusillanimous, but I am not ungrateful.

How do you feel about Mrs Simpson. I cannot decide in my mind which in the long run one should prefer. A defeat for Baldwin and the damn church now, or the possible good effect of a dull reactionary King Albert. The trouble is, we like dull reactionaries. In any reasonable country Albert would mean revolution in a year, especially as Albert-Jacob after Edward-Esau; but for all I can see we shall support him securely through all the days of his doddering life.

Why it should be worse, of course, to get sexual excitement from an American lady than from an old pair of fur bedroom slippers will remain a mystery to me. But apparently the church will bless the one little foible and not the other. And Mrs Baldwin is undoubtedly more like the slippers than the Simpson, so Baldwin's sympathies would naturally be with Jacob.

Anyhow it is all very interesting. I wish I were in London, hearing what people in trams and buses say.

43

TO STEVEN CLARK[1] *16:v:1937*   *24 West Chaldon Dorchester Dorset*

... we have got the new house, at least I suppose so. Yesterday we met our landlady there for a final discussion. She was most obliging to us, lowered the rent by two pound ten, and agreed to put in all the electric light at her own expense. She went round the house with us, being most lavish, power points in every room, she was even prepared to give us six bells. And she is a most detestable woman. An Anglo-Indian,[2] small, obtuse, capable, bossy, and without a glimmer of intellectual day. I have rarely disliked a benefactor more. However, once we are in the house I suppose we shall not see much more of her, and a great deal of the electric light and improvements, and I hope it will turn out for the best.

We certainly like the house better and better, and have found some asparagus in the garden. While we were walking round the outside of the property with Mrs West her upper-class eye caught sight of that innocent picnic bottle, lying where we had laid it. And she immediately broke into a bristle, How did it get there, What impertinence, enquiries, trespassers, lower classes (in the face of that elegant bottle, too, the idiot!) et patati et patata. And we looked on, like the goats in the story, with a sorrowful eye, and then gently removed her from the subject by an enquiry about the rubbish collection in Maiden Newton.

TO PAUL NORDOFF[3] *4:vi:1937*   *24 West Chaldon Dorchester Dorset*

Dear Mr Nordoff,
    Your letter reached me this morning; and I am afraid there is no chance

1. Born in 1913. His working life has been divided between an inherited family business at Street, in Somerset, and a family philanthropic enterprise centred in Wilmington, Delaware. In October 1936 he was in Barcelona with instructions to make a report to a society in London that was arranging medical aid to the Government side, and he was lodged in the same suburban villa with STW and Valentine Ackland. He fell seriously ill with influenza and they, with the help of a Spanish woman named Asunción, took care of him.
2. That is, an Englishwoman who had lived in India.
3. (1909-77), American composer of operas, symphonies, chamber music, ballets, and song cycles. From 1935 to 1943 he was head of composition at the Philadelphia Conservatory.

that we can meet before you sail on Sunday. I am not sure if I shall be in England or not during the later summer, so I will not suggest any plans for meeting then. I am sorry for this, as I should like to hear your music, and I should like to hear about Polynesia too. For you have been more conscientious than I. I wrote *Mr Fortune* with a placid disregard for fact. It happened that I very much wanted to write the story, and did not feel inclined to postpone the writing of it, or even compromise my views on how it should be written, by seeing Polynesia first.

After this confession, I can hardly reproach you for doing your opera before you wrote for my permission, can I? I think it will be quite all right, I certainly will not put any spoke in your wheel. But as a matter of prudence and etiquette, may I suggest that your librettist should write to my American publisher, and ask permission to make a libretto of the book with a view to possible performance. It is a formality. But I believe that there are certain matters of copyright, and as I don't want any possible performance of your work to be jeopardised by a last minute hitch over libretto rights I hope you will let me advise you to do this.

To Oliver Warner 28:vi:1937   *Guilford Street* [*London*]

Dearest Oliver,

A couple of little jobs. We may—extremely doubtful—be going to Spain on a writer's delegation to the congress of the International Assoc. of Writers in Defence of Culture, which is being held there.

Just in case we are conveniently encountered by a Ger. Ital. bombardment, you will remember, won't you, that you are my executor; and that our wills are in the top drawer of a walnut chest of drawers in the pink sitting-room of 24 West Chaldon. N.B. it sticks.

I would rather Nora[1] did *not* help in going through my things: she isn't likely to want to, but in case of trouble keep this letter to show my wish.

The other little job—much more probable—is, that if the Foreign Office should ring up tomorrow to ask if Valentine Ackland and Mary Kathleen McCrory Ackland are the same, you will assure them that they are, and that Valentine is a pen-name. The reason for this being that her passport is M. K. M. and her invitation to attend the Congress is addressed to Valentine Ackland.

I shall give them your name, but to be on the safe side would you pass the word to Ian[2] and Chatto.

1. Her mother, then Mrs Ronald Eiloart.
2. Ian Parsons.

To Naomi Mitchison[1] *17:vii:1937*   24 *West Chaldon*
                                               Dorchester Dorset

Dear Mrs Mitchison,

I have just got back from the Writers' Congress in Madrid and Valencia. Among the delegates I met a friend of yours, Mr Seu, who asked me, on my return, to write to you and give you his greetings.

I am sure that you will be glad to hear that Mr Seu looked very well—even under bombardment in Madrid he continued to look as serene as a water-lily; and that his speech as delegate from China was one of the best speeches of the congress . . .

Now that I have given you my message I should end my letter. But I have something else to ask you. And I will not beat about the bush, I want some money. The circumstances are these. There is a very serious soap shortage in Spain. The hospitals still have a little, but ordinary civilian and military life is soapless. And I undertook, at the request of Dr Hodann of Valencia, to try and get soap sent to Spain as soon as possible. Actually, the first consignment has started; for the Comité Sanitaire in Paris have sent £25 worth already, which I have guaranteed.

But of course much more is needed. And I am now trying to raise money for another consignment among women writers. Women, for some reason, are supposed to be particularly concerned with soap; at any rate, we have a reputation for being practical. It seems best that the soap should go from France, both because of time-saving and the pound-franc exchange; and the Comité Sanitaire are ready to do our buying and sending for us, being experienced in such things.

But we must raise the money, amongst ourselves, as I hope, and by the odious activity of soliciting our friends. It is really a serious matter, this shortage, and entails much suffering on all classes. It is heart-rending to see the women patiently *rinsing* children in that very hard water; and of the finally discouraging and demoralising effects of being dirty against one's will I need not speak, nor of the danger to public health. I hope I can count on your sympathy.

To Oliver Warner *27:vii:1937*   24 *West Chaldon Dorchester*
                                          Dorset

Dearest Oliver,

I have been a Hog with Bristles not to have written to you before—though I got back ten days ago I have not had a moment to turn around in since, not to turn around with any feelings of leisure and amplitide, such as I would want when I write to you.

1. Scottish novelist, short story writer, and poet.

46

Well, it was all most satisfactory. I expect you know that we went illegally, the F.O. having most definitely refused to grant that cultural reasons were valid reasons for going. We delayed a couple of days just to arrange that a protest should be made at our being not allowed to go, and when that was nicely en train, entrained ourselves, at least actually en-air-linered ourselves. I knew I should be frightened of flying, so I thought it was a good way of getting myself in order for what might occur later.

We went to Barcelona again, to Valencia, where the Town Hall where we had our sessions has had a bomb through the roof which just missed the two most magnificent cut-glass chandeliers I have ever set eyes on—like two frosted walnut trees hanging upside down in a pale blue and pale gold saloon. And I think it is typical of Spain that I had been twice in that town hall before I happened to notice that the marble steps had a great scar across them, that the ceilings all round the gallery were showing their lath-work, and that the walls had great pits and gashes in them.

And we went to Madrid. Three nights of bombardment, one pretty heavy, and a superb view of an aerial battle, when our fighters went up straight into the formation of fifteen Caproni bombers and scattered them. I have never seen such flying, such speed and precision. We came into all this because the Government were carrying on an advance. Whenever the Government forces do well the Fascists always shell and bomb the centre of Madrid, in order to break the civilian morale. Poor muts! For they don't. People in Madrid are very quiet, no swagger at all. But the women, on whom these persuasions of shell and bomb are lavished, wear, one and all, whether they are old or young, stupid or intelligent, whether they look well or tired— and most of them look deadly tired—the same expression of indomitable concentrated rage. If you talk to them they are as friendly, as kind, as you please. But the moment they leave off talking this look of whitehot bad temper comes back. It was the most impressive thing I saw in Spain.

We were the guests of the Spanish government, and they gave us a strange fairy-tale hospitality, very generous, beautifully thought out, and with a kind of wild romance running through it . . . For instance, when we arrived at Madrid, after days of motoring, our cars turned into a sort of park, where, galloping down the dusky avenue, three mounted sentries met us and heard our qualification of being 'los Intelectuales.' Then we were turned out in front of a sort of Petit Trianon, and went into a grand room where there was a long table spread with wine and dishes of cold snacks. And this was a 'lunch' (lunch is any minor meal, irrespective of time) pre-sented to us by General Miaja, whose secretary told us how sorry the General was not to be there to receive us himself, but that he was busy at the front. While we sat eating lovely snacks and drinking the best Manzanilla it has ever been my fortune to drink, we could hear the distant grumblings of that front.

And think, Oliver, of hearing those words, *los intelectuales*, spoken, and never dreading them, never feeling the usual awkwardness and confusion of being a representative of culture. Think of hearing soldiers and people in small country towns, and peasants harvesting, speaking those words with genuine enthusiasm and understanding and kindness. Think, in fact, of being able to be, at last, genuinely glad, genuinely unembarrassed at being a representative of culture—not, as in England, a mock and scorning, not, as in USA, a sort of circus animal; but something that is really a credit to the human race. *And this is the reception that we got from everybody*. Not just from representatives, who might have been trained (though it was unmistakably echt); not just from other intellectuals; but from sentries, from shopkeepers, from hotel-keepers, from the people in the small towns where we stopped for petrol. Think, my dear. And then remember how our Foreign Office does not accept culture as a legitimate reason for travelling to Spain. If you are an accredited journalist, yes. If you go on a humanitarian errand, yes. If you go for business reason, YES! (This is what they told me there) But if you go for cultural reasons, NO.

Meanwhile, there is being a dinner for Arthur Machen. And thank you very much, I will come with great pleasure if I possibly can—the proviso is only that there is no date, and I may have to be in Paris for a few days in October. But Valentine, with an equally grateful heart to you, unfortunately can't. The reason, between ourselves, being that she has no evening clothes, and we fear that the hospitality of the National Liberal Club could only fit her out with a white waistcoat, and this, though probably becoming, Would Not Do.

To Paul Nordoff 5:ix:1937   *Frome Vauchurch*
                                   Maiden Newton Dorset.

Dear Mr Nordoff,

I am so very sorry. But I cannot get to London, and I cannot ask you to come down here. A friend of mine who was travelling in the west of England was taken sick on her journey, and is here being nursed, and it ties me here.

It is a real disappointment to me, both not to hear your music and to meet you. It is so very nice of you to want me to hear it, and to have been ready to make a journey so that I might do so; and I feel very mean not to have responded to your kindness as I should have liked to.

But please do not carry into action what you too impetuously say about not feeling licensed to carry your music to performance without my approval. I know enough about music—indeed, when I was young I composed, and was convinced that music was my metier—not to know that a work of music is a complete and separate thing, and that the libretto from which it springs is only the earth in the pot that the flowering plant grows from. I have manhandled enough texts for my own purposes to know this; and I beg of you to feel as I do on this matter.

To Steven Clark 6:ix:1937

Frome Vauchurch
Maiden Newton Dorset

Dear Steven,

You see, we are really here. We have been in for about a fortnight, quite long enough to know if we are going to like it or not. And we like it extremely.

It is a most accommodating house, took our furniture to its bosom without any cavillings. The cat likes it, we like it. The river is full of trout (Valentine has become a passionate Piscator, studies Hardy's catalogue day and night, and has a new weapon on the strength of it, a small silvered kosh called demurely 'a priest', with which to whack trout over the head) and chirrups with moorhens and their broods and contains a water-rat who swims under our windows looking like a half-submerged bulrush.

This last visit to Spain was infinitely happier than Barcelona. It was like Barcelona with a great many Asunciós and no O'Donnels[1] and Feas. No that is not quite true. We had Stephen Spender with us and he is a kind of O'Donnel in the flesh, an irritating idealist, always hatching a wounded feeling; but positively no Feas.[2] O Lord, we met such a lot of nice people, people in hotels, people in shops, our chauffeurs and so forth. I find myself deeply at home with the Spanish, I cleave to their particular variety of practicalness. For instance, when we had a tyre blow-out between Valencia and Tarragona, and the spare tyre was found to be as bad as the injured one, our driver, wasting no time in useless acrimony or lamentation, went off, gathered a large handful of walnuts, hammered them open with a stone, and fed us as we sat by the roadside.

---

1. Probably Hugh O'Donnel or O'Donnell. 'Hugh O'D had, I think, some position of authority in the Spanish Medical Aid Committee (a London body) and carried that to Barcelona. In spite of his Irish name, I think of him as being one of the British in Barcelona in those weeks and a fish out of water.' Steven Clark to the editor, 7 October 1981.
2. Fea is not a proper name but the feminine of the Spanish adjective for ugly. 'She was one of the English in Barcelona in those weeks 45 years ago, and though her sympathies may have been in the right place, she could not, unlike Sylvia, love Spaniards.' Ibid. Because Asunción once referred to her as La Fea, STW, Valentine Ackland and Steven Clark took to speaking of her by that name.

... I must apologise that I did not send that note on our non-union writers. I had it all drafted; and have been so taken up this last week with that sub-committee for Spain that I never got down to the final licking. And when I thought I saw the hour I found myself invoked to write recipes for Basque children (who were, so the invoker said, becoming horribly constipated on wholesome English food); and Martha-ed instead of Mary-ed, which will not surprise you, I daresay.

We entertained Professor Shelley Wang at the week-end. He arrived with a large suitcase held under one arm, and the handle of the suitcase in the other hand, like a talisman. The suitcase had given way under the weight of books in it, we had to go to the local leather shop to find him another, and Mr Pouncy's mind opened unwillingly to the idea that suitcases should be used for other objects than suits. However the East wore Mr Pouncy down, and Shelley Wang went on to Exeter (which he insisted on calling Executor) leaving the broken suitcase under the spare-room bed and the handle on the mantelpiece. We loved him very much, but I am afraid his Dorchester audience found him perplexing. He told them stories of the Chinese revolutionary spirit, but did not make it clear that the stories dated, many of them, from 3000 BC, and had, naturally, become stylized in course of time.

One of these stories I saved for you, it was so beautifully Marxian. A Chinese dictator, determined to have peace in his dominions, took away all their weapons from the peasants. The metal thus collected he had melted down and cast into the shapes of twelve massive religious figures which adorned his palace. In the end the peasants overthrew him with sharpened bamboos.

You will see that this seemed all rather odd to the Dorchester Labour Party.

1. Poet, essayist, biographer, and editor.

1938

To Steven Clark *11:v:1938*

... This place is most beautiful. We love it far more than we thought we should. The river is an incessant pleasure, and is always handing us small nosegays of beauty or entertainment. The latest nosegay is a posy of three fat young water-rats who have just learned to swim. They cross the river swimming with every limb, their tails lashing about, their eyes heady with purpose; and swarm up the bank and sit in a clutch, pressed close together, chewing the same iris stalk. Now the nightingales have just arrived. They came on a night of sharp frost, it was curious to hear their passionate excited voices singing of summer on that rigid silence of frost.

I have developed quite a talent for public speaking, and ornament the platforms of Wessex. I enjoy it very much, especially the applause. The first time I got an audience to interrupt my peroration by cheering in the middle of it I thought I should grow wings. It is a rapturous sensation. My great trouble is, to remember, after my moving closes, not to sit down looking like a cat that's got at the cream, which must modify the effect, even if it shows an endearing candour and humility. I have also developed a record speed in gutting trout. Valentine hauls them out most skilfully, and we eat them every day.

... As for Mexican cook-books ... Go to, Master Steven! There are larger fish to fry. And every diletante (two ls?) in the English-speaking world must needs trot into the kitchen and trot thence to a publisher, the language is lousy with cook-books.

To Oliver Warner *25:viii:1938*

... How soon, dear Oliver, should I start being a nuisance with the firm about the dust-cover of my new book?[1] Having written a long book about Spain without a single mantilla in it, so to speak, I do not want to be belied by a Sandeman's port picture on its outside.

1. *After the Death of Don Juan.* '... a parable, if you like the word, or an allegory or what you will, of the political chemistry of the Spanish War, with the Don Juan—more of Molière than of Mozart—developing as the Fascist of the piece.' To Nancy Cunard, 28:viii:1945.

You are luckier with your orchard than we. We pruned most attentively in January, and had a delightful show of blossom; and just as the fruit was setting we had a thirty-hour salt south-west gale that blew off all the fruit and blighted all the leaves a dismal brown; and now we have exactly five apples in the garden, if they have not fallen off overnight. Adam and Eve could be put in this part of the West country in perfect safety this year, there is not an apple worth looking at, and it would take a serpent to hunt out the few miserable specimens we have.

Trout, on the other hand, have done nicely, and the priest has been busy at his consoling functions.

1939

To Oliver Warner *30:iv:1939*

Dearest Oliver,

It was my great-grandfather.[1] I am pleased to know where he was educated, I never knew before. But the medal must remain unclaimed, as far as I'm concerned. He was a holy evangelical character, had a poor parish in Leeds, and a cough; and his loving parishioners felt sure he was dying, so they presented him with a gold watch inscribed Redeem The Time; and an affectionate subscription; and he went off to Torquay with his poor chest, and lived to a ripe old age, and married the lady who should have bequeathed me the public house called The Black Dog. But it was sold—low, I suppose.

Now you will please write me a little letter saying that I am by character and finances a suitable person to be granted a visa to America. I'm not sure that I'm going, but I'd like the visa to help me make up my mind.[2] Write it all grand on the firm's paper, and that should do admirably. I don't seem to know any clerics or Justices of the Peace.

To Paul Nordoff *21:vi:1939*   *26 Jane Street. N.Y.C.*

Dear Paul Nordoff,

I am sending back your copy of *Mr Fortune* with an inscription.

I wish I could convey half the pleasure and excitement that your music gave me. I have been talking of it ever since—and demanding of my friends that they should demand a performance of it.

I have had various songs set by various people; and on the whole I have been lucky in my composers: but as a rule I have a private feeling that I could have set the words better myself, and my appreciation has a twinge of self-sacrifice in it, as though I were giving way in an argument.

I want to tell you that in your setting of *Mr Fortune's Maggot* I had no such reserve. From the first phrase of the prelude (which incidentally I woke up the next day remembering as though I had known it all my life)

1. See letter to the editor, 20:xi:1962.
2. It was a question of attending the Third American Writers' Conference in New York, called to consider the loss of democracy in Europe.

your music carried me with it. It does seem to me that you have written a most beautiful thing, and I am proud and happy to be in the centre of it.

There are innumerable things I could specially praise: the economy, the absence of fuss, the power of inventing the right device (like that beautiful arioso and chorus in the bathing-pool scene); but I would rather praise the *unanimity* of the work; for plenty of music has good qualities, fine details of invention, and yet is not good and fine music; but yours both has, and is. It was a wonderful evening, and one I shall never forget.

I seem to be writing all this very belatedly, but the truth is I went into New England for the week-end, and did not get your parcel till my return yesterday.

I stayed in a queer place. A country house with large grounds about it, the whole thing only about twenty or thirty years old, and already the forest primaeval is getting back on it. The kitchen garden is gone back to pasture, the pastures have gone back to woodland, little trees poke up on the lawn.

To Paul Nordoff *14:vii:1939*   *24 Jane Street N.Y.C.*

My dear Paul,

I am so sorry that you are having all this worry and trouble—and I don't see how you'll avoid it. When I read your words 'it will be necessary for me to stay here in the city till some sort of order is restored' I grinned a dry grin. Isn't it odd, all artists are supposed to be so impractical, unbusiness-like, and so forth; and the moment anything befalls that has to be sorted out, who does one see stripped to waist in the midst of the mess? the artist.

Is it possible that you could get time off later on to come and stay in Warren County, Conn? I shall be sharing a house there for the next six weeks with two other petticoats (both of them, of course, wearing trousers). It is a completely plain-headed house, no instrument of music except a melodion in the attic, but it is lovely country, full of wild raspberries and red-haired butterflies sitting on pink flowers, and cool mountainy airs, and a general feeling of Robert Frost. I only know the charms so far, no doubt when I'm living there I shall know the drawbacks too; but it promises well, and anyhow the country is lovely—so if you could come for a week-end or so, it would be a great pleasure to me. I am going there on Monday, the address is c/o Walter Kibbe, Warren, Conn. There is a letter box under an apple-tree.

It is so gratifying of you to say in your letter that you like me. Things of that kind, which can be very important, people usually omit to mention. Personally, I have no use for unspoken affections, and so I will most readily reply that I like you a great deal, and look on my meeting with you as one of the best things I have found in this country.

And I am so sorry that you are having all this worry, plus that disappointment about the engagement. And I wish you, in the language of the English liturgy (you'll have to borrow that prayerbook again), a happy issue out of all your afflictions.

To WILLIAM MAXWELL[1] *30:ix:1939*   *Hotel Latham, 28th Street*
at Fifth Ave. New York

. . . It seems that in the depths of my being I am an unappeasable idiot. I have the profoundest doubts about this war. I don't feel that it is being fought against Nazidom, and while Chamberlain is around I doubt if it will be. And I can't suppose that going back will better it or me. But for all that I feel that my responsibilities are there, not here.

To OLIVER WARNER *12:x:1939*   *Frome Vauchurch*
Maiden Newton Dorset

Dearest Oliver,

Just a line to tell you that we got home yesterday. After a safe and painless passage on the Manhattan; painless, that is to say, except that owing to the absence of cargo and the fact that the usual ballast of pig-iron could not be used as pig-iron might be considered munitions, the ship rolled like a dog.

And then, just when we were in port, and sitting waiting for the immigration officers to come and give us landing tickets, all of us sitting in glum patient rows in the saloon, the most terrible thing occurred. For a fulsome voice with a strong Irish accent upraised itself in our midst and began to intone *Land of Hope and Glory.* For a moment it was remarkably like being torpedoed. And people who had looked perfectly brave and sedate during the voyage suddenly turned pale, and looked round for escape. There was of course no escape. The singing came from a large fur-coated white-haired lady surrounded (rather like Britannia) with a quantity of parcels. And she sang all through that embarrassing stanza. Then she paused, and looked round challengingly. We all pretended we had heard nothing unusual, nothing, in fact, at all. After a while she sang the doxology. After that she sang no more.

Mrs Keates (who with her old husband and her small foster-child) is evacuee here, greeted me with: Oh Miss, thank God you're safe at last. An odd implication, and one that would have seemed queer to some of my

1. American novelist and a fiction editor at *The New Yorker.*

55

more excitable friends in USA. Except for the Air Raid Precautions it certainly seems safe enough at present. But it is frightening to go out at night and stand in total darkness and hear the Wardens go tearing past in search of something to do—like the Gubby Hounds in Cornwall only the Gubby Hounds are usually overhead.

TO PAUL NORDOFF *27:xi:1939*

Dearest Paul,

Your letter came this morning. I can't tell you how glad I was to see it, letters from the States take so long and it is a melancholy feeling that every day one becomes more isolated, more cut off and mentally endangered by isolation. And your letters have the particular grace in a time like this of being as natural as though there were no more than a town-line between us . . .

So you went back to Colebrook. I don't wonder. I have been back there many times. I remember every leaf on that locust tree, every apple, every twist of that ramshackle gipsyfied vine; and the view from that dining room window the evening of our last dinner, the green meadow darkening, the white flowers turning to scattered clots of sea-foam, the outline of the stand of corn stiffening against the remains of daylight in the sky. And the cricket in the window-screen, and that absurd spinning-wheel, the cradle with the logs in it, Franklin's[1] arrangements of petunias, the wooden doors so thin and the wooden flooring so massive. All my life I shall remember Colebrook and how happy I was there - - a happiness one could dive into and never be threatened with grating one's nose on the bottom of it. What an amazing fortune, as amazing as the hazards in music, that brought us into our harmony there, in a place we had scarcely given a thought to in our respective life-times.

I can only compare it to music. This is the shape of the leaf and this of the flower.

TO ALYSE GREGORY[2] *3:xii:1939*

. . . It is very difficult to apprehend it. Llewelyn for so long had defended Llewelyn from death that I can scarcely believe the wall is breached.[3] I

1. Franklin Brewer, Nordoff's friend.
2. (1884-1967), American essayist and managing editor of *The Dial*, and the wife of Llewelyn Powys. After his death she stayed on in Dorset for a dozen years and then moved to the village of Morebath, near Tiverton, in Devonshire.
3. Llewelyn Powys died in Switzerland of a massive stomach ulcer, having been in and out of tuberculosis sanatoria for years.

often thought of him as deadly ill—but never as an invalid. He always seemed to me in those Chaldon days to be the healthiest, the most vital person in our society. We might be sad and bewintered; but Llewelyn, as on the day he was carried into court on a litter, always had a daffodil in his buttonhole, and news of some enjoyment on his lips, always shrewd, positive and alert. If nature could mourn, she would mourn for Llewelyn, and there would be a train of foxes[1] at his funeral.

1. See letter to Julius Lipton, 3:v:1935.

To Steven Clark 3:ii:1940

Dear Steven,

It is disgraceful that I have meant for so long to write to you, and put it off for equally long. Blame it on the war, not me; there is something oddly inhibiting about this long spell of death in the icebox, one develops the feeling that since one has nothing blood-curdling to write about one must put off writing till there is. And the thought of the poor patient censor almost forbids the usual trivialities of correspondence, it is like lighting a cigarette in church.

However, I purpose to light my cigarette. USA is still my favourite subject of contemplation, and at the moment I am brooding contentedly on Cambridge, Mass: where the city council ordered that the name of Lenin be purged from every book in the boundaries (including mentions of Leningrad), and where a young man sat for seven hours in a tree in order to demonstrate his love to a young lady. But I do take pains to remember that there must be people equally silly in Cambridge, Cambs. And that probably the main difference between them is that the local idiots do not command such good publicity.

And this afternoon the Parish (or rather the Abbotsbury Rural Deanery) Magazine arrived, and so I have been very happy with my tea. The earliness of Lent is causing these parish priests considerable concern. 'Lent is so early this year' remarks the incumbent of Langton Herring with Buckland Ripers 'as almost to take one by surprise.' At Puncknoll and Swyre this underhand punctuality is also creating alarm, mingled, I think, with resentment. 'Now, with Christmas barely over, Lent is rapidly approaching.' At Cattistock with Chilfrome the prospect of Lent rouses more philosophical thoughts. 'Lent in wartime has a double appeal, as already, whether we like it or not, we have to make many sacrifices and go without much we have the right to enjoy in normal times' Take in all in all, I perceive a certain revolt against Lent in the clergy of the rural deanery of Abbotsbury; what one might call a *movement*. 'On the other hand we thank God for the safe return of little Violet Dunford from Weymouth Hospital.'

At Longbredy with Little Bredy the coldness of Christmas is still the dominant impression on the mind of the church. 'The weather still pursued us—we will not say malevolently, for it has been helping the Finns—when we held our Christmas Tree.' I cannot but compare this approach to omnipotent mercies to that remark of Samuel Butler's that in making the rain fall on the sea God is like the actor who blacked himself all over to play Othello. I think that is all, except that a household hint for making a more economical marmalade by mixing it with sago is immediately followed by 'Look up at the stars, they have a cheerful twinkle.'

Now I am afraid I have made England seem too amiable; for part of the purpose of this letter is to ask you to do what you can to prevail on Janet[1] to stay in USA. She keeps on manifesting an odd desire to come back, and I am convinced that she could not do so without being horribly disappointed, and very much worse off than she is now. England is not nice. The rich may be richer, but the poor are certainly poorer, and above all it is no place for the young. This kind of war is an essentially middle-aged pursuit; its aims, its ideals, its methods, are all middle-aged. It is like a great sprawling pater-familias with all the young running errands. And I really cannot see that Janet should come all the way back in order to run errands.

As for *how* Janet stays on, that is another matter. It seems to me that Perry Street may pall, and I would like to think of her seeing more varieties of American life than she is seeing just now. But that is just a matter of wanting the apple enough to pull it from the tree, and so I feel it is her concern, not mine.

You have been very kind to her, I know from her letters, and have nourished her with a great deal of pleasure and companionship. Will the plan of going to Celo come off? I would love to hear more news of that place, how Curtis Earl Dwight[2] is holding out, and *if the baby's grave* is grassing over. Did Janet tell you of that distressing incident? Just before we left she remarked musingly that she believed from what you had told her that there was a baby buried just under the place I had chosen for a tidy rubbish burning. The moment she suggested this I felt sure she must be right. I am not lucky with buried babies, the only time I lifted a floorboard in London I found a number of probably baby bones under it (I replaced the board saying firmly that the femur looked to me more like a cat); so my last evening was spent in anxiously removing smoke-blackened stones, pieces of partially charred orange peel, etc., and strewing handfuls of fresh fair grit over the spot, while Janet and Valentine stood round reproaching me for heartlessness and irreverence, and not being humbly and quietly content to throw rubbish away under the bushes.

I remember Celo more intensely than any other place we saw. I suppose because it was the most static and classical. That half-hoop clearing and the woods rising above it, and the pasture full of white michaelmas daisies and morning mist is a thing I can call up as clearly as though it were still within a step's reach.

1. Her cousin, Janet Machen, who had joined them in America and was spending the winter in New York City.
2. A kitten that Valentine Ackland had rescued half dead from a garbage pit in North Carolina, nursed back to health, and found a good home for.

I am reading the *Mémoires* of Saint-Simon, and enjoying them a great deal. The society is so limited, the passions are so parochial and so parochially intense, that it is like sitting in some dream public-house, where the village gossip pours out his whole burden of scandal, surmise, and rancour, only wearing a peruke and the most polished manners and speaking in sentences as polished and labyrinthine as the convolutions of a shell. It is a perfect book to be reading just now, its loveliness crowned by the fact that the small print un-annotated edition is in twenty volumes; and I thank my providential lack of enterprise that I have never read it before. C'étoit un de ces insectes de cour qu'on est toujours surpris d'y voir et d'y trouver partout et dont le peu de conséquence fait toute la consistance. It is full of things like that. A Babylonian hanging garden of a book.

TO PAUL NORDOFF *16:ii:1940*

. . . Snow is nothing to you, I suppose, except that snow is always snow; and it's not much novelty to us this winter, for we have had it on and off since before Christmas . . . we went out for a walk across the water meadows this evening . . . a dull small moon, but most of the light came off the snow . . . There was not a sound except our creaking footsteps, and the rattling roar of the water running through the sluice; an old wooden contraption, sleek and darkly glittering in its ice-coat. The water was charcoal black, curving through the flat white meadows it was like the artist's first serpen-tining stroke on the white paper. Suddenly in this black and white world we saw a clear marmalade-coloured star, slowly, it seemed, descending towards us. For a moment we were completely baffled, then a friendly noise explained that it was the evening train, coming down over the hill. Valentine said: Look how it shows up! If there were an air-raid we shouldn't stand a chance. I answered mildly: Perhaps the air-raid might not coincide with a train . . . which is indeed quite a possibility, since ours is only a minor line with few trains. These discussions about being killed from the air have become like a very slow game of chess in which I handle the defensive, countering Valentine's pessimism with an exasperating pawn, or some forgotten bishop rushed up from the corner of the board. Our standpoints by now have be-come purely conventional, it is Valentine's part to try and checkmate me, and mine to throw out her moves by inventing little words of cheer and comfort.

. . . I feel sometimes that my eyes will give out, perish, if they don't rest on a Latin outline. I would like to sit on a hot stone wall, smothered in dust and breathing up the smell of those flat-faced roses that grow along the edge of Latin roads, or perhaps the rich harmonious stink of a heap of rotting oranges thrown in the ditch; and look at oxen, and small dark men with alert limbs and lazy movements, such as cats combine. And I would like to sit outside a café of atrocious architecture, drinking a pernod, and looking across at some Jesuit great-grandmother of a church that I shan't go into. And I would like to touch small hard dry hands like lizards, and hear people saying Tss, Tss, when a handsome girl goes by. And see small proud boys making water against notices that say they're not to. And awful dogs of no known breed being addressed as Jewel; or alternatively as Bastard and Sexual Pervert.

To Paul Nordoff 16:iii:1940

... My life just recently has not been quite so tranquil as I could wish. I have had to go ... up to London to see a solicitor about my cousin's divorce, she couldn't go because her child was sick. And in addition we have been rather more seriously domesticated than we usually are. We have two very nice soldiers billetted on us, and one of them was pining because he loves his wife and she was pining, so we suggested she could come and stay here for a visit to us, which would enable her to see him. But it makes us feel rather more concerned about hot meals and clean floors.

The nicest thing about London just now is the black-out. It is indescribably moving to see that city just quietly abandoning itself to darkness, as though it were any country landscape. Meekly settling down in the dusk, shutters going up in windows, walkers pattering home, here and there a few modest mediaeval little lanterns being fetched out and set at the threshold of the subways entrances; and the darkness falling, and the noise thinning out from a mass of sounds to individual sounds, as though the night combed it.

I will tell you a nice thing the solicitor said. Divorces, said he, would be half the price and half the trouble if men who are being divorced would not insist on trying to be a hero to both women. But he didn't seem to think there was any cure for it.

To Paul Nordoff 30:v:1940

... It was thanks to Valentine I had this lovely spell of solitude and industry. I was trying to get the book finished and sent to USA before the war crashed down on it; and just at the same time we had a letter from a friend of ours saying she had been ill and had been told she must convalesce in the country. She is poor, and we had to have her; but I groaned in spirit, knowing what a toll the harmless convalescent can extort. Then Valentine most nimble-wittedly, and most nobly, packed me off to Rats Barn and stayed to prop the convalescent single-handed. I felt the only possible return I could make was to enjoy myself a great deal. So I did.

The war cast a queer colour over one night while I was there. I had been out walking late, it was about ten o'clock and quite dark except for starlight, when the noise of guns began and the sky lit up with flashes. Gunfire light is quite different to lightning, it doesn't twitch, it just glares and goes, glares and goes. I hadn't seen a paper for two days, owing to my shameless seclusion from the world. I walked on speculating, over these bare solemn hills so oddly disturbed, and deciding that this was too irregular to be anything but a real engagement, for a practise is usually metronomic, and hoping that when I got back I should not find those two riding horses having hysterics in my doorway; and all the time with the queer feeling that somehow I had got into that picture of Ryder's called Death and the Pale Horse, and that if only I knew it there was a fine lithe serpent snaking along beside me. When I got back the house was rattling like an old buggy. Then all of a sudden everything was quiet, so I knew it had been only a practise, more realistic than usual.

The thing that really depresses me about the future, my own immediate future, I mean, is the thought of our local ARP. Recently we have had two rehearsals. It is like a knock-about farce film done in slow motion, and at intervals some member of the local gentry pipes up to say, 'Well, let's hope it will never be needed,' or 'We can't really get on with it without Mr Thompson,' or 'Has it started yet, do you know?' The most melancholy thought is, that if there is a real raid they will all dauntlessly turn up to mismanage it, for their courage is as unquestionable as their artlessness. I think myself Tennyson's *Charge of the Light Brigade* has a lot to answer for.

To Paul Nordoff *1:vi:1940*

... We had to sell our car. Owning a car became beyond even an expensive joke. Instead, we have bought two motorized bicycles. Like ordinary bicycles with small two-stroke engines attached. I am the only person in Europe who never learned to ride an ordinary bicycle, now I am in the absurd state of having to learn how to remain upright on an engine that I can drive perfectly well. It is like those religious conflicts when the spirit knows exactly how to behave and the flesh just won't. I expect to enjoy it a great deal when the flesh will. What an unusual expectation! The first time I have ever experienced it this way round.

Dearest Paul, it is so good, so patient and generous of you to ask us to USA on the Pulitzer. Particularly, patient: for I hardly dare to imagine how *exasperating* we must seem in remaining here. But you must just somehow go on believing that we are in our right minds. Put it this way. It's not patriotism, and it's not obtuseness. It's realism. It is a modulation inherent in the tune, it's a variation that the ground bass demands. Sometimes I am blue with fear, but it is always the quality of fear one has before a difficult passage that has to be dealt with; and I remember the flat-headed alleycat cautious yet passionate curiousity I felt driving over that bony plain towards Madrid, and how the driver suddenly halted the car, and told us to get out, and stood squinting upward towards a group of approaching aeroplanes, and how in an instant I had noticed a ditch under a few scrubby trees, with ants crawling around in it, and was thinking quite serenely, Well, this time I'll overlook the ants . . .

Another thing I appreciate very much, darling, is that you don't say how anguished you are about England . . . I hope you will never have to know how, when the thought of your country is like a toothache, the sympathy of people whose country is not like a toothache can wear holes in one's self control.

To Paul Nordoff *3:vii:1940*   *The Hill. Winterton. Norfolk*

. . . Valentine has told you, I think, that we are here: with a few remarks on family life. As it's not my family I get considerable philosophical entertainment from the set-out here. Ruth is a good woman, but Riddled with Christianity, and never happy unless she is suffering more than anyone else or doing more than anyone else. Preferably, of course, both. She reminds one of that Byzantine view of Jesus called 'Jesus Reigning from the Cross.' Just now she is about 250 yards away, but I can hear her quite plainly. She is talking to a Medical Officer about her First Aid group, and rapidly getting him down. Her tactics could teach Hitler quite a bit about overpowering resistance by surprise envelopments and bombs fitted with megaphone devices. Just now I heard her ejaculate 'stockings!' at the top of her voice. This surprises even me a little, and I know her tricks. The Medical Officer doesn't, and so on him the effect must be even more unnerving.

This place is very beautiful, and you would love it. It is right on the coast. As I look out of the window I see on two sides nothing but pale sand-dunes and pale sea. Inland the country is flat as a chessboard, a thrifty sandy soil, patterned with pale corn and oats and barley, and broken with great stretches of inland water, called Broads. Windmills and church towers stand up all around. One can see for miles and miles, and everything is pale and severe. It is so flat that it might just as well be mountains. No boggy valleys or Walden Ponds.

The people have bony noses, and cunning grey eyes, and talk in snarling rasping voices, like foxes barking. They have obstinate upright characters and violent tempers, and are as proud as Lucifer, and very nice and easy to get on with, because thay are all as good as you are, and better.

. . . I am well and cussedly serene. As my dear uncle by marriage Arthur Machen observed to me: There are always idiots but war makes them more noticeable. So when I have fits of thinking that soon the British Government will compel me to scream, I calm myself by remembering that the fault is mine, not theirs. They are just about what they have always been, but I have fallen into the habit of noticing them. And there is always a silver lining to every bomb. For instance, when I feel a little peevish, I think of Sir Samuel Hoare in Madrid, and how the heat must be affecting his bowels. And then I go on so bravely and calmly, nourished by the sufferings of that good old man.[1] Long long ago, when I was a happy little rich girl and taken every winter to sport in Switzerland, I met him. And he wore the most peculiar stockings, like gloves, with a compartment for each toe.

To Paul Nordoff *13:viii:1940*   *Hill House. Winterton. Norfolk.*

Dearest Paul,

Was it to you or to Franklin or to both of you that I described this Caledonian Market of a house? Anyway, I was describing what now may be called historic: for the place has been requisitioned by the army (or as Ruth goes around saying 'I have been seized') and we are all being turned out, and the contents stored.

Oh my God, you never saw such an eyeful. Ruth has no more sense of order than a magpie, and goes trotting and breathing heavily from her bedroom to the potting shed in order, say, to restore a gimlet she's found in an old right-foot boot ('How did it get there? I must have been hanging up a picture') and leaving a long trail of little booklets on spiritual healing, litanies for the Mothers Union, nut-crackers, balls of string, all the God knows whatses which she carries around in a sheaf, and lets fall like affrighted Proserpina, on the smallest movement—and she's always on the move.

1. As Secretary of State for Foreign Affairs he tried to appease Italy in the Italo-Abyssinian War, and negotiated the agreement whereby Italy was virtually given Abyssinia as a protectorate.

Yesterday evening, and sans blague, I heard her turning out a drawer and murmuring: Now whose teeth can these be?

. . . The clearance is ruthlessly being carried on by us, a sort of grinding alla marcia basso obstinato, to which Ruth supplies a florid descant. Fill up the background with billetted soldiers, commandeering officers (who come out at intervals to say that it hurts them more than it hurts us to evict a poor widow—and *when* will we be out?) chorus of holy women from the village trooping up for a farewell prayer-meeting, distracted furniture removers, and a grim silent man grimly and silently going on with the inventory, and you have us for the last week. Don't forget the four cats, all perseveringly trying to get packed in the linen-trunks.

As a result, Ruth is going to a small house in the village, and Valentine and I have rented a very small cottage, built of flint, and exceedingly out of repair: which we shall furnish with a horse hair sofa, and a couple of seicento virgins, and a jampot or two. Where we expect to be very happy. The wooden virgins are mine. They seem rather unexpected, but they have been housed here because Frome Vauchurch is not the sort of house one can put seicento virgins into. In a cottage with no bath they will be perfectly at home.

(Don't worry, by the way, about addresses. This village is so small that the post-office always knows where one is, and distributes the letters accordingly. Meanwhile, *Winterton* Norfolk will do).

19:[1]

But it is called Beach Cottage. And we are in now. It is all very much according to plan except that the door was too narrow to admit the horsehair sofa. It is really a very well-contrived little house, and furnished like Mole End with *windfalls from aunts*, and providential last minute looting. Except for a teapot, and a bucket, we've scarcely had to buy anything.

Its name is a misnomer, for it is nowhere near the beach. It is at the low end of the village, where the street peters out into sand dunes, and where the village leaves its tins and broken bottles. The dunes we can look at, but can't walk on, as they are dotted with defensive landmines. One of these went up the other day, when a tired soldier accidentally stepped back on it. There was an enormous stately tree of smoke and sand that hung on the air, slowly dissolving; and presently another soldier came running from far away, stiffly holding at arm's length a boot with a piece of bloodied bone sticking from it.

This has been a week of great air-battles, but nothing has come this way except a few raiding planes, an occasional rattle of machine-gunning overhead, a bomb dropped—in a field about a mile away. Everyone has been getting in the harvest as fast as they can, in case incendiary bombs get it first. Farmers give just the same mistrustful glances at the blue clear sky as they gave in other years to signs of rain.

1. Date of continuation of letter.

. . . Meanwhile a real incendiary bomb has fallen through the roof of the spare room at Frome Vauchurch, and eaten up a piece of a bed and a very nasty bookcase that came to us by accident and we have never remembered to give it away or otherwise get rid of it. Kit Dooley, who is living there, put it out in ten minutes. She says the mess is indescribable. I feel how providential it is that I was not there, as I hate cleaning up. Everything really is providential. Ordinarily a poor old solitary widow-woman sleeps in the spare-room because she doesn't like being alone at night in her own place; but she was not there; and ordinarily the spare room mattress is the most comfortable and expensive mattress in the house; but Kit had moved it to another bed a little before. After all this I don't see how any one can help being an agnostic.

I *am* doing a novel, but it isn't in a state to be talked of yet.

Just below me sits Valentine, by a fine fire, writing a poem perhaps, or perhaps reading the memoirs of a pirate called Shelyock, whose first captain shot a black albatross off Tierra del Fuego and was subsequently read about by Wordsworth and mentioned by him to Coleridge and thus got themselves in the Ancient Mariner . . . I wish you could see the searchlights. They are like swans with stiff necks—at once intensely moving and grand, and slightly comic in the way they make their rigid darts and pounces . . . Valentine and I spend hours in the garden watching them, while the cats fly round in the apple trees and send the apples down on us.

Valentine sends you her love, and she too assures you that you can have a peaceful mind about me; and adds that you are not to suppose she has laid me as a sacrifice on the family altar, on the contrary if anything is mincemeat as a result of being here it is the altar.

We talk of you so often. And never in the past tense.

To Paul Nordoff *17:x:1940*   *Winterton. Norfolk.*

. . . This bloody black-out! You can have no idea how exasperating it is, from indoors, and how hunted one feels as every evening one has to begin a minute or so earlier to go round letting down blinds, drawing curtains, putting up screens, all the maddening expedients for turning a room into a shoebox . . .

It makes me feel like a ghost to think how much of London is gone. Some of it in the ordinary course of nature. The last time I was there I found that the block I lived in had been pulled down; but now so much more by bombing. There are just two prayers I put about London. That St Paul's may be spared and that Sir Edwin Lutyens may not . . .

We have four Londoners here. My old charwoman, and her even older husband, who is really her lover and not her husband at all, and their youngest daughter and the daughter's baby. They are in our wicker cottage. We went round the village collecting furniture and fittings for them, and the village people were extremely kind and open-handed and efficient. The organisation that is supposed to deal with rehousing the bombed-out was none of these things, six pie-cloth blankets was all I extracted from them.

When they arrived they looked like shadows. I felt like a hostess in Hell, welcoming the dead. But I had seen them all before, in Spain. They have all settled very well except the girl. Her husband is still in London. They have only been married a little over a year, and she loves him considerably more than she loves the baby. I expect she will go back, I certainly shaln't try to stop her. Of all damnable offences preaching prudence to the young is the most damnable.

. . . My mother, hearing that Buckingham Palace had been bombed, instantly hoisted the Union Jack above her porch. It is a small porch, and no one visits it except the postman and a small child who brings the milk.

To Paul Nordoff *17:xi:1940*   *Frome Vauchurch.*
                                  Maiden Newton. Dorset.

. . . We have not looked at a single bloody bright side of anything since we got back. As a result, of course, we are in the sweetest possible humour, and being at liberty to see the drawbacks to everything we find everything satisfactory. The back stoop of our house has water all around it, and in order to get anything from the shed we have to wade through a flooded rubbish-heap. It is extremely cold, and for three days the hot-water boiler has been out of action (mended now). The house is full of feathers, because when the incendiary ate up the bed it loosed great quantities of stuffing from pillows and eiderdown, quantities of which are still floating around like unwieldy gossamer. And with wet feet and cold hands and mouths full of down we exclaim to each other (through the down): Isn't it lovely to be home? Everything's so comfortable! [censored] morning we were got out of bed at [censored] bombs falling sufficiently near to wake me. If a bomb wakes me, it can be assumed that it is too close to be disregarded. When no more fell we wondered if we would make tea, then we decided we would go out in to the garden. Oh it was so lovely to go out of the house, which wore, as all houses surprised too early do, a rather surly and dishevelled expression,

67

into that sweet night air. The sky was marbled with flat pinkish clouds, exactly like the pattern that sea makes of sand at low tide. The little river, heavy with rainfall, went by with its full hushed spinning-wheel voice; and I said to Valentine, being full of platitudes and great thoughts as one is if one wakes up too early, how extraordinary it is that one feels this profound difference between things like bombs, which one can only partially assimilate to one's experience, and things like a cloudy moonlight sky and the naked boughs of an apple tree, which are commonplaces, and part of one's ordinary being. For all its violence, war is papery-thin compared to a garden with apple trees and cabbages in it. Even when it's forced down one's throat, one can't swallow it. Whereas one goes out and eats great mouthfuls of cabbage and apple tree and moonlight. In fact, I shouldn't be surprised if in the last analysis it turns out that the horror of war is tantamount to the horror of boredom; it is the repugnance one feels to being compelled to attend to things that don't interest one.

Afterwards this lovely late moonlight turned into a sunrise with the eastern landscape banded with grey and faint golden vapours, and in the western sky a terrific tall navy blue raincloud with a rainbow climbing up it, and the elm-trees like gold inlay, and the postman coming up the drive shaking off the rain like a cat and saying that all four bombs had fallen quite close, and fallen in fields and done no harm to any one. So perish all warlike heroism: for it is undoubtedly heroic to go out on bombing raids, it is even more dangerous than going out on a horse to kill foxes. If more deeds of heroism could just fall flat there would be more hope for humanity. It is interesting how almost all working class people seem to know this without having to bother to hold it as a theory. They have almost endless fortitude, but whenever they get involved in some act of obvious or showy bravery they instantly begin to disinfect it by saying it was a bloody nuisance, or that they would never have done it if they'd had time to think, or that they've never felt such a fool in their lives. This is so marked in the eighty per cent of our population that the remaining gentry percentage have more or less to follow suit, though they very rarely achieve the true grumbling note of the working class hero malgré lui. But the essential difference goes much further when you come to think of the spectator. Working class spectators of the brave acts pour on as much disinfectant as the performers, and say that they never saw Bert run so quick, or that Alf was unlucky from a boy, always getting mixed up in things, or that his trousers will never be the same again. Gentry spectators just can't or don't attempt this, they'd as soon part with a trump.

Do you ever think of the Censor? I don't mean from the point of view of muttonising your language, for it's obvious you don't do that. But do you ever think of him as roomfuls of ladies and gentlemen, all engaged in the embarrassing occupation of reading other people's letters? What will they do when they can't be censors any longer (for they can't all become village postmistresses or go into the C.I.D.)? Will they pine and languish, and feel themselves suddenly cut off from humanity? Or will they spend the evening of their days reading Madame de Sévigné and the Reverend Leman White (I think he was called that; anyway, he loads the shelves of every second-hand bookshop, letters to ladies about their souls)? Or will they demonstrate their freedom by never opening another envelope, not even envelopes addressed to them, whitey brown envelopes marked On His Majesty's Service and containing income tax demands? Valentine had a terrible time when we got back a year ago, yearning to go into the censor's department. She has always been perfectly shameless about reading letters not meant for her, and, as she said, she was ideally suited for the work by never having much inclination to answer letters back.

To Paul Nordoff *27:ii:1941*

. . . I knew you'd like Edward Thomas. There is a very prosaic Scotch business man who runs a bookshop in London, and I discovered he'd known Thomas, and asked him what Thomas was like to know. After a pause during which he looked as though he were engaged in striking an exact percentage, he replied, He was like the rain. I believe this, don't you? The sort of sad quiet rain that is full of fine smells and bird songs.

It is all very well for you to read my stories in *The New Yorker*, and I am glad you do, and that they are there. But *which* were they? I have not heard anything from *The New Yorker* since last autumn, when they sent me a cheque for a not very good piece called *The Water and the Wine*. That was in late September, I think. Since then I have sent them five stories and several poems, and I don't know from Adam which if any they've taken, nor what they have paid me.

Mails are quite awful. Clippers take a month at least; and if *The New Yorker* sent me a cheque by boat it is probably at the bottom either of the ocean or of the censor's tray marked Immediate. Sometimes at night I become prey to the gloomiest suspicions, remembering how dear to my country is the sight of a dollar cheque; and I wonder if what *The New Yorker* has designed as a reward for my earnest persevering talent hasn't just gone straight to a Spitfire fund, labelled Anonymous.

Tonight armed with whistles, perhaps fortified with whistles would be a better term for it, Valentine and I will be out firewatching. It is a most pastoral and contemplative pursuit. We walk up and down a section of quiet country lanes awaiting the descent of possible incendiary bombs. If they did, it would become our duty to blow a series of short blasts on our whistles. Probably, being of meddlesome characters we might try to extinguish the fires too, but strictly speaking all that is required of us is whistling. The only snag is that—as you will readily understand—one cannot rehearse the series of short blasts, in case the rehearsal gave rise to false alarms and despondencies. I have tried mine out very quietly in the toilet, it seems to go all right, but how am I to know if a mezza voce whistle is going to be as good ff? The other temptation is resisting being owls. Valentines whistle is just a whole tone lower than mine, and the same interval exists between the male and female owl, and we might have such lovely conversations. It always seems to me that owls are very happy in their married lives, perhaps because they never speak during the day.

To Ben Huebsch *29:iii:1941*

... Lack of sleep, lack of fruit and vegetables, weighs heavy on children, and often they are further oppressed by overhearing bugaboo and horror-stories told by their parents. I have a small careworn neighbour, aged ten, who assures me at intervals that there will be no food at all next week, that the police will come and take his mother away to work in a factory, that the Germans have marked down Maiden Newton as their next target—and so forth. We are thinking of teaching him to shoot; he is just about the right age to learn, and it might be very upbuilding.

... This village has been perfectly quiet all the winter except for a few scraps high overhead, which perhaps we should not even have noticed if it had not been for the wild Euclidean demonstration in white chalk on a blue board written by the trails of exhaust.

To Paul Nordoff *2:vii:1941*

. . . Better than one cuckoo, two cuckoos. A pair, shamelessly amorous. They pursue each other among our appletrees, with *growls*. And the cock bird, instead of the usual trochee, has invented a charming wobbling coloratura version of his own. Beginning *forte*, CUCK-wook-wook-wook-wook-coo! Then his mistress comes growling past, and he falls off the tree and goes after her.

It is a little after midnight, our midnight, which is really 10 p.m. We have only just come in from the garden, where it was still light enough to pick flowers, though just dark enough to examine the moon through field-glasses. She has, poor thing, a sad appearance of being made of pumice stone; and tonight looked so near, so clear, that it seemed ridiculous that we could not buy a ticket at Paddington and start off to visit there. Partly pumice-stone, partly a snowball that has just begun to melt. It has been a beautiful evening, oddly veined with death. We had the wireless out under the trees, and were listening to a good performance of *The Barber of Seville*, and then, bump, bump, in the middle of the second act, we heard bombs falling just so far off that in the still air they sounded like ripe apples falling off a tree. Presently, going fast and straight, a pair of swans went overhead, and another pair, and this gave us an idea where the bombs had fallen. Meanwhile, we went on listening to *The Barber*. How delightful it is, particularly that fooling about escaping down the rope-ladder. I always enjoy his ruthlessly practical modulations. He is like a cat carrying a kitten in her mouth, he just bumps the tune down where he pleases and leaves the poor little thing to find its feet there.

There has never been more beautiful summer weather. The air is full of the scent of cut hay, and now the smell of the elder blossom has been added to it. And our garden is crammed with clove pinks, and presently we shall be crammed with raspberries. Perhaps it is a trifle like the hearty breakfast you get on the morning you are going to be hanged; but that is no reason for not enjoying it.

How ghastly, my poor darling, that departure, and all those farewells . . . nine farewells out of ten are artificial, most of one's real goodbyes are said to people who haven't any idea they are being parted with and don't know what one is saying.

To Paul Nordoff *28:vii:1941*

. . . Is it the realisation that people recently psychoanalysed tend to be dreadful bores which makes the USA army reject them for the draft? Over here it would never be taken as a valid reason for not being conscripted. I often think your country is much more humane and intelligent than mine.

We have eleven rabbits, and six rows of peas, and five rows of broad beans, and as many of french beans, and a stand of sweet corn, and a vegetable marrow bed which is positively alarming, and a fine crop of onions and a crop, not so fine I'm afraid, of potatoes, and a demonstration of a hayrick it is so exemplary, and millions of raspberries and possibly twelve apples, for it was a bad setting season for them, and all the fruit fell off: and a lot of globe artichokes, and vast quantities of greens for the winter; and I have been up to my elbows in canning and preserving and conserving, and drying of herbs. And next week we shall have a young woman and her boy of six. I am not perfectly sure about whether this will be nice, but I am sure it will be good. And at any rate she is very nice to look at, which is a considerable matter in someone who is always about the house. When we had *The Cat's Cradle Book* and lived in luxury[1] she was our servant—till she gave us notice, which she did almost immediately because it was so dull, and no young men available except a young man of her sister's called by the odd nickname of Tulip (all the fishing people in Norfolk have these extraordinary given names, and are quite seriously spoken of as Mr Starchie George and Mr Tulip Goffin). Since then she has got married, so her young men will be no concern

1. i.e. at Frankfort Manor.

of mine, and that will be a great weight off my mind. I found it very tiresome and harassing having to brood over virginities, yet if they get mislaid you are held more or less responsible. She was evacuated to a place where there was no chance of the child getting regularly to school, so she is moving herself here instead. It means turning the whole house upside-down, which is fatiguing but interesting. So many things reappear which one had lost years ago. But both the animals are steeped in woe, being under the impression that we are going to move house again. I feel it might be rather nice having a child around, he will cover everything with stickiness, no doubt, and throw balls through all the window-panes which will be irreplaceable—but with any luck he should resemble his mother's side of the family, and they are all very nice-looking, with wild bright eyes, and a great deal of dash and physical arrogance. They are most of them bad hats with good hearts. And completely equalitarian, which will make it all much pleasanter.

Yesterday Radio Paris was appealing to French householders to take badly wounded soldiers for a month. This looks as though the German losses were considerably heavier than they had reckoned for. The broadcast had a dreary flavour of Children's Country Holiday Scheme about it, when the German propaganda tries to be winsome it is like a clown with homicidal mania—ludicrous and terrifying both at once. And it is melancholy to hear it in French, and coming from Paris. But I think we said we would not write about the war unless we really had something to say about it. So I won't say any more except that I wish with all my heart you could see the searchlight effects. In the country especially among the trees and rural outlines they are incredibly beautiful and exciting. What a pity that they are not just turned on for glory and delight, like the fountains at Versailles.

To Paul Nordoff *5:ix:1941*

... Now that you are home again, and have time for a reasonable existence, and are in the literate zone of the US again, do get Virginia Woolf's life of Roger Fry. Because though a great deal of it is made parochial even to me by time, being an overlap with my own lifetime; and to you would be parochial in space too; it is worth reading as an example of how the creative mood imposes desinvoltura in the most improbable characters. For there was old Roger, brought up to be a little Quaker, with every impulse put through a sieve of conscience and scruples, and moving on to be an industrious copycat of all the Mandarins; and ending up as free and rapscallionly and outrageously honest as any man might be, sitting on benches in dusty cheap parks talking to burglars, and laying down the law with all the bravura of the lawless. Such a nice comforting story.

Isn't it pleasant to think that in all the sermons that have been preached about the Prodigal Son no one yet has mentioned that his final, his crowning act of prodigality, was to go home?

... Just as you are congratulating me on my sense in not gestating a novel I rather suspect I'm that way again. At least, for the last six weeks I have found myself pestered by some characters in search of an author; and one of them who at his first appearance was merely an unpleasant and baleful hypocrite keeps on producing strange traits of anxiety and idealism; and is, I suspect, one of those exasperating butter-fingers who havock everything, and in the end, just when you are standing over them with a hammer, there is some word, some gesture, some fidget over the well-being of a cat or a neglected geranium that freezes the hammer in your hand ... my books are apt to announce themselves in this way. But the incubation may last for years. I towed that Minna and that Sophia[1] around from 1926, God pity me, a restless pair. If things were normal I would be resigned enough, and prepared to be pleased later. But in war-time I am rather like the clerks in Valentine's office who say: 'Oh, you couldn't have one in war-time could you?—except, of course, it gets you out of being called up.' Unfortunately a novel does not get you out of being called up: or what a lot of people would now be buying bargain bundles of paper.

One bedtime story before I end this letter. A friend of mine was attending a lecture given by the organisation of the Red Cross (which is, in this country, a terrifically wealthy and autocratic and the Lord is with us affair) on first aid. For a long while the Red Cross has ignored the possibility of aid between the waist and the knee, contenting itself with a general aspiration that first aiders should not be prudish. However, air-raids are forcing them to relinquish their modesty, and this lecture was dealing with how to undress a wounded man. First of all,' said the lecturer boldly, 'you remove the trousers.' Cries from the audience, matrons and virgins' voices mingled. 'No you don't! You take off his shoes.' 'Yes, yes. Of course. You take off his shoes. The next step is to pull down the trousers.' Renewed cries. 'You've forgotten his braces.' O tempora! O mores! How could they use an old maiden so, as the song says. To tell the truth, it's like that all over the place. The tales I hear from London would make the big tears course down your innocent nose.

To Bea Howe 4:xii:1941

... and the everlasting problem of finding something new to cook or some new way of cooking the old. Supplies are very mingy and monotonous

1. See note on *Summer Will Show*, p. 39.

here, as this is a district crammed with evacuees and baggage-waggon ladies, with the population always soaring above the allotments of foodstuffs. And if it were not for the local ocean casting us an occasional crab, and what we rear in the garden, we should be living on tinned turnips and breast of mutton. I work two days a week at the Dorchester WVS—a nice office in an old house with Portland Flag floors and soothing proportions; though the county hags who come in and out don't seem to react so readily to the soothing effect of Georgian measurements. However, I can sit filling up forms like the Mole in the Blue Boudoir, and saying little more than Yes, and No, and How very inconvenient for you; for no one else in the office likes forms, and the PAC[1] keep us endlessly supplied with them, so I hope to go on wrapping my papery insulation round me while high-bred passions rage.

In between I do some lecturing for the Workers Educational Association. I have a college of young secretarial ladies near Bridport. It is a nice walk over empty hills, and I arrive as blouzed as Lizzy Bennet,[2] and talk to them about Queen Elizabeth and *The Vicar of Wakefield*, and they are very sweet and attentive, and sometimes even attend enough to ask questions afterwards. I have also lectured to over a hundred ATS. I thought that was going to be terrible, and indeed the sight of so many depressed tunics was soul-searing; but when we parted we were under the impression that it had been quite a nice evening. But the poor things were living in such horrid chilly hencoops, and it was melancholy to hear them leaping to their feet as their officers walked in, their two hundred odd uncomfortable Heavy Oxfords thundering as one—all the disadvantages of being soldiers and none of the fun.

. . . I have just come back from Weymouth this afternoon. There was a thick seamist, and all along the front one could see nothing but rows on rows of barbed wire billows fading into vapour. The seagulls must think we have gone mysteriously mad.

To Paul Nordoff *17:xii:1941*

Dearest Paul,

Your letter came this morning; and in between the writing and the receiving USA is at war. I still find it very difficult to adapt my mind to this. It is like packing when one has already begun to journey. I keep on finding things I have left out, I remember people whose reactions I had

1. Public Assistance Committee.
2. See *Pride and Prejudice*, Chapter VII.

not thought of till now, and things and projects. And I wonder how the people will be feeling, and what will become of the projects and the things. I think of our nice neighbours at Warren, the Kibbes, and the eldest boy who used to bring Valentine tributes of live snakes; and how I went into their kitchen one afternoon in late August, the wireless was blaring out news of imminent war in Europe, and Mrs Kibbe was packing string beans into jars with an expression of resolute deafness, and the old hired man was leaning back in his chair with his hands folded across his stomach, attentive and detached like an old God. Then I think of all those dear slummy Italians in Houston Street, the old grandmothers in black wrappings, and the babies in bathing slips rioting as the water-cart went by. Oh Lord, I hope they are all right, and that no one is persecuting them! . . .

I try to imagine, and can't in the least, how it would feel to be at war with the war going on so far away, and the whole enormous extent of the Middle West and the Mississippi and the Rockies between where you are and where it is. Here for so long we have been accustomed to the idea of wolves on the doorstep that paradoxically I feel it must be far more alarming for you.

I am too full of questions to be able to write. And at the same time I am sick of being interested in bigger and bloodier wars. Though I think the US is perfectly right to fight on this issue of China (and I suppose really we have all been expecting it for months) I am thankful to think you stayed out so long as you did. Two whole years of being able to call one's mental processes one's own is something well worth having had. I also reflect with pleasure on all those good Pulitzer clothes you bought. Hold on to them, guard them as your life. War makes wool grow very thin on civilians. And if you have five dollars to spare spend them on a stout pair of shoes, now, before leather goes from you. Mark these words, it is the voice of the bard. There will also be a shortage of razor blades. O, and music paper. My God, yes. *Buy a lot of music paper immediately*. And don't, my dear, unless you have already done so, hazard a great deal of money in getting a copy of the *Maggot* piano score across to me. It might just as likely go down. And I would much rather you had the money, and I got along with a very sound memory of the music. Luckily, I have a tough memory for what I like, and I have most of it tucked away somewhere behind my ears.

Valentine's mother is coming for the New Year. She always comes for the New Year. She likes seeing it Out. And In. One year, when we were all patiently grouped on a freezing doorstep waiting to hear some bloody chimes the cat rushed out and began to fight another cat. Another year, though we didn't know it at the time, an old man who had come home drunk from the inn had fallen into the river and was being drowned a stone's throw away.

. . . Scarcely a bomb all this winter—very different to last year. The only incident that came at all close was one of our own bombers that came down near by, and just before coming down went over our house with every appearance of being about to remove the chimney-pots. All its occupants bailed out and landed safely, the pilot in the same field as the plane. He had a nasty moment, as while he was in the air the plane, also still in the air, blew up below him. He heard the roar, and thought to himself, Surf. How cold the sea will be.

To Elizabeth Warner *8:i:1942*

... My hands are so cold I can neither type nor spell. Following the advice of *The Allotment Holder's Guide* I have been taking advantage of frozen ground to wheel dung over it. The dung is home produce, from our dear table rabbits; and the only reliable profit we get from those animals, since we get so attached to them we can only rarely bring ourselves to eat them. At intervals we can just bring ourselves to sell them to good homes. It is providential that our humanity stops short with the animal creation, and that we can still contrive to cut and cook the cabbages we fondled as seedlings.

To Paul Nordoff *9:iv:1942*

... Of course your music won't go. The only irreparable loss is the loss of one's private solitude. One loses one's hearing and goes on with the posthumous quartets, or one's official wits, and writes such lovely poems as Clare's in the madhouse, or one's hope of heaven, like Cowper, and keeps hares and laments felled poplars. One's powers are most home-keeping cats, whatever happens overnight they are round again by the morning, looking for their milk in the usual corner by the stove. The worst thing about losing a love ... is that, for a while, one relinquishes that personal solitude; as you say, you can't bear to be alone. But one morning you will walk into an empty room and be thankful. Then on, you will be all right again.

I have just come in, wet as a water-rat, from carrying the washing to its local depot. No more vans coming to the door now, in this new austerity of petrol. One carries most of one's things, and also one carries bits of newspaper to wrap them in—unless one chooses to be perfectly natural and walk around clutching a nude fish. On the whole it all seems to save a lot of trouble and mental wear and tear. One can't visit, or be visited, that is very nice and makes one feel unusually warmly about one's acquaintances. Housekeeping is child's play when one just buys what one can get. I don't at all object to being simplified, and personally I feel domesticity just slipping off me. It is a choice. Either one can let it go or one can intensify it. The people who intensify it seem to get quite a lot of interest out of that, too, and are as preoccupied as pirates. There is a great deal of release in hardship, people slide out on one side or the other, according to their natures.

It is a lovely day. There is a terrific south-westerly gale raging, it is lashing with rain, the fields get greener and greener as one looks at them, deepening like a thunder-cloud, they seem to be swelling with colour and moisture, the river is tearing past my window, mud-brown with silver wreaths and writings on it, the swifts, who came last week, swoop down to the surface of the water and up again, and the catkins blown off the hazels fly through the air like soft bullets.

Please don't mind if I write back to you on the verso of your letter, it is not heartlessness or inattention, just paper-saving. I still have quite a fair amount of paper, but I want to husband it, as I seem to be really writing a book[1] this time. After endless false starts and false scents. It is about four-teenth century England, almost all the characters are professionally religious, nuns, or parsons, or bishops. I am interested to find how much I know about these people, there is practically no love in the book, and no religion, but a great deal of financial worry and ambition and loneliness and sensitivity to weather, with practically no sensibility to nature. If you have no sensibility to nature the rain seems much wetter, the cold much colder, etc. It is not in any way a historical novel, it hasn't any thesis, and so far I am contentedly vague about the plot. But it is being very obliging in the way it presents itself to me as I write it, lots of good fortunes about counter-subjects that turn out to be invertible or perfectly good canons, and so on.

For a long time we wondered what we should do when we had no more stockings, now we wonder how we shall keep our last pair of stockings up when there is no more elastic. Valentine has a theory that it can be done with little tabs of adhesive tape. It worries me, I must admit, a good deal. My work takes me much among clergymen, so I must have stockings and I must keep them up. Unless the church throws itself open to women, and I can become a dean and wear gaiters it seems to me I shall have to give up my work. Why my work takes me so much among clergymen is because it takes me into villages, where clergymen still abound. They are not even rationed yet, there is one to every village. The last one I saw combined being a clergyman with what is called being a village leader. That is to say, if his village were cut off from the world by invasion, he would then have to take charge of a lot of things like deciding whether cows should be milked or slaughtered, scorched cows policy, and whether Mrs Tomkins of the local first aid should or should not have priority over Mrs Bumkin of the local air raid precautions. When asked if he was village leader he hesitated before replying, and then explained that he did not care to spread the news as he had heard that village leaders would be the first people to be shot by the

1. *The Corner That Held Them.*

79

Germans, so naturally he did not want too many people to know about it. I thought this very nice and natural of him. It is becoming my belief that if our local villages were invaded, nobody would have time to notice the enemy, they would all be too busy taking sides over Mrs Tomkins and Mrs Bumkin, and storming the village hall, that is to say if the local first aid is in possession the emergency cooking squad will be storming it from one side and the ARP personnel from another, and the boy scouts will be making their way in by the chimney and the home guards will be tunnelling in from below. There is not enough accommodation in our villages for all the things that are going on, or may be going on. Often, too, there is not enough personnel for all the various patriotic doings. I know many people who are in charge of so many different activities that the whole of their faculties will be absorbed in vetoing as one person what they wish to carry out as another. Valentine's mother is a case in point. In her ardour for service she has undertaken the charge of so many things that as far as I can reckon she will be essential in five different places at once; and as she attains terrific velocity, fells whatever stands in her path, and is permanently fitted with a screaming device like a German bomb, she will create incalculable havoc amid both defenders and attackers, besides spraining her ankle and getting very much out of breath. I often think that Mrs Ackland is the real reason why Hitler has not yet tried a landing on the East Coast. She thinks so, too.

It is very odd to look at all these poor consequential idiots and remember that war might at any moment make real mincemeat of them. Even under the shadow of death man walketh in a vain shadow. People often mention with surprise the flippant behaviour of animals in the face of death, how the live frisks over the dead animal and doesn't seem to know it's there. I don't know why they find it surprising, for in the next breath they are doing it themselves.

[PS] The Philipine news is just coming through! Oh God! God damn!

To Ben Huebsch *7:xi:1942*

. . . It was very interesting to see St Paul's among the ruins, and London, at least that part of it, looking so like Madrid, with stretches of dusty rubble and half broken Baroque churches standing up amidst the remains. It was a searching comment on our civilisation that one could not see those Wren churches with an unimpeded view till they had been half knocked to bits. Even in bits they are superb. His naves are quite as grand as his towers and spires, and the proportions of the whole buildings a rapture. Some of the working-class districts give one very different sensations. It will take generations to blow away the smell of dirt let loose—air-spun, like Mr Coty's powder. St Clement Danes is a most romantic ruin, exactly like a Piranesi print. One expects to see hooded shepherds from the Campagna sitting around it.

Another thing that was a new light on London was to see, after a showing of *The Battle before Moscow*, a perfectly respectable middle-class house leap to its feet and stand to attention through the *Internationale*. Today, to celebrate the 25th anniversary of the Soviet Revolution the BBC has performed that well-known air right through, on a gramophone record. First performance by Broadcasting House.

The news from Egypt—it took us a day or two to believe it was really there—has had the most extraordinary effect. Everyone, so affable, you wouldn't believe it was them; and a general squaring of elbows and feeling of Where do we go next?

To Harold Raymond *14:xi:1942*

... I am in just the same state, thin, busy and well. I continue to educate HM Forces with great fluency, you would never believe what a lot of subjects I can talk about. There is one group I have been doing weekly since last April, and I haven't repeated myself yet, though we are getting wilder and wilder. Next time I discourse to them it will be on How Bugles Blow; and I still have theology up my sleeve. And I have learned to drink army tea (lovingly offered and impossible to refuse, and almost always with affectionate dollops of sugar in it) without blenching. I have also learned how not to shrink or blink when saluted by a sergeant, but that took a lot of doing.

To Alyse Gregory *26:xi:1942*

... Here are some poems I would like you to see. They are by a young man who came to me out of the blue. He saw a thing of mine in *The New Yorker* and sent me a present because he liked it. As you will see by the letter he is in a sanatorium, poor boy. It isn't a manner of poetry that I care for, by nature; and there are too many words. But it seems to me he has got the emotion of vulgarity, the overtone of fairs and bank holidays and crowded summer parks, and people coming back in the evening from their day out. Verlaine has it essentially, but I can't think of any Anglo-Saxon poets who can do it. They always tag on a cause or a complaint or a moral—or else, like Whitman, they are too strenuous and good-hearted to convey this particular smell of bruised public grass.

Dearest Alyse,

Here, with much love from us both, is a small Christmas present for your evening teapot. I think I remember that you like matte.

I wish I could send you the bush. 'This large white-flowered shrub grows wild near streams.' And its old English name is Jesuit's tea, which carries an agreeable suggestion of sly domesticity; and now we don't even spell it properly. With its proper formalities it is drunk from a sort of hookah, and passed from drinker to drinker. The Jesuits must have looked very pretty at their maté-parties.

Valentine asks me to beg your forgiveness that she cannot write herself. She has been a little better today; but it is a bad bout of influenza, and I have been very worried about her, and am not easy yet.

While I look after her, and find, even in wartime, how tolerably well supplied our storeroom is for such cups and trays, I am haunted with the companionship of the innumerable people in Europe who also nurse some loved one dependent on them, and have nothing for them, nothing beyond the barest coarsest husks and hedge-brews. I feel as though I should be deformed for the rest of my life with this inequity of man's making to which willy-nilly I consent and willy-nilly profit by.

1944

To Nancy Cunard[1] *28:ii:1944*

... I am hoping very much that the possibility of the coastguard's cottage at East Chaldon will materialise, because I think you would be very happy in that landscape. It is especially fine at this time of year, when the sea is painted in oils and the land in the thinnest distemper. The pale cliffs seem to *float* on the sea, scarcely heavier than buttresses of foam the sea has cast ashore. It is country for poetry, so bare, so wide, that an old roller at the side of a field with its shafts in the air, or a wisp of straw caught on a thorn tree is something that brims up one's mind for hours. You will hear the foxes bark at night, and the vixens yowl, and presently the first dusty-white blossom will come on the blackthorns that have filled up the old chalk-pit where the shepherd throws the dead lambs. The coastguard cottages themselves are as ugly as a government could make them; but at least they are weatherproof, and not picturesque.

Disgracefully I forgot to thank Norman Douglas for his message that came in your letter. Now it is too late to make amends for I doubt if you will see him before you leave London.

I have had an obliterating cold in my head, and sneezed away all my better parts. They are beginning to creep back again now, like those poor devils that were driven away by spring cleaning. The house swept and garnished still means to me what it meant when I was a child and first heard the phrase: a very clean bare house trimmed here and there with bunches of parsley. Charming, don't you think?

To Nancy Cunard *28:iv:1944*

... I wish you were not going away. I wish the later half of your visit had

1. (1896-1965), poet, translator, memoirist, printer, and editor. The fine editions she printed at her Hours Press helped many young poets to achieve recognition. During the War her unoccupied house at Réanville, in Normandy, was vandalized by both the local peasants and the Germans. Because of her public quarrel with her mother and her own unconventional behaviour she moved in a cloud of notoriety, and no place was her home for very long.

not been blasted by the Ban,[1] and all of it nibbled by our hideous, our obscene, our disgraceful lack of leisure. I sometimes feel exactly like a bombed building, with a cloud of dust rising up from my ruined chambers. And when this metaphor seems too magnificent, then I compare myself to a member of the royal family, incessantly keeping appointments of no significance, and marvellously recognising people I have never set eyes on and wish never to see again. Now I have a notice on my table telling me to attend at the Labour Exchange with a view to taking up employment of national importance—which means they will try to put me into a laundry. If I had taken to myself a husband, lived on him and made his life a misery (as undoubtedly I should have done, as no man has ever been able to bear me as a continuity) I should not be troubled with any of this. Being kept by a husband is of national importance enough. But to be femme sole, and self supporting, that hands you over, no more claim to consideration than a biscuit. The great civil war, Nancy, that will come and must come before the world can begin to grow up, will be fought out on this terrain of man and woman, and we must storm and hold Cape Turk before we talk of social justice.

I feel that our ghosts will appear regularly on the bench outside the Strangeways Arms on each 24th of April, talking against time. How strangely we have met at last! How pell-mell, and how inevitably. I am endlessly glad we have met; and sure we shall meet again.

To Harold Raymond 25:v:1944

. . . I flourish, but with flattened ears. We are occupied by the US army, and they play rounders with baseball screechings all day in the meadow by the house, and half of them are in the garden looking for their plaything, and the other half are scrambling over the fence which it took me five months to get mended, and as they are all from the vast open spaces of Wyoming there is no hope of them learning how one feels about one's fence or one's standing hay or one's young onions. I notice that every one says: I'm sure one ought not to get into the way of abusing these poor young men, they are terribly homesick I believe: and then takes a Bath Club launch into streams of injurious anecdotes. I often wish I could hear a good consecutive statement of what the poor young men think of us. It would be like comparative religions, always so full of striking similarities, no doubt.

1. In March, 1944, because of the likelihood of an invasion of Normandy, non-residents were obliged to leave the area of the South Coast and residents to remain within it.

To Nancy Cunard and Morris Gilbert[1] *9:vi:1944*

. . . Our little house at Chaldon[2] is gone, Nancy; the little stocky grey house that sat there looking so mittened and imperturbable. A vagrant bomber dropped a two thousand pounder in the field just behind it, blew it to smithereens and cast subsoil clay all over its garden. May and Jim and May's small brother who had come for the week-end had the most extraordinary escape. May had just got them downstairs, very unwillingly because there was only a little gunfire out to sea, and they were standing in the doorway when it happened. Blast blew or sucked them out as the house fell round them. But they have lost most of their belongings, the summer's food in the garden, and a house that they loved and looked on pretty much as their own, for they knew we would not move them out unless we absolutely had to. And the only decent cottage in that village, the only cottage kept in order, gone, while the hovels belonging to the Weld estate, God damn it, are untouched in all their filth, scarcely a bug shaken out of them.

To Alyse Gregory *7:vii:1944*

Dearest Alyse,

There is a young American, Corporal Christopher Blake, who is very anxious to meet you. He had found Llewelyn's letters in the Dorchester bookshop, was enchanted by them, and began to tell me about a wonderful English writer called Llewelyn Powys, then remembered that my name was in the book, recovered himself with admirable dexterity, and asked innumerable questions. As you will have guessed, I gave him your name and address; with the qualification that you did not always feel equal to visitors; and some stress on the inaccessibility of Chydyok.

He is a young man of parts, I think. He writes, and not badly, and ambitiously, which at his age is a good sign. He talks a great deal, and often about himself, and is full of confidence, and internally, I suspect, often riddled with fears. In fact, as I say, he is a young man of parts, with all that it implies. If he does come to see you I think he may bring a chaplain with him (he is attached to the regimental chaplain, a chaplain's orderly, or whatever it is called). I said that I did not think you would want a chaplain. He assured me that this was an exceptional chaplain, a Congregationalist, an intellectual chaplain, the sort of chaplain you could take anywhere; then in a burst of candour he added that his only hope of getting to Chaldon would be to

---

1. Reporter (*New York Herald Tribune, World Telegram,* and *The Times*) and foreign correspondent. He also published a novel, short fiction, and verse.
2. See undated letter to Harold Raymond, summer of 1930, p. 17.

drive the chaplain's jeep, with incumbent, thither. The chaplain in fact, is the equivalent of a horse, a sentient means of transport.

To Nancy Cunard *26:vii:1944*

. . . with the lifting of the ban we became flooded with evacuees. I spend day after day conferring with Public Assistance, Relieving Officers, Billetting Officers, WVS ladies; and hastening from one Rest Centre to another saying words of comfort such as soap flakes can be made out of solid soap by means of a cheese-grater, nobody need be ashamed of lice nowadays, salads will not be appreciated without vinegar, Londoners seldom like porridge, pubs open at six, nettle stings are not the same as nettle-rash, fish and chips will come out in a van, lost prams shall be traced, those are *our* planes, Londoners can't be expected to go to bed before eleven, the old lady will probably leave off crying if you can get her to take her shoes off, cows don't bite, have you put up a washing-line, nursing mothers must have early morning tea, buses run on Wednesdays and Saturdays, etc. . . . I have forgotten how all this began. Anyway, this is now my life, and on the whole welcome to it, for I'd rather be overworked than rot on Lethe's wharf. But as part and lot of this I shall have two women in the house from this week-end onward. A big melancholy woman, a little like the searching Demeter, and her eighteen year old daughter who has asthma, not improved by stifling in an Anderson. It is so shameful, so disgraceful, that one is expected to *choose* them, to pick as in a slave-market. I don't feel as if they could ever forgive me for having chosen.

I expect it will be hell. The two previous lots, full of virtues, irreproachable, were hell. The first set made the house stink of breast of mutton, it stank so for months after they'd gone. I've forgotten what was wrong with the second lot, nothing I think except that they were here.

To Nancy Cunard *11:ix:1944*

Dearest Nancy,

Poems for France[1] came this morning. I like its looks very much, the empty capitals on the cover are an elegant balance. How well you correct proofs.

1. *Poèmes à la France*, an anthology of poetry written in praise of France during the Second World War by British writers, edited by Nancy Cunard. It contained a poem by STW.

How strange it is to read these poems now with the sun of today flashing on the page. It is already a historical document, this anthology of yours.

Dorch. even poor draggle-tailed Dorch. had the FFI film of Paris. How lovely it is, that gesture of the woman holding up the gun as Titian's daughter holds up her platter of fruit. Dorch. watched it through, and remained in its seat placidly awaiting the next film, which was called *Rookie Cookies*, to the best of my memory. These provincial digestions . . .

Our search-light site on the opposite bank of the river has packed up and gone. We feel extremely sad to see them go. When Valentine went by this morning all was gone except some furniture. There were three old arm-chairs ranged along the hedge, and each had a cat on it.

To Paul Nordoff *2:x:1944*

. . . Just now we lie mutilated and bleeding on the altars of family affection. Ruth has been staying here for a week, and for the greater part of that week Valentine has borne it alone, for I had to go and visit my mamma. My mamma is stone deaf, ravaged with evil passions, and talks incessantly; and is, as you can imagine, fatiguing; but nothing to Ruth . . . she emphasises every other word so that the cat claws at the door screaming to get out, mirrors splinter, glasses leap from the table, and bedroom doors at quite the other end of the house rattle on their hinges. She also sticks like a gramophone record; for a while speaking with every appearance of deep feeling her attention strays and till it comes back again she will go on re-peating the same adjective. . . .

To Ben Huebsch *21:xii:1944*

. . . My cousin Hilary Machen (old Arthur Machen's son) is a prisoner in Germany (no fault of his, for he has made two attempts to escape). We try to send him books but the book shortage, of which I have so often told you, makes this increasingly difficult. As you probably know, books to prisoners of war have to be bookstore copies, or I could send him some of mine. Will you please send him some from time to time, a small parcel: contemporary fiction, poetry, short stories? It would be a godsend to him, and to his friends in the camp, and it would be a great weight off my mind. You cannot, of course, enclose anything to explain why they are coming. But if he sees your wrapper he will probably put two and two together, and even if he doesn't the essential that he gets the books will remain. You will use the

87

ordinary discretion about choice, books that are political or that contain anti-nazi material just don't get through and the fact that they have been sent may re-act unfavourably on the prisoner.

This is his address. Pte. Hilary Machen. Gefangennummer 267074. M. Stammlager iv D. Germany.

I will be extremely grateful to you if you will do this. He is not a character that finds captivity easy, being by nature a wild and solitary bird. He was taken prisoner a little before the fall of Tobruk and sent to an Italian camp. When Italy capitulated he was one of the men who escaped in order not to be nabbed by the Germans, he was out for about three months, walking over the Gran Sasso, and nabbed when he was only a couple of miles from the Eighth Army. He made his second try in Germany, and again very nearly made it. As he is married and has children we hope he will not make a third attempt, pertinacity is dangerous.

About my book (yes, it will be a longish one; longer than me, I sometimes think in moments of despondency). You will find a lot of blotches like the one about Gothenburg. I have not much time to write in, and what I have I dare not spend in looking things up. There will have to be a Day of Wrath, a Washing Day, when I get down to that sort of thing. Meanwhile I shall be very grateful to you for noting anything that catches your eye as a boner. Some more will be coming across presently. At this moment you should have up to p.182. I have killed off a lot more ladies in the next bit you will get, so much creating and killing off makes me feel as providential as Providence. Ralph, however, is still with us. He is to live into an old age serene and bright and die without a pang of conscience.

1945

To Nancy Cunard *13:iii:1945*

... Thanks to you, your wire about Aragon, and thanks to Aragon, we met for lunch on Thursday. My first impression, that he was little changed; that was when I saw the coup d'oeil of the spirit; my next, that he was grey as a cobweb and extraordinarily fatigued; but then, I reflected, I [have] never seen him not looking fatigued; in Paris, in London, in New York, he has always looked at the brink of death and spoken like an angel from a cloud. My final impression, that I had seen a new Aragon, new to me; triply distilled, and aromatic with pride and a queer happiness.

I think he found little here to please him. Our intellectuals, he said, seemed to him to be exactly where he last saw them, planted in the year 1939. Our comfort, ease, solidity of living—like a museum piece; handsome, perhaps, and admirable, but with no relevance to the present day. Our ruins, of course, impressive, and regrettable; but only a background to people looking as usual.

To Nancy Cunard [Undated]

... Thomas Cadett on the BBC has just said that in Paris people are relieved that the Syrian shooting is over and at the same time have few illusions about the purity of British motives in intervening. Neither have we. But how characteristic of our idiot government's astigmatism to get the ports at the price of inflating Hitler's Arab Boys League! It does seem rather hard that besides being rogues they should also be so persistently fools.

We are both well. Slightly perturbed because our landlady came last week and announced that she wished to occupy this house at Christmas. Valentine remembered the rent restriction act, and the local solicitor says that she will find it necessary to prove *greater hardship* in order to get us out. As she has a house already she would not have a very good case. On the table in his waiting-room a copy of *Country Life* lying on a copy of *The Field* was balanced by a copy of the *New Testament* lying on a copy of the *Book of Common Prayer*.

Dearest Nancy,

How could you tear yourself from Cahors just when the autumn crocuses must be coming out in those meadows? Yet I who ask it saw them and
was torn on; though I have seldom left a town with more regret. It is insane
how one is dragged through life as if through a hedge backwards, leaving
tufts of bloodied wool on every thorn-tree.

I suppose I shall shortly be leaving some more of my wool in Edinburgh.
For we are going there next week to look at the house we almost certainly
shan't take, the house on the Water of Leith. I have had to take a lot of
cuts in my first beaming outlook on living in Edinburgh, that it would be so
easy to leave it by air. So it is. The air-service is good and will be better.
But it will be a long time before it is cheaper, and fourteen guineas for a
there and back to London would soon become very isolating. Meanwhile
several responsible people have assured us that it will be very easy either to
let or to sell this house; so I think we shall probably close with it, do it up
(it will be a great pleasure to obliterate our landlady's penchant for decor-
ating/Irish in/Stew)[1] and love it as something we can leave. A very good
reason for love, anyway.

I am longing to know what happened across the mountains. Many good
Cats and Comrades (so said a letter we had a few days ago from the camp in
Lancashire where the Spanish Republicans are in a sort of protective custody,
just not sent back to Franco, but meanwhile treated as mauvais sujets) many
good Cats etc have been munching garlic and raw onions from our garden.
We sent an enormous parcel, arranged like a funeral pillow by Anthos, an
outer ring of shallots, an inner ring of onions, a breast-knot of garlic. Of
course they have had nothing but wholesome English mutton and custard.
I wish we could have them munching *in* our garden.

Your invaluable Strachan[2] has lent me *Les Caves du Vatican*. What a
strange and hollow talent! Gide appears to be completely indifferent to
human nature, none of his characters have characters, and he hangs bits of
behaviour on them just as one hung different paper dresses on flat paper
mannequins. The hanging is most ingeniously done, and I am enjoying
the book as a performance. But a meal of stewed spillikins would be as
nourishing.

1. Possibly meaning 'in the manner of Irish stew'.
2. Walter J. Strachen, poet, translator and Head of the Modern Languages
Department, Bishop's Stortford College.

To Paul Nordoff *5:i:1946*

. . . No one feels well or happy just now. No one in wartime can quite escape the illusion that when the war ends things will snap back to where they were and that one will be the same age one was when it began, and able to go on from where one left off. But the temple of Janus has two doors, and the door for war and door for peace are equally marked in plain lettering, No Way Back. And the dead are not more irrevocably dead than the living are irrevocably alive. Only yesterday I had an invitation which began, Now that the war is over and things show no sign of getting better I hope you will come and stay. Which puts it into a nutshell well enough.

My book, my long book.[1] With luck I shall finish it this spring, revise it this summer. I still incline to call it People growing Old. It has no conversations and no pictures, it has no plot, and the characters are innumerable and insignificant. I shall be very much astonished if any one likes it, personally I think it is fine. Anyway, it has a remarkable vitality, for it has persisted in getting written through an endless series of interruptions, distractions, and destructions, it has been as persistent as a damp patch in a house wall. It is like a damp patch in other ways, too: the same kind of patterning and colouring. The house has several damp patches in it because though it has rained and ruined just as much through the war as through any other six years, it has been impossible, being war time and now being post war time, to get either men or materials for mending it. So when I speak of damp patches I know what I am talking about.

Last winter I read the whole of Balzac—except *Seraphita*; and was left with my mouth as open as the Queen of Sheba's . . . Have you ever thought of making an opera from Balzac? *La Duchesse de Langeais*, for instance, or *Ferragus*, any of the impassioned social ones, ought to work up into a grand opera like eggs into a sauce Bearnaise, the duchesses so shrillingly soprano, the villains so profoundly basso, the situations floating in moonlight and limelight, and Balzac's genius roaring through it all like a quartet of saxophones. A total absence of refinement . . . I suppose that is his secret. All I know for certain is that the works of Balzac kept me from death last winter.

1. *The Corner That Held Them.*

To Nancy Cunard *9:iv:1946*

. . . You are lucky to have your furniture in a warehouse. Did I tell you how Valentine and I went to inspect the Ackland family furniture, which had been stored by HM. Govt. when the house in Norfolk was requisitioned? It had been stored, nice and safe from bombs, in a deserted Victorian-Elizabeth mansion (I have never seen more ridiculously bogus chimneys) and HM Govt another department of same had stored quantities of dried milk there too. The cartons of dried milk had been put on top of the furniture, the roof had leaked, the dried milk had returned to its native element and dripped down through the furniture and solidified on the floor as cheese, the rats had come after the cheese, the cats had come after the rats, the dogs had come after the cats, etc. The first impression was of an overpowering stink and everything covered with a thick blue mould; then, when they began to move the stuff out, it just fell to pieces. You've never seen such a ruin; and the repository people who had let it all happen under their noses handing out perhaps a fumed oak hanging medicine cupboard from the wreckage and saying hopefully, Well, *this* doesn't seem to have suffered so much.

So I hope your Vernon warehouse won't have had anything more than a bomb or two. I do assure you, dried milk is worse. The waste of dried milk, too, on the fringe of a starving world, was an agreeable spectacle to our eyes.

Darling, it is impossible to go on with this letter because the cat is winding his tail in the type writer and every time it gets caught he looks at me reproachfully and I have to leave off, disentangle the tail, give a brief explanation of the theory of cause and effect, and smooth his feelings.

Valentine will write soon, and tell you more. The house is still being redecorated and they have just fallen through the kitchen floor. As no one was hurt I look on it as providential, for now the floor will have to be mended, permit permitting or no.

To Ben Huebsch *24:iv:1946*

. . . It will be long—about 180,000 words I believe. It is also what one calls powerful. If dropped from a suitable height it would wipe out the state of Vermont.

To Paul Nordoff *8:v:1946*

Dearest Paul,
I loved to get your long letter and all this news of you and your family. It sounds so happy and well-set for more happiness. And I loved the snaps

of Sabina and Anthony and you looking like the Lion Tamer just about to spring from his loincloth. I think Anthony is like you down to the tip of his nose after that he gives himself to Sabina. I am glad he is musical and likes tunes . . . Soon you will be like David Garnett, who looked at his eldest son sucking at the breast and said, It is rather difficult to make out whether he will prefer Keats or Shelley.

Aren't dandelion fields marvellous? I have just been seeing some magnificent ones, for we spent the first week of Valentine's holiday motoring in Somerset where the soil is rich and cultivation has been short-handed during the war, and as a result the fields are golden now and in a fortnight's time will be silver with dandelion clocks. 'A braver thing was never seen to praise the grass for growing green.' Everything was praising the grass for growing green or else praising itself for growing pink and white. All the cider orchards were in bloom, the trees were so thick with blossom that they looked as solid as masonry. The horse-chestnuts were heavy with bloom and heavily revolving, and the gardens were packed with stocks and wallflowers. It was lovely. We have not had such a holiday for years, not since the war, a carefree holiday with enough petrol (we had been hoarding it for weeks) to go without incessantly measuring and calculating.

I thought my novel was almost finished; then I went back to the beginning, and now I find I want to rewrite a great deal of it, perhaps the whole of it. Because having spent so long on it and written it at such divers times and under such distracting circumstances, though all the characters in it are solid and consistent, the lighting, so to speak, has an inconsistency, the shadows are sometimes to the east sometimes to the west of an incident, and it needs a long study as a whole to put these discrepancies right. One might almost think that the material of a work of art has the awkward individual vitality of timber; and warps and changes its contours after it has been sawn and fitted and put together.

To a friend who was of two minds about
            remaining married *21:vii:1946*

Stop, take thought. Consider the lilies. Whatever [   ] fell in love with it wasn't a Mother's Help. You say that you have been too much together. What you mean is that you have not been together enough, that you have been incessantly chaperoned by a fatal spirit of helpfulness and unselfishness . . . I say it with my true heart, the worst injury one can do to the person who loves one is to cover oneself from head to foot in a shining impermeable condom of irreproachable behaviour.

93

. . . a commission to write a small book about Somerset. Just now I am in the midst of reading the many books about Somerset which have already been written. I am consoled for the numerousness by not finding one among them that I can enjoy. They all hurry like anxious Satans over the face of the earth, and never once do these breathless authors stop in a wood and smell the smell of the country. I hope I shall manage to do better.

Perhaps if I write it very beguilingly you will feel that you must come and visit Somerset yourself.

Meanwhile you are going to Central America. Oh, how I envy you in my cold bones! I have not been decently warm since the beginning of May, and that was really no more than a chaste salute, a surface compliment. A flood has been whirling round us, and lapping over our doorstep, and all the wretched garden has been made into a puddle, the fat gardener who comes once a week will not be able to set foot on it till God knows when, he would sink and be swallowed up, and that would be a great pity since his wife loves him and so does his cat. Please send me a hamper of pawpaws, a jar of Guatemala honey, half a dozen hibiscus bushes, an Indian Baby, some snow off a volcano, three humming-birds, and one hundred and forty four (twelve dozen) yards of blue convolvulus. And a pink sunshade. You can send me the lot, if you please, in a small Latin tram. Trolley-bus to you.

I hope the trip will be a terrific success, violently profitable, and just long enough to make you pleased when it ends. I wish we had your itinerary, I would look it up in the map. Will you conquer Peru? I hope Dolin dances better than he used to in this country, when he bounded like a curate in liquor entertaining a Children's Sunday School Treat. I remember her[1] with respect and rapture, she managed her head so beautifully, it was as much hers as a serpent's is.

To Alyse Gregory *23:xii:1946*

Dearest Alyse,

Usually one begins a thank-letter by some graceless comparison, by saying, I have never been given such a very scarlet muffler, or, This is the largest horse I have ever been sent for Christmas. But your matchbox is a nonpareil, for never in my life have I been given a matchbox. Stamps, yes, drawing-pins, yes, balls of string, yes, yes, menacingly too often; but never a matchbox. Now that it has happened I ask myself why it has never happened before. They are such charming things, neat as wrens, and what a deal of

1. Alicia Markova.

ingenuity and human artfulness has gone into their construction; for if they were like the ordinary box with a lid they would not be one half so convenient. This one though is especially neat, charming, and ingenious, and the tray slides in and out as though Chippendale had made it.

But what I like best of all about my matchbox is that it is an empty one. I have often thought how much I should enjoy being given an empty house in Norway, what pleasure it would be to walk into those bare wood-smelling chambers, walls, floor, ceiling, all wood, which is after all the natural shelter of man, or at any rate the most congenial. And when I opened your matchbox which is now my matchbox and saw that beautiful clean sweet-smelling empty rectangular expanse it was exactly as though my house in Norway had come true; with the added advantage of being just the right size to carry in my hand. I shut my imagination up in it instantly, and it is still sitting there, listening to the wind in the firwood outside. Sitting there in a couple of days time I shall hear the Lutheran bell calling me to go and sing Lutheran hymns while the pastor's wife gazes abstractedly at her husband in a bower of evergreen while she wonders if she remembered to put pepper in the goose-stuffing; but I shan't go. I shall be far too happy sitting in my house that Alyse gave me for Christmas.

Oh, I must tell you I have finished my book—begun in 1941 and a hundred times imperilled but finished at last. So I can give an undivided mind to enjoying my matchbox.

[PS] There is still so much to say . . . carried away by my delight in form and texture I forgot to praise the picture on the back. I have never seen such an agreeable likeness of a hedgehog, and the volcano in the background is magnificent.

1947

To Alyse Gregory *22:ii:1947*

. . . I have been reading *Les Amitiés Particulières* by Roger Peyrefitte. Have you read it? I was transfixed by it . . . It has set me down on my knees all over again before that French talent for dealing completely with a subject —and with nothing else. It is like canneton à la presse: not a moment's let up till the last atom of juice has been expressed, and not an atom of anything extraneous allowed to get into the machine. It makes me hang my head and feel like a rag-bag.

Not that they can all do it; but more of them try to, and those who succeed, succeed most triumphantly.

Though I tell myself that nothing could be colder than we are my mind misgives me that you are even colder. I have passed from realisation to incredulity, from incredulity to acceptance. I can't believe it will ever be warm again . . .

Every morning I wake thinking of the birds who must have died in the night. Some such waking thought has sat on my pillow for so many years that I wonder if I ever woke with an untainted conscience.

To William Maxwell *14:iv:1947*

. . . This really should be a letter to your private address. I want to ask your advice. I have had for two years a First Reading Agreement with *The New Yorker* and this ought to be my dearest possession, but I don't find it working out quite like that. They take what seems to me a very long time[1] before they let me know what they have rejected. I can assume after four months or so that they do reject, but till I am told I can do nothing about sending anything elsewhere; and I am beginning to feel as though I had plighted my vows to a refrigerator. If this degree of delay is accidental, or due to misplaced kindness, or something of that sort, I can adapt myself to it, and write tart letters of enquiry. But if it is a recognised part of the First Reading Agreement I

1. The occupational disease of editors is procrastination. I had left *The New Yorker* a couple of years before in order to write a novel. At the time this letter was written I was filling in for somebody who was either away or ill. Eventually I insinuated myself back on the staff as a part-time editor.

96

don't think I like it and if I am asked to renew my vows I think I won't. But till I know which it is I am in a slight quandary; and I shall be extremely grateful if you will help me out of it, in whatever direction.

To Paul Nordoff *30:v:1947*

. . . Well, darling Paul, we have been extremely cold; and now we are blissfully hot, all the air smells of May blossoms and lupins and fat green grass tawny with buttercups, and it is almost dark, and the birds are still singing and there is going to be the hell of a great thunderstorm presently. And I finished my great long book, so long that it will be years before it gets published, and meanwhile having thought it was finished I have sent for it back again and am making a lot of alterations . . . And I have had influenza, a vile stealthy unimpassioned kind of influenza that never got really bad and almost never got better—however, it is gone now; and I have had a little tussle with *The New Yorker*, at least with a gentleman there who was supposed to attend to me and didn't and have emerged with a lot of extra dollars in my hair; and in a Schubertian fit of inspiration I tore through a short novel all about a young girl; and really she is charming; and after that I became completely exhausted and could do nothing, except try and play the piano.

Valentine's mother has been staying with us, with the usual devastating effect on Valentine's health. She *always* comes in May—for Valentine's birthday, with the result that it is only by the skin of our teeth that Valentine survives to be a year older. I think the word 'trite' must have been prophetically invented for her. This is the kind of conversation we have.

R. 'And who did you say she is?'
V. 'She is Mary Tomkins. She lives with her brother John on the Dorchester Road.'
R. 'Oh. She lives on the Dorchester Road?'
V. 'Yes.'
R. 'With her brother John?'
V. 'Yes'.
R. 'And is he her brother?'
V. 'Yes, he's her brother. She's his sister. They live together on the Dorchester Road.'
R. 'On the *Dorchester* Road?'
V. 'Yes. The Dorchester Road.'
R. 'And she's his sister?'
V. . . . .
R. 'How delightful!'
Really it's like this. Only worse. Much much worse.

To Nancy Cunard *4:vi:1947*

. . . Valentine had to go to Norfolk last month, to see about the family house. We thought that John Robertson Scott might buy it (he is leaving Idbury) and she went there to show it to him. It has only just been relinquished by the War Office, and this was the first time any one had got in and gone right over it.

It was a sombre experience. They have totally ruined it; and deliberately. Not merely the usual war damage of broken floors and ceilings and lost door-knobs and fallen slates and the banisters stolen to make fires of. They have broken everything that could conceivably be broken, a lot more you would think unbreakable. Every single chimney-flue in the house, for instance, and both the boilers and all the hot water pipes. Naturally, there was not a chance of John buying it. It would take ten years to put right, and he is eighty. God damn the Army, say we. Valentine said that the only thing she had seen comparable to it was some of the damage done in USSR —like the photographs of what was left of Yasnaya Polyana.

To Ian Parsons[1] *22:viii:1947*

Dearest Ian,

Just when you have heard that no more paper is to be issued to publishers, here is my loving anaconda back again. I have revised all the part between p. 121 and p. 299, and taken a great deal out, especially convent politics and the changes of post, which you found confusing. (It was the breath of life to them, poor wretches, as good as a voyage to Africa or the death of an aunt.)

To Steven Clark *28:xii:1947*

. . . I can't at this moment answer your enquiry about Borrow, because I only came back last night after a grilling fortnight of trying to settle my poor mother, whose eccentricity suddenly flared into a *nova* of rapid senile decay. Now she is in a nursing home in Paignton, and the doctor tells me her general health is excellent. Have you ever seen Paignton? It is full of yuccas, that clash their claws in north-easterly gales. Even if you have seen Paignton, I suppose you have not seen the entrance hall of the Windemere

1. (1906-80), C.B.E., partner in Chatto and Windus and later head of the firm; Joint Chairman of Chatto, Bodley Head and Jonathan Cape Ltd.

Nursing Home. On the usual Torquay Baronial side-board there is a modest brass cross (ready for Peace be in this house and those that dwell in it) flanked and surmounted by an array of gigantic antlers and tusks. Even after a fortnight of the vagaries of a disordered mind (and it had been an eye-opener), this made an impression on me. It was of the same kind as that modern cathedral in Barcelona you were so much attached to.

To Alyse Gregory *29 : xii : 1947*

. . . My mother is in a nursing home. It specialises in old people, so I think she has every chance of being skilfully looked after, since there will be no more alluring cases, childbirths or interesting operations, to call off attention. She has a very kind homely young nurse, who manages her far better than I could. I hope she will settle there—as far as she could ever settle anywhere: for even now the most burning spark in her ashes is a desire to assert herself. If I can find a suitable nurse-companion for her, and she still wants to go back to Little Zeal, we will try that. But the companion will not be me . . . And if this course leaves any specks on my conscience, and I daresay it may, I will rub them off at my leisure. But go down quick into the pit I will not . . .

I had been meaning to write to you long before this, about a passage in Enid Starkie's life of Rimbaud. It would be better, of course, if we returned the book, but Valentine is still reading it. It shall come back, I promise.

But perhaps you remember how she writes of the last verse of *Michel et Christine*,

Et verrai-je le bois jaune et le val clair,
L'Epouse aux yeux bleus, l'homme au font rouge, ô Gaule,
Et le blanc Agneau Pascal, à leurs pieds chers

and how, having been very industrious in identifying Michel et Christine with a vaudeville of the date, she says it is clear that the young man of the poem is wondering whether he [will] ever see the autumn woods and fair valleys of France, and whether the pascal lamb will be killed for his feasting, and Agnus Dei qui tollis, and so forth.

But when I read it, knowing that it was a poem of the date after the first amours with Verlaine, in the cheap bedroom, I thought of the yellow wood of the wardrobe, the pale view from the upper window, the sheepskin mat at the foot of the bed, and the jokes of the blue-eyed Rimbaud and the flushed Verlaine. And don't you think that this is much more probable, and that Michel and Christine were the petits noms they gave themselves? 'A leurs pieds chers' seems to me to be the key of this verse, this stance à clef for Verlaine's reading. How Miss Starkie could get feet on to a eucharistic lamb of God, even a Hebraic one would be skinned, passes my understanding. Only a very wise virgin could be so very ingenious and so very ingenuous, I think.

God, as I exclaimed to Valentine, has the woman never been in a bedroom of accommodation? And really, I don't think it is too much to ask of some one who sets out to write lives of the poets, do you?

To Paul Nordoff *17: iii: 1948*

... I have just been listening to Mr Truman. It was depressingly like waiting to listen to Hitler in 1938, 39. The same sensation of What the hell this time? I can't believe that the ordinary quiet coca-cola citizen is behind all this pontifical roaring and stamping, or wants to hang over Europe like an allegory in a painted ceiling, with a bun in one hand and a bomb in the other. It is such a pity, and such a nuisance, because the rock-bottom result over here is that the earlier sensible feeling that Americans were the sort of people you didn't need to take sides over is melting away, and now there are pro-Americans or anti-Americans, and all as cantankerous as a church assembly; and a deep and growing sensation that it would be nice to put cotton-wool in one's ears and have a quiet fortnight without overhearing any more of these threatening platitudes, and never, never, NEVER again hear that tedious word democracy. And no doubt these sensations are reciprocal, and you must put your fingers in your ears and scream whenever you catch an English accent.

Valentine wraps herself up in reading Plotinus. I have yet to find any philosopher who will console me for the deep religious feeling which makes statesmen and politicians so ready to throw other people under the car of Juggernaut. Whoosh, they cry, their voices throbbing with piety, Under you go! Meanwhile, I am glad Anthony is too young to be conscripted.

Did I tell you I had, at last, a letter from Franklin? It was long, and kind, and told me all about his cottage at Carmel, Calif. with a plan, and photographs: it was everything it should be; and yet I felt that it was all wrong, too. Something's happened that shouldn't have, that's how I feel. It was just such another go as your meeting at the Latham, when he wasn't there. Photos, letter, all the rest of it. But Franklin wasn't there. I do feel worried about him, and there doesn't seem to be anything at all that I can do about it. I feel like Cassandra. I smell death. I smell calamity. But one can't write and say so—at least, I can't now, with an ocean and a continent in between, and this dishevelling sensation that they have somehow been put there on purpose. Do let me know anything you hear about him. Before I got that letter, it was such a long time without any sign from him, I had got around to thinking that perhaps we had offended him somehow, or he had had a change of heart and hated the thought of us, or anything normal and understandable of that sort. But the letter quelled any such cheerful suppositions.

It was affectionate, remembering, all that sort of thing: but ghostly, and unreal, and *not there*.

And no address, either, in spite of the plan of the house. Don't you think that's queer? —as if in spite of writing he had to slide in this intimation that he didn't want to be written to.

To Paul Nordoff *27: iv : 1948*

. . . I am never out of one or the other of your shoes. Just at this moment I am wearing the brown ones, and presently I shall be putting on the black ones to impress two New Zealanders who are coming to lunch. I have never seen either of them, so my anticipations are not clouded with the usual gloom that waits on country entertaining. We are in a burst of conviviality. Yesterday we had a junk-shop dealer to tea, and he took away a selection of very disused objects, and left us twenty pounds, which was unusual behaviour in someone who comes to tea: usually they take many more books than they will ever trouble to return, and leave their umbrellas. And before that we had Janet and her baby to stay . . . She is in the stage of proceeding everywhere on her bottom, like a dog with worms, but much faster. I have never seen anything speedier, except a tortoise going towards the lettuce-bed: the same unobtrusive velocity, in both cases.

O God, how I wish you could see our cherry-tree. It is like nothing but a cherry tree, only more so. There is a thick border of blue lung-wort just below it, and between the lung-wort and the tree there is a thick border of bumble-bees.

To Nancy Cunard *17: vii : 1948*

. . . I was so sorry that I did not see you while you were in London. I was staying at a house in Gloucester; partly because some old friends live in it, partly because my cherished Mrs Keates, my cockney charwoman, is now in all the glory of 'old family remainder' there, and wished with all her passionate and commanding heart, to see me. Heavens, what hours of stitching, shoe-shining, and manicure did I not undergo in order to make a presentable appearance and be a credit to her! By the grace of God I happened to have a new hat, and to have found a pair of pre-war gloves at my mother's.

I see that your mother is dead. Out of my own present experience I can only assure you that a mother who dies in possession of her senses is less painful than a mother who lives on without them. Since we are both undutiful daughters, I suppose we are both exposed to the same vexed variety of filial emotion, and I can sympathise with you both in feeling and the constriction of lack of feeling. Does it make your finances any easier? I hope so. Valentine has been stretched on a different type of the same filial rack. Her mother has just been broadcast: in a BBC feature programme about the WVS. It was indescribably awful—two and a half minutes of vertiginous embarrassment, followed by a pat on the back from Wilfred Pickles. What one goes through!

As for the house, it will soon be invisible. Valentine's willows, thanks to the wet weather, grow enormous, and she continues to set more and more of them. I look forward, tranquilly and indeed happily, to a day when there will be nothing to do in the garden except sit down and weep. Meanwhile, they look very graceful, smell deliciously of quinine, and are full of tits and goldfinches.

To Paul Nordoff *29 : vii : 1948*

. . . a loquacious thunderstorm this morning which was oratorical without a pause for breath all through breakfast, and having finished what it wanted to say, took itself off . . . a model to all loquators. The coffee tray beside me, being made of metal, is too hot to touch. And I am too lazy to wish to move it, and the sun streams through my large and rejoicing geranium and outside the elder-berries on the bush which grows out of the wall above the river are turning purple as I watch them. All this is very nice. We live on raspberries and artichokes, gooseberries (small red ones) and green peas, and that is very nice too. There is not a visitor on the horizon, and that is nicest of all.

Next week, packing the black suede pumps and wearing the drab gaberdine jacket you sent me, I am going off for a jaunt. First to stay with a very nice, exceedingly dry old lady in Kent (perfect specimen of the English spinster, full of quiet stories about what she said to the policeman in Constantinople, and that pleasant bandit they met in Macedonia), and then on to stay in the Essex marshes. Sukey's[1] country; and I expect I shall get terribly homesick for it. If I find the right solitary black-tarred farmhouse, with quantities of old corn barns, and a black ditch round the property, I daresay we will buy some mosquito netting and move there. That is one of the advantages of having bought the house you live in, as we were forced to do. Once bought, it becomes much lighter on your hands, and you feel you can up and sell it if you wish to. I travel, alas, alone, because Valentine has nobly taken on a job with a near-by doctor, to bring in some money (my mother's

1. The heroine of *The True Heart.*

nursing-home expenses mop up what used to be my allowance, and *The New Yorker's* volte-face (they have taken nothing for a year, the recent Finch piece was dragged from their cupboard by William Maxwell when he went back to them as a stop-gap) has made us extremely lean. *The N.Y.* is a great sorrow as well as a loss. I am assured, I don't know whether to believe it, that they are being purged of Stalinists by Edmund Wilson,[1] and I am one of them). Well, to get out of this forest of parenthesises, Valentine is being a secretary to this near-by doctor. Fortunately, he is a very nice young man, and so considerate that he won't employ her till the evening while the weather is hot, and pays well for quite short hours, and positively venerates her opinion on how things should best be done. But even the easiest job is Adam's Curse when it comes to things like jaunts into the Essex marshes; and I wish to heaven that she need not be noble.

As for my poor mother, there is a ghastly gaiety about her senile fantasies: and to hear her, hanging out of the window and looking down into an empty sunlight garden and holding airy conversations with old swains who have been dead and gone for the last thirty years, is grisly indeed. She seems perfectly happy in her disconnected way, and will live, they say, for a long while yet, years and years, probably, swimming in fantasies of grandeur and fantasies of love. But I hope I will remember to cut my throat if I ever begin to go that way.

To Steven Clark *30:vii:1948*

Dear Steven,

I think we can safely rely on the Longobardic Sisters. I had a very warm-hearted letter from Mrs Erani (almost as perplexing as if it were from our phonetic friend Hidalgo, but that is my fault, since I know even less Italian than I do Spanish—and Spanish only when I am trying to know Italian). She tells me that she has received the thousand lire, and also a parcel which I sent to her presso suoro, early this month.

I have not heard from Mr Carlini. But he is an orphaned father, no, I mean he is a widower with a family; and I daresay this leaves him little time for writing letters. I sent a Carlini parcel at the same time I sent an Erani one, and both were acknowledged on the part of the Longobardic Sisters by an English-speaking Dame of Good Works. They seem to receive both safely and punctiliously. So we can feel confident that both the families will

1. Harold Ross, the editor of *The New Yorker*, was indifferent to the political convictions of its contributors so long as they did not use the magazine to proselytize. Edmund Wilson was reviewing books at the time and had no say whatever in the policies of *The New Yorker*.

get the food and the clothing parcels you ordered for them. This was very kind; and I am so grateful for this, and for all the trouble you have taken to such good purpose.

I break off to remark how very agreeable it is to be able to be grateful for trouble that has worked out to good purpose. So few people seem to be able to bring good results out of their trouble taking. Did we ever tell you of the parcel, so kindly and painfully packed and sent us by Valentine's mother which contained a packet of cigarettes, a ripe Camembert cheese, and some lavender?

Lovely Verona! I was taken there as a child. I sat in the arena with my grandmother, a slow-moving scholarly woman. We sat there for hours, while she meditated on The *Decline and Fall*, no doubt, and I watched the lizards. Then we went and bought figs in the market, and then we went and sat in the shade in a garden whose name I don't remember. There were quantities of cypresses, the parterre was laid out in patterns of coloured stones, still in the Austrian colours, and I made speechless friends with the gardener's little boy who was called Silvio. When Lydia is old enough to travel (say about nine or ten) you will remember, won't you, the importance of sitting for hours while Lydia expands? My grandmother was unsurpassable at sitting. She would sit on tombstones, glaciers, small hard benches with ants crawling over them, fragments of public monuments, other people's wheelbarrows, and when one returned one could be sure of finding her there, conversing affably with the owner of the wheelbarrow.

To Paul Nordoff *17:viii:1948*

... It might amuse Sabina to know some of our prices. Rationed things of course are cheap; butter, margarine, cheese, bacon, tea, and dried fruits— not that these latter can always be got. And meat is rationed, and mostly very poor, so poor that one doesn't mind how little there is of it. Fruit, except apples, is appalling, raspberries and strawberries a dollar or a dollar fifty a pound. A pheasant—if you have a friend in the black market and can get one—costs 26/ and a guinea-fowl 30/. Guinea fowls used to be 3/6, and one bought them when one felt too mean to buy a chicken at 5/. A lot of these prices are just ramps. In London you pay five shillings a pound, say, for green peppers at a west end store and in Soho they are one and sixpence. Our district is not cheap, because there are two army establishments in it, the tank corps at Bovingdon and an RAF place at Warmwell; both messes shop in our market town, and prices are up accordingly. As we have a garden and have learned to be good gardeners, we can walk past the fruiterers and the greengrocers during the good part of the year; and for the bad part of the year we make out with my sorrel-bed which usually has something edible going on in it, it is a blessed vegetable, and the garlic and shallots we have grown ourselves, and that debated greenstuff, the Brussels Sprout. My worst headache is how to keep the garden soil alive after ten years of intensive cropping. At this moment I am on hooks as to whether or no I shall get the load of stable manure I am negotiating for. Composts heaps are all very well, and I keep a grand one; but they only put back into the ground what has been taken out of it, and it is too much like the Scilly Islanders earning their precarious livelihood by taking in each other's washing to be a long term method.

Eggs, controlled, are 3/ a dozen—a little behind your 81 cents, or is that for a single egg? You get them according to the season. Sometimes three a week, and then in winter, it may be two or one. The people who are worst off are the small respectables, the retired, and the pensioned. Their lot is hellish. The people who are in clover and have been all through the war, are the middle-sized and large farmers, who get government subsidies on what they set out to grow, whether or no they grow it, and wallow in black market, and, in addition, are allowed all the petrol they like to ask for provided they remember to ask for it in the name of agriculture. Our local farmers can be seen driving out to do a little agriculture at the Dorchester cinema and pubs almost every evening. Farm labourers are doing pretty well, too—a pleasant change. At last they are getting decent wages, and they poach and fiddle a bit in their spare time.

So far we have scarcely fiddled at all. We had to fiddle a tyre some years ago, or Valentine would not have been able to get to her work. It was, as near as possible, fiddling a hymn-tune. I fiddled a chicken once, when we had a visitor and nothing to feed her on. I have no particular conscience about it. But I loathe the kind of company it gets one into; my virtue is due to nothing more than social prejudice and spiritual pride. What I shall do when cigarettes get shorter I don't know. Paganini, I expect.

To Nancy Cunard *1:ix:1948*

. . . Every one here is more or less rheumatised. I should think it is largely due to the general feeling of depression and oppression brought on by Mr Bevin's war of nerves on the British people, and the bleak consequences of Marshall aid. There is now no tinned fish, no tinned meat, no biscuits, no cigarettes (unless, like us, you have had a regular order, in which case with luck you get some of it still)—nothing but plum and apple jam and a copious crop of potatoes. The latest disappearance is paper-clips. No paper-clips. Presumably they are all attached to Notes from the Western Powers. There is also No Enthusiasm. General de Gaulle is again pictured in our newspapers, looking as usual like an embattled codfish. I wish he could be filleted, and put quietly away in a refrigerator. It is regrettable that having been, in his hour, the man that was needed (though perhaps one should confine oneself to saying that he was the man who got in where a figure was needed before anyone else did), he should remain as a large life-like mascot to be marched around by the Catholic reaction.

TO IAN PARSONS *23:x:1948*

Dearest Ian,

Yes, indeed. Please tell Aldo Martello that I would be delighted.[1] And I think we need not try to raise their 9% to 10%. I should feel rather like skinning my mother just after she had been kicked downstairs by a burglar, to be asking for another one per cent from an Italian house just now.

Would it be possible to intimate to Aldo Martello that I would prefer to pick up my advance in lire on the spot? I am rather hoping to be in Italy early next year, and I could see more and stay longer if I had that advance to spend there.

I feel very pleased about this. For one thing, I might learn a little Italian off the translation. Of course it wouldn't be very practical, but one degree better than adapting quotations from opera, which is made harder because I can never remember the words unless I sing them.

1. See letter to Ben Huebsch, 25:xii:1949, p. 115.

To Nancy Cunard *19:i:1949*

. . . How difficult about the houses: the non-existent one you long for, the existent one you don't like so much. I feel for you over the ruin: there was a ruined house in Wiltshire that I found when we thought we should lose this one that I still long for. It was out of the question, then; permits, and all that; but what an angel! There it lay on the hillside, facing south with wide open windows, and fragments of its burned thatch littered on its stone flagged floor. c. 1750, I suppose. Walls like the breast of a horse, and its stone-work tabbied with casual brick and flint.

We shall see you in March or April, and then we shall know more about whether or no a trip to France can be squeezed out of 1949 finances. Of course I want to come; but I am by no means so sure that I want to attend any sort of Congress or Committee or Gathering. My mood is *centrifugal.* I can't at this moment of history warm to the thought of a congress about anything, Why, indeed? There is so much to be anxious about: but somehow I can't believe that anything will come of congressing and gathering just now. A sitting on already boiled eggs, a clucking of past hatchings. No, a quiet dust-bath is more to my mind, a dust-bath and a minding my own business.

To Paul Nordoff *4:ii:1949*

Dearest Paul,
We were so very glad to get your cable with the news of your daughter. I hope she will be very, very happy; and I hope she will be without fear. I am quite sure that to be fearless is the first requisite for a woman; everything else that is good will grow naturally out of that, as a tree has leaves and fruit and grows tall and full provided its roots have a good hold of the ground. Bring her up to be fearless and unintimidated by frowns, hints, and conventions, and then she will be full of mercy and grace and generosity. It is fear that turns women sour, sly, and harsh to their neighbours. It was Shakespeare's Constance who said she was 'a woman, naturally born to fears.' Not naturally, I think; but hereditarily; and so to be guarded against fear before all else.

The libretto, yes, certainly a man; and certainly no message; and the man, some sort of Quixote, yes. And the time, presumably, some sort of rough and ready Now. But there must also be a framework, a story; for just a character and incidents is not substantial enough to support the weight of the music. We do not want a Symphonic Variation opera like *A Village Romeo and Juliet*, or a tone-poem opera either. So from now on till when I come back from Italy I shall be devising this framework; and when I get back in March I shall send you the draft of it. Of course I have ideas already, dozens of them; but equally I am sure that Italy will give me better ones. Isn't it fortunate that just at the moment when I want to bear you a nice libretto I should be going to Italy, with all the stimulus and excitement of mind that will mean?

I would like to know roughly your Columbia resources? Can you have a chorus, or is the stage too small? A semi-chorus then? I must know this, because if you can have neither, then the libretto must allow for the orchestra taking over at the intervals when the solo voices are off. Have you any particular experiments you want to try? Are you thinking in terms of dialogue and arioso, or will you include trios and quartets? I hope, the latter. It is so ravishing when the voices flow into polyphony. This, too, would justify the devices of stanza and rhyme, and the pleasure of being a Metastasio, everything flowering into a madrigal. I have always admired the way Walter Prude managed this in *Mr. F.* No. Certainly no damned folkery, no *Oklahomas*. Two hours would fall normally into three acts, or so, and I suppose Columbia will not crave for many changes of scene. Five hundred dollars, my God! That seems extremely handsome, and will be extremely timely; for though I have just hooked another Finch into *N. Y.* the wolf's cold breath was playing on my ankles from under the door, and the Italy trip would have sent us back to whistle for a wind. With five hundred cushiony Columbian dollars I can sit at ease and let my genius flow. I hope they are being equally handsome to you, my dear.

To Marchette Chute[1] *8: iii: 1949*

Dear Miss Chute,

Thank you very much for writing to me about *The Corner That Held Them*. What you say of the prevalence of books that breathe heavily down the reader's neck applies to letters written to authors too. I have several times been felled by approbations which by their hearty inattention to the book involved have been more painful than the sharpest criticism could be.

So it was a particular pleasure to be praised by some one who has worked

1. American biographer and literary historian.

in the same century, and found it comfortable, and I am most grateful to you for telling me that you like the book—and disagree with the reviewer in *The Spectator*. I agree with you, I may say, on both points. But as I write my books in an attempt to please myself I really cannot complain if they do not also please reviewers. I imagine the *Spec* gentleman (I did not happen to see his review) was one of those people who prefer their fourteenth century at a more gothic degree of perspective. It is wounding to a strong twentieth century amour propre to admit that the course of time has not made vast differences in the development of human nature.

Has your book on Chaucer been published in this country? I would like to read it. Please tell me—or tell me the USA publication, so that I can ask the Viking Press to send me a copy. I love him so much that I had the greatest difficulty in keeping him out of Oby.[1] His shadow was always tipping over the threshold.

TO PAUL NORDOFF *12:iii:1949*

Dearest Paul,
I found your letter and the beautiful spectacle of the Columbia advance when I got home.

That was four days ago; but I have waited to write to you till I could tell you something about the libretto.

After some false starts on other themes, I am sure of it . . . the theme is Shelley's last summer, at Lerici, where he and Mary, and the two Williamses, and Trelawney went, to suffer their sea change, as Trelawney prophetically said. They are all falling most beautifully into place. Did you know that early in that summer Shelley saw the vision of a child rising out of the sea and beckoning to him? And that after the shipwreck, when Trelawney went to see Mary, 'he did not attempt to console me, but launched forth into an overflowing and eloquent praise of my divine Shelley, till I felt almost happy'? That will be the last scene of the opera—an extended arioso (Trelawney is obviously a baritone) which will answer your idea of a long conversation with some one invisible, either an angel or the devil; for Mary will have no singing part at all in this scene, and the pauses in Trelawney's arioso will be answered by—so it seems to me—by a wordless melodic line, perhaps Shelley's high tenor vocalising, or a solo fiddle; which will comment on the strain of the arioso and lead it further.

There will be only one set: the upper room at Casa Magni with the french window opening on the view of the bay; sometimes this window will be open, sometimes shut, according to the scene. During the scene

1. *The Corner That Held Them* is set in the fictitious convent of Oby.

of the wreck—which will be left entirely to orchestra and chorus voices off—the window will be open, and the three women, Mary, Jane Williams, and Claire, will be silhouetted against it, shaping a group of intensified anxiety and hopelessness. From this window they will see the arrival of the ship when she first comes from Leghorn, newly built for their summer's pleasure. All the ship business, and Trelawney's seafaring talk, and Shelley's enthusiasm, is going to be lovely. Think what music you can have for the ship coming smooth and full-sailed over the water, the solo voices expatiating, and the chorus of the fishing-people of Lerici on the beach below the window. This device of the upper room is going to be a godsend, because you can have your chorus, all the chorus you want, without them crowding up a small stage. Then there is Jane Williams, and her guitar, another lovely motive of the lyric voice, the light jarring guitar notes, and the sea-continuo supporting it. And for my fun in the job, there is one fascinating strand: that Shelley, who in all his poems was obsessed by rivers, by rivers flowing to the ocean, by rivers traversing underground caverns, is himself expressing this river's hastening compulsion to be lost in the sea.

Shelley and Trelawney will be the two dominating parts. The women interpose, or supply little lakes of duets and trios. Edward Williams I hear as a *serene* bass; the exponent of the feeling of summer, of natural enjoyment of nature, of the blueness of sky and the amplitude of days. I think what lovely full cantabile one can get from a bass if he is not being misused as a grunting Hunding, or a pop-pop-pop merry peasant.

So now, darling Paul, give your mind to the Mediterranean, and write and say you love me for this.

. . . I will write and tell you about Rome, and Assisi, and the journeys presently. But except to tell you, I cannot write anything that is not the libretto just now, for it is washing round me and islanding me from anything else.

To Paul Nordoff *7: iv: 1949*

Dearest Paul,

Here is scene iv of the opera, with everything going all out, and the ravishing moment when the ship's sails (they must be red, I think, for one will want a trumpet for the eye) fill the whole backstage, and Shelley's voice climbs through the whole texture of chorus and orchestra, and holds (don't you think) his high note as the rest subsides.

About the sextet. I have planned it to build up from two sopranos, and Claire's contralto interjection, to quartet of tenor, bass, two sopranos, increasing to the sextet with the contralto and baritone entry. This sharply broken off by Shelley's exclamation, which should burst out of the close.

Then a relaxation of Claire and Trelawney. Then the sextet renewed, this time with all the voices going it, and again as it reaches its close a solo voice emerging, this time, Mary's soprano, as exclamatory as Shelley's *A Sail!*—but extended into fierce arioso. Because I think this will be a lovely way of getting over the difficulty of the close of a concerted movement not seeming the traditional, 'Now-we-will-all-bow-in-a-row-and-get-our-breaths-back' business.

I wish I could write librettos for the rest of my life. It is the purest of human pleasures, a heavenly hermaphroditism of being both writer and musician. No wonder that selfish beast Wagner kept it all to himself.

To Alyse Gregory 5: vi: 1949

... So in a month or a couple of months Valentine and [   ] will be living together. Here, in this house, I hope. It seems much the best plan. It will assure Valentine a continuity of work and trees growing and books, some of her roots will remain in the same ground. It will settle [   ] with a certain degree of responsible domesticity, which will be much more settling to her nerves than flitting from hotel to hotel; and for my part, I would rather have the sting of going than the muffle of remaining. Practically, too, it is much easier to find a roof for one than for two.

Our plan of a holiday in France thins to a dandelion clock, and I am sorry about this: though I never quite believed in it. And the new solitary life I shall lead has come suddenly nearer, like the leap the moon makes from a sky of wind and vapour. And that, too, I cannot really believe in. I can visualise everything about it except myself in it. It is like looking into a mirror that reflects everything but one's face. For all that, I believe I welcome this sudden gesture of time. Yes, certainly, I do. The attrition of waiting is as dangerous as a wound that may turn to gangrene.

But the main reason why I am telling you all this is that for the first time I have been able to feel a living and in-my-flesh belief that Valentine may one day return to me. Till now I have assented to this belief with something more calculating than hope and more tremulous than reason; and chiefly because I love her, and cannot bear to disbelieve her assurances. But yesterday I saw her, not only more shaken by the news in the cable than I (that could be accounted for by her doubled state of mind, and the burden of two loves she has to keep her balance under), but—what is the word?— the word is very nearly appalled. It seemed to me as though this was the first time she had realised herself living without me, that, until now, solicitude had always presented it to her *as me living without her,* but now for the first time solicitude for me was swept aside by a personal realisation of how this would affect her. Yes, it was as though, after endless concern for

[   ] and for me, she had suddenly become aware of herself, and fore-saw herself, not me, bereft and intimidated by what is to come.

It was not for long . . . But it was there, and I saw it. Even if I never see it again, I saw it. I cannot tell if it will make the immediate future easier. In some ways it will make it more painful. It slams the gate of resignation in my face . . . I feel tired, and unbelievably stupid, with a flat staring peasant stupidity. But it was there, and I saw it, and so I want to tell you.

To Paul Nordoff 6: vi: 1949

Dearest Paul,

One good turn deserves another: and you and Sabina have sent us so many kind parcels, that now we have just had the great satisfaction of doing up a box for the Nordoffs, and tomorrow it will go off.

It is a very rum assortment, made up partly from a parcel of clothes from USA which in a most timely way reached us about a month ago, and partly from the remains of my mother (who now, poor soul, needs only nightgowns and bed-jackets) and partly from our own die-hards. Not, alas, a shoe or a pair of pants among them; but I will try to remedy this with a later parcel. I really have put in all sorts and conditions, and don't, please, judge my taste by some of it; but I thought what can't be worn as it is might be made up into clothes for the children.

As country people say, when they give one a cracked teapot, or a totally unwieldy pumpkin, we hope you will accept it in the spirit in which it is meant.

. . . I think I have the subject for our next collaboration. It is a legend of the Irish church, very simple, about the mercy of God. It would not make an opera, for there is no development of action; but it would be perfect for voices discoursing with a small orchestra, even, perhaps, a string quintet. I was so glad to come on it, and to recognise it at once as a meeting-place for us. It is as you say, we must meet in that lonely desperate beautiful place, where we can tell each other the deepest, the *impersonal*, secrets of the heart.

We agree about Shelley. It is his despairing and tragic poems that are the essential. I would love him for ever for those two lines, 'Bright reason shall mock thee, Like the sun from a wintry sky', and some of his satires, brilliant as the heart's blood.

It was the libretto which intervened between telling you about Rome. My dear, I had forgotten it was possible to be so happy, so released, so natural, as we were. It is the most beautiful city in the world, I think, and the wisest and the kindest. It was like the lap of a heavenly grandmother, full of all the toys of time. There was only one black patch, when we went to Assisi and, the day after our enraptured arrival, Valentine suddenly went down with influenza. It was the local kind: violent and aggressive; but she is as wise as a snake in illness, and with that, and the kindness of a dear old chambermaid, we came out into the light again, and our last days, back in Rome, were full of marvellous things, new-fallen snow flashing on the Alban Hills, the fountains in the piazza before St Peters blown sideways like willow-trees, and all the baroque figures on the sky-line ready to leap into the air and flutter up to heaven. And when we came back, we were so full of happiness that we still glowed, and had no feeling that our holiday [was] over and done with.

Oh, and the oxen, darling, so stately—one young one, unharnessed, that I saw stepping through an olive-yard like a thoughtful god; and the landscape, clasping its hands in ecstasy, its mountain hands above its valleyed breast. And everything enriched with art and poetry and history, and so deeply aristocratic, with no airs and ten thousand serious graces; and all seen hand-in-hand with Valentine.

If I should ever write to you and complain of my lot, remind me that in the February of 1949 I went with Valentine to Italy.

To Alyse Gregory *14:xi:1949*

. . . Thank you very much for letting me see the photograph of Stephen Tomlin. I think it is the best likeness of him I have ever seen. I wish one saw more heads of that kind nowadays . . so serious, and so open a regard. Looking at it I realised with dismay that I have not seen a young man with *a classless face* for many years. I suppose the moderate settled middle-class aristocracy that produced such countenances has not the vitality to produce them now.

To Steven Clark *21:xii:1949*

. . . Of course you love Mme du Deffand, but do you know the story of how, when she was old, so old, and had read everything, known everybody, stored decades of unbeguiled seeing behind her sightless eyes, her companion, feeling, Well, now, at last — read her one of the epistles of St Paul — and the old woman in her eared chair listened attentively, and when the reader had quite finished, said, Well—And what do you make of all that?

. . . I am having a very happy Christmas, because I have discovered that I am ripe to re-read Proust. It is heavenly to see that vast and palpitating zoological garden extending before me and to be saying to myself, 'as best I can remember, the tigers are round this corner, and the macaws just beyond them'. And then finding the tigers even more striped and supple than I supposed, and the macaws brighter than even memory painted them.

And the Italian translation of *The Corner* has been giving me a charming delusion that I can read Italian. They have given it the most touching dust-cover, with a pair of Benozzo Gozzoli nuns conversing in a *pink* cloister under a Tuscan blue sky. Aldo Martello if you are interested to know whom.

I think it would be very nice to have a letter telling me how you all are. Did you hear that Charles Prentice died last summer? In Africa, of all deplorable places to die in. There was never a man more plainly designated to die in his own bed in his own country, and he must needs have to die in Africa . . .

. . . Every idiot on the face of the earth seems bent on making a disastrous year of it, but I still hope that the common-sense of commonplace people may outwit them. Still, a murrain carrying off *all* the Distinguished Persons of every nation might not come amiss.

To Paul Nordoff *23:iii:1950*

... If any one could feel for you, God knows it is I. Write? I could as soon
do trick bicycling. The other day I thought I'd got the knack again. I
pulled out the book I was working on a year ago. I thought it was lovely. I
began where it had been broken off. Do you think I could do it? I wrote
as well as ever for six pages and then fell off my bicycle amidst universal
silence.

I think Sabina has put her finger on it. You have been composing too
long, and too steadily, and *Lost Summer* has just about finished your capacity
for the time being for that kind of composing. And I think another thing.
I believe that tiresome fellow at Columbia who cavilled at *The Sea Change*
did something equivalent to banging you on the womb. Your *Sea Change*
died of it—unborn. It's there—for certainly it was there last Spring, it
engendered: but now it has been killed in you, and you can't possibly give
birth to it. There are times in the inception of a work of art when the least
shock from outside will finish it—and if that shock had come a month later,
if the house had caught fire, if an earthquake had rolled you into the ocean,
if a flying saucer had scorched all your hair off in passing, nothing,
NOTHING, would stop the work of art going on. But that fellow came just
at the ticklish moment.

That is one reason, the chief reason, the immediate reason, why I think
we should not try to alter it or cut it about. I am sure it is the right libretto
for you in a certain mood. I still think that you may be able to compose on it
at some later date. I felt so sure of your music, I almost heard it, and in a
way, I feel the music has taken place. But not for now—and it would be
much better to put it behind you. Also I am physically averse to having
anything to do with it myself just now. I was so happy and in such a state
of grace when I wrote it, and immediately after, in such stony despair, that
I don't want to foist myself back to April 1949. But chiefly, I feel we must
both turn away from this last twelvemonth, and have the courage to admit
that in our different ways we are afraid to poke up its ashes.

To Alyse Gregory *29:iii:1950*

... No word from you could ever disturb me. I think soon I can tell you a
great deal; could now, even, without caution withholding me, or super-

stition about the edge of woods; but it is so new, and Valentine's part in it so agonizing and so upright, that reticence hangs round me like a morning mist . . .

I think Valentine has never loved or needed me as much as she does now, or I her. We hold on to each other like convalescents.

TO WILLIAM MAXWELL *29:iv:1950*

. . . I have never yet had a praising review that did not send me slinking and howling under my breath to kneel in some dark corner and pray that the Horn would sound for me and the Worms come for me, that very same night. The horn doesn't and the worms don't, and somehow one recovers one's natural powers of oblivion, and goes on writing. Not that I am an example of that just now. I have been a barren figtree for the last twelve-month. A novel I was working on died half-baked, I can't settle to anything else, and I can't revive it. If you are anywhere near 25 W. 43rd St. though, ask Mr Lobrano for a short story called *The Children's Grandmother*. It is a good one, though he don't think so,[1] and I would like you to read it.

And then, after all, I did not go to Paris. I had to stay in London instead. You should come to London soon, before all the ruins have been cleared away. When I was a child I used to go to a house that had all the Piranesi Views of Rome hanging along a corridor, and I was much affected by all those romantic ruins, fallen columns, gapped peristyles and so forth. It is extraordinary to find one's native capital offering a whole new series of Piranesis. There is a row of grand houses, backing on the Green Park, which is beyond all: the great silent dusky dining-rooms with their mahogany doors weathered to a dusky grey-green, fern sprouting from their busy basements, and the tusks of the grand staircase rising tier above tier to end against the pale London sky. I wished that Byron and Thackeray (who have much more in common than their critics suppose) could have been seeing it too. But each time I go back there are fewer of these spectacles, and if you are coming to England you really must not leave it too late.

TO NANCY CUNARD *28:v:1950*

. . . I have begun many letters to you in my mind, and some even on paper, but never finished them. This one should be more lucky as I have taken the precaution not to begin it till near midnight.

---

1. He thought well enough of it to choose it for *The New Yorker*'s second anthology of its short stories.

Soon after you left I had to go down to Devon, where a cousin of mine died suddenly. I had been till a few months before her daughter's guardian, and twenty-one is a young age to find your mother dead in her bed, to be alone in the house when it happened . . . So I stayed for a few days, and found myself doing a great many odd things in a dreamlike way, packing and unpacking, and listening to the undertaker's life-story. My mother died in February, our dear cat in March, last month my cousin . . . today is still the 28th of May, and I look rather cautiously at the calendar. But why I began on all these funerals was to tell you how, coming in to the room with the usual set of consolatory tea-things I saw the affecting picture of this long-legged young woman lying on the floor before the fire reading the bible and eating a meringue . . . and felt rather as if I had come on the bittern booming or some such rare aspect of nature.

My mother's probate is still not through, and thank heaven my mother's tenants are still in the house; but I am afraid they will not be there much longer. He is in the Marine Commando lot at Plymouth, and they have Malaya hanging over them. So before long I shall have to unwind my Sloth's embraces, and go down there to wrestle with sales and disposals. The magpie's nest . . . photographs and ostrich feathers and papier mâché boxes and twenty thousand bits of china, and all in a place quite inaccessible and the devoted gardener sighing round the house like a banshee.

TO ALYSE GREGORY *10:vi:1950*

Dearest Alyse,
It would be asking very little of Valentine—to borrow the Kinsey report. It would be asking a great deal of yourself to read it, *me judice*. I for a little tried, liked it not, and tried no further. I am coming to be of the opinion that information about the sexes is boring to those who know already, and ruinous to those who don't. Sexual experiences are nothing if they are not amazing. Hymen without his saffron robe looks pretty much like any other forked radish. And when I looked at Kinsey, my heart began to grieve for all the young men and maidens who will read it, and when they come to go to bed with each other it will be no more than anything else they have read up for, a Little-Go, or a School Certificate. I mistrust instruction. I think it folly to be wise. I remember [   ] and [   ], as promising a Daphnis and Chloe as you could hope to find—and then they got hold of a treatise by a person called Haire, and learned about all they should do and all they should feel; and conscientiousness descended on them like a blight and from then on they began to make each other miserable . . .
Meanwhile, I am comforted to remember all the embracing couples we

118

saw while we were in town. It was too hot to do anything in the evenings but sit in Kensington Gardens. The grass was strewn with lovers, and the heat made them graceful and indolent, it was as though they had been placed there by Claude or Giorgione, perspectives of them under the ranks of trees. I was particularly delighted with one young man who, after a long and passionate embrace, sat up, and raised one languishing hand, and caressed his own hair. Another pretty couple was two young men who had had a baby—or so it seemed. We met them twice running, and each time they were placidly adoring a small baby, waving the flies away from it with a green bough, refreshing its naked body with a damp handkerchief, and dandling it. I have never seen the verb to dandle better expressed. And once, while one of them was holding the child on his knee the other, who had been reclining on the grass beside it, suddenly and ingratiatingly stood on his head, though whether to please the baby or express his own satisfaction I have no idea. Then, when at last the park-keepers began to cry their *All Out*, they put the baby into its pram and walked demurely away. Perhaps they had found it under a gooseberry bush.

It was pleasant seeing people so hot and so happy; and being able to love one's kind again. I cannot love people in the country, I discover, because there is always this danger that they may be acquaintances, with all the perils and choleras of acquaintance implicit in them; but in London they seem as charming as rabbits.

To Nancy Cunard *26:vii:1950*

... By the grace of God I sold a longish story to *The New Yorker*, and the money will see us to wherever we go and back again. Otherwise I would be sitting on the sea-wet rocks and combing my Spartan hair—for by the usual series of legal ingenuities my mother's lawyer, whom she was demented enough to appoint as her executor, is still finding fresh reasons for boggling and buggering over probate, and by the time I do see my inheritance I do not expect to have more than threepence half-penny, the rest will have gone into his gorge ... The only thing the lawyer cannot take is the house in Devon, where all the ceilings have just come down.

I think that is the main outline of my woes, except that the magpies have eaten the peas of this summer and a rabbit has nipped off with the greens of next winter ... So much for the winter greens. It is more to my pleasure that the hollyhocks are eight foot high, and have been inter-marrying since I first got them, and now have hit off some very fine imitations of Rome: apricot-tawnies, and burned milk, and one just the colour of Tiber mud. How frustrating it is not to be able just to enjoy seeing the

Americans whacked in Korea!—a simple childlike harmless pleasure, one would think; but impossible to s'attabler to, with one's heart in one's mouth about what may happen next, and one's pride down the w.c. because of our own draggled part in it.

To Marchette Chute *28:viii:1950*

... *Please* don't write a life of Milton. It is such a melancholy subject, the way the English Angel, flourishing about in Italy, degenerated into a public figure, generally cross about something. There is quite enough to depress one as it is, without being reminded of Milton.

To Paul Nordoff *31:viii:1950*

Dearest Paul,

How are you, and how do things go, and how is The Codicil, and how tall are the children? And how do you like High Mowing, and is your bursitis cured?

Three weeks ago, my darling, I was in Ireland, looking at a house in Co. Clare, and very nearly buying it. Which I should have done, if it[s] rooms had been fewer and larger, and if its windows had looked out on the loveliest landscape I have ever set eyes on; instead of staring at frantic trees planted to break the Atlantic gales, and if it would have been feasible to live in its stables instead of itself. O my dear, it was a very strange and poetical house, ugly, isolated, inconvenient, with great gaunt black granite hearths, and noble passages, wide enough for two coffins to go abreast—but a house that would lie on one like a weight of melting snow, a house in which one would begin a hundred things, but never be able to go on and finish them. Still, it is not the only house in Ireland; and later on I shall go with Valentine and look for another.

All of a sudden, we began to feel potbound. I think it may be the tickle of the healing of the [   ] wound—you know how a new clean tissue announces itself by feeling like an ant-heap. Anyhow, we wanted to move. And though not to Ireland, I think we shall have a wonderful winter in Great Eye Folly. It is on the north coast of Norfolk, on the extremest edge of it, sea from the forward set of windows, and marsh and saltings and the sad stern mainland from the others. It stands on a little hummock, and looks like a dear little police-station. It has a Bechstein, two bathrooms, three very small bedrooms and no drinking water. We found it almost by accident about ten days ago. It was to let for the winter months, and we instantly decided to take it—much to the bewildered exhilaration of its owners, who do not often find such maniacs. It will be as cold as cold, and very likely if the winter seas are high it will become an island.

In between then and now, we are going to France with the car. We start next week, and make for the Auvergne. All these are very nice things, and I scarcely know myself with so much going on. And I have a wonderful story coming out in the New Yorker soon, called The Childrens Grandmother. Such a sostenuto, my dear, and such a enharmonic twist at the end.

But I am tired, O God, how tired I am. It has been a tranquil wettish summer, nothing to tire me and a great deal to please me; but it is as though the whole fatigue of last year had settled on me. Once we have got to Ossel in those Auvergnes, I hope to find a nice extinct volcano (it is all extinct volcanoes) preferably with a lake in its crater (lots of them have lakes of unknown depth containing legendary fish) and sit on its slopes for days and days and days, quietly emptying myself of an infinity of crumpled yawns and deferred groans. And in the evenings I hope for a nice kind proprietor to tie a bib round my neck and feed me, and send me to bed early, to a sober-minded French mattress with harsh linen sheets, and to wake me, not too early, with coffee in a bowl and grilled breads.

To Marchette Chute 30:ix:1950

... You are filling your closets, and we are emptying ours: but the state of man is the same. Isn't it appalling how much property gets into one's pockets? How many clothes one has, and how many, many note-books, all with just enough blank paper in them to make it a matter of conscience to save them, and none blank enough to be given away? For we, with our eye on Great Eye Folly, are clearing this house enough to let a furnished tenant get into it. The furnished tenant comes tomorrow, to look over the place; and for the last two days Valentine and I have been sugaring it to the best of our ability: whitewashing the damp places on the diningroom wall, polishing the floors with a frotteur which we brought home from France, snatching down cobwebs, and arranging large bunches of Michaelmas daisies (full of earwigs) in dubious corners. I am now in the proud state of having crossed off every item on my list but the last two, which run: mend the sitting room grate: ennoble the hall.

France was heavenly. We rolled in romanesque churches and extinct volcanoes—we went to Auvergne, which abounds in both. We saw the Lascaux caves with their prehistoric paintings. We found a mediaeval village called Martel that nobody seems to know about, even the all-knowing Michelin, has nothing to say of its beauties; we sat repairing ourselves with ices on a terrace looking down on Rocamadour, where there was a day of reparation going on, with plainsong ringing through loud-speakers; we learned a great deal more French, because of the sweet conscientious way that shop-people in France always try to throw in a little information along with the change: one said to Valentine, who had become confused, Madame, il y a des biscuits, et des biscottes. And at our poorest hotel they gave us a packet of coffee, because we had praised their brew, and at our richest, we found, when we opened the picnic meal they had put up for us to take away, that the waiter had inserted half a pound of the hotel's butter. We also saw, at long last, a Marshall Plan tractor. As we had been through mostly agricultural country, we had expected to see quite a lot of them; but this one did not meet us until we were on our way back, running through the edge of the Côte d'Or. It was standing beside a field of vines, it has two of those vast tubs on it into which they empty the baskets of grapes; and there it would remain, no doubt, till the end of the day, when it would duly carry them home to the farm. It is so like the French to grasp the essential thing about a tractor: that it doesn't mind how long it stands still. Meanwhile, they were ploughing with oxen, just as usual, half a mile further down the road.

To Alyse Gregory *20:x:1950*

. . . we sort, and clear, and make inventories; and at intervals display the house to people who do not see its beauties, and see at a glance (as indeed they could scarcely fail to do) that there is no stair-carpet. Most of them were so very uncongenial that as we saw negatives start out all over their blanked countenances we were more grateful that they would go away than saddened that they would not come.

I think Valentine will have told you about Great Eye Folly. I have the oddest impressions of it, since we were only there for about fifteen minutes, and conversing all the time with its owners. But the first five of those minutes was enough to enchant me. It is the sort of house one tells oneself to sleep with, and sometimes I almost suppose that it is really one of my dream-houses, and no such solid little assertion of the rectangle breaks the long sky-line of salt-marsh and sea. But things tether it to earth, again: a post-card, saying, 'I forgot to tell you that the butcher is called Arthur.' An inventory, listing 'seven mugs, one glued.' And such facts as that today I packed the four grey and white cups and saucers Valentine bought to take with us, grey and white to complement the view of the sea from our windows: It looks straight out on the sea: fifty feet of a low wind-bitten cliff, and then the shore. At dusk we shall see the ships' lights passing, and the intermittent fixed stars of the light-buoys: and from the south windows, the small far-away lights of the village, and the few head-lamps travelling along the coast-road of what one must think of as the mainland; for the salt-marshes in between have that equivocal character, one cannot really look on them as solid earth. Next Friday, at this time, we shall be there. I can hardly believe it.

To WILLIAM MAXWELL *3:xi:1950*   *Great Eye Folly. Salthouse.*
                                                      Holt. Norfolk

. . . I would like to live here for ever—the owners come back at Easter—but that no one could do, for in five years time the sea will have eaten it. The young man who came out from Holt yesterday to bring another cylinder of gas for the cooking-stove said to me, talking of the rate at which the sea is advancing, that his father could remember loads of corn being drawn inland over the bridge. What bridge?—said I. *I* can remember the bridge, said he. It was there. And he pointed to where our track runs out on the shingle, and the high water mark ribbon of seaweed is.

At the other end of the track is the coast road, and the village of Salthouse, where every one is most humanely solicitous to make our flesh creep. It was unaccountably delightful to be told that I need not worry at all until I saw the cattle being taken off the marsh (there has been nothing on the marsh but geese for the last two days), and to be told by the grocer about underground passages between the pillbox on the beach, which the sea has already undermined, and the pillbox that is fastened to the side of the house, and how, if I go and listen at high tide—but I have, and not an underground gurgle did I hear, so I'm afraid it is the usual monkish underground passage story, but brought a little up to date.

Another remainder of when this was a fortified coastal point is a tight little brick hut, with a door lettered: Bomb Disposal. Private. I like the English moderation of this. The door is fastened, but the cat goes in by a crack in the threshold—and knowing how bombs get left about and over-looked I was rather nervous at first. He is the happiest cat in the British Isles—three pill-boxes, and a whole system of trenches to play in, and the spindrift to chase and the sea-tangle to explore.

To MARCHETTE CHUTE *16:xi:1950*   *Great Eye Folly. Salthouse.*
                                                      Holt. Norfolk.

. . . To the seaward we see gulls, and sometimes seals and porpoises; to the landward, there is a heron that lives in the marsh, and a kingfisher, and three horses, out for a tonic bite of pré-salé, I suppose; and in the mornings

123

there is the post-girl, coming on a windblown bicycle. That, really, is all, except for sea and sky, and a long sharp-edged pebble beach, where we go out at low tide to see what may have been cast up for us. The flotsam etc is very odd, one would think that people on this north sea did nothing but eat coconuts and brush their teeth.

To Ian Parsons 26:xii:1950   Great Eye Folly. Salthouse.
                              Holt. Norfolk.

. . . It is a lovely book; and a beautiful bit of editing.[1] It is so valuable to have those letters of Mme Straus's to him, and the illustrations are divinely chosen. They gave me a queer Zeitschmerz. Waves from this cross-channel world touched my childhood—the young man who played the Valse des Roses and strummed l'Après-midi, hats of the same type if not quite the same hats, and a photograph frame which the young man presented to my mother, a replica of the frame of the little Fauntleroy Marcel with fleurs de lys on it—purple of course.

I noticed the inadequacy of the reviews, and was sorry. The truth is, my dear, there are not many reviewers who would be at home with the book, and even fewer editors—and of those few, half would be ashamed to admit it. It takes reckless resolution now, to admit that one has known a more civilised age than the present. It is painful to admit it to oneself, and apparently shameful to mention it to others. Every one is busy pretending that even if they once or twice went out to tea they always drank the tea from a mug. I can well understand that you sat down at the end of the year and felt discouraged. At the time when we first knew each other there were the usual number of fools about, I think—but at least those fools did not feel it incumbent on them to be boors too. As for the novels that pay and the novels that they pay for, that is a matter between you and your conscience, I don't interfere, I only venture to say that I can't think of any other publishers who have done so very little evil that good may come . . . and, at the same time, avoided that other pitfall in which the highly respectable wallow—the pitfall of being so consistently bores that one can tell beforehand just what books they will bring out next year and the year after. The firm has done such a lot of queer things as well as good things; and personally, that is what I most admire about it. For between ourselves, dear Ian, it is not very difficult to be on a consistently high level; all you have got to do is get up there somehow, or be dropped on it, and then remain in the same place raising the right and the left foot alternately.

1. *Letters of Marcel Proust*, translated and edited by Mina Curtiss, which Chatto and Windus had published, and which he had sent to her as a Christmas present.

To Paul Nordoff *31:xii:1950*   *Great Eye Folly. Salthouse.*
                                      Holt. Norfolk.

. . . We have been snow-bound and ice-bound for days at a time. It has been strange to look across the marsh, and see the chimneys in the village with slow twirls of frost-bound smoke, and sometimes a lorry or a reeling bicyclist inching along the icy coast road. A devoted baker brought us bread twice a week; we had our woodpile, and the sea kept on adding to it with driftwood; once, when all the water froze, we melted snow (it took hours, and was dark grey when we'd got it, and precious little in comparison with the billows of snow it started as) . . . I have not seen Valentine so happy nor so much herself for years, and all her beauty has come back to her, and she walks about like a solitary sea nymph . . . a sea nymph who can split logs with an axe and manage a most capricious petrol pump, and cut up large frozen fish with a cleaver.

It was a brilliant idea to come here. It has avoided all the small regretful uneasy niggling ghosts that were still sitting about in our house in Dorset, sights from windows that suddenly present you with how you were feeling when you saw them on such and such a day, latent remarks in the familiar noise of a door shutting or a chair creaking.

To Nancy Cunard *7:ii:1951*   *Great Eye Folly. Salthouse.*
                                               Norfolk.

. . . I am sorry that the yellow house has turned so awkward. It may be
better when you have lit more fires in it (Oh—but does the chimney smoke?)
and gone into it to get out of the rain. In the end, it is the animal aspect of a
house that brings one to love it; not the views, nor the view of it, nor the
guests, nor the absence of guests, but the times when one has gone into it for
shade or shelter, or in darkness, and it has put the box of matches into one's
groping hand. But when it is teething, and needs its diapers changing, and
yells for workmen who don't come—God, how detestable a house can be.
Even in our perfect house, our darling apple-scented Frankfort Manor, I
remember one day when I hated it so much that I wrote a poem about the
tranquil house that hangs upside down in the pond—'securely drowned'—
and its antithesis of the real house full of banging doors, care, and the laundry
basket, with only one pillow-case sent back.

Now—did Valentine tell you?—we are confronted with another housing
problem. Her mother's doctor gave a confidential report that Ruth is in a
bad way, and that her heart is so dot and go one that she might die of any
shock or exertion (and that it would be injudicious to tell her so, since this
might provide the very shock). Ruth is a person who lives for shocks and
exertions. To spring from a running bus in order to break her heart at a
funeral is her idea of the good life. Also, she refuses to have a servant in her
house, or to live in a hotel or service flat. The upshot of it is that our very
casual views on getting a house in Norfolk some time or other, when we
found the right one, has been intensified into a grim search; since the alternative seems to be an endless series of cross-country rushes from Dorset.
Of course we almost instantly found the almost ideal answer to prayer; a
house to let unfurnished, large rooms, not much upkeep, and very easy to
nurse Ruth in, if she comes to need that; . . . The landlord is palpably a shifty
dog, and we dare not trust ourselves with him without a very well-secured
agreement, and this he won't give us . . . Meanwhile, we go patiently looking
at Little Eases, or great gaunt rectories with contaminated water supplies
and poltergeists.

To William Maxwell *17:iii:1951*   *Great Eye Folly. Salthouse.*
Holt. Norfolk.

Dear Mr Maxwell,

A magnificent ham arrived, and I should have written before to say how wonderful it looked against a background of grey sea; but I hoped to combine the letter with another story, and have been hanging on to that hope. It is all done except for one sleeve, like the nettle-shirt in Hans Christian—but then a lot of noisy things began happening, and now we are packing to go home, so I shall have to put it off until I am unpacked and in my right mind again.

One of the things that happened was that we nearly became an island. There was a wonderful concatenation of new moon and northeasterly gale and telephone conversations with the coastguards at Cley . . . the coastguards asked me, 'What's it like down your way,' and I was proudly enabled to reply, 'About two hours ahead of its usual tide-mark, and coming in very full now.' All this was very much as I liked it, and the sea was lovely to see, I have never seen anything enjoying itself more. But the car is all the car we shall ever have, and it became obvious that we could not keep it dry-foot much longer unless the wind shifted, and when the coastguard finally and rather obscurely remarked, 'Well, I should say that prevention is better than cure,' we made a hasty dusky get-away, with the dog, the cat, and a carcass of chicken—for I was determined not to waste the goodness in its bones; and as the wind bowled us along the causeway we saw the spray jumping up over the shingle ridge like hounds, and the water just beginning to lap across.

We went inland to friends, and I made chicken soup that same night. (The ham? It was in my bedroom, I knew the sea wouldn't get at it there); and when we came back two days later, some morose waves were mumbling away at a completely re-shaped beach, with a lot of gaunt remains of tank traps unburied, and looking like some sort of mineral nettles. You could tell that man had been there.

We leave on Monday; and today I have been going round tearing myself away from fishmongers and greengrocers and bakers, and Mr Morris the saddler. It is very painful for me to leave them because they like me so much. I am much more of a social success in East Anglia than in Wessex, and I don't look forward to being just that peculiar Miss Warner again, after being loved and laurelled all the way down Holt High Street, and knowing the Christian names of every one's cat.

To Paul Nordoff *27:iii:1951*   *Frome Vauchurch. Maiden*
Newton. Dorset.

Dearest Paul,

The record followed me here, and in the midst of the horrors of unpacking we sat down and listened to it. I don't know which of us was most moved It is such exquisite music, and so thrilling to hear it like this, with your

127

voice speaking to me, as though your disembodiment had come with it. I think the Shelley aria is one of the most moving, most heavenly, most profound things I have ever heard. I had the extraordinary sensation while I listened to it, *that I knew it*. This was partly that I know your idiom, perhaps, yet I feel that it is more than that, that in some way we have really been together in this work, and perhaps I have heard your music in my dreams, so that it has this strange quality of being something both new to me and already part of me.

Heavens, it is so beautiful! So wise and so mature. But hearing it, and having heard your voice, I could have wept, for there is such a charge of experienced sorrow in it. O my dear Paul, we are so many years older since I last heard your voice, and we have suffered so much in those years, grief, fatigue, anxiety, disillusionings. But your music . . . your music. And the lovely duet, so classically spare in its grace: and that heart-rending introduction to the last scene . . nothing could better convey the feeling of all over and now all to begin, the acceptance, the endurance of despair, life beginning again, patiently, inexorably beginning again, the earth heavily wheeling to another day, the blank light patiently fingering through the shuttered window. It is ravishing—only no instrument could possibly be as *right* as your whistle! Never was such desolation in a whistle.

My darling Paul, I embrace you with my whole heart.

It is strange to be back here, in this gentle air and beside this sly subtle river, after that long stay in rough air with the noise of the waves a continual pattern under one's living. I miss Norfolk people, who are so brisk and upstanding compared to these Wessex folk; and on the other hand it is like the Kingdom of Heaven to be back in my own clean convenient kitchen after struggling with the world's worst gas-cooker, great iron frying-pans, and chipped crockery. I had no idea how luxurious we are; or perhaps I had no idea how very badly some house-owners supply their tenants. Our tenants were worthy of our good providing. They destroyed nothing, left the house clean and tidy, and rescued Valentine's tortoise into the bargain (he woke too soon, unwary creature, and they found him trying to dig himself in again on hard frozen ground).

Calamities go on having a buffet at us. I think I told you that Valentine's mother is a great anxiety . . . Every time the telephone rings, we expect it to be bad news about her; yet, as far as I can see, she will probably go on like this for a long while yet; for she is set in her ways, and one can stay almost indefinitely at Death's door if one has planted one's camp stool in a sunny corner of it.

. . . The garden is a swamp, and we must buy a new donkey boiler, and three parcels of books have got lost on the railway, and five needless people have come to the door since I began this letter; and so on. But my mind is so full of your music that all this flows round me rather than over me.

... O my dear, I know that state of feeling dead-cold, living in an ice-coffin, seeing too clearly, hearing with delirious accuracy and detachment, everything neat, precise, scissor-sharp: and within, that unavailing unavailed unused tenderness and sensibility. The May frost: and it half kills one. It is an after effect, I think. In your case, after the shock of Columbia. There is a beautiful passage in one of the Chinese philosophers about how, if one wants to enjoy the possession of an oak-tree one must plant it in the village of nowhere in the province of nothingness, and only then can one lie down and repose in its shade without care and anxiety. There are times when I find this exasperating piece of advice extraordinarily restorative and convincing—and always beautiful. One is so grateful for good advice that can be completely accepted without having to run about putting it in action ... and thereby finding that it doesn't apply and won't work.

I should love to write a violin and piano sonata, commissioned or no (actually, I have enjoyed all my commissions, there is something rather appealing and tidy about a commission, as if one put on one's best wig and waistcoat for it). But if I did, I know it would be very monotonous, for I should never be able to drag myself away from the satisfaction of using the violin for the lowest voice; and it would be like a soliloquy from a person of great eloquence under a mosquito net. As for anything called a symphony, I am with you. Something has happened in our lifetime to the symphony, and now it seems totally uninhabitable—like a hotel. Or else like a chain of hotels, which is worse.

To a friend who had inconveniently fallen in love *11:v:1951*

... Because happiness is the root of all, even of tragedy, I begin with your happiness. Though it were brief as a rainbow, it is there, it is imperative, it has been accepted, and you must accept it. To accept what one has accepted is sometimes the hardest thing in the world. All the burned child in one flinches, refuses, shies away. That you haven't done. You are too much of a salamander for that, my darling. But that is not all the catalogue. There is also conditional acceptance, acceptance with one toe still cautiously clawing at the underwater sand. Hurrying to my old pulpit, I adjure you, I implore, say no more, think no more, about perhaps losing [   ] to some one else. To think of losing is to lose already. To consider a rival fattens an insubstantial into a real being. Since you are in the river, darling, SWIM! And if that hypothetical younger person comes into your mind, think of me. Here I am, grey as [a] badger, wrinkled as a walnut, and never a beauty at my best; but here I sit, and yonder sits the other one, who had all the cards in her hand—except one. That I was better at loving and being loved.

To William Maxwell *5:vi:1951*

... England has never been herself since motor mowers came to us. Lawns, that used to be all peace and eating white raspberries on seats painted green, are now disorderly scenes of strife, with mowers, the human part of the mechanism, jolting round the corners or falling off into the rhododendrons, or—worse—galloping along after the horrible thing with their mouths choked with daisies. We have a nice old-fashioned one, and a little boy called Colin is all the motor it has, and afterwards he goes fishing in our reach of the river.

I haven't had time to see our tortoise lately. When I saw him last he was eating forget-me-nots and Niou was trying to wash his back. He is called Manisty, after Valentine's great-grandfather, Mr Justice of that ilk. *He* was considered, even in the most strictly sensuous reading of the word, an ornament to the Bench, and remains in marble and duodecimo in ivory. I don't think our Manisty lives up to that; but he has a nice dry tidy little countenance. Through Manisty Valentine is related to Shelley's Lord Eldon, and so almost to Shelley, in a Court of Chancery way; and through Lady Manisty to Mrs Gaskell, whose correspondence with Charles Eliot Norton so much resembles ours.

To Alyse Gregory *7:ix:1951*

Dearest Alyse,

A story demanded to be written, and that is why I have not answered your letter before: a wrong-headed story, that would come blundering like a moth on my window, and stare in with small red eyes, and I the last writer in the world to manage such a subject. One should have more self-control. One should be able to say, Go away. You have come to the wrong inkstand, there is nothing for you here. But I am so weakminded that I cannot even say, Come next week.

I am preparing to enjoy Delacroix very much, but I cannot do so just yet because the L. L.[1] sent him in a translation and a truncation, and I want him in his own skin and at full length. Not that I can't skip like a flea, and

1. The London Library.

do so; but I like to choose my own jumping-off places. The editor has left out all the cookery part—the lists of paints, the ponderings as to whether to glaze the Repentant Magdalen in Naples Yellow or Raw Siena, and that seems to me a mistake, since artists without French might want to read just that. And even if one is not an artist there is something crazily elevating in overhearing just that sort of studio talk; not a word of the general effect, the emotional content, but a steady happy mumble about that dash of cobalt under the left breast of the Venus.

Do remember, even among your thousand affairs of departure, that the gentleman in Bournemouth's Powysiana should include a Gertrude.[1] If nothing else, the fact that I so often find myself disliking one of her canvasses at first sight, convinces me that she is the true artist. One's hackle never rises except before the real threat of real art.

To Nancy Cunard *9:xi:1951*

. . . about ten days ago I got started on a new book, and am completely, brazenly devoted to it: my hair is uncut, my letters are unwritten, the house is a shambles, and I sit here as happy as Mrs Jellaby, though I am in 1836, not Africa.

It won't go on like this, I shall fall over some obstacle, and wake out of my dreams with a black eye and broken shins: but while it does last, I daren't interrupt it. I haven't had such a spell of writing for nearly three years.

To William Maxwell *6:xii:1951*

. . . Yes, it was caution that kept me so non-committal about the book in hand,[2] and also astonishment, incredulity, and lack of breath. I got out of my bath and began writing it about the middle of October, and have gone on at a canter ever since. While I was in my bath I had been speculating about my great-great-grandfather, who stayed in a pious East Anglian family just long enough to beget my great-grandfather, and was swept off to die on a voyage to the West Indies, while the pious family constructed a sort of inscrutable grotto round his memory, alleging that he was a mauvais sujet and never supplying any evidence for it. But except for the date, any resemblance to the facts stayed in the bath.

1. Sister of Theodore, Llewelyn, etc.
2. *The Flint Anchor.*

To William Maxwell *12:ii:1952*

... Poor Niou has just had his first affair of the heart, and of course it was a tragedy. As a rule he flies from strange men, cursing under his breath, and keeping very low on the ground. Yesterday an electrician came; a grave mackintoshed man, but to Niou all that was romantic and lovely. He gazed at him, he rubbed against him, he lay in an ecstasy on the tool-bag. The electrician felt much the same, and gave him little washers to play with. He said he would have to come again today to finish off properly. Niou who understands everything awaited him in a dreamy transport and practising his best and most amorous squint. The electrician came, Niou was waiting for him on the window-sill. A paroxysm of stage-fright came over him, and he rushed into the garden and disappeared.

He'll get over [it] in time; but just now he's dreadfully downcast.

I hope you noticed the heights of unconventionality achieved simultaneously by the late king and his daughter. One of them spent the night in a tree, and the other in dying unattended, thus bilking the bishops. There has not been such a death in the succession since William Rufus. I tell people that the Archbishop of Canterbury's indisposition is entirely temper and mortification; but this may not be true, though I like to think it. I am in a desperate state of mortification myself, for I can only mourn up to the waist. But I can keep my temper, which is more than the Archbishop of Canterbury can. They say that Lambeth Palace rings with oaths and execrations and that he has gnawed his way through five bolsters and the private chaplain.

To William Maxwell *5:iv:1952*

... Your garden is ahead of ours. But that is because our second row of peas was frustrated by the blizzard. We had set out for a small holiday in the car the day before it blew up, and by driving as fast as we could into the teeth of an easterly gale we always managed to keep about an hour ahead of the snowdrifts filling up the roads behind us. When we got to Yarmouth on the coast, there were sanddrifts instead. We were in a friend's car, of great magnificence with central heating, so we had all the elation of being very hardy and daring while remaining in perfect comfort. I have never heard anything finer than Coke of Norfolk's avenue at Holkham. It is a double avenue of live oaks, two miles long, in full winter plumage, and the noise was oceanic. The wind was so steady that they scarcely swayed at all, they just bowed themselves and bellowed.

To William Maxwell *9:iv:1952*

. . . It was in the north of Scotland, and the traveller was sitting before the peat fire under the wide chimney, making conversation with the inn-keeper. 'I saw a strange thing on the road today,' he said, 'I saw four cats carrying a little bier, and cats walking before and behind in procession, keening like Christians. And on the bier was a coffin about eighteen inches long, and on the coffin was a small gold crown.' And the cat of the house, lying on the hearth, started up at these words, and exclaimed, 'Then I am the King of the Cats', and vanished up the chimney.

To William Maxwell *8:vi:1952*

. . . After a slight setback of entertaining Inescapables, I am so much better that at any moment I may begin to write again . . . I could perfectly well have begun earlier, if I had not decided to polish a bureau. Having polished it so beautifully, I was rash enough to turn my admiring proud gaze round on the rest of the house, and then of course it was my grandmother and the biscuits all over again. Brought up sternly in Charlotte Square, Edinburgh, my grandmother was allowed down from the nursery to see the dining room arrayed for one of those dinners after which it was quite customary for some of the gentlemen guests not to come up to the drawing room at all, but the word would be given by my great-grandfather, and my great-grandmother would give a tactful low whisper to one of the ladies, and she would presently rise unobtrusively and go downstairs to where her respected lord had been propped up to wait for the moment when he could be guided to his carriage. Well, there was the sideboard with the dessert set out on it, and among the dessert was a dish of sweet biscuits. My grandmother took a light nibble from one of them. Replacing it, she saw that the nibble was only too plain. She nibbled all round the biscuit, with a hope that it would appear to be no more than a decorative edging. This only emphasised the undecorativeness of the remaining biscuits. Mad with terror, frantic as a rabbit biting its leg off to get out of a gin, the child nibbled round every damned biscuit on the dish.

Fortunately, my great-grandfather was a very intelligent humane man, and though he could not do much to restrain my great-grandmother's sense of duty—and certainly not about the dark room that followed the biscuits—he saved her from complete slavishness, and she grew up a very intelligent and enjoying woman. I say this, in case you lie awake all night, wishing you could get at my great-grandmother. For myself, I have come to the conclusion that these wishes, though laudable, are vain; and that children experience terror however they are brought up; in some generations it is better and in others worse, but it always has to be gone through, and when it is put off from childhood it is only to pounce down on adolescence. Oddly enough, I can't feel that this is any reason not to want to get at my great-grandmother. If one's impulses did not perpetually war with one's conclusions, I daresay one would be senile in a week.

Further Advice to the friend who was of two minds about remaining married *3: viii: 1952*

. . . Now instantly, let me nip one of the fleas that is biting you. You say of your children, whatever will they think of me when they grow up . . . they will grow up as we did, trampling lightly on codes of morality, fanatical about their own code. What that code may be, we can't tell; but we can be perfectly sure it won't be like any other in the world before. But the judgement of their hearts is foretellable. They will judge you as a person who . . . had a light step, a long look, a comfortable way of laughing, who could hoist one into a tree and lift one down again at the right moment, whose coat's shoulder had a particular smell. That is how. I don't think you need worry yourself over that.

. . . I don't believe in this chat about 'broken homes' . . . Children make their own homes. They are at home in the womb, they are shaken out of that, they construct a new home of breast and cradle, they are hauled out of that, they make a new home of nursery, of playground, of society.

It is impossible to stop children making homes. They make them in woods and under tables, and round the garbage cans at the bottom of the alley. They make homes as they make flesh and make bone. Have you considered what quantities of people in my country have had their homes broken? I mean the thousands of children from Anglo-Indian families. They are transported, at the most fragile age, from a hot climate to a cold, from black faces to red ones, from mangoes to apples, from monsoons to drizzles. They do not merely change one parent, they change a whole world and a whole method of existence; and they change—perhaps the most influencing change of all—impalpables: the frames of mind that surround them, the waves of thought that flow over them, the chemical influences of race and civilization. Those children grow up into those very English we scorn because they are so very reliable and level-headed—or if you please, so stodgy and respectable. But whichever you prefer, they are not nervous wrecks.

To Leonard Bacon[1] *11:viii:1952*

. . . I have never seen a natural moose, or a tarpon; but I once saw a whole herd of financiers, and it made an indelible impression on me. I was a young lady, and a rich friend had taken me to an after-dinner music at the Gulbenkians'. We went up to a drawing room full of creditable easy chairs with ladies sitting about in them, a rather depressed seraglio. And then the door opened, and the financiers came in from the afterdinner sitting; and I have never in my life seen such a strange assortment, they looked as if they had come out of a swamp. They clung together, too, in a timid clotted way, as one would expect of some form of life whose natural habitat was a swamp.

To Leonard Bacon *23:viii:1952*

Dear Mr Bacon,

I am so very sorry to hear of your illness—and its concomitants. Saltless meals, denicotinized cigarettes and bathing with female assistance sounds as though you were following some obscure sect of Epicurians; and it must be misery to belong to any sect, though I daresay the smaller, the better. There is more moral snobisme about it. I hope you will soon be better, and that you will be sly enough to dodge another attack of the same thing.

Though when I saw a collection of Shaker antiques at Litchfield (I think; you will see that I am returning to the question of sectaries) I felt there was something to be said obliquely in favour of a sect that drove its votaries to such beautiful abstract, faute de mieux of representational, pictures. I remember a view of coloured spokes and circles that was as lovely as anything on a Persian dish. And I liked that ascetic furniture, that had renounced every intention of collecting dust; though I would not care to live long with it, and certainly not in a large strange continent. Can you explain a thing that has long puzzled me?—why the early American art—

1. (1887-1954), American poet. He taught at the University of California and was awarded the Pulitzer Prize for one of his volumes of poetry.

135

17th-18th century—is so aggressively pure and plain? If I were Governor Winthrop, making a large fortune out of wampum, with the cold sea roaring on one side of me and winds from a wilderness blowing on the other, nothing would have supported me but the most emphatic baroque. It wasn't Puritanism—Puritans who could afford to in this country sat on chairs carved all over with lions and barley sugar twists, like so many Lauds and Cosins. Can it have been that they struck only hardwood? Even so, they might have gilded it. And since I am on the subject, what is wampum?

Your mention of Ralph Hodgson and his broadsides swept me back to the public at fisticuffs. Broadsides were what one bought at Munro's Poetry Book-shop, only I think we called them rhyme-sheets. Like galley proof, as you say, with rough coloured woodcuts heading and tailing them, often drawn by Lovat Frazer. And we tacked them on our walls, above our beds and our baths. I remember one I was peculiarly attached to, that began

Oh, what shall the man full of sin do,
Whose heart is as cold as a stone,
When the black owl looks in through the window,
And he on his deathbed alone?

I can't remember the author, which is ungrateful of me.

But afterwards the method was taken up by the tea-shop anglo-catteries, and so fell into disrepute.

It was in 1913, I think, and I sitting in the Café Royal feeling amazingly grand, when a young man came in who had a great air of beauty and walked like a panther—and the person I was with said, There's Rupert Brooke. The only time I set eyes on him. Do tell me about him. It was a year when everything was happening, Cézanne, Moussorgsky, Claire Dux singing Pamina, and my hat like a flowerpot with a single waterlily growing straight out of the top of it, but nothing ever got between me and my impression of the young man walking like a panther.

To William Maxwell 27:ix:1952

. . . Did Emmy's Lachaise fire properly? I can't think of a more agonising constraint for the artist. It is bad enough to put one's dear cake in the oven. I suppose dramatists suffer next worse. But at least, the dramatist can get into the oven during rehearsals. I remember a dress rehearsal of *Heartbreak House* when Shaw bounded on to the stage and became a young girl. He was infinitely better at it than the actress, even when she had studied him, he far out-girled her. He had a tirra-lirra twirl of the waist that I went home and practised by the hour. I couldn't do it either.

To William Maxwell *21:x:1952*

... I am in a fidget about the election, too. I would be easier in my mind about Stevenson's chances, if there were some little scandal or dash of black-guard about him. People with votes develop that odd mixture of patronage and quixotism that swings them towards handicapped candidates, provided the handicap is louche or ludicrous. If Mr Truman had been of godlike form and intellect, he would not have got in last time. Personally, I cannot endure Eisenhower, the man is perpetually in tears, even for a military man, he cries too easily. Whichever way the election goes, I suppose he will cry on Stevenson's bosom, and that must be a disagreeable thought for Stevenson. I think I am giving way to national prejudice, though. Public characters in this country are not supposed to weep in public, except about cricket.

To Marchette Chute *19:xii:1952*

... Valentine has burst into commerce. Early last summer she was led away into attending the local auction rooms, and came home with treasures knocked down for next to nothing in mixed lots, or just lots that were engaging by their mixedness alone. After a while of this, we looked round and saw that very soon we should be camping on the lawn, because every inch of the house was taken up. So then, in a flash of genius, she decided to start an antique shop. The long room with the piano in it was cleaned, if speciously, and the auction room treasures laid out (of course, they looked very meagre, so we ran madly round the house soliciting ourselves for con-tributions) and while we were still looking blankly at each other and wonder-ing how one attracted customers, the rumour of our eccentricities spread, and so many customers came that Valentine felt justified in buying a bell to put on the door. Indeed, it has gone surprisingly well, considering how painlessly she set about it, and there have been several agreeable trans-actions—perhaps the one that pleased her most being a picture of Dorothy Wordsworth (a copy of that portrait in the mutch) in a purple velvet shrine, which she found in a tin bath, together with some old fire-irons, a home-made truncheon, and a potato masher ...

As for me, I have finished the first state of my novel; and early in the new year, when I have forgotten the sharpest edge of my feelings towards it, I shall start revising it.

To Leonard Bacon *11:i:1953*

... I went to Olney last summer for the first time in my life. It is so near London that of course I never went there until I had quite got out of the sensation of being a Londoner; and learned too, for the first time in my life, that it is pronounced Oney, and that the Sofa was one of those bleak affairs of wood and meshed cane that it is now the custom to call day-beds. Olney is charming, mostly built of that calm dove-coloured stone that makes Northamptonshire so full of demure dignity, with an immensely wide street and a long bridge that shows how wide the river can be when it floods its water-meadows. The Cowper house, however, is of brick, tall, and rather florid in its stone trimming and fenestration; and inside, much more modest and poky than one would expect from the exterior (he lived in one half of it, only) with two small parlours to the front, and a handsome stair-case, and a long narrow garden, walled, and extremely fertile, and very much *laid out*; a grass plat, wall-borders, fruit trees, vegetable plots, and such a sense of thrifty planning that by the time one comes to the summer house, one is almost as travelled as when one comes to St Peter's between the colonnade. It is kept as a museum, and the custodian who lives there has become completely Cowperized, though as much from affection as from study, he knows him from the heart, and as a neighbour, which is delightful. I suspect that before long he will be keeping hares himself. No one could doubt that Cowper was a poet after seeing the lock of his hair: the typical English poet hair, very fine in texture, extraordinarily young looking, the kind of hair that escapes from control and dangles over one eye in a kind of pensive uncontrollability. There is also part of the wig that was clamped down on top of the poet. It looks harsh and scorched, as if he kept it too near the candle. It touched me to the heart to think of that gentle spontaneous hair growing from a head tormented with religious nightmares.

I cannot agree with your tutor who was made to think of dressing-gowns and gruel. He was historically wrong, because at that date a dressing-gown was aristocratic and at Olney slightly defiant. If he had known Cowper's yellow satin waistcoat (still preserved, I think, in the Johnson family) he would have revised his outlook on Cowper's negligé. It—the waistcoat—is a most ravishing shade of white wine yellow, and most delicately dandyfied. But I daresay he (the tutor) was misled by that peculiar muffle of thick grey approbation that the nineteenth century evangelicals cast over a person so tragic and so sophisticated that without such a muffle they would have been hard put to it not to shudder at him. I wish someone would write a sensible book about Cowper. David Cecil's, that is considered so sensitive and sympathetic, is really shockingly sloppy, and filled with what my grandmother called glimpses into the obvious.

TO MARCHETTE CHUTE *5:ii:1953*

Dear Marchette,

Your lovely parcel came, thank you very very much for it. Valentine, like a wasp, has already got at the maple syrup. You send the most understanding parcels, it is as though your astral body came across to inspect our store-cupboard. We got so tired of our incessant colds and coughs that next week we start for a fortnight in Florence—where it *may* be as cold as here, but at any rate, the sun will be so many degrees more south. In Rome, at the same season, we basked in the Forum though there was snow on the hills.

Our departure is clouded by these floods along the east coast, and the ruin of Salthouse, that dear village where we wintered the year before last. The first I knew of it was an aerial photograph, named for another village; but as I looked at the picture, I recognised a lane that used to run up from the marsh and now from out of the waves. About fifty cottages gone, more than the village; and it is such a small place that it will never be able to come together again. It all happened in half an hour, they could save nothing but themselves. The loss of life would have been as bad, cent per cent, as Canvey Island in the Thames, only the Salthouse people always lived with one ear on the sea, whereas the poor Canvey Islanders were mostly sub-Londoners, and to them a stormy night was just a night to go early to bed in. One old woman only was drowned at Salthouse. A wave broke down their door, filled up the kitchen, and knocked her over. Her husband dragged her up, and put her on the kitchen table, but the next wave swept her off it and swept her away. The strangest thing is, that crazy Great Eye Folly, right on the sea's edge, where we stayed, still stands. The sea was all round it, but the force of the tide smacked inland. It was like a dream, hearing the first bits of news. Someone drowned at Wiveton. Wiveton is a village five miles inland, and we used to go there on very cold days, and say how sheltered and safe it seemed. Meanwhile, Valentine's mother is not half a mile from the same sea, and her village is perfectly unharmed. The defences had broken in the last great flood, and for the last fifteen years they have been rebuilding and solidifying, and not a trickle has come through. Most of the other places in Norfolk would have been safe, too, I'm afraid, if the seawalls had been kept up. But they were knocked about as coastal defences, and since the war, nothing has been done about them—no money to spend on such tame things. It makes one very angry. Yet defences aren't everything. Holland kept up hers much better than we did, and they went like paper; the only thing is, they will be easier to repair, when they can start on it. Ours will be like darning an old stocking—mend one place, and another will rend.

I must be getting old; for when I heard the news, for the first time in my life I didn't begin throwing things into a bag to get there immediately.

To Alyse Gregory *26:v:1953*

... the shop still does very well, and Valentine will feel justified in spending more on things that she knows she can dispose of.

It is very interesting what people *do* buy. There is an inexhaustible demand for plated spoons and forks, coming from people who must be weighed down with family silver. This we could never have foreseen, just as we should never have supposed that early nineteenth century flower-prints and china should hang on our hands unbought. My chief function seems to be as a touchstone; for the things I admire, and would buy, nobody else does, and Valentine has only to see a particular expression of uninterested dislike on my face to be sure that a delighted customer will follow soon afterwards ...

I don't wonder at your mood of self questioning, if you have been typing out old journals. Of all Pandora boxes, the worst is the box one keeps journals, letters, unfinished manuscripts in. I have mine, too, and merely to open them in search of some specific thing is enough to send me tossed and ship-wrecked into that strange unchartable sea of Time Past. Sometimes I cannot even recognise the woman who did these things, knew these extra-ordinary forgotten people, entertained these jejune great thoughts or these absurd ambitions. But one thing I have pulled out with reasonable certainty: the fact that no journal, no record of one's days, conveys the extent of the garment on which these nosegays and sodality buttons and crape bands were worn. An old teapot, used daily, can tell me more of my past than anything I recorded of it. Continuity, Alyse, continuity ... it is that which we cannot write down, it is that we cannot compass, record or control. And I daresay that an intimate, unconscious acknowledgement of this may account for the pleasure so often felt in very dull day-by-day diaries, such as Woodforde's; it is not the mutton nor the goose nor the flounders that he consumed, but the fact that he was always there, at the same table or tables, to consume them, which, in some odd way, pleases us to know.

To William Maxwell *16:vii:1953*

... As a rule, very happy marriages are achieved through thickets of every-body opposing them, but I don't think it can have been like that with you and Emmy, for you have not learned the Concorded Tarradiddle. You tell me that it will dishevel *The New Yorker*'s book-keeping to deduct the price of that bath perfume, and Emmy assures me that there was never any question of paying for it, it was a gift. You are both revealed as incompetent. I will not dwell on it. I shall ask Steven Clark who has banking accounts in both countries to deposit some money with you the next time he visits New York. I can't imagine why I have not thought of this before. It was so transparently simple, I suppose, that it escaped my notice.

Poor Niou has been alarming us, his head suddenly swelled up, his eyes closed, he looked like a pugilist and fell into a stupor. The vet thought it was concussion from a blow on the head, and during the night I put ice on him every two hours. By the morning he was near enough to his own contours again to see that it was an abscess on his forehead, and penicillin has put him almost right again. A scratch from a cat-fight, I think. I wish he would not be sans peur as well as sans reproche. There was a dreadful night in May when we were roused by hideous cries, and hunted all through the garden, and finally traced the cries upwards. He and a ginger cat of the locality had rushed up a tree, and were fighting in its summit. We could do nothing, of course, short of getting the fire-brigade. The branches swayed, twigs fell down on our anxious upturned faces, the beam from the electric torch showed us sometimes a white and sometimes a ginger form. Some hours later, Niou came in without a scratch on him. It had been moral expostulation only. He licked off the dews of night, ate a large meal, and fell blamelessly asleep on my bosom.

To William Maxwell *23:vii:1953*

... after Valentine's mother's visits, when I am tidying her room, a work of hours because she is a woman of many letters, and habitually tears them across and across with terrifying energy, into the smallest fragments, and then throws the fragments like confetti round and about the waste-paper basket, not to mention a way of giving herself early morning tea in the middle of the night, which leads to crumbs, tealeaves, and quantities of caster sugar in bureau drawers, and several other timetaking mannerisms— well, as I was saying, when I am tidying up after Ruth I sing that poem of Emily Dickinson's, The solemnest of industries enacted here on earth,[1] to a

1. 'The Bustle in a House
   The Morning after Death
   Is solemnest of industries
   Enacted upon Earth...'

hymn tune I made up for it; and it makes me appreciate my blessings, and passes the time. Otherwise, I am seldom heard to sing.

To William Maxwell *31:vii:1953*

. . . What became of the Rosenberg children? I do not like to think of them exposed to Uncle Greenbaum's remorse, and I am sure he is the kind of man who would have a great deal of remorse and need to rub it off on people for the good of his soul. How respectable the despicable were in the old days, before it was de rigueur to be so full of noble intentions. I suppose the parent Rosenbergs made some arrangements about the children, but such arrangements are not always respected. If you don't know, don't trouble, I will write to the Embassy. I feel that this sort of thing is as much my business as it is anybody's, because such things are every one's business, or should be.

For the last thirty years I have been saving up the de Goncourt *Journal* for my old age. I have now broken into the larder, and find it perfectly entrancing. I follow Valentine about the house, telling her the latest gossip of 1874. What deaths, and what horrors! The vultures after the battle of Isly, who fed delicately on the eyeballs of the dead, and fell inebriated from the heavens. I feel as if I had fallen asleep in the cemetery of Montparnasse and were dreaming it.

To Harold Raymond *7:ix:1953*

Dear Harold,

I think you should know the latest development with Theodore. A week ago he decided that he would not go back to Sherborne Hospital for his operation—or to any hospital for any form of treatment. Except that he was not told he has cancer (the word is ulcer of the bowels) he was very honestly informed by his doctor, and with the alternatives of living perhaps another year without the operation, and another two years if he did have it, with all the miseries of a collostomy, he has chosen the shorter life . . . Although he did not much dislike the hospital while he was in it, from the moment he got back to Mappowder he began to feel the most intense fear and melancholy, threatened to hang himself, could only be got to sleep with sedatives, and only for a few hours then. He was, in fact, the condemned man from sundown to sunrise, and not much better during the day. I saw him three days ago, and he was looking not merely resigned or stoical, but even rather gratified. He told me it was the greatest possible comfort to have known his own mind and gone his own way. So there it is. Personally, I feel he has chosen rightly, though I'm afraid the choice may not go on being a panacea as it is at present. But at least, he has given himself a platform to die on.

To Marchette Chute 9:x:1953

... Valentine and I have been staying in Scotland. We went up by car, and as we crossed the Trent and saw the limestone outlines of the Derbyshire Peak scrolling in front of us I realised with rapture that from there on to John of Groats (though we were not going so far) one need never be out of sight of a mountain skyline. However often I did it (I have not done it often enough) I could never lose the excitement of seeing SCOTLAND declaimed on the road-sign, and the little line, no wider than a half-ribbon, painted across the road. It is an astonishing frontier, for, as Valentine said, it is not only the frontier between England and Scotland but the frontier between England and a province of France. I thought a great deal about this while we were there, and of how the Scotch went on drinking claret when England took up port, and of how the Scotch feeling for litigation is so close to Racine's comedy and so far from the trial scene in *Pickwick* or the Court of Chancery in *Bleak House* and how easily one can imagine Villon dodging about the wynds of the Edinburgh Old Town; and having this thought in my head, I went on seeing more and more resemblances—the demeanour of waiters, who are, as in France, native and not imported, the use of grey and pink in interior decoration, the clanking resonance of church bells, the fact that people speak in sentences, and end them instead of leaving them hanging in air, the gravity and self-possession of the children, the largeness of table napkins, the stylishness of common domestic objects, like breadboards and casseroles, even in poor shops, the death-devotedness of graveyards, the total absence of the cosy, the odd occurrences of the splendid—the very small inn where we stayed in the Ettrick Valley, for instance, had plate-glass windows and linen sheets. Thinking of all this, and of the equalitarian good manners of all the people I talked to, it darted in on me that from the day of Jamie's departure until somewhere in the first third of the last century, Scotland really existed as a species of republic, with church and law of its own, and what went on at St James's and Westminster no more to it than the arbitrary behaviour of some distant cousins by marriage.

To Leonard Bacon 18:x:1953

Dear Mr Bacon,
    How you delight me with your remark on Edith Sitwell's book about Pope—that she mothers him too much. 'It is the duty of a biographer to

explain, not to exculpate,' was what I dared remark myself, reviewing the book long ago, apropos of her twiddle-widdles round the business of the letters. I wish to God that heaven had put the word *mothers* into my inkpot. But as I did not say so myself, it is a great consolation that you do. Between ourselves, I do not think that women make good biographers. Mrs Gaskell did a classic in her unorthodox way (one excellent recipe for doing a classic at any time), and that queer old stick Ethel Colborn Mayne wasn't too bad in her life of Byron, for she had the candour to be cross with him. I could never feel much about Amy Lowell's Keats. Once in my youth I stayed in a house in Berwickshire where I sat every evening on a sofa entirely covered with an embroidery of beads not much larger than homeopathic pills; and afterwards it came back into my mind as I read her painstaking book, with all those explanations of how and why and whence he wrote as he did. Just now I am reading a biography by a woman that I *do* think good. Marchette Chute's life of B. Jonson. I think it better than the other two, though I suppose I shall be almost alone in doing so. But it is good historically, rather than biographically. I wish she would write a history proper, indeed, I have just been urging her to fill that vast ungrateful gap in letters and set to work on a history of Scotland during the 17th cent. Unrivalled sources, and an unrivalled opportunity to remain impartial and cool-headed; which is, I think, her real talent.

You should have seen the house in Berwickshire. It was a small and conscious castle, it had little cannon mounted among its battlements, with wire netting over the mouths to prevent birds nesting in them; and its garden had almost as many summerhouses as Stowe, some classical, some practical—that is to say, with water-closets in them. There were also some very remarkable dining room chairs, Scotch Gothic revival, made of black and massy oak, with scenes from Scottish history carved on their backs in far too high relief to be comfortable. I shall never forget the sharpness of the axe poised above Queen Mary, it was situated exactly where my shoulder blade met it, and being newly décolletée at that time, my shoulder-blade was both sensitive and unwary.

If I did not feel so well towards you, I could not endure to know that you have got Boswell's Grand Tour volume before I have. It isn't out here yet, and every morning I bound downstairs to see if the post has brought it. How very apt of him to find that quotation from Madame de Guyon; a contemporary Boswell (Oh God, if there were one, lurking unseen, mortality would be an even sharper thought!) would be finding something very similar, for there is a great fashion for illuminati just now, and so many Clouds of Unknowing being read that I am sure the climate is perceptibly damper than it used to be. I have one dear friend engaged in making a Roman Catholic of me, and another leading me towards Zen Buddhism, and yesterday I had two astrologers to lunch, and the air was vibrating with the Major Arcanae and malign aspects. I was interested to learn that the heavens are not infallible. Three separate astrologers wrote to the Air Ministry of the time to say that the R101 (an airship) would come to grief if she set out on the day appointed. The Air Ministry was unimpressed, the R101 set out, and did come to grief. This would appear (it did to me) a clear proof that one cannot fight against one's stars; but I was assured that everything would have been all right if the astrologers' warnings had been attended to . . .

The thing that struck me most about Boswell's Dutch Diary was his desperate courage—the courage of a fly in the milk. I love him, of course, but I also esteem him. A man whose heart is a black pit of terror, black as a Geneva gown, and who yet can attend to the colour of the waistcoat he puts over it is a man after my own heart.

To [Dorothy?] Hoskins [undated, 1953]

. . . This must be a short letter, for I have many others that I must write, including a letter of congratulation to my old London charwoman who, well on in her seventies, has just married her third husband. She will lead him by the nose—but as he is a man, I don't suppose he will have any objection to it. She was the joy of my life while I lived in town, for one thing she was an unsurpassable polisher, and for another, she was one of the best Cockney speakers I have ever known. I have not time for more than one of her flourishes just now. It was a lowering foggy January day, and she walked in, and began with relish, 'The way they're dying of the influenza in our street, Miss, it's like a fairy-tale.'

To William Maxwell 28:xi:1953

. . . We have just come back from Theodore Powys's funeral. He died sooner, and with less misery than any of us dared expect, probably because he had made up his whole mind to it. I do not mean that he was resigned; but he was resolved. There was a great deal about the funeral that he would have approved of. To begin with, because of the lay-out of his front door, the coffin came out upright, as though it were walking out on its own voli-tion, or rather, as though he were walking it out to its burial. It was a mild grey-skied day, the doors of the village church were open during the service, and while the parson was reading the lesson from St Paul a flock of starlings descended on the churchyard and brabbled with their watery voices, almost drowning the solitary cawing rook inside the building. The parson, an old man, and a friend of Theodore's, must have believed every word he said, and after the blessing he stood for some time at the foot of the grave in an oddly conversational attitude, as though, for this once, he had got the better of an argument.

To Alyse Gregory *7:i:1954*

. . . Today bereaved me, for this morning I heard of the death of Leonard Bacon. Rather over two years ago he sent me his translation of *The Lusiads*, and out of that we developed a friendship of correspondence which had, as he said in one of his letters, the freedom and innocence of a conversation at a masked ball. We knew a great deal of each other's tastes, whims and prejudices, and next to nothing of each other's circumstances, except when he had to explain that a stroke of paralysis forced him from pen to pencil. We had a number of friends in common, almost all of them dead, so that we could discuss them without caution or affectation. We gave each other a great deal of pleasure, and that exceedingly rare satisfaction of an intercourse between male and female uncompromised by particular man and particular woman. . . . Under my mask, I could still hear myself praised for being delightful without thinking myself a fool for believing it.

He died, so his daughter's letter told me, suddenly and peacefully. An enviable death, and I am sure he deserved it. Not that I assume that a sudden death is necessarily a peaceful one. A tumult may be packed into a minute's apprehension, and the peacefulness may often express no more than the fact that the standers-by had no time for alarm. But I believe that this man's death may have been peaceful, since his brief account of having a stroke was so perspicuous that it was obvious that his intelligence had mastered what he referred to as 'a misadventure.' Feeling the syllables dissolve in my mouth and my left arm detach itself from my body, he wrote. That seems to warrant a hope of a peaceful death.

Last night the Amadeus were playing in Dorchester, and the programme ended with the *Death and the Maiden*, which they did exceptionally well, as though it were news to them. It struck me, as I listened, that with Schubert one has, more than with any other composer, the sensation of holding the music in one's hand, feeling it flutter and burn and strive there, as though one were holding a wild bird.

To Paul Nordoff *4:ii:1954*

Darling Paul,

How heavenly, I am as pleased as you to think of another performance of *Lost Summer* (performances of *Mr Fortune* mean so much that I have

scarcely given it a thought, just put it straight under my pillow). And of
course change the needle. My trouble is to find a metallic tom object in two
syllables: there is hatchet, but nobody wants to sing hatchet, and anyhow in
USA I think it is always axe. The *spade in the patch*, or rake, hoe, fork: there
is trowel, but men as a rule don't use trowels, not manly enough and means
too much bending; *the tractor in the field*; or *the scythe in the orchard*—one
does scythe orchards in May, if one keeps that kind of orchard. These are the
best that Valentine and I can do at the moment, if you and the tenor can find
better, have with you. Anyhow, don't hang up a performance over such a
trifle.

Of course it is a pity he can't sing, *the money in the bank*, which is
perfect. But it would Not Do.

Have you ever thought of making a cantata from *Prometheus Unbound*?
Scene 11, Act 11 is so ravishing, and it would be a pleasant change to begin
with the chorus work and close with the arioso music of the two young
fauns.

Here I sit, looking out on snow and ice and a blue sky. The children are
sledging down the field, and the furry brown hedge-row, all withered and
unkempt, looks on like a kind dog. No more now, I want to get this off at
once. A thousand loves.

To Alyse Gregory *2:iii:1954*

... There was a heavy fall of snow yesterday, and a hard frost last night, and
now everything is dazzlingly unreal, the sun shining, footprints of hare and
heron drawn in blue pencil on the snow. I have been wandering about,
sucking small icicles off the ends of twigs, delicious!—and depositing
coveys of pork fat and raisins which I hope the birds will find delicious too,
while Valentine spreads hanging tables.

I think we must leave off planning to go away in the car. The last spell
of winter weather came when we had everything arranged for a journey to
Norfolk, and two days ago I was working out a route to Saint David's.

We have found a place we must take you to see. It is called A là Ronde,
a small circular cottage ornée built at the turn of the 18th-19th century by an
aunt and a niece called Parminter. Everything that can be done with pointed
scissors, neat gum-brushes, fairy-like needles, with shells, seaweeds, and
feathers, they did excellingly. The drawing room walls are decorated with
feather-work: small breast feathers laid on in geometrical patterns, looking
at first sight rather like mosaic, but keeping a softness and vague sleekness of
something animal. At the top of the house, under the lantern which lights it,
there is a round gallery with its walls entirely covered with rocaille, except

where there are windows and between the windows panels, each panel with a bird made of feather work heraldically displayed. It is extraordinarily beautiful in colouring—the shells mostly pale grey, dull pink, sand-colour, relieved with scrollings of dark mussel-shells, and the birds, crow-blue, rook-black, the brown and dark green of drake-feathers.

The problem of a round house was majestically overcome by the elder Miss Parminter, and in a way that I am sure must have been entirely satisfactory to her female mind. In the centre of the house there is a small hexagonal hall, lit by the lantern, and six rooms give into it. The rooms, except for their outer walls being part of the circular design, are right-angled. If you will now shut your eyes and do a little geometry, you will see that in order to get this result, you will be left with six architectural gores, a space, shaped like a slice of rounded cake, between each room. Each of these gores is a cupboard; each cupboard has its little diamond-shaped window, and a narrow door giving into its neighbour room. Think of living with six commodious well-lit cupboards . . . what happiness!

The property has descended from one female Parminter to another, a dynasty of nieces and cousins once removed. The present one is very severe—and very old, and I am afraid very poor—but she thawed by the time we were in the second room, and conversation had somehow got around to the inferiority of modern shiny scissors which don't cut, only maul and fumble, compared to the old scissors which were made of dark grey steel and never lost their edge.

To William Maxwell 5:vii:1954

. . . I gather you didn't see the poor eclipse. We were feeling just the same, the morning was cloudy, and anyhow the eclipse was being blown on because it wasn't a total one. Valentine had to go to a junkshop at Stourminster Newton, the only place where Mr and Mrs Thomas Hardy were happy together and therefore, as they didn't stay there long, rather a sad one; and after that we drove the car into a field gateway and ate cold sausages and cherries, and when I got out to shake off the crumbs it occurred to me that I might as well look up to see how the eclipse was getting on. The cloud was just the ideal thickness, and we had a very good view of it. The sun was silver, like a moon, and very much smaller than usual, because of having its disk defined. And while I was watching, I had a rush of astronomy to the head, and realised that the round shadow on the sun was not a shadow, but the moon. There was the sun, here was me, and that was the moon between us. For a few seconds I felt myself an inhabitant of the solar system—a delightful and enlarging sensation. I daresay Thoreau felt like that all the time.

I daresay you know that The Times demurely listed the eclipse under *Arrangements for Today*.

Yes, I knew the remark about the wolves;[1] indeed, I am very seldom either astonished or disbelieving before quotations from my books. They fly back into my heart like the scattered bones reuniting in Donne's grand passages about the resurrection. I write so hard, you see. I hatch with such intensity. You know *The True Heart* very well, was it the first S.T.W. you read? How silly, how exasperating, I was in New York that winter, guest-critic for the Herald Tribune, we could have met and had the pleasure of each other's acquaintance that many years earlier. You know it very well, but did you recognise the sub-structure?—it is *Cupid and Psyche*, from *The Golden Ass*. I wanted to do some serious technical study—to develop my wrist for narrative. So I thought I would write on a canto fermo, as one does in learning counterpoint. *The True Heart* is on a canto fermo, and so is *Elinor Barley*, for which I chose a folk-song, by the sortes Virgilianae, from a collected volume; but *E.B.* was a slighter exercise, as the canto fermo was a much sketchier and undemanding affair. I was very happy when I identified Queen Victoria with the Winter Persephone. I stuck clues all over *The True Heart*—Rew and Grieve in the rectory kitchen, being ferried over to the island by Zeph, Mrs Oxey's peacock; but not a single reviewer noticed them. My mother was on it at once.

To Paul Nordoff *18:vii:1954*

Darling Paul,

It was worth waiting for, all those many years, wasn't it?—the confirming pleasure of meeting again, and being just as much delighted with each other's company as ever. After your train had swallowed you, Valentine and I drove down to Weymouth through a tearing gale, and praised you the whole way there, and continued to praise you while we waited for Mr Cole to come and open his shop and sell Valentine the jelly-mould and the candlestick, and talked of you with praises all the way back. It was only when we entered the house that we fell silent: it felt so extremely bereaved of you, and the old rose by the garden gate had been blown off its support and was lying prostrate on the lawn, as devoted and bedizened as an Indian widow. The cats were full of reproaches that we had not brought you back with us, and the C sharp in the treble clef is mute with grief, as if to imply that it did not want to be played on for the present, it would prefer to ruminate under its lid all the heavenly music which had been fetched from it.

---

1. '. . . she was weeping because of the cruelty shown to wolves. No one ever, ever, showed to them the least spark of human kindness . . .' *The True Heart*, p. 120.

149

To Dorothy Hoskins *30:vii:1954*

... I find drinkers very congenial. There is a generosity in their recklessness. We had a drinking old lady as a neighbour for many years, and I had the greatest esteem for her because she knew what she wanted (not many women do), and was so grandly ready to hazard her health, her last thirty shillings (she was very poor), her peace of mind (for, pious pressure being what it is, she was always exposed to waking up in the middle of the night and thinking, I've done for myself, I shall fall into the oilstove or get cancer), for what she really wanted. As for respectability, and all that, she had thrown it away long ago. In the upshot, she was very well thought of by all the village boys, who ran her errands and ate her apples, and died as tidily as you could wish of heart failure. If there is a heaven, I am sure she went there like a cork from a champagne bottle.

To Paul Nordoff *17:ix:1954*

... I listened to *The Turn of the Screw*, it came through extremely well. The form is very interesting. Both acts consist of eight scenes, with orchestral interludes, which have their own connections, as they are a set of variations, developing with the opera but also in themselves. The scoring is very light, the tessitura inherently high, as well as his usual high tessitura, as the voices are two straight sopranos, a boy treble, and two dramatic sopranos: nothing lower, till the tenor comes in in scene 8 of the first act. This entry is marvellous. Quint has appeared before, mute, but conveyed by a twirligig passage for the celesta. In this scene 8, when he is on the tower looking down at the two children, the celesta twirls are developed, there is no interruption of other singers, and then the tenor enters on a pedal note, very quietly, and the note so ambiguously in his middle register (perhaps B flat or A) that it might be anything, the bottom note of a soprano or a viola. By the time a moderate crescendo has established that it *is* the tenor, the effect of something supernaturally dominating and yet furtive is overwhelming. It is exactly like what one is told of bad ghosts appearing: the growing sensation of intimidating cold. And the moment this is established, Quint begins a series of leaping, flickering coloratura phrases: the sort of coloratura one finds in Taverner's virtuoso masses. Another most beautiful device of the sinister is in the scene where the boy is having a latin lesson with the governess, and begins to sing a rhyme, apparently nonsense-mnemonic—like Common is to either sex Artifex and—whatever the other word is, I don't remember. But each line of this rhyme begins with the word, *malo*; and for each repetition there is a new, slightly stiff angular melismata on the first syllable, ambiguous, then perverse—a devil's plainsong, sung in this innocent soulless treble.

The boy sang magnificently, and somehow gave the impression of singing with a hallucinated attention to what he had learned in fear and trembling and now was defiantly sure of. And it was so delicately done by the composer, with such bleak avoidance of appearing to dwell on it or turn blue that it was as matter of fact as a snake, an interval of terror and gone in a flash. Lovely! So was the scene of the piano, with the smooth glib single-line of étude de la vélocité passages protecting the child like a skin of slippery ice against the governess's human agitation.

To Alyse Gregory *16: xii: 1954*

Dearest Alyse,

I will not be so old-fashioned as to ask how you weathered the last gales, for since then I have heard of a worse calamity. Valentine read to me from the *Western Gazette* that there is a proposal to drill for oil near East Chaldon, on land belonging to Mr Cobb's farm; and that a road is to be made over the downs to the experimental drilling site. Where is this horror to take place? Will it be near you, will you have the road and the wire netting and the cement blocks and all the rest of it in sight? I feel so agitated about it, thinking that it may destroy your peace of prospect and Katie's peace of mind. It seems the height of fortune's malice that living so far away, with none of the amenities of the common lot, walking through mud for your letters and groceries, your telephone snapping in the wind like a vine, only rabbit holes to put old bottles in and all the rest of it, you should now be threatened with the nastiest (except perhaps the Army) development of science and progress. Even if they don't find any oil—which I sincerely pray—they will make a havoc; and if they do . . .

Please write and tell me the worst, and put me out of the discomfort of a generalized sympathy, which always feels so flapping and incompetent.

I am leading the strangest double life, experiencing the oddest, most unexpected possession. Europa swept off on the bull's back could not feel more astonished, proud, and powerless. Alyse, when I was in London a few weeks ago I was asked by Chatto and Windus if I would consider translating *Contre Ste-Beuve*. If I had considered, I must inevitably have said no. As it was, I said quite calmly that I should be delighted to. Since then, there has been the usual mystical doldrum which descends on any negotiation with Gallimard—only not so long as usual. Chatto and Windus had, of course, asked for and got an option, and had confirmed it by cable, by letter, by telephone; but with Gallimard that could mean nothing, and in fact we should still be exactly there if Madame Mante-Proust had not told the editor of *Vogue* that Chatto and Windus were the English publishers. Apparently this is the word of a goddess, and can more or less be relied on.

Meanwhile, I had started translating just for love. It is the strangest most entrancing work, rather like reading the *Recherche* in a dream, and finding several characters, or scenes which one had not read before. As for Ste-Beuve, there is very little about him, and what there is is a more eloquent version of Calvin Coolidge's preacher on sin. It all began—as I expect you know—as an article for *le Figaro*, and then extended itself through bedrooms and into the Jura and Venice, and the Faubourg, and the weather, and altogether there is about 300 pages of it, followed by some critical articles—a ravishing one about Chardin, and some very queer early ones, embarrassing praises of Saint-Saëns, the Critic about Town; but every thing shot through with his zigzag illuminations and heavy with his imperturbable richness of sensation. As I translate, I feel as if I were following a fish through the depths of a lake.

Another aspect of it amazes me: that I can be interrupted, and that when I go back, the thought is still there, I have only to run my fingers through my hair once or twice and then go on. After writing one's own work, this seems indescribably luxurious and majestic. As luxurious as heaven, where moth and rust do not corrupt nor thieves break in and steal.

I am telling you this because I know you will be pleased by it. But it is private. For one reason, because there may yet be a slip. For another, I cannot work at my best with anyone looking over my shoulder. I hate my doings to be known. I have a superstition that it brings ill fortune on them.

1955

One last word of Advice to that friend who was of two minds
about staying married *9:i:1955*

. . . I beg and implore you, above everything else, *to clear your mind of
conscience.* If things are wrong, it's not all your fault, nor can they be put
right by you alone. Run away, dear, like a wise man. Turn your back, shut
your ears, Agamemnon was not happy in his family life either.

To Alyse Gregory *Feb. 1955*

. . . Valentine with her sensitive pointer's nose for old ladies has found
another one who could not be more appropriate; for she knew my mother,
my aunts, my grandparents, even a great-aunt or two, saw them all with the
attentive large clear eyes of a little girl in a provincial town. She made me
feel like a sexton, or a Raven; for every one she asked after I had to reply,
Dead. Really, the mortality in my family is what if I had the unfettered use
of my native tongue that every charwoman possesses, I would describe as
chronic. I even began to wonder if I had eaten them: there seemed no other
way to account for it. However, Lady Spencer Smith did not look un-
towardly depressed, in fact all these deaths, here there and everywhere, were
rather as if I had tossed another little billet on a good hearty fire. So am not
I, said the cookmaid; and as she was seeing us off at her door she pointed to a
basket of just such little billets, applewood, and said lightly, That's how I
keep warm. They were very well sawn, they would have been a credit to
anyone, any mere sexagenarian; and she, as I reckon, must be near her
eighties, if not in them. Welsh stock. Her maiden name with a careless
indifference to plagiarism was Mary Tudor, and the bright red-gold hair
that I remember my mother describing still smoulders at the point of a fine
long knob of hair at the back of her head.

One of the pleasantest things that has happened to me lately was a few
nights ago when without the slightest preliminary there were two long
magnificent astonishing peals of thunder. After that, nothing. The world,
having stood still to listen—went on. Winter thunder is always the best,
though I don't know why. Better produced, and more majestical. These were
superlative, I have never heard their match. They did not crack the silence;
they emerged from it.

I am deep in *Contre Sainte-Beuve* and very very happy. It is in itself a fine and typical piece of Proust, full of lovely things, and with a poignancy in some passages which there isn't in the *Recherche*—because of being that much younger, I suppose, and because of not being worked over to the same extent; a sorrowing over himself, over his ill-health and the discrepancy between his ambition and his hopes of carrying it out which is extremely moving. But the thing that fascinates me most of all as I get further into it is to see what he took on from it into the *Recherche*; some passages almost entire, though not many; many passages used as the bones of the soup, and some very entertainingly; for instance what he disliked—and a most personal degree of dislike—in Beuve comes out wickedly and schoolboyishly parodied in—M de Villeparisis. But the most interesting thing of all is what I can only describe as invocation of sacred mounts and founts. For instance, do you happen to remember his references to little residues of holy water in stone stoups?—there are several, including the oysters in a dinner at Doncières. In *Contre Ste-B*. there is an exceedingly grand, too grand paragraph, quite untranslatable and apparently quite unmanageable for he did nothing more with it; but in its last sentence is the original stone holy water stoup. He carried it like a talisman, or perhaps truer to say, like one of those objects that infallibly procure an erection for sexual neurotics—the late king's fur bedroom slippers etc. I have found several instances of this kind of thing though the holy water stoups is the most striking.

As for the peace and quiet of writing some other person's book, I cannot say enough for it . . . though I know that I am uncommonly lucky in my lot of the other person. But the beautiful calm of knowing that it is there on the page and not at the mercy of the winds and waves of one's own daily life would apply to whatever the book, and that is a considerable proportion of the peace and the quiet.

Now I have written you an entirely egoistic letter, I think you should do the same by me. But it will probably be more difficult for you, as you will have more to tell.

To Alyse Gregory *28:iii:1955*

. . . Two days ago we saw the first swifts, and that makes it more possible to believe that sooner or later we shall crawl out of this interminable and most jading winter. I nauseate wool, I hate the very sight of a hotwater bottle, artificial warmth is a weariness to me, I am ready to revolt at my dependence on such things. If I had not had Proust, I really doubt if I could have endured these last two months, for I have felt far too battered and exhausted to do anything of my own. But Proust has been rather like those conservatories that opened out of Victorian drawingrooms: a limited release, since though one can have many explorations of thought within the boundaries of some one else's mind one cannot fly off into the danger of an uncharted air; but still, an available other world, a foreign climate, and an absorbingly different flora to contemplate. I long for your return for there is so much I want to consult you about.

Meanwhile, here is something to amuse you—not from P. himself, but from someone called Bernard de Fallois, who wrote a long preface. He is describing the place of Proust's mother in this early version—where she is still only herself, no bifurcation into mother and grandmother—and dilating on her modesty and self-effacement—comme cette héroine de conte de fées anglais dont il ne reste plus qu'un sourire—in other words, the Cheshire Cat. Valentine's comment was that it was nice to have the Cheshire cat's sex determined at last.

Valentine's shop is doing very well, and today we have been to Bridge-water to hunt for hidden beauties. We found one true hidden beauty shop, and another only one degree nearer self-consciousness, both had second-hand sewing machines in them, and my heart leaps up when I behold a second-hand sewing machine. I am attached to Bridgewater, it has that Mark Rutherford quality of decent brick terraces, a look of being worn but not decayed, a tradesman standard of self-respect, and no trace of the picturesque; and then among its hardheaded North Streets and West Streets and Church Streets one finds a street labelled Pern Orlieu. And today the air was as cold and as clean as wet linen on a line—true sea-level air, the air of the country round Wisbech and King's Lynn that I love so devotedly and grudge so savagely to the Air Force, who have made a noisy desert of it. One feels it is a No Popery town, like Yarmouth. We lunched at a very pleasant small hotel about three miles out, with a dining room overlooking the River Parrett, that stretched away between its high green banks looking as shiny and as unanimously pale blue as if it were painted on a tea-tray. The food was uncommonly good, the mustard, for some reason, was in shallow little bowls, and the waitress carrying one of these bowls to a table where an elegant middle-aged woman was sitting by herself, tripped, and the mustard bowl flew out of her hand and the lady and her table were spattered with it. When she, the waitress, had gone off for a cloth to mop with, the lady raised her voice and said to a young man rather like W. B. Yeats who was sitting at a further table, 'I've been covered all over with mustard.' 'Oh God!' said he, looking even more like W. B. Yeats, and went on reading his book. A ritual rather than an engaged expression of sympathy; as he might have replied Et cum spiritum tuo. It seemed to satisfy her, however.

I have so little to say that I must be like the Sluggard and tell you my dreams. A few nights ago I found myself with Hester Johnson and Mrs Dingley, indeed I almost found myself *in* Mrs Dingley, since the whole dream was from her angle. We were in Dublin lodgings, dirty and shabby and with a half-unpacked look on everything, and Swift, so I knew in my

Dingley consciousness, had abruptly insisted on spending one night with Hester, and she was getting ready to set out for it—it was to be spent somewhere in the Dublin suburbs. She was in a state of intense nervousness and was showing it by an incompetence to get dressed, to make up her mind to anything, to find what she was looking for or even to know what it was, or to let herself be helped or straightened in any way. We both know that it would not do to keep the Dean waiting, and when there was a knock on the door we both felt extremely abashed and apprehensive. But it was not the Dean, it was his manservant, who handed in two small parcels from him. The parcel for me, a very well-adjusted acknowledgement of my share in the business, thus far and no further, was a sachet of dried violet petals. Hester unwrapped the sheet of paper from a smaller object, and took out a ring with one opal set in small brilliants. The opal was almost a fire-opal, but very blue, a smarting sparkling blue. She cried out, 'Look! He has sent me an eye.' Now I shall always feel that I know the colour of Swift's eyes when they were terrible.

Dearest Alyse, I send you my love, and my thankfulness—odd as this may sound—that you are still away. You would have perished in this cold.

To Ian Parsons *14:vi:1955*

Dearest Ian,

Thank you for the royalty cheque. I see with pride & relief how majestically I have swept beyond that handsome advance payment. It is a matter of deep satisfaction to me that the firm is not a loser by *The Flint Anchor*.

Proust goes on. I love him as much as ever—but between ourselves he is not a very impressive critic. Rather like Valentine's intelligent poodle with grapes. She adores grapes, and can do everything with them except bite them.

To William Maxwell *26:vii:1955*

. . . We have never had such a crop of strawberries and raspberries, the strawberries can't be eaten and only the raspberries from the top of the canes; for ten days ago we had six and a half inches of rain in less than twelve hours, and the river flooded as never before. The cable that carries our electricity from the pole across the river was burned out by lightning, we had, thanks to Valentine's Robinson Crusoe disposition, some oil lamps and a few candles, and it was with a candle blinding me that I walked into the back-kitchen and found water racing over my insteps. The river was flowing on both sides of the house, as usual, making a noise like a blowlamp. When I looked out in the first light, all the garden was under a streaming flood, with a few debauched-looking opium poppies rearing out of it. When all this had gone down, everything indoors and out was covered with thick black mud, and swarmed over by bluebottles. It was all very disagreeable, and all foretold by the cats; who came in several hours before the storm, their eyes black, their hackles up, their voices sharp with anxiety. The house is straight again now, it was only the two lower rooms that really suffered, but the garden still looks like the remains of a slag-heap.

But I cannot really sorrow, for the weather is hot and fine again, and the process of throwing away old rugs that would have been thrown away long ago if I had more strength of character, and cleaning out ancient hoards, and casting empty jampots to the wind, is reviving. Indeed, I found the river quite helpful, once it was back in its own bed, for it was like having a perpetual refuse collection flowing past.

TO WILLIAM MAXWELL *12:x:1955*   *Pensione Sitea, via Terme di Diocreziano 90, Citta* (!)

Dear William,
Yesterday I did what I have dreamed of doing for years, and went to the Villa d'Este. We went in splendour, hiring our car and driver through the American Express, and got there so early in the morning that we had it all to ourselves, painted rooms, and cypresses and fountains, and gardeners snipping at box-hedges. I realised that such fountains come out of the same vein of Italian genius as the immense crystal chandeliers that fly like swans in the roofs of baroque churches and hang in a ladder all the way up the transepts of St Peter's. The water that falls in a fringed curtain from the goblet fountain is not so much water-works as water-sculpture.

TO WILLIAM MAXWELL *19:x:1955*   *Frome Vauchurch Maiden Newton   Dorset*

Dear William,
You guessed right. Unpleasant news is best received at home. We came home yesterday, to find that the well-intentioned woman to whom we had lent the house for her change of air had slaughtered my dearest geranium by leaving it out all night in a hard frost (she had thought the beautiful midday sun would do it good, and forgot the kindly action as soon as it was performed), had not liked to use the fridge in case she damaged it, but inadvertently turned off the switch, so that when I came to open it the inside was like that hell of Dante's, I can't remember which storey it was on, that

157

was a cold puddle and stank, had unearthed the caddy in which I keep our best tarry Souchong, and used it for making the gardener's tea, only she had to use more than twice as much because it was so pale otherwise, and hidden all the letters that came for us with such care in case it had really been a burglar she thought she heard going upstairs that it was some hours before she could be quite sure where they all were; so, dear William, by the time I came to your letter, the bitterness of death was past, and I learned that you, collective you, were not taking *The Snow Guest*[1] as calmly as a water lily, the uppermost thought in my mind being that *The New Yorker* would never have forgotten my geranium, etc, nor made a milk jelly on purpose for our supper, either.

This is rather a protracted sentence, but not more so than I felt at the time.

To Alyse Gregory 23 : xii : 1955

... Our poor old gardener had a stroke the week before last, he recovered, but his eyesight was affected, and he was convinced that he would be blind. Yesterday Valentine drove him back from the hospital. He stared out of the window, overjoyed because he could recognize things, saying, 'There's the weir. Oh, thank God! There's the garage, there's Frampton Church. Oh, thank God, thank God!' All the way home he kept up this enraptured soliloquy of thankfulness and relief. At his own door his pursy gossiping old wife stood waiting. When she saw him the tears rained down her face, her lips trembled, and all she could do was to stammer, again and again, My darling, my darling. We have always thought them a very stodgy platitudinous couple—and so, I suppose, they are. But having no skill in words, no range of language, they have no figleaves to pin before their feelings.

1. Included in *A Spirit Rises*.

To Ben Huebsch *1:ii:1956*

. . . [P.S.] *I* don't think four thousand copies such a wretched sale.[1] You should try to take a longer view of it. If you had sold four thousand female tortoiseshell kittens, for instance, you would think you had done marvels.

To Alyse Gregory *6:ix:1956*

. . . We went out to tea last week at Bettescombe, the house of the celebrated Screaming Skull. They did us the honours of the Skull—a remarkably small one, elegant and compact, and patina'd to a beautiful shade of natural mahogany.

After tea, having discovered that one of the people there, it was quite a party, was an astrologer and Tarot specialist, I suggested that he should do a Tarot reading for the skull. So once again it was taken out of its box, and laid on the floor, and the astrologer dealt twelve gaudy cards in a circle around it, pondered, while we sat round in respectful silence (incidentally, the 12 cards taken at random produced some singularly apt comments). One of the party was a French girl, smooth-haired, well-brought up, on holiday in Dorset. And I thought what a fine story she would be able to tell her grandchildren about how the English amuse themselves on country afternoons.

To Paul Nordoff *18:x:1956*

My darling Paul,

No! I did not know that the Phila production of *F.'s Maggot* was definitely off, and I am smitten to the heart, for you, for myself, for it. I thought it was completely in the bag (a vain thought ever to entertain, I suppose); and when Franklin was here last month I told him about it; he shocked me by saying he did not think it was so certain, but when I asked him how he knew that, he said he had heard it from your cousin; and this I

1. Probably referring to *Winter in the Air*.

discounted as being probably no more than the sort of thing one's relations always say about one—no, it is ungrateful of me to say that, for I have numbered two cousins both of whom would swear black-white for me; but still, relations as a rule are not unapt to take a poor view of one's career. Franklin's words did make me uneasy, but as I heard nothing from you, I decided it must only be a rumour. Oh blast and damn, my darling! What an autumn to what a spring! When I think of your happy visit in April, all those gay vistas, all that work, how hard we worked, and with what confidence and what brilliance—and now this! One blight, one calamity after another. And you, my poor Paul, so battered you scarcely know what you are about, and yet so full of fortitude, it breaks my heart . . .

I meant to write about Franklin's visit, but immediately after that we had to go to Norfolk to see Valentine's mother, and on the way there Valentine caught the kind of seasonal influenza that had been raging through the land, and I got it after her, and went on feeling extremely dazed and done for, and just able to crawl up and down my daily life, nothing more. Franklin was the greatest surprise and satisfaction. I had never thought to see him again, even when he wrote to ask if he could come here, I did not think he would, even when I was meeting his train at the station, I felt as though I were waiting for a ghost to materialize. And then looking down from the bridge over the track, I saw a composed, elegantly-overcoated stranger carrying a great deal of hand luggage that plainly didn't belong to him but to the untidy exclaiming woman beside him—and it was Franklin, just the same Franklin, but matured and so to speak, set—like a jelly sets, or a pavement. It was a very brief visit, only a week-end; but we all met so instantly, so freely that no time was wasted in seat-slamming lines. We listened to your records—the third and fourth songs in *Lost Summer* many times, he was enthralled by them, and overcome with admiration for their orchestration, and deeply moved by the last song—just as Alec Robertson is, you know. In some mysterious way he had grown considerably taller—unless I have shrunk; for I always retain a very exact recollection of how far up a person I reach. The army, I suppose.

I have finished the Proust translation, all but a few final titivatings. I feel extremely desolate and oddly unprotected. It had gone on, a secure private life, all through the period of Valentine becoming a R.C. and now I feel that I must come out of that life and face to face with what she assures me is not a new order, not different, not inconsistent with the past—and which I still go on finding full of unexpected jabs and pitfalls, and a completely unresolved perplexity as to what on earth a mind and a heart like hers can require from that extraordinary mingle-mangle of pettifogging little ordinances and assumptions of such incredible ambition—ideas, I mean, like the sacraments, and a priest cast [sic] dispensing or withholding a deity in a wafer—that when I think of them I feel swamped and over-shadowed by some nightmare variety of tree, a perambulating tree with no roots, such as I used to dream of when I was a child. But there it is, she doesn't waver, she seems encastled in it; and I realise more and more sadly that this could not have happened to her without a long spell of previous unhappiness and dissatisfaction, which perhaps I was instrumental in, and in any case was incapable of mending.

To William Maxwell *6:xi:1956*

... I have really finished it ... but I can't let go of it because paper flowers are still giving final little untwists, and it is so entrancing to watch them at it. I spent a great deal of last night in a dream where I met the Duchesse de Guermantes, grown old but remembering Marcel very affectionately and merrily and breaking out of her harsh speaking voice to sing a little nursery rhyme in a robin's treble. It was a house-party, and it was at the Château de Guermantes, with an endless series of kitchen courts and laundry courts and wellheads and granaries scarcely altered at all from their 14th century, and all these we traversed in our best clothes on our way to a garden party, our social squawks echoing off the stone.

To George D. Painter[1] *12:iv:1957*

Dear Mr. Painter,

Your corrections and suggestions were so valuable that I am shocked to realize that I have never written to substantiate my preliminary letter of thanks. I have used all of them, I think, except in the *Sainte-Beuve et Balzac* article, the phrase about Balzac's arrangements *pour trouver en hâte des mines de romans*. I did my best to agree with you: I re-read *La Recherche de l'Absolu*[2] to see if I could find a trace of Balzac looking for mines of novel plots. But I don't think he does anything of the sort. Claes is all he cares about, and he only makes perfunctory attempts to give the story the appearance of a novel—the *mien* of a novel. I think one is forced to read *roman* in the singular.

. . . But I am still at dead scent over that mysterious sentence in the George Eliot essay: *des équivalences morales à travers l'échelle humaine, d'une passée ici*, etc. If it were not for that previous *échelle humaine*, a flight of birds would be dictionary-right, at any rate; but dictionary-right would then oblige me to go on to a shady church path, and a washing day. I know you are right about *passée*. One says *trépassé*. Am I to assert that P. *did* say *trépassée?* I feel completely foxed.

But I have made a most interesting identification. In the Jesse-window, the scene of the dying Princess who replies *Je te comprends* is the old Princesse Mathilde, in her last illness. (There are times when P. reminds me of an economical Quakeress I know of, who during the war put the sardine-tails in the soup, alleging that it all added richness.

To William Maxwell *4:v:1957*

. . . Our summerhouse is being built: I can hear the mason's clink and clatter as I type. It will have three windows, and the best of them will open straight

1. C.B.E., biographer (of Proust and Chateaubriand) and incunabulist. Keeper of 15th-Century books at the British Museum 1954-74.
2. One of the 'Etudes philosophiques' of Balzac's *Comédie humaine*. In his effort to find the philosopher's stone, the hero, Balthazar Claes, a Flemish weaver, ruins himself and his family.

into a box-tree. The other two will look at the river. The front, as I think I have already told you, will have a commanding view of the coal cellar.

Happy Kate on the merry-go-round. I went in a splendid merry-go-round at Portland Fair last autumn. It was velvet barouches, though, immensely dowager, and the machine was a mountain of gilding, carving, and let-in panels of classic and tropical views. Signed and dated by the maker, who made it in 1860. It must be the oldest m.g.r. in existence, and the general effect was like something preserved by the National Trust. The barouches rose and dipped so much and so fast that it was quite breathtaking. My companion was a little girl called Phillida Stone, and she sat there like the heir of the ages.

To WILLIAM MAXWELL 18:vii:1957

Dear William,
. . . You find *Mado* and *The Rectory* 'too fast, or simply too strange, or just not quite real' while I, reading some of the stories in *The N.Y.* find them too slow, or too familiar, or not quite strange enough to be real. There are these swirls and by-currents in taste, and just now in Europe we are swinging away from the probable and the well-knit. Ionesco is only the striking tip of the tail of the general cat.

Fortunately,—fortunately I hope I can always appease my craving for the improbable by recording with perfect truth my own childhood (Have you observed that nobody ever had a probable childhood?).

To WILLIAM MAXWELL 24:ix:1957

. . . Today began with a friend of Valentine's saying: 'I can't stop. I've got to pick apples, and the hurricane is coming at twelve'—as though it were an aunt, Valentine remarked. I think you may like this example of how the English, though they have no pound, and no future, and no nothing, are prepared to deal with any hurricane that comes along.

However it did not; but yesterday, even before we had been told what to expect, was a very queer and alarming day: classically still and brooding, and both our cats with staring coats, and slinking about at my heels in the most woe-begone way. They have a wonderful talent for being Cassandras, only unfortunately they cannot prophecy with any explicit detail, so we never know whether to expect floods, lightning, or visitors.

Have you read Nancy Mitford's *Voltaire in Love?* It seems to me to be a very satisfactory, well-adjusted book. She knows a great deal, and doesn't make too much of it, and she sees Voltaire steadily, though no one, I suppose, could see him whole. There is an account of the Court of the King of Poland (in Lorraine) which is as funny as anything in Voltaire himself: all the state and frippery of a court, and all floating *in vacuo*, unsecured by any obligation to rule, keep in with other courts, breed heirs, or open bazaars. If Saint-Simon had been put there for a week, he would have *burst*.

I have been sent a diary, and on the title-page is printed: The moving finger writes, and having writ, moves on—Which of course is indisputable, but yet casts a rather sombre shade over the dotted lines on which I shall note that Mary Tomkins is coming to tea, that the chimney sweeper is coming to sweep.

To Janet Stone[1] *17:iv:1958*   *Lourmarin, Vaucluse*

Darling Janet,

Your heavenly long letter got here a day after we did; and we got here on the day we planned to, which was indeed a marvel, for we came through the wildest kind of weather. We had icy winds from Chartres onward, and I expected to see the Cathedral take wing & whirl into the air at any moment. It began to sleet soon after Bourges, & when we paused at Moulins a car parked beside ours, heaped with snow, snow plastered all over its behind and hard frozen on. A priest got out, like an old woman, bundled in coats and shawls over his long skirts. I asked him where he came from. From Vichy, said he. So much for our hopes of better weather as we fared south. All the rest of that day we met hundreds of cars coming towards us, fleeing hell for leather from their nice spring holiday, and the snow got thicker & thicker, & crossing the Mont Lyonnais was like crossing the Alps. Finally we were driven to stop at St Etienne, of all horrible places, and crawled into bed in a commercial hotel, Valentine feeling like death, and I feeling like indigo.

However, next morning the snow was over, & we had nothing to contend with except a terrific mistral that came sweeping up the Rhône Valley, one of the noblest & most dramatic storms I have ever seen. And thence on, though it was cold & stormy, it was cold & sunny too, and we were so entranced by the rapture of Roman arches, castles on every hilltop (why did our grandparents pant so about the Valley of the Rhine?) acres of fruit trees shivering in white or pale pink muslin like a dancing-class, and the amazing colours of the earth and endless succession of new mountain profiles ahead, that we felt quite consoled for being nearly blown off the road every ten kilometres or so.

And we were lucky in finding the most enchanting places to stop, delicious meals everywhere Except at the Three-Forked *Le Provençal* in Orange (where the service was so bad we nearly ate the coloured table-cloth, & the food when it came extremely shabby). And as usual, retired cordons-bleus cropping up in the most obliging way. We spent a night at a sweet little town called L'Isle-sur-la-Sorque where the patron of the inn had been a cook at the Dorchester, where the inn itself dated from 1710

1. Photographer, wife of Reynolds Stone, the engraver. They lived in the village of Litton Cheney, in Dorset.

and had barely been touched since, & where the church was entirely ornamented inside under Louis XIV—such gilding and such painting and such prancing splendours as I have not seen since the Gesu.[1]

The mistral is still about, but we dodge it. The sun shines, I have just been picking wild narcissus, and we drive from one Cezanne landscape to another in a state of rapture, besides meeting countless Cezanne portraits.

Today we went to Gordes, which looked incredibly stern and pale & embattled on its rock with the wind banging away at it. And then, inside the church, Oh, how I longed for the Stones to be with us! For in a side-chapel was a *crèche animée*; and when we dropped 10 fc bits into a collecting-box held by a toy angel, the angel wagged his head, the light went on, a little musical box began to play, the wheels of a toy windmill revolved, and a procession of carved and painted & dressed figures began to revolve round the holy family. There they all were, early 19th cent. I suppose, the chasseur with his game-bag, the baker in his white nightcap, the waiter at the auberge, the notary in black, the shepherdess knitting her stocking as she walked, the village intellectual, or possibly idiot, the ménagère with her provisions, a farmer with his ducks under either arm, the midwife with her bag and wise face—about twenty figures, perfectly carved, and so living that one felt one knew their very nicknames. Round & round they went, & the Holy Family remained unmoved in the middle, entirely taken up with admiring the baby & entertaining the Magi.

To William Maxwell *13:v:1958*

Dear William,

We are back—except for the part of me which has stayed in Provence. It seemed blasphemy to come away from a place where I was so entirely happy. Your green guide—it was invaluable—has been carefully put by against another visit. Now, looking back with perspective, I realise that the thing that gave me the deepest and most continuous pleasure was the light; that clear, unambiguous, candour of atmosphere in which everything had its due place and due proportion, and stood exactly where it was, each row of cypresses, each hill town, each sunned apricot farm on its chess-board square of ownership.

At S. Remy we stayed at the Ville Verte—like Gounod—so we were in the middle of everything that went on. The first thing that went on was a fair, with St Mark in a gilded cage carried out on to the church steps by four strong forains to bless it. And the day before we left opened into a bicycle race. The bicyclists rode thirteen times round the town, and it was

1. The principal church of the Jesuits in Rome.

ravishing to see them flash past and stream away down the avenue like a flock of macaws. After all this excitement we went and said goodbye to Les Antiques. And I think the part of me which has stayed in Provence has joined that conversing calm couple at the top of the mausoleum, and looks out over the plain towards Mont Ventoux. It almost stupefied me to think that while Les Baux was being built with all that medieval fear, frenzy, and ambition, Les Antiques were standing there, with the trees swaying round them and the wild boar rushing through the thickets and the wolves howling on winter nights and the huntsmen and the charcoal burners knowing all about them and paying not the slightest attention because they had always been there.

Our garage which has long been falling down was rebuilt while we were away. It is much improved, and now it must be paid for. So will you please send me that reassuring eight hundred dollars which you wrote to tell me of. It is now more watertight and snug than any part of the house, so next winter we shall probably live there ourselves.

TO PAUL NORDOFF *13:viii:1958*

Darling Paul,

Ralph Vaughan Williams has just left, and I have enlisted him and his wife, the more active and fostering, perhaps, of the two, since she is half his age and not engaged in composing, on behalf of an English performance of a Nordoff opera. They had heard about you, but all askew, as usual: that you were writing an opera on *The Flint Anchor*. I explained that you had written an opera on *Mr Fortune's Maggot*, and that it was glorious, and we talked about its chances of production; and then, because, as usual, the problems of producing a GRAND opera reared their ugly heads, I said artfully, But he has also written a most beautiful chamber opera, about Shelley at Lerici. Chamber opera, as you know, is one of V.W.'s enthusiasms; and Ursula immediately sat up, and asked a great many questions, and then said, It sounds just the thing for the New Opera Company. A very good company, too, said V.W. but aren't they insolvent? Not at all, said she, they've planted a hook in television, and that will make everything all right.

And she is going to write to Peter Hemmings of the New Opera telling him about *The Sea Change*; and as V.W. is its honorary patron and president, she will certainly be attended to. I am to write to him too, sending a copy of the libretto, and telling him that you will be over soon.

All this is a gift to us from the Cerne Giant.[1] Joy Finzi wrote to say that Ralph V. W. wanted to see him again, and that while she was driving

1. An 80 ft prehistoric figure carved out of the chalk at Cerne Abbas.

him and Ursula to Dorset, could they come and see us too? They were coming after a picnic lunch; but about one o'clock, there they were on the doorstep asking if they could eat their picnic in front of the house, because it was so wet everywhere else. And with the open-handed generosity that ever marks me I said they could eat it in the dining-room, so down they sat with their sandwiches and their mugs, refusing nice boiled eggs but gratefully accepting a bottle of Beaujolais, and by the time we had whisked through our omelette overhead they were as warm and happy as well-buttered cats, and our lovely joint party began with coffee and went on for a long time, Ralph, much to my pride and joy, refusing any suggestions about lying down for a rest on the grounds that he would prefer to go on talking to me since we had so many heresies in common and both loathed Clara Schumann. I used to meet him on and off when I lived in London, but never for long till this happy day . . . He had asked me, a little sternly, why I had left off composing, and I explained that I had come to the conclusion that I didn't do it authentically enough, whereas when I turned to writing I never had a doubt as to what I meant to say. But if I were reincarnated, I added, I think I would like to be a landscape painter. What about you? Music, he said, music. But in the next world, I shan't be doing music, with all the striving and disappointments. I shall be being it.[1]

To George Plank[2] 4:ix:1958

Dearest George,

I remember Anne[3] more often than I ever remember dates—but I have not forgotten that a year ago she died. I feel as bereft now as I did then—more bereft, perhaps, with twelve months' realisation of how dulled and dimmed I grow, lacking her to turn to with all the random nonsense I could talk with her, and with her alone. She made trivial things into dewdrops &

1. He died about two weeks later.
2. (c 1892-1962), American artist. He designed a great many of the covers of *Vogue*. Soon after the First World War he settled in England, and was a friend of Henry James and Logan Pearsall Smith, among other persons of consequence. He lived near Mayfield, in East Sussex. 'He was a neat, brilliantly blue-eyed small man, with a worried expression—perhaps because of the deafness—and invariably dressed in a sky-blue jersey to match his eyes . . . and he was one of the cosiest people to sit by the fire and pour out one's troubles to that I have ever known in my life, being extremely sensitive where he was fond.' Norah Smallwood to the editor.
3. Anne Parrish, American novelist, author of *The Perennial Bachelor*, etc.

dragonflies, she could knock the stuffing out of solemn hypocrisy with the whisk of a feather. And all these charms & graces & flashes of wit grew straight out of her heroic, tragedy-beaten heart. Surely there was never anyone like her, no one so revivingly, disconcertingly truthful, so generous in her enjoyments, so philosophically acid in her dislikes.

I have found one thing to thank this wet summer for. I have never known the conditions so ideal for getting up dandelions. They come up as affably as carrots, one would think it was their vocation. I lay them on the path in rows, patriarchal mandrake rooted specimens, long tapering specimens in their prime of dandelion-hood, and even those poor skinny little infants that hide under blue primroses & pretend to be blue primroses themselves.

Of course if I thought that next year there would be no dandelions at all, I should be very sorry. But I don't doubt there will be quite enough left to give me that particular pleasure of the dandelions that appear like defiant ancient Britons and have the first pure honey-scent of the year.

The day before yesterday, I appeased a life-long ambition: I held a young fox in my arms. He was an orphan—in other words, the vixen had been killed—a small rickety orphan, when he was given to Mrs Cox six months ago. Now he is the elegant young friend of the family; gentler than a dog, more demonstrative than a cat. I held him in my arms, & snuffed his wild geranium smell, and suddenly he thrust his long nose under my chin, and burrowed against my shoulder, and subsided into bliss. His paws are very soft, soft as raspberries. Everything about him is elegant—an Adonis of an animal. His profile is intensely sophisticated, his full face is the image of artless candour. His fur is like rather coarse, very thick, swansdown, & he wears a grey stomacher.

Heavens . . .

To Ian Parsons *18:ix:1958*

Dearest Ian,

The Royal Society of Arts has asked me to lecture (11th Feb. 1959) on *Women as Writers*, & has further asked me whom I would like as my chairman.

Whom I would like is Leonard Woolf. But do you think I could ask him? What daunts me a little is the thought that he might say yes out of a sense of duty, & kindness, & then have to spend a whole afternoon doing something that he would rather not.

Consider this for me, & be candid.

To Marchette Chute *25:xii:1958*

... Owls sing sweetly to us at night (it is open weather & they are delighted in their hunting) But a few nights ago I woke up to a much rarer sound— the belling of a stag. I felt as though I had woken up in another century, in one of Marchette's centuries. Herrick with his woods near by must have heard it as a familiar thing, & Shakespeare in London may have dreamed he heard it—but it was only the watchman.

To George Plank *30:xii:1958*

... You asked me if I knew Reynolds Stone. Yes, we know him very well, he is a neighbour of ours—as country neighbours go, about ten miles away—and a delightful neighbour, since there is always something going on, two hand-presses, and a great long table heaped with blocks, tools, paintbrushes, books, leaves, specimen papers, an indescribable confusion with Reynolds serenely finding whatever it is he wants, like a bumblebee over a flower-bed; and outhouses and rooms over the stables with the larger works. The first time we went there, he was working on Duff Cooper's memorial: a slab of black slate, eight foot long, three foot high, heaven knows how thick, and engraved on it the words, THIS PERISHABLE STONE . . . a lovely example of English hyperbole. I am very fond of him, and of his charming handsome family, which includes a grey cat called Luke and a donkey called Fanny. He is tall and—not fat, not plump—opulently built, a very light noiseless mover and looks like a portrait by Veronese . . . that gentle, sumptuous, sleepy look. He looks at trees with an astonishing degree of love and trust and penetration; almost as though he were exiled from being a tree himself. Janet, his wife, has a genius for recasting English idioms. She spoke the other day of someone barking up the wrong shin. She also told me, in a moment of confidential distress, that they were tethered to smithereens by finance.

1959

To William Maxwell 6:i:1959

Yes, the de Goncourt *Journals* .. what rapture; and you and I have both been well-starred, coming to them rather late, so that one knows so many of the people, has thought them over, formed surmises and conclusions; and then one meets them in the journals, contemporarily, they come out of the great picture à olof whore they have been heads and numbers, 1, V. Hugo, 19, P. de Chavannes, they come out as they were, complete in every everyday detail, smelling of tobacco, smelling of sausage. And as well as this, counterpointing this, is the unintentional portrait of the Goncourt brothers. I am especially devoted to the pages where the servant Rose is discovered to be the fiend in human form that one might expect to inhabit that horrible little den on the top-floor. It is the best story Maupassant ever wrote.

How scantily we would exist if it were not for 19th century France. I realised this all over again the other evening when a local boy came to consult me about becoming an artist (I hope he may. He had got some promising faults). He is the son of the local builder and decorator, he has never been outside Dorset, barely outside Maiden Newton, he has seen nothing except reproductions and the pictures in the Dorchester art shop which he took a firm breath and assured me he didn't think much of. He talked about Cézanne and van Gogh and Degas and Picasso as if they appeared familiarly to him in visions every night.

To Marchette Chute 21:i:1959

... I have been reading Mary Wordsworth's letters. They are a great argument for celibacy. Everyone is married, & intermarried, and domesticated; and children languish and die, or can't spell, or can't find a curacy; only Mr Samuel Barber 'an eccentric bachelor' goes on being perfectly happy adding improvements to his house, & building oratories & Swiss bridges in his garden. I don't think this is the moral the editor means one to draw; but it forces itself on any reflecting mind.

To Leonard Woolf[1] *12:ii:1959* *Inverness Point Hotel*

Dear Leonard,

It was very kind of you to preside over me yesterday. It made me feel proud and enabled me to feel confident. I wanted to say at the beginning of the lecture that all women writers owe you a debt of gratitude for what you did for one particular woman writer. But I don't think these things should be said in public; so let me say it now. I have long wanted to.

To George Plank *20:iii:1959* *Maiden Newton*

. . . I went to the Nat. Gallery & spent a couple of hours discovering all over again that Rembrandt is a marvel. I discovered, too, that his people who sit there thinking, really think. I had been looking at old Margherita Tripp; and there she was, reflecting about her larder, & her cellar, & all the provisions she had put by, & knowing every gherkin & every firkin of them. Well, I moved on, and looked at the old man in the patterned gown whose hands, whose old veined discoloured hands, are painted *like a brocade*; & after a while I went back to Margherita Tripp, & her thoughts had taken a long journey, & this time she was thinking about her childhood. She hadn't moved, & her features were set; but her expression was totally different. Then I made another discovery. His portraiture is so total that it comprises different ages of the sitter. There was that serious-faced young woman with folded hands. When I looked back at her from across the room, she had grown twenty years older, she was the woman she would be in twenty years' time. In the end, I said to myself, Rembrandt is not a painter at all. He is a creator, who creates his beings, three dimensional living beings, on a two-dimensional flat surface *which acts as a mute*, and enforces silence on them.

To George Plank *29:iii:1959*

Dearest George,

As a contribution to the spirit of Easter I have just cleansed the refrigerator. It is now quite as clean & neat as any sepulchre should be. And before that I rang up our dear Stones, saying that we did not think this would be a suitable evening to let off rockets on their lawn (it is pouring with rain,

1. (1880-1969), Political historian, writer and editor; co-founder, with Virginia Woolf, of The Hogarth Press.

and lawns of any ownership are spongy morasses). The news was received with well-concealed relief by darling Reynolds, who is afraid of fireworks anyway, with frank annoyance by his children; & no doubt will be a great comfort to the Warden of All Souls, who is staying with them. Not a man to get his feet wet for mere feux de joie.

Anyhow, there is all the summer before us, & fireworks are much more enjoyable as a summer diversion. When I was young & lived in London, I gave a wonderful midsummer party, fireworks at midnight prompt. My flat had a small back-yard, just large enough for dustbins & fireworks, & I cannot tell you how lovely those rockets looked, soaring up through the quiet Bayswater night, nor how interesting it was to see my neighbours' faces at their windows, tinged a beautiful shade of green by Bengal Flares. No one minded—but in those happy distant days no one did mind. The world has grown considerably crosser since, I'm afraid.

To William Maxwell 22:iv:1959 *Hotel des Voyageurs.*
Carnac. Morbihan.

Dear William,

I am sorry to have bothered you about my traveller's cheques, but since they are not at the Rennes Crédit Lyonnais by now, I think something must have gone wrong. My nice landlady who telephoned the Crédit this morning for me with the abstract ardour of a Frenchwoman who venerates all money, whoever's it is, was of the opinion—by the time she'd finished with them— that if a bank can make a bungle it will; but since it all happened so smoothly last time I didn't take her defeatist view as 100% right. Anyhow, dear William, the delay does not matter in the slightest, for we had already decided to stay on here for several days more. The hotel is cheap and charming, the Atlantic disporting itself a mile away, everything smells of gorse, it is quite incredible how well I begin to feel after less than 48 hours of this, there are also two abbeys just beyond the twenty thousand menhirs where they sing very well, and innumerable things we want to look at. As for the menhirs, *les alignements*, they look as if the Druids in a prophetic ecstasy had laid out a good crowded French churchyard. It is not a beautiful spec- tacle, but so baffling that it has a sort of conundrum majesty. You must have my night-letter-telegram framed. It was the first transatlantic ever to leave the Carnac post-office, and took forty-five minutes of general research, since at first both demoiselles were convinced that what I needed was an air-mail letter. Then the Guide was opened, its virgin pages riffled through, new lights burst in, inestimable memorandums were made on sheets and sheets of scribble paper. But *collect* was too much for them. They snuffled at the lascivious idea, but decided with morality, *Not in France*. In another hour we might have come to it, but the sun was shining and I wanted to go to the tip of Quiberon. So it was weakness of the flesh, not of my ungrateful memory that did not avail itself of your noble recommendation.

Anyhow, we have plenty of money as well as plenty of honey and tomorrow we go off looking at Calvaires, and langoustines appear on every menu, and wistaria dangles from almost every doorway, and perhaps it is very crude and selfish of me to insist on how happy we are—but as you have a loving heart, perhaps it is not.

To WILLIAM MAXWELL *24:iv:1959*   *Carnac.*

Dear William,

With your details, which came this morning, everything worked out a charm. Mme Catroux, who was longing for another go at the Rennes Cr. L., rang them up this morning, reduced them to saying the order had just arrived, which we none of us believe for a moment, & then said with decision that everything must be transferred to Vannes, since I could not waste my time going in & out of Rennes. Later, we went to Vannes where an *enormous* envelope, sealed up to the ears, enclosed another envelope, also sealed up to the ears, & inside were the T. cheques, so we drove home rejoicing & Mme Catroux has a sparkling eye & put a special trophy of wistaria on our table.

To GEORGE PLANK *20:v:1959*   *Maiden Newton*

Your prayerwheel was oiled at the exact moment, for we flew over on April 20th, both of us feeling so tired and done for that we each wondered in our private bosom whether it was really worth the effort. And from the moment we arrived, thanks to P.W., we began to recover. I recovered that very next morning, because as it was cold and the hotel very plain and way-side, we were invited into the kitchen for breakfast, where we had slices of bread on a clean American cloth spread, and a great motte of butter, the size of a Victorian blancmange, and a fire at our backs, and a kind hostess in a woollen wrapper, and other people coming in and out; in these circumstances, I found myself able to keep up quite a fair conversation, to ask questions and to answer them. Valentine did not recover quite so rapidly; but the same evening in Carnac the smell of gorse and the sound of the sea, and a great dome of chestnut tree standing beside a church like its heathen godfather did the trick for her, abetted by the P.W. And from that moment we never looked back. After a week in Morbihan we drove slap down to Bayonne, and from there scorning St Jean Pied de Port, which is massacred by popular buses and visitors knowing the picturesque when they see it, we went on and found St Jean le Vieux. Here, we saw mountains with snow on them, while at the same time we sat in a hedge under an acacia tree; and heard innumerable bells, for every horse, ox, cow, sheep, goat, wears a bell around its neck, gently dong-donging; and slept in an enormous room with floorboards two feet wide and heaven knows how many inches thick; and ate our dinner while at adjoining tables two sets of men played belotte, one set in French, the other in Basque, and eight such physiognomies, so brown, so strong-featured, so Cezanne, you could never hope to better.

And everywhere it was roses, big strong climbing roses, clambering over houses and overwhelming archways, and filling the air with their strong pure scent. And where it wasn't roses, it was wistaria, the lovely old-fashioned pale wistaria, or lilac, or acacia groves. They fill the clefts in the mountain sides, and carry their ivory white almost up to the white of the snow.

And that was not all, for on our way back we dawdled in the Saintonge, looking at Romanesque churches, and listening to nightingales.

To Paul Nordoff *21:v:1959*

... So what with roses, & oysters, and music, & snow topped mountains— we got to the Pyrenees—and cream-coloured oxen, & sea air and more Romanesque churches than you'd believe possible, we came home well & truly restored. I feel so well I can't believe myself. I must, indeed, have been near the edge when we set out. Now for the moment things seem a trifle less hysterical in the Ackland family. Ruth has found a doctor she abides by—a woman's last love-affair is with a doctor or a priest—and so she is abiding in his presence, & staying for the moment quietly PUT with some kind half-Irish nieces who have a large old farmhouse in Sussex, and who are very nice & patient with her, & manage her far better than the anxious Valentine can. Of course it's too good to last, but for the moment it's lasting, & we are enjoying it while we can.

Our garden is a wilderness of weeds & slugs—there wasn't a long enough frost last winter to kill them off at all—and we shan't have a green pea or a lettuce that we don't fight to the death for.

To Marchette Chute *30:v:1959*

... yesterday evening I went to read poetry at a local school called Bryanston, & one of the people I met there is a Wordsworth ... I always enjoy looking at him because of the family type. He is really astonishingly like William: the same long narrow head, and mouth like a malevolent sheep. I gaze at him and think how astonishing it is that he should have written the *Intimations* and known Coleridge.

I shall probably be gazing again in ten days time, when the school are giving a performance of Eliot's *Murder in the Cathedral*. The producer told me that of their chorus of twenty-two women of Canterbury eight have bass voices, and that the effect is very noble. The school has a Greek theatre in its grounds, with a beautiful surrounding of trees; & there we shall sit, vainly slapping at the midges, & wishing we had come in trousers. Habituées arrive reeking of citronella & such-like deterrent essences; but by the second acts the midges have always got the upper hand.

To George Plank *31:vii:1959*

My darling Un-Sainted George,

You are worn out with clipping yews and bays, so this is not a tactful moment for me to tell you that I have eleven little bay trees, self-sown, self—so far—grown. But I am rather pleased with them, for such a thing has never happened to me before; and I am pleased in my prudence, too, for I see a vista of painless Christmas presents . . . . I may even keep two for myself. Being on their own stems, so to speak, I imagine they will grow up straight and formal. Their parent is enormous and glorious, and quantities of birds nest in it, and if I were cooking on the bedroom floor and wanted a bay leaf I could have one very easily without going downstairs for it; but as it was a struck cutting, it will never be a Forest Tree, only a Forest Bush. Two polite bays in pots might add that touch of formality to the front porch which would convince strangers that it is a front porch, instead of which they go all round the house looking for something that would fit in with their preconceived ideas, and in the end hammering vainly on the door of the coal cellar. But what with Valentine's fossils, the landing net—a thing one has to have at hand if one lives on a river bank, my weeding baskets and watering pots, the coffeepot, a congerie of endeared shells draped in cobwebs, the old broom that I haven't the heart to throw away, etc., I doubt if the addition of two restaurant bay trees will be indicative of anything except perhaps that this house is a failed restaurant.

This is a delicious day, hot but not too hot, and not clammy; and made all the more delicious because tomorrow our visitor may go away. She isn't too bad, indeed, there is nothing really to complain of except that she talks with a great deal of emphasis and in a loud rather hectoring voice, and knows a lot of anecdotes about distinguished people, and saints.

TO GEORGE PLANK *25:viii:1959*

. . . It is just the weather for Mawk, and I am wallowing like a tranquil hippopotamus in Augustus Hare's *Life with Mother* & *Life without Mother*. He was really rather a savage little weevil at heart, & in *Life without Mother* it is nice to see it coming out. I also like musing on all the stately homes he visited, and adding details of my own—the stately water closets with blue china bowls, mahogany surrounds, and brass handles you pulled up—often repeatedly, I fancy. And the puddings in the Pugs Parlour that had so much more maraschino in them than the corresponding puddings that went up to the dining-room, and the amazing tribal customs peculiar to each of these establishments. A tribal custom that I saw as a child, staying in an Irish stately, was the way gooseberries came in for dessert. First, you took a wide platter on a stand. On the platter you laid a pavement of red goose-berries. Above this, and one gooseberry less in circumference, a pavement of green gooseberries; & so on, in red & green layers, symmetrically de-creasing, till there was one lone gooseberry on the summit. This the butler, with every muscle and sinew braced not to topple the erection, his lips tightly compressed, his breath held in, placed in front of my great-aunt, who took it as calmly as if it were some simple unaesthetic matter like a buttered crumpet.

TO WILLIAM MAXWELL *25:viii:1959*

. . . TWO bathrooms! What splendour. No wonder you mentioned it. I am reminded of a man I know who was invited to lunch with some Italian friends. They had a flat in a tenement house, overlooking a river. It was a humble home, lunch was rather humble too, and mainly served in its native cartons. At the end of the meal the host rose, gathered all the cartons together, and hurled them out of the window with a splendid gesture, remarking, 'Ogni commodita'.

TO JOY FINZI[1] *20:xi:1959*

. . . The river has a voice again—a very low confidential one, with a slight stammer. What you say about this house being like an old boat stranded fills me with delight. One needs to be reminded from time to time of the quality of the house one lives in. Force of acquaintance tends to make it split apart into rooms only.

1. Artist. Her drawing of Ralph Vaughan Williams is in the National Portrait Gallery. She is the widow of the composer, Gerald Finzi.

Dear William,

The stereoscope has started out for you, and here is its bill. I told Valentine who writes twenty letters where I write one that I would look after it. I discovered that I had been wrong to assure you that the box was inlaid. Instead, it has some rickety little victorian carving on it—but I hope that won't affect your reactions; and that Kate and Brookie[1] won't be scared out of their lives by the spectacle of a view of humanity being so unnaturally three-dimensional and so unnaturally motionless.

While you are getting a stereoscope, we are playing with a tape-recorder, a small Grundig, equally of course a period piece. Valentine manages it as M. de Guermantes managed the stereoscope—a slightly solemn domestic diversion. When I heard myself played back, a casual remark about ears for music and eyes for measurements I was instantly persuaded *that I was dead*. To be there on record, preserved like a fossil, made me feel completely posthumous; and I am in two minds about my existence still. Later, when we have grown cleverer at the distance-intensity ratio, we hope to get some very fine recordings of our cats singing for their supper. Valentine meanwhile has recorded the *Gloria in excelsis Deo*, in order to examine her latin accent.

1. Our two daughters, then aged five and three.

To George Plank ('My Beloved Wilberforce') 1:i:1960

I am glad you have liked George P.'s[1] book. I met him while I was in London, Norah[2] asked him to dinner. He is tall, thin, dark, with a very fresh and ruddy colouring and short-sighted spectacles, through which he sees and sees. He looks about 20, and is either shy or too interested in what people are saying to say anything himself. He works at the British Museum, where he is the authority on incunabuli, and lives at Redhill with his wife and two teen-age daughters. He works impassionately on his incunabuli, goes home by train, has *an hour* to himself in which he writes his book on Proust; he has Saturday afternoons and Sundays, but then he does some housework and gardening. Soon after Norah had got this out of him he rose like a Cinderella and went off to catch his train to Redhill. I liked him very much, a kind of infra-red intelligence, invisible but powerful, glows from him; but I do not suppose I shall ever be able to like him more extensively unless I can get myself into the B.M. disguised as something printed before 1500. Once or twice during the evening when I noticed his attention dwelling on me with dispassionate ardour, I had a feeling that he was considering whether or no I had contributed something to the character of Mme de Guermantes; but as he will have to discard this hypothesis, I attach no hopes of a ripening interest to it.

To George Plank 5:i:1960

. . . I scarcely know myself, the house is so neat. Since Saturday when Valentine bore away her mamma to Sussex, I have been *passionately* clearing away. Three large sacks bulging with paper-litter, two large cats bulging with oddments out of the larder, one small postman staggering under a load of outward parcels, rugs airing themselves at every window as if for Corpus Christi. Oh, what a clearance, what purging gales! Mrs Carlyle could not have been more waspishly active than I, not even when she was driving the bugs out of the red bed. My great-grandfather, George Moir, knew Mr & Mrs Thomas C. when they were in Edinburgh. He even stayed with them

1. George D. Painter. See p. 162.
2. Norah Smallwood, her editor at Chatto and Windus. Later Managing Director and Chairman of the firm.

at Auldmuckle or whatever that farm was called, and did a drawing of it which was afterwards sent to Goethe. He gives me this small link with Goethe, and another with Coleridge—not so direct, but much more interesting and creditable. He was a German scholar like all the fashionable intellectuals of his date, and had made a translation of *Wallenstein,* which was actually at the printers, when he heard that Coleridge was translating *Wallenstein* and withdrew it. My grandmother loved him so devotedly and so appreciatingly that it often seems to me that I knew him myself; and when I read *Tom Jones* or *Clarissa Harlowe* or *The Beaux' Stratagem* or *The Way of the World,* I like to think I am reading and handling the pages he did. He kept these shocking works in his study, where his pious sad wife couldn't get at them. He was a very small thin man with a long ugly face and an inexpugnable Aberdeenshire accent, the ugliest of my forebears —which is saying a lot—and the most engaging.

6:i:1960

No—except in always getting what she wants, V.'s mamma is not like your sister. V.'s mamma is the iron hand in a moth-eaten rabbit-fur glove; she appears to be warm-hearted, full of understanding, a brave old poor thing with an Anglo-Catholic smile. Strangers in trains think her quite wonderful and carry all her luggage for her (she never travels without at least seven bits of luggage, some heavy as lead, others, paper-bags at their last gasp. . She does, however, arrive when she pleases, regardless of the feelings of the arrived on) . . . She is descended from Lord Eldon; and makes me feel as if I were descended from Shelley. That is enough for now of an inherently painful subject.

To GEORGE PLANK *14:ii:1960*

Dear George,

I have just seen off a week-end visitor, and washed up lunch, and heeled in a William Lobb and a Nevada who were sent off much more briskly than they needed to be because their growers were thinking of the railway strike; and now I will sit down to tell you about two very old & distant cousins of mine, brother & sister, who live together. She is in her nineties: he is a trifle younger. They were sitting together, he reading, she knitting, Presently she wanted something, and crossed the room to get it. She tripped. & fell on her back. So she presently said: Charlie, I've fallen & I can't get up. He put down his book, turned his head, looked at her, and fell asleep.

It is a relief to my feelings that the railway strike has changed its mind, because I like hearing our trains at night. There is a pair that meet between 12 & 1, like Shakespearian lovers, or Drydenic or any other variety for that matter, and converse in low whistles. They are as pretty as owls. I suppose they are inviting each other to tea. And in winter how lovely it is to see a sudden burst of steam, so warm & white and glowing, burst up in the bare unflowering landscape. All the same, I think the strike was well-justified. It is an outrageous anomaly when grey-headed engine-drivers take home £8, or less, and every lout in his teens who likes to be an unskilled labourer can take home £12. It seems a queer development of a mechanical age that it should be so much more profitable to have strong legs and a strong back than to have skilled hands under an experienced head.

We still have some sweet little branch-lines. I am always expecting them to be abolished; meanwhile I have the tenderest feelings for them. There is one from Taunton to Castle Cary which ten years ago I used very often, coming back from visiting my poor witless mother in her nursing-home. I caught its last journey of the day; and at each little station the guard got out, locked up the ticket office, looked round like a mother to see that everything was as it should be, put out the lights, and no doubt said God Bless You to it. This idyllic artless journey ended at Castle Cary, the train took itself off to sleep in a siding, and I waited half an hour for the express to come dashing & flashing in like something of a different breed. There is also a God-fearing train from Yeovil to Taunton that doesn't run on Sundays, and our own local pet from Maiden Newton to Bridport that has the best blackthorn brakes I know, and trots like a horse under the neolithic fort of Eggardon, & crosses a quantity of narrow bridges with screams of apprehension. As for the primroses along the cuttings . . . you can lean out of the window and smell them. There was also a very nice system from Tenby to Penally. The road was curly & hilly, the railway track was straight and flat, so naturally everybody walked along the track. And Mr. Jones-Station once explained to my Aunt Purefoy that one could not expect the trains to run up to time because the pedestrians were often so engaged in conversation—impassioned conversation, being Welsh pedestrians—that they wouldn't move out of the way. So the engine paused, and puffed till they were kind enough to notice it.

To Norah Smallwood[1] *16:ii:1960*

Dearest Norah,

I have now gone through the first part of *Swann's Way*[2] for corrections

1. See footnote on p. 179.
2. 'Chatto and Windus are considering a revised edition of *Remembrance of Things Past*, and want me to have a hand in it, if it hatches.' STW to the editor, 16:ii:1960.

and emendations, and made a list, with page & line references, of what I think should be set right.

I found a few total misunderstandings and mistakes; what is more serious and harder to trap is S.M.'s habit of gratuitous insertions. Some of them are the insertions of enthusiasm; he is so entranced with what he is translating that he has to put in little *fiorituri* of his own; but the majority are of the nature of doodles: modifications, qualifications, and above all, amplifications. And as a result, his version is much more long-winded and muffled than the original.

A certain amount of circumbendibus and *um—er* is proper to English style, and I don't think S.M. should have all his loops and twiddles removed; but where Proust is obviously trying to make a plain statement of an intricate train of thought, I have re-cast and tightened, since not to do so is to betray the original.

I have enjoyed all this intensely. It has been like a superlatively engrossing spring-cleaning, and the joy with which I have seen my heap of throwouts increasing is only to be surpassed by my raptures at getting rid of the cobwebs and removing dead mice.

But now I would like to think that a fellow-spotter is on the way. Have you got your hooks into that young man[1] yet? I don't know that the work would be done faster if two people were doing it, but it would be done more securely.

To George Plank 4:iii:1960   *Maiden Newton*

Something has been brooding over me. For that vile cold I wrote to say I had got the better of turned round and bit me in a most black-deathly manner, and for over a week I have been in bed suffering no pain in particular but with a temperature that would not lie down, and our good earnest little doctor looking more and more like a terrier halfway down a rabbit-hole, barking out that he must get to the bottom of it, and specimens of my blood and my spit and my urine distributed over half the county, so that in the end I said to him in my best die-away voice, Would you like a lock of my hair?

However he is now at peace, his penicillin has worked at last. So he thinks. I draw no attention to the fact that I aided it with garlic sandwiches, and quantities of surreptitious aspirin. And tomorrow I can get up and go out, and be rational again.

1. Andreas Mayor.

To Norah Smallwood *9:vi:1960*

Dearest Norah,

The Mayors have come to lunch, and he & I have been going over each other's problems, and emending each other's emendations, and discussing method, & sharing out the spoil, and generally having a cosy sit.

I like him, and think well of him. He is extremely conscientious, observant, and sound. I have seen enough now both of his S. M. emendations and of his straight translations (the new material in Pléiade) to feel that he knows what he's about, and is a Proust scholar. And he is *tidy*, a tidy worker, most essential in anything of this kind. So I think it will all go nicely, and it will be a comfort *and* a stimulus to work with anyone so conscientious and exact.

We shall need to collaborate to a certain extent; as he says, there are certain phrases, idioms, turns of expression which Pr. refers back to, or harps on, and these will have to be made to correspond, whether they are in the volumes he is doing or those that I am doing ... Altogether, there are a thousand fine problems, but we think we shall manage to control them.

To George Plank *1:vii:1960*

... I am much attached to *Goethe's Conversations with Eckermann*. Have you ever read this odd work. It has more platitudes to the square page than you could believe possible, and Eckermann is *so* enthusiastic—even more loving and toadying than Boswell; and Goethe is *so* bland. Perhaps it is a book more enjoyed by women than by men. It supports that feminine theory that when men get into a tête-à-tête they are as foolish as two stuffed owls ...

Valentine is walking about upstairs yawning like a tiger, and obviously it is bedtime, but I shan't go yet. I have been paying bills, doing up parcels, writing duty letters—I cannot go to bed with all my virtues seething in me, or whatever it was that Hamlet used as an excuse for not killing his uncle just then.

To Nancy Cunard *4:vii:1960*

Dearest Nancy,

I am appalled by your news.[1] I had heard nothing about it, read nothing about it. What date was the case, which court were you had up in? If they

1. After creating a series of disturbances, Nancy Cunard was committed by her cousin Victor Cunard and her doctor to an insane asylum in the East End of London, from which, through the intervention of friends, she was removed to more bearable surroundings at Virginia Water, in Surrey.

decided you were drunk, it would have been in order to send you to jail, but I cannot understand why you should be where you are. Are you being given any form of treatment—I think this would be the usual procedure—or are you just 'in reclusion'? And what for? What form of insanity are you said to be suffering from?

It wrings my heart to think of you among these unfortunate creatures of decayed wits—dirty habits too, I suppose, poor things! What a black page of the human story you are studying! You are in a ward. Does that mean you have no privacy, except for the cocoon one's mind can spin round one? A very frail cocoon, at best, and the spinning a most painful labour.

I wish I could come at once to see you. We would—I hope you know it—but we are in another variety of fix ourselves. Valentine has a recondite and horrible thing called temporal arteritis (it can make one go blind) and has been given cortisone for it since March. No improvement, and now they want to operate—what is called a biopsy. Meanwhile, I have written to Roger Senhouse. One's publisher is a sort of parent, and I think he should know of this. And it has struck me that Diana Duff Cooper would be the best person to approach R. A. Butler. Though I haven't much faith in Cabinet Ministers. They are so wound up in their underlings that they can scarcely move. But Diana might do something, as being a transcender of the usual routine approaches.

I will think more—your letter only came an hour ago, and I am still feeling as if it were the earthquake in Chile—and do everything and anything I can, my darling, to help you out of this hideous entanglement.

To George Plank 6:ix:1960

Dearest George,

You know me before and behind and search out the secrets of my heart—how else should you send me that message not to write to you? Indeed, I have felt as sodden as a drowned owl and as dumb as a worm. After Norah's visit, too, when I should have been re-starched & newly-gilt. When the Mistletoe Gipsy appeared at the door this afternoon bearing a roll of bright red carpeting under her thin wiry arm she gave me one glance, put by the carpeting, & concentrated on selling me a scrubbing-brush. And from the fervour and profusion of her assurances about how well I am looking I began to think I must be looking even more of a death's-head than I feel.

Yesterday ought to have whipped me into a more active thankful state of mind. We went to a lunatic asylum, what is called a Mental Sana-torium, to visit a friend of ours, who was clapped into it a couple of months ago—no, more. Four months ago, poor love! She is said to be better, she may soon be let out, even. They have been treating her on pull Devil, pull Baker lines. First they fill her up with sedatives & depressants, then with vitamins and tonics. As she remarked, I have had everything except the chaplain. She is a creature with a very brilliant violent character—it is still there; but lying round her like leaves round an autumn tree. I don't know if she will ever be reclothed with herself. Yet when she came into the waiting-room & looked at us with her quizzical bird's stare she seemed to me to be the only sane person in the place, & I embraced her as if she had come down into hell to rescue me.

It is one of the classy loony-bins: lots of very clean windows, lots of bedded-out plants, flower-vases everywhere with not a drooping petal in them, excellent colour reproductions on the walls (flowers again, or Côte d'Azur landscapes) smiling faces, suggestion boxes, announcements of events in elegant calligraphy—and really hot bath-water, she said, & quite tolerable meals. Yet the impression, George, was of a dowdy cheerfulness only to be matched by the most uplift chats on the BBC. Everything was so reasonable, so unbendingly normal. Surely it must be very bad for people out of their minds to be smothered in normality?—not a dark corner to mope in, not a companionable horror to stretch out its supporting hand. Nothing, NOTHING to justify & mitigate that noise of keys being turned in locks.

To George Plank 10:ix:1960

. . . We have more apples than we can give away, because everybody we knew has more apples, etc. The musk rose, if you please, is covered with berries as though it were a holly. I reap off as many as I can reach, but as it is ten foot high & twenty foot long, I must take the long-handled pruners for the upper storey. Fertility dogs me. When we came here the house was as bare as a hat-box. Then came the time when I was proudly training the jessamine & the clematis and fostering the musk-rose. I love them as much as ever, probably more; but I clip the jessamine as if it were a yew; & even so, a long wand of it has crept in above the hinge of the side door and is turning itself round the top of a cupboard. And next year the passion-flower will be coming indoors too. It was given me three years ago, by Reynolds Stone—a weedy little sucker torn up with practically no root, because dear Reynolds is no gardener, and would never sink his fingernails in the mould. Now it has designs on the chimney-pot.

To George D. Painter *5:x:1960*

Dear George Painter,

I was very sorry that yesterday's frustrating evening[1] involved the further frustration of my hopes of conversation with you. I had looked forward to that with great pleasure. Anticipation of pleasure is a pleasure in itself.

But by midnight I was thankful that your train had carried you away from an exhibition you would have found extremely distasteful. Accuracy of text is nothing to them; preservation of their uncle's translation is nothing to them. Respect to Proust less than nothing. Scomo clung like an embattled limpet to his cronies at the Saville Club and Miss Scomo asked if Virginia Woolf's books still sold. One of the things they prevented me doing was to ask if you can get me a new Reader's Ticket to the B.M.—or rather, if you will get me a new ticket, for I have no doubt but that you can. I want to do some research into *Emily da Liverpool*. She is an early 19th Cent opera & I suspect she may be the incentive for Balzac's remarkable statement that women in Lancashire are so passionate that they die for love.

To William Maxwell *20:x:1960*

... Mme de Genlis was governess to the little boy who ultimately became Louis Philippe, alias M. Poire, the last King of the French. She was born of a somewhat down-at-heels flighty provincial family, she was taught to play the harp and to say her catechism, she harped her way onward and upward into court circles, and became the mistress of Philippe Égalité, Duc de Chartres and then d'Orléans. She had an insatiable talent for improving people's minds, and her own. When she wasn't practising the harp, collecting a mineralogical cabinet, writing little plays, and planning improvements in industry, she was teaching other court ladies about astronomy and spelling. Philippe É. made her governess to his daughters, then to his sons. She educated them from head to foot, from religion to gymnastics. She plunged them in cold baths and took them out into the streets of Paris to become acclimatised to the common people. She was a prig and a fidget, and

1. 'After a discussion at the Garrick Club with George and Joanna Scott Moncrieff, Ian Parsons, Norah Smallwood, STW, and myself present, on the project for STW to revise Scott Moncrieff's Proust. They refused permission. (Just as well, as this enormous task would have affected her last two decades of creativity, but disappointing to her at the time.)' George D. Painter to the editor.

her memoirs are only accidentally amusing (though they contain the hermits who lived in a forest supporting themselves by making silk stockings) but she is a fascinating picture of that immediate pre-Revolution period, riddled with incompetent good intentions. In a way, she is for that period what Chateaubriand is for the post-Revolution. They are like supporters to a coat of arms. She has all the common sense and intellectual enterprise he hasn't, and none of the passion and poetry . . . When I have told you that if one wants to be knowing one sounds the s in Genlis, I will leave off being like Mme de Genlis.

To Norah Smallwood *22:xi:1960*

Darling Norah,

This morning I had a letter from Andreas Mayor, who has heard that I shall be in Sussex this week-end, and now asks me if we can meet & talk about the Proust translation.[1]

You'll remember that after the scene of Embattled Scott-Moncrieffs I said that A.M. ought to be told, since he is so much engaged in the project. And you & Ian, more hopeful than I of the S.M.'s said, Later on.

So here I am, confronting a really horrid problem. It's obvious he doesn't know, for his letter is full of how well he has been getting on with *Cities of the Plain*. What the hell am I to say? It goes completely against my stomach to go on as if nothing were wrong. Equally, it is now too late for me to tell him. So much time has gone by, and for me to tell him now would be to assume an elder statesman attitude which is quite impossible between one collaborator & another. And Ian is in bed.

I see only one way round. Will you write to him—before this week-end —giving him an explanation of what happened at the Garrick dinner; what has been done since to bring them round; what hope there is of a happy issue (not much, I imagine, since I have heard no more since Ian's invocation of those joint acquaintances); and what chance there is that he could go on with *Le Temps Retrouvé*, since that is out of the S.M. juris-diction.

And could I have a carbon of your letter so that when I meet him I may know what he has learned?

Otherwise, I shall either have to go behind Ch. & W.'s multiform back & tell him (which I don't wish to do *at all*) or have my face blackened for having treated a collaborator as a no-account.

1. In the end Andreas Mayor finished retranslating *Le temps retrouvé* and his translation rounded out the unfinished Scott Moncrieff translation until 1981, when Terence Kilmartin's revision of the whole work became the standard text.

I am very sorry to heap all this on your plate when Ian is away & you are doing all his work as well as your own. But I think you will understand how I feel, & what a really vicious fix I am poised over. For without any of us meaning it, and damned Old Time abetting, I must now seem to have behaved in a very dishonouring way to A.M.—whom I suspect to be extremely sensitive. For that matter, if he were a rhinoceros, the dishonour would be just the same.

To Janet Machen[1] 8: xii: 1960

. . . It seems to me that any holy harms the child might pick up in all this surplicing & choiring is more than outweighed by the sheer physical advantages of singing. There is no exercise so wholesome. As William Byrd remarked, 'It openeth the pipes'—it warms one's blood, it loosens up one's ribs, it strengthens one's jaw. Oh, I am all for singing. If I had had children I should have HOUNDED them into choirs & choral societies, and if they weren't good enough for that, I would have sent them out, to sing in the streets. Besides, the child's paid for it—weddings on the nail. Payment is almost as good for the spirit as singing is for the body.

I don't wonder he comes back radiant from practices.

1. Social worker. Daughter of STW's mother's sister, Dorothie Purefoy, née Hudleston, and the novelist Arthur Machen.

To William Maxwell *7:i:1961*

Dear William,

I am perfectly able to like *Truth and Fiction* as a title for the Clive story. Indeed, I like it much better than my own. I have always envied Goethe his version, such a perfect designation for all such works of remembrance that it should have become a generic, like symphony, and all subsequent reminiscences just have opus numbers or Koechelverzeichnisses . . .

I am very glad you have taken it, and that it is liked. I like it too. That terrifying little boy alarmed me so much when I began on him that I was obliged to break off and go to bed with the two cats and George Eliot to recompose myself. Normally, I am as happy as a ghoul with my horrors—but Tony was too much for me. It may amuse you to know that the whole of this story sprang from a house that happened to catch my eye as I was travelling from Lewes to Worthing en route for Valentine's mamma in her nursing home (she is now out of it, and fit to tear up tigers); my mind divided between the pleasures I was leaving, and the boring goodness that I was approaching (I am always perfectly conscious of my own goodness), I gave it a glance, noticed that it was darkish, square, sat among its shrubs among sallow fields. That was all.

A few days later, I had the whole story, all I needed to do was to transfer it to a landscape that has not so many literary associations as Sussex. These impregnations are very odd. Inattention seems to be an essential element. just as it is in seeing ghosts. In the matter of seeing ghosts, I suspect that water is important too; a pond or a river nearby, a damp house, a rainy day.

To George Plank *10:i:1961*

. . . Except for a dog, two cats, and a mysterious being that walks about overhead when I am downstairs, and on the ground floor when I am upstairs, I am alone. Valentine's tiresome sister has lost her job. And created over this as if she had lost her hair, her teeth, her legs, her good name, and her latchkey. So much so, that Valentine felt obliged to drive up to London at a moment's notice in order to condole with her, and listen to her sorrows and sit on her head. And now, on the principle of being killed by two birds etc, she is in Sussex, visiting her Parent. Nothing is perfect. Valentine has relations. Really worst of all, she missed the swans this morning. Eight of them, flying round and round the house, and surging up through the garden as if they meant to fly in at the window where I stood watching them. I was deafened & blinded with swans and glory.

To George Plank *20: iii : 1961*

. . . As we went from Shropshire to Gloucestershire it was like going from one country to another. The skies suddenly becoming dramatic with light and shade, the landscape paling and shrivelling, and fat flakes of snow hitting the windscreen.

We came home full of virtuous intentions of painting as much of the outside of the house as we could reach without falling off ladders. That was yesterday. This morning our accumulated letters came from the post office, and among them a totally unexpected invitation to spend three days in Paris with an old friend,[1] a Pennsylvanian like you, as his guests from here and back again. Unlike you, he is incapable of writing a letter, and for years we don't hear from him, and scarcely even know where he is, or whether our letters reach him. And then suddenly he descends in a shower of gold and kindness. My dear, we shall stay in the rue de Rivoli. I cannot believe it—we who have always skulked in cheap hotels on the Left Bank, and once even—and very nice it was, too—in such a low lodging house off the rue de la Gaiêté that we had a gas cooker in our bedroom and a stern notice to say that if we offended against decency or made an inordinate noise we should be turned out on the spot, and where the water closet was one of those gaping seatless pits where the whole of the Seine pours out when you pull the string, so that you have to leap for your life in order to avoid being swept down the pit yourself.

Well, there we go on the 28th, by the night ferry, snoring in comfort all the way in one of those wagon-lits you dislike so much.

I cannot get over my surprise. It is the sort of thing that I have always assumed only happened to other people.

No woman was ever less well prepared in her apparel to lodge in the rue de Rivoli than I. Fortunately, I have three very beautiful pairs of shoes, all in mint condition since I haven't gardened in them; and with that, and Mrs Warre-Cornish's[2] reflection that I am a British subject, born in wedlock, and a member of the Church of England, I shall hope to oar myself along. It is one of the solid advantages of old age that as no one will expect you to look elegant, you needn't feel guilty if you don't.

1. Franklin Brewer.
2. Wife of Francis Warre-Cornish, Vice-Provost of Eton College.

Do you know that Eton had another Mrs Cornish, almost as good? And that on the morning when the first news of the Titanic had reached England, she was met in the street looking very sad and worried, and said to those she met, I hear there has been a most dreadful boating accident.

To Paul Nordoff *2:iv:1961*

Darling Paul,

I waited to answer your letter till I had seen Franklin. He was waiting for us on the station, and from the moment we met his kindness enfolded us, and I think none of us were conscious of the lapse of time since we last were together—five years ago, almost. He is too thin, and it alarmed me to see how he suddenly looks dead tired, for no apparent reason—for I don't think we were the reason—and his colour drains away, and his skull shows through his face. He has an awful cough, and he explained that this is because he has a lung condition called, I think, emphysemia; however it may be spelled, what it means is that he doesn't empty his lungs sufficiently, so that he chokes from superfluity of breath, as ordinary chokers choke from insufficiency. I hope the sea voyage he is going [on] will do something to improve this; but as he has had it for so long, since the war, I don't suppose it will ever be quite cured.

He was an angelic host to us, and we were cosseted from head to foot during three marvellous days; two of them blue and gold, the other silver grey. Not having been in Paris for so long, I thought I might feel a shabby stranger to it. But not at all. That stretch of time was obliterated too. It is extraordinarily little changed, the same trees look over the walls, the same couples seem to be sitting on the quays, the same children darting like swallows, the same sense of *knowing how to live* meeting one everywhere. We walked in the Tuileries gardens and by the river, we sat talking in cafés, we ate the most delicious food, and one evening, since Franklin had not seen *La Dolce Vita* and we had not seen the whole of it, we went to the last cinema showing it—a minute little box in the remotest part of Montmartre, which must I think have dated from the earliest Wild West and *Broken Blossoms* period, decorated in blackberry juice purple and faded gold, with two such enormous chandeliers that they almost filled the auditorium—a queer frame for that intimidating film. Have you seen it? If you haven't, then for God's sake, do.

To George Plank *7:iv:1961*

... You have the nicest hand with a parcel. I can't think of anyone to match you in parcelling except perhaps Henry Tilney, to whom I attribute *all* the graces. Mr Knightley's parcels would never come undone, true; but think of all the paper & string involved. Elinor had to do up all Edward's: Edward required a good deal of buttoning and unbuttoning, though she enjoyed his dependence on her: the butler did all Marianne's & Colonel Brandon's. Mr Darcy did exactly three parcels a year, for Lizzy's birthday, for New Year's day, & for their wedding anniversary. The product was excellent, but he took *hours* to achieve it. And locked the library door.

To George Plank *11:v:1961*

Dearest George,

Don't be so sure about my mother. She was not a *man-eating* tigress, she had no need of that, since every man who set eyes on her hurled himself into her jaws. She had a delicious bite or two, & then spat them tidily out again. But she was quite a considerable tigress. The best portrait of her is the Duchesse de Guermantes. Like her, she was brilliantly witty, autocratic, mocking, with several areas of her heart as hard as a stone. I wrote cold, and amended it to hard. *Nothing* about her was cold. She was intensely, savagely loyal, very hard-working, with a hand that could turn to anything. The thing that was most eminent & glorious about her was that *she had not the smallest drop of vampire blood.*

Hogarth did quite a good portrait of her when she was old: Mother Needham, the procuress in the first plate of the Harlot's Progress. The same stately sailing port, the splendid little nose emerging from a face that had grown heavy, the same *cerne's* eyes, and melancholy yawning eye-sockets.

During my youth I was terrified of her, and one reason why I couldn't afford an account-book was that the alternative, after my father's death, to penury in London would have been to live with her, and incessantly exasperate her, in Devonshire. Fortunately, she married again—my kind, simple-hearted, sweet-natured stepfather, fifteen years younger than she, and no match for her in anything, except a kind of obdurate goodness & justice which he imposed on some of her wilder vagaries.

After I had left off being afraid of her, I was able to feel love, and great esteem, and to accept her illegitimate charms without a priggish sensation that they were unjustified. I imagine your Lady Sackville,[1] or was she Lady S. West, was much such another. I am sure you would have loved her —*madly*, albeit with occasional pangs of disapproval.

O George, how I envy you! Not to have felt anger since you were eighteen. I go on being angry to this day, frantically unavailingly angry at such things as fox-hunters, otter-hunters, Valentine's vampire relations—

1. See letter to Bea Howe, 23:v:1965, p. 217.

and often the demands made on her by her vampire Church. The best I can say for myself is that now I am more often saddened than infuriated. But I could not be my mother's daughter without containing a considerable charge of dynamite.

To George Plank *18:vi:1961*

Here I sit, full of strawberries & virtue, having dispersed ten gallons of life-blood & water to ALL the roses, my grateful communicants. Grateful they are; bringing forth good works, such plum-colour & crimson in the moss roses, such heavenly scents in the damasks and the bourbons and musk-roses, and, as lovely & gratifying, such splendid new shoots coming up beneath this year's flowering wood. When I think that this is not a rose soil—no vestige of good nourishing clay in it, and far too much chalk—I am amazed at their kindness to me.

But the prettiest thing in the garden today (and now no longer in it) was the little girl who came to tea. She is an infinitely distant cousin of mine, and her grandparents and I shared a London house in the twenties, and her mother was the baby of whom Mrs Burroughs the charwoman said, 'She ain't half a saucy little cow.' The saucy little cow is now about thirty I suppose, and I found it extremely confusing, since I could not get it out of my head that the little girl eating strawberries and putting more and more lumps of sugar into her mug was also the baby I had held so often, squirming like a salmon; and made nursery curtains for her (very pretty pink and white toile de Jouy) and been a next-door mother to.

And then the household was dispersed by calamity. The saucy little cow's mother went out of her mind, my cousin Oliver locked himself in a W.C. and slashed his wrist in an attempt at suicide; and though he was rescued, and Dorothy was soi-disant cured, they never lived together again. Not long after she died of pneumonia, saying, 'Let there be no remorse', and he married again, and the saucy little cow was brought up by a kind stepmother in the country, and married herself, and went to live in Ghana with a very amiable young husband . . . and now they are home. And as we sat under the Japanese maple this afternoon, there was no trace of the old tragedy—except Dorothy's pure grey eyes looking at me out of the child's face.

And isn't it astonishing, my darling George, what quiet elderly women living in the country with their cats and their roses have to look back on? And what a lot of ghosts come sit round a tea-table on a lawn?

Some of the ghosts this afternoon were very antiquated; for Oliver & Dorothy and I had all crossed each other's paths in the 17th century. He is descended from Oliver Cromwell, Dorothy was descended from Mrs Grace

Lane who helped Charles II to escape after Worcester, and my removed great-uncle was Father John Hudleston, who confessed that monarch on his death-bed.

That is like your statistic on Mr W. Shakespeare. One has only to go a few trifling centuries back and we are all in each other's pockets and pedigrees.

TO WILLIAM MAXWELL 23:vi:1961

. . . Valentine's mother died early this month. She was in her eighty-fifth year, she had been failing for some time, it wasn't a shock. Yet it was. When people are as old as that, you accept that they will decline but you don't accept that they will go out. Valentine was the last person she recognized, the last thing that gave her pleasure, and she died like the fall of a feather.

TO GEORGE PLANK 28:vi:1961

. . . Valentine had a way of doing Tarot fortunes, with the sum of the date of the fortune-told's birth, which was blood-curdlingly accurate—accidents and changes and so forth which could not possibly have been foreseen. When we were in Madrid in 1937 (as part of a deputation) one of the entertainments supplied us was a visit to a part of the front on the Guadarramas. It was a hot siesta afternoon, except for crawling among thistles when on the sky line there was no danger in it. The fascists had plenty of ammunition, of course, so they kept up a vague sewing-machine of machine gun fire; the loyalists, having to count every bullet, were sitting in their shallow trenches, hollowed out from the hillside, and in between us was a beautiful narrow stretch of watered valley with a row of peaceful poplars beside the little water course. But the thing I remember most sharply was seeing a pack of Tarot cards, scattered on the dry earth in one of the trenches, the remains of an interrupted game, I suppose. There they were, those mysterious fateful characters, the Hermit, the Fool, the Emperor, the Hanged Man. And so many fates in the balance there, or dismissed already.

TO GEORGE PLANK 26:viii:1961

. . . It is not credible how oppressed we are by the prospect of going to Norfolk. We don't start till the 4th, there is still plenty of time for us to die in before then; but the cloud reaches out and chills us. For a grisly week we shall be finding moths in blankets, blue mould in bread-bins, mice in bookcases, cracks in china, and damp in everything. The house is exactly (except for the increment of mould, moths, mice, etc) as it was when Valentine's mother left it, two and a half years ago, saying she would be back next month. Since then, it has been in the charge of her stone deaf gardener and factotum, whose devotion will have made him keep everything exactly as she left it, including the right hand glove she dropped in the hall and the packet of sandwiches she left beside the clock . . . At the end of this—with lawyers, second-hand furniture dealers, grieving members of the Mothers' Union dropping in to impede and contend—we bury her ashes.

To Martha Bacon Ballinger[1] 23:xi:1961   *Maiden Newton Dorchester*

. . . . once, when I was a young lady and on a night express, with a whole compartment (you know our un-Pullmanned trains) to myself, and stretched out in blameless slumber, I was awakened by a man coming in from the corridor and taking hold of my leg. Perhaps he meant no ill. Perhaps he thought I was part of his luggage. I gave this no consideration at the time. Quite as much to my own astonishment as his, I uttered the most appalling growl that ever came out of a tigress. He fled, poor man, without a word: and I lay there, trembling slightly, not at my escape but at my potentialities.

To William Maxwell 3:xii:1961

Dear William,
    Swans on an Autumn River came yesterday. I am being taken by Valentine for a week's holiday in Cornwall tomorrow (a very stately and expanded birthday present), so I will take it with me, and see what a change of air will do about that ending. At the moment, I incline to the opinion that the fault lies in its insufficient weight. Operatic, you say: that set me off on this line of thought. When I was studying musical composition, on one occasion I took in an unfinished exercise in which I had left a gap of several black bars, and the man who was teaching me remarked 'those are the most promising bars you have done so far, Sylvia. They show that you have developed a sense of form.' I looked at him most carefully, but he meant

1. (1917-81), American poet and writer, daughter of Leonard Bacon.

what he said; and If I hadn't developed a sense of form before, I did then. So now I will apply this to the last page of *S. on an A. R.*, and see what comes of it.

Yesterday we learned that this house is threatened. A by-pass road will be carried through our meadow, & possibly right up against us. Not yet, but within a few years. We have yet to see the plan, but I'm afraid we're dished. Incessant noise & stink, lights all night (it will carry a great deal of the Midlands to Plymouth traffic), trees felled, and the house shaking to pieces. It's curious. When we came here, over twenty years ago, we never meant to stay: we looked on it as a convenient little pis-aller; and now, when we have grown into it, grown very fond of it, and had every intention of dying in it, we discover that we were never meant to stay. It is the trees and the garden I grieve over most, because I feel a hopeless responsibility towards them: Valentine's red willows, the aspen with its rainy voice, the balsam poplar. Trees we have planted and nursed up; and the yew trees that were here before us. But we must look for something else, & hope to sell this to someone who likes a lively outlook. Somewhere in this neighbourhood, we think, so that we can retain the practical advantages of being cherished as old inhabitants by tradespeople. A devoted grocer, a fishmonger who remembers one's taste for bass and John Dory are not lightly to be parted with.

But all this is the decisiveness of shock. My hair hasn't even lain down yet, and here I am talking of plighted grocers.

Who knows, we may find ourselves fastening on a house in Cornwall (Valentine has a passion for inspecting impossible houses, I for seeing possibilities in them). But I hope not. It would be very inconvenient, and silly too, to plant ourselves on a peninsula among Celtic Methodists who stone strangers.

To William Maxwell *13: xii: 1961*

... But, dear William, I'm afraid you will have to believe about that road; though you can come to it gradually, the bulldozers will not be in our meadow ... for some years yet. This was discovered for us while we were in Cornwall by a sympathetic neighbour who is a county councillor, and has approaches to the department that will do it. It is a large scheme, and will be done in sections, and Maiden Newton is towards the end of it. So for the moment, we are reprieved, we shall have time to look about for something we can like, we shall not be hurled incontinently into the outskirts of Bournemouth, among the conifers and the dog-breeders. Look we must, however. As Valentine says, if we wait too long we shall be too old for such sports ... When I think of the garden, the old roses that I have nursed back into a new lease of life (only last summer a nameless timeless old Methusalah rewarded me by displaying itself as a Camille de Rohan), when I ask myself, But who will feed the birds? I am in despair. But I have to admit that flashes of infidelity traverse my mind when I think that there are other fish in the sea. When you come to write your book on the English, dear William, and dedicate it to my memory, you will enjoy yourself in the exposition of our polygamous devotion, our quite genuine mandrake howls when up-rooted, our equally genuine exploration of a change of soil. So grieve for the ruined water-meadows as I do, rather than for us, since we do not sorrow as those without hope. By the way, Toller Fratrum will be untouched, you can still walk there and not grieve.

⸻ 1962 ⸺

To Martha Bacon Ballinger 23:i:1962

... I expect we shall recognise each other, we shall see that peering unrecognised look in each other's eyes. Or we could carry—too late for a rose, I'm afraid—we could carry a peach. The first time I met Nancy Cunard she walked, the picture of elegance, into the lounge of a very respectable provincial hotel holding a large Spanish onion. But that was in 1941, when onions were ingots, so all she aroused was envy and speculation as to where she could have got it.

To George Plank 30:i:1962

... Isn't it a strange thing how falls resound? There's Ady,[1] the size of a squirrel, and weighing little more, falling down five or six steps—and sounding like a roof and two ceilings. And when my mother, not much heavier, fell from top to bottom of a flight of circular stairs (in itself, no mean feat of agility) the cook rushed up from the basement and said, Oh, was it you ma'am? I thought it was the coals coming in. I am glad that when I followed my mamma's example in an inferior way, for our stairs are straightforward, I was alone in the house and so spared these invidious comparisons.

It is a thing very much to Jean Untermeyer's credit that she has not become a vampire. She has most of the requisites; misfortunes, egoism, domineeringness. But some kind of personal honour has restrained her, or her Jewish uprightness perhaps. I am afraid she is very unhappy. I am afraid she has always been more or less unhappy, though often enjoying and elated. I blame her odious Prussian mother for a great deal of it. The Prussian mother of the child of a Jewish father would have enforced self-pity on the child. And if one learns to pity oneself as a child, and poor Jean certainly had good reason to learn it, self-pity will dog one for the rest of one's life. I don't often wish to drag people out of their graves and tell them what I think of them. But I admit, I have sometimes played with the idea of doing so to Jean's mother. Airy fancies, visionary gleams! One doesn't do it, even with people still going round ungraved.

1. George Plank's sister, who lived in the United States.

To William Maxwell *23:iii:1962*

Dear William,

   Don't be sad. The burden is unevenly distributed. You have to say the story won't do—with nothing to mitigate the painfulness of saying it; except a good conscience, and we all know how much comfort that is. I had three weeks of rapture, selfish remorseless rapture such as I had thought I would never feel again. Of course I'm sorry that you don't take it, and I am sorry without any of course that you had to tell me so. But perhaps I feel a trifle like a Bacchante coming home from a night on the mountain and saying, 'Did I tear up Uncle Lysander? Oh dear, I'm so sorry.' I don't suppose it will recur.

To William Maxwell *31:iii:1962*

   . . . I hope Brendan Gill will enjoy himself in Normandy, but I can't help feeling he might enjoy himself more if he went to Saintonge or Auvergne. I did once enjoy myself very much in Normandy, that was one night when we went out for a stroll in a hot little public park and I tripped over a lump which I took to be a haycock, and subsided on it and it turned out to be a camel (resting from a circus). But don't tell him that, it's not typical. I feel that Normandy is rather ground down, partly by fighting armies, partly by fighting holiday makers. Probably the way to grow to love it would be to go through it on a barge, emptying out enamelled coffeepots and hearing dogs barking in distant farms.

   . . . my address from April 16 to 23 will be Taverna Antico Agnello. Orta S. Giulio. Novara. Yours too.[1] I believe you should bring a raincoat because of the mountains.

To William Maxwell *27:iv:1962*

   . . . I don't know why I tell you all this, since you were there too. But as I have started, I will just at least remind you of the Easter Eve ceremony; how the west doors were suddenly shoved and wrestled open by panting acolytes, and the air from the mountains rushed in, and there, in the porch, was the sharp light of the new fire, and the priest blessing the Easter candle, and peering through his spectacles at his book, and the dark silhouettes of the acolytes and the congregation clustered round, and an extraordinary

1. Since I was tied to New York City by my job, and liked travelling, we enjoyed the fiction that I travelled with them.

sense of danger and urgency and secrecy; and behind all this, at the foot of the steep hill, the lake and reflected lights and the mountains beyond. The candle was lit, and carried into the dark church (at this moment, you remember, some rash twiddling hand turned on the electric light and guiltily switched it off again); and then here was that combat à l'outrance of every one scrambling to get his candle lit as soon as possible; and when we had all sat down in our pews with our candles, a new figure dominated the scene: a sturdy lay Hercules, holding the seven foot candle, and wearing a magnificent knitted pullover new for the occasion, white, like the candle, and like the candle, decorated with birthday cake ornamentation, hoops of bright stars and roses round his splendid girth. His expression, William, complacent, reliable, sternly benevolent; and his look of mistrust and uneasiness when he had to hand the candle over to that shortsighted priest for further blessings; and finally, when he had got it back again, and fixed in its stand beside the altar, how he stood warding it, with tutelary familiarity, one arm clasped about it, and his legs in an easy posture with one standing and t'other akimbo; with all the dignity and repose of one whose duties had been rightly performed and whose trousers were faultlessly creased. I suppose he was some sort of church-warden; but he seemed to me much more likely to be a genus loci, who had affably come in to lend a hand. What was your impression?

To George Plank 20:v:1962

... We are also rather concerned about our moorhen who went mad while we were in Italy and began to build a nest in a tree. No reasoning of ours, of course, could stop her. She finished the nest, laid her eggs, in [it] and now has hatched out two small balls of black fluff. These fall out, at intervals, and have to be sat on by their protective Mum. We daren't put them back, and heaven knows how she manages to. But apparently she does, for when she isn't being a black umbrella on the path, she walks about in the tree, looking as uneasy yet persevering as a district visitor in a brothel. Her feet flap as she staggers from branch to branch, you never saw a moorhen look so silly and so disconsolate. Though they often look both, poor bodies! Did you know that trout tease moorhens? They swim up from below and bite their feet.

To William Maxwell 10:vi:1962

... I have been leading a series of double lives, rushing to bed for another assignation with another Tractarian. It began with a most astonishing change of heart towards Newman. I have always disliked Newman's Newman, the *Apologia* makes me grind my teeth. But I had the curiousity to read a new life of him, that takes him on into his career as a Roman Catholic; and his adversities were so ludicrous, and he bore them so handsomely; and the slights put upon him were so outrageous, and he took them with so much dignity and ease; and he lived among third rate minds and his own mind was enlarged by it; altogether, he turned from a trumpery little silk purse into a honest respectable pig's ear. Then I read a very dull life of J. A. Froude—but *he* wasn't dull. Then I had a wallow with Faber, whom I had previously supposed had been created for the specific purpose of annoying Newman; but there was more than that to him; a pleasing habit of referring to the Virgin Mary as Mamma—which I sparingly practise on Valentine when I think the moment is propitious; and one amazing flash of poetry; and now I am sadly happy with Clough, who with better stars and some money might have worked out as well-nourished as Goethe. And Pusey lies before me, and Keble, and Ward, What bliss. When it is all over, I shall re-read the 39 articles. Never a dull moment.

To Marchette Chute *20:vi:1962*

. . . Valentine has broken out in tortoises, and a testudodrome occupies the lawn, to keep them from eating the green peas and the strawberries. One of them, he is the original tortoise, of several years standing, has now become so expansive that he can declare his affection for her. When she steps into the testudodrome, he hurries towards her, lays one paw on her shoes, raises the other and looks up—not quite in her face, that is more than he can manage—but as far as her knee; with devotion. We have a grass-snake too, a gift from some nice naturalising children we know; at least we hope we have it, but we never see it.

To William Maxwell *31:viii:1962*

. . . I am still going to bed with Pusey. He is an old man. Every one he loved is dead, every one he attached himself to has failed him (or disagreed with him, which amounts to the same thing); all his hopes have failed, all his plans have miscarried, he has been cruelly disillusioned in Mr Gladstone; and throughout he has remained patient, polite, sweet-tempered, honourable, he has borne no malice, he has harmed no one. And suddenly he staggers into action, and spends his last energies, his last breath, in defence of—of the Athanasian Creed, dear William. There had been an impious proposal to make it non-obligatory in the Church of England liturgy.

Have you ever read this remarkable production? My father once described it as 'Hitting freely all round the wicket.' It reconciled Pusey and Mr Gladstone, however.

To George Plank 12:ix:1962

Jorge de mi alma,

We have just been doing a little rescue work by moonlight; for it suddenly turned so smitingly cold that I thought of my tender vegetables, and what the brisk smack of frost could do to them. So the cocoa beans were housed in Indian bed-spreads, and I brought in a trugful of courgettes, and both the oak leaf geraniums, and the baby myrtle and the even more baby tangerine, and things I can't get in till daylight helps are overdecked with sheets of *The Times*. And what the garden will look like tomorrow with its paperings and Indian bedspreadings to the morning postman I know not and care not. Anyhow, as he brings the letters into the hall, he already has the American Gentleman's hat to occupy his mind.

The American Gentleman, with two American ladies, turned up over a week ago, having heard of Valentine's antique shop and found their way to it. They didn't buy anything, but they were all very nice and amiable and well-beseen. And after they'd driven away, Valentine found that the gentleman had left his well-beseen hat behind him. We had to go out that afternoon, but we supposed he would come back for it, so we left it conspicuously disposed in front of the house, in shelter and on an eminence where the cats would not sleep on it . . . but when we got back, there it was. So then we supposed, since one of the ladies had taken Valentine's shop card with the telephone number, that he would ring up about it. Not a ring. And next day, not a letter, not a postcard.

So it sits in the hall, where for a few days it was a feature, and now is imperceptibly melting into the general aspect of the things we keep in the hall—including the machete I prune trees with and the chapeau de paille d'Italie I walk round the garden in when we have visitors; and I suppose it will end by being another of the things I dust from time to time.

Such a beautiful hat—I don't know how any man could forsake such [a] hat, all the more so since he had scarcely taken its virginity. It is a homburg, made of a solid, slightly furry felt (I think the term is brushed), a subtle shade of green olive on its way to becoming black olive, with a fancy Petersham band round it and a feather incident—and a lining of turquoise blue. Dunn's, Piccadilly. I long to wear it myself. It is only a trifle too large for me, and immensely becoming. But I can't persuade Valentine to agree, she says it would make me conspicuous. What else does she suppose I want a hat to do? What other purpose has a hat? But there it is, I am too kind to wear a hat that would even incidentally associate her with conspicuity; and the gentleman won't reclaim it, I despair of him now. Unless he has had a motor accident and only when consciousness returns to him will he cry out, My hat, where is my hat? And by that time they will have mislaid Valentine's card, and he will be carried onto a Jet airliner on a stretcher and never see his hat again.

If he hasn't reclaimed it before Christmas, would you like it? It is a very handsome hat.

To William Maxwell *16:ix:1962*

. . . Please explain to Mr Shawn that why the dealer entered his own name against the purchase of the mirror was just doting on my part, and nothing more recondite. We must expect these little slips to become more frequent as I approach my hundredth year.

Carpet. Certainly the carpet. If you *must* keep it—plunk, plunk—then throw all the cushions out of the window, and arrange all your glassware on the dining-table. An old-fashioned tin saucer-bath suspended from the ceiling also makes a good resonator. Probably it would be simpler to roll up the carpet and coil it in the bathroom. Unless you move the piano into the bathroom. But then you can only have cold baths, humidity muffles pianos too.

As for love, my dear William, love means little to a piano unless substantiated by deeds.

Thank you for those cuttings. I have never read any provincial reviews before. I am pleased to see that they lay stress on my moral tone. I sometimes think that I am alone in recognising what a moral writer I am. I don't myself, while I am writing; but when I read myself afterward I see my moral purpose shining out like a bad fish in a dark larder. Have you ever seen this?—the bad fish, I mean. You'd never think a mere haddock could look so elfin.

What will I do when I have killed Pusey off? I shall go on to Keble.

To George Plank *24:ix:1962*

. . . You went to your doctor about your breathlessness. You know, that seems to me the most astonishing tribute to your doctor. He must be an uncommonly amiable man if you go to him, unkicked, so to speak; readily and naturally, as one would go to the baker. I have only once had a doctor I felt like that about; and I had him so long ago, and my health was so unquenchably good, that I scarcely had a reason to go to him. He had a soft commiserating Highland voice, and a considerable bee in his Highland bonnet. The bee was gas. He was convinced that everyone in London was suffering from an undeclared gas poisoning, because the gas system, from gas-vats to the fixings of domestic cookers, was so old that it all leaked. In the end, he retired very much sooner than he needed to, and went to live in Egypt, to get away from the gas.

To William Maxwell 27:x:1962

Dear William,

I think of you so often. You might turn round in the street and see my anxious ghost looking after you. But with the look of anxiety on every face, how should you recognise mine?

There could be a great deal to say, but this seems no moment to say it—though I certainly never thought I would be tongue-tied in a letter to you. What is needed is a Mauve Fairy, to cast everyone into a sleep. Meanwhile, I suppose, every day that the surface of an every day is preserved is a day's step towards sanity, and a chance for the U.N. to speak it. I was saying this last night to Valentine, and five minutes later the ten o'clock News assured us that an invasion of Cuba was all ready to go. Now I am waiting for another such sedative draught. I think I will leave off now, before the cup comes to my lips.

O my dear William—we don't deserve it.

To Helen Thomas[1] 30:x:1962

Darling Helen,

The people who sat in darkness . . . I was listening to the programme on Sunday which the BBC broke into with the news. I went up to tell Valentine, I went up a hundred stairs and opened a door of stone. I could have yelled; but I could not speak. Seeing me look so stern—*such* thankfulness, Helen, is a stern thing—she turned pale, thinking I had come to tell her the worst.

I wish I could kiss that short-fingered peasant's hand that turned back destruction. What magnanimity, what courage, in that plain, total, unbargaining acceptance—for he must have known the mistrust and enmity of so many of those who would hear it, there must have been some cautious corner in his mind that whispered, 'Don't give yourself away.'

I still feel un-housed in myself. All through that week my heart was rent

1. (1877-1967), wife of the poet Edward Thomas, and living at that time in Bridge Cottage in the village of Eastbury, near Newbury, in Berkshire.

in a hundred bosoms; here an old woman, who in this last year has seen her middle-aged daughter suddenly blossoming in a rapture of first love; there, an enchantingly gifted little boy, who in his boundless trust and expectation of the riches and variety of our hospitality, asked me if I had a dead body in the house; there a rose; there a tree; and wherever I looked, the agonised dissembling faces of parents. And the parents of projects and works of art. Spence, thinking of Coventry Cathedral. Israel.

And all the time everything looked so beautiful in its autumn composure.

Valentine has possessed herself of your book of prayers. But I thank you for my pleasure in her pleasure. Do you remember Byron in the cemetery at Genoa (I think it was Genoa), and how the tombstone saying Implora Pace took hold of his imagination.

To William Maxwell 20:xi:1962

. . . The painters and decorators come tomorrow—to paint my walls and ceiling, to back a small wall-cupboard with a piece of tarnished looking-glass, to tear out an ugly grate that is never used. For two days I have been clearing away, and carting books, and disposing of geraniums, and in course of this I found a bundle of old Warner letters, never properly read through; and among them a letter from my great-grandfather to my grandfather, then at Cambridge, which is a match for any Pontifex. I will send you a copy. It is a blackmailing about going to the opera, 'if you insist I cannot prevent you, but at least, do not stay for the ballet'—from his affectionate and anxious . . . .

I hope my grandfather went to the opera—if he did, he certainly stayed for the ballet, which is the only thing he would have enjoyed—unless the opera had been about a cricket-match; which of course it might have been, since pre-Wagnerian operas had far more scope.

Since this letter I shall never again, even for a moment, regret selling my great-grandfather's gold watch, presented to him by his admiring congregation in Leeds when he was a flushed curate dying of consumption (he married a rich wife, moved to Torquay, and lived to a ripe old age). It was engraved: Redeem the Time; I thought it pointed to the pawnshop, but I was obstinate, and sold it.

In *The Flint Anchor* he was Mary's son Johnnie. The characters one deprives of their development can weigh on one's conscience, can't they?

Now I sit in a bared room; empty bookshelves, the table I write at, a neat grey suitcase (so full of gramophone records that it must wait for the painters to lift it); and on the stained, shabby walls, my shadow. I swear I never had a shadow in this room before.

To Martha Bacon Ballinger *11:i:1963*

. . . Life since New Year's Day has consisted of regular or irregular ceremonies: The regularity supplied by me, the irregularity by circumstances beyond my control. Sometimes the uncontrollable circumstances are very agreeable. This morning, for instance, the laundry man came shouting into the house. He has to come over a great many hills to reach us, but today was the first time he could do it since Christmas. So I can leave off wondering what I should do when I was down to the last clean sheet.

It is not that the roads are impassable. Most of them, except the kind of road the Ordnance maps call Unclassified, have been cleared of most of their snow; but underneath the snow is the ice of the frosts that came before the blizzard, and it is a very unpleasant surface; only Fools and Heroes go out on it. A strong man who came here yesterday from the next village told me he was going back across the fields. Snowdrifts, said he, at least stay where they are, they don't turn into avalanches and chase you, whereas he had twice had to leap for his life from a skidding lorry.

If it weren't for Valentine & the wind, I would even be enjoying it. The wind is from the East, fanged with all the frozen leagues it has blown across. Valentine is in bed. Ten days ago she slipped on a patch of ice, and fell bang on the doorstep. She isn't crucially broken, for she can walk and sit and stand; but the doctor says there must be a crack or a fracture somewhere, and until she can be got into Dorchester for an X-ray she must lie flat and be kept warm. I think he actually said, keep quiet. In fact, she lies in bed with her heart in her mouth whenever she hears me go out, convinced that I shall fall and break myself. For the first few days, when the thought of being the only pair of functioning legs weighed heavy on me, I was so exceedingly cautious that it is a marvel I didn't perish by it. Now I feel less apprehensive, and am that much safer.

. . . The real sufferings—the sheep freezing to death on Exmoor and the famished foxes eating at them, the hawks and the owls dying in hundreds, the marsh birds unable to break through the ice, are too appalling to write about.

To William Maxwell *27:ii:1963*

. . . I heard something so beautiful that I long for you to have heard it too.

I desperately hope you have, for I cannot see how I can manage it for you from my own resources. A Radio-Television programme from Paris of people remembering Proust: people who had known him, a little girl who had been fetched out of bed, to the fury of her English governess, dressed and sent down to the salon to meet a gentleman—with a beguiling voice— who urgently needed to meet the fledgling model for Mlle de Saint Loup; an acquaintance at Cabourg whom he questioned about all the passers by, explaining *Je suis un peu concierge*; a friend who had studied him so intimately that he could assume his voice and launch into one of his interminable entangling sentences; and at the end of all, Celeste Albaret recounting his last days and death. Twice she broke down and wept; and took courage and went on, always with the same impassioned dutiful accuracy—as though this were something too sacred to be falsified.

To Martha Bacon Ballinger 22:iii:1963

. . . I remember my mother feeling much as you do about her growing daughter. She had no son to compare me with, or no doubt she would have felt even more strongly. I certainly deserved all her disillusionment. I used to get up at 7 a.m. to play the piano, and refused to do a hand's turn about the house. I also insisted on wearing black and looking like a femme fatale; with horn-rimmed spectacles. But yours will wear through it, and come out quite as charming as you or me. Meanwhile, you must keep your heart up and in your blackest hours say to yourself that Simone de Beauvoir was worse. Or you might call to mind Mrs Bishop Moberly of Salisbury. She had twelve. Besides a Bishop. You've not had a Bishop, and I trust you never will. Not that I don't esteem and enjoy Simone de B. (as an autobiographer; her novels bore me). But her estimable, well-founded, impermeable French self-righteousness leaves her strikingly unaware of what a headache she must have been to her parents.

To Joy[1] & Marchette Chute 21:v:1963

I do apologise for writing by hand—and so badly. I shall soon be like Helen Thomas, notoriously illegible. In her last letter only two words stood out plain; 'Blood pressure'. Subsequent research demonstrated that what she had actually written was 'Beloved friends'.

1. American short story writer, sister of Marchette. Member of the English faculty of Barnard College.

To Helen Thomas *1:viii:1963*

. . . we went up on the White Horse down, and saw all the plain below as blue as a willow pattern dish, and the view of down after down, with the look of sleepwalking in the heat haze. And we walked a little way along the Ridgeway between banks of scabious and bedstraw and the little pink bindweed that smells of almonds; and talked of Edward, and agreed that his poetry is essentially the poetry of someone who walked, and came home with a poem or a thought or an image that had fastened itself in his mind as burrs had fastened themselves in his trousers or pollen lodged in his boots.

To Alyse Gregory *5:ix:1963*

. . . For I am by no means sure that Valentine is well enough for the jaunt. She is better, she is undoubtedly better; but I don't feel that she is well. She does far too much—a bad sign. People in perfect health never do all the things they ought to do: they scamp this, or forget t'other. And another thing; if one is below par, duties *grow on one*, like moulds and mildews on sickly plants. Still, I hope there will not be so many duties and obligations once we are across the Channel.

Have you read *Journey from Obscurity*, by Wilfred Owen's brother, Harold? It is a book of the utmost integrity—and horror: the account of a childhood spent in the direst respectable poverty, struggles to be clean in filthy surroundings, struggles to be well-behaved among degrading companions. It is like an accusation pressed into my heart to realise that while I was growing up in a world that seemed all promise these children, my contemporaries, were writhing up, no other word for it, in a morass of squalor and emotional destitution. Art saved him. He found he could draw, made his way into a night school, and knew at last a reason to exist.

To William Maxwell *22:ix:1963*

. . . It will be very awkward if the real Hat-leaver reads *Some Consequences*,[1] and recognises his real hat, and writes to reclaim it. Because I gave the hat away last Christmas—as a stocking, filled with trifles; and the receiver put it on experimentally, found it a perfect fit, and is I believe wearing it to this day.

1. See letter to George Plank, 12:ix:1962, p. 202. The story that accompanied this letter was published in the November 9, 1963 issue of *The New Yorker* under the title *Some Effects of a Hat*.

. . . We had a heavenly holiday, and Valentine was well the whole time, and sloughed off her conscience from the first morning in Siena, where we discovered—no one tells one these things—that the Duomo is paved with Sibyls: inlaid on black marble, with graffiti work . . . We went to Pisa, so that I could keep a long appointment of the heart with the curve of the Arno through the city. It is *perfectly* beautiful: the arc of the curve, the width of the river and its walks, the height of the houses on either side are in an ideal proportion. Like all perfections, it is profoundly melancholy. The Duomo, the Baptistry, & that tower, all white as wedding-cakes and standing on a green lawn, are like a garniture de cheminée. If gigantic glass shades descended over them, you would not be in the least surprised.

The moment we got to Rome something quite extraordinary happened. Our hotel was in the Pantheon quarter, we walked out of it and there, in a chemist's window, a very nondescript and back street chemist, was a cake of *White Rose & Cucumber* soap (see *Bathrooms Remembered*). I had not seen it since my childhood, and whenever I enquired after it I was told there was no such soap, that it was glycerine & cucumber I meant. But there it was in Rome.

We travelled from Florence to Rome in the same compartment with an elderly Canadian couple, in Europe for the first time. They were amiable —and I would have said, as unenlightened as blancmange. But the man, after staring at the rows and rows of vines, looping from tree to tree in heavy swags, exclaimed: All the trees are holding hands. Which shows what Italy does to people.

I was as good as my word. I enjoyed myself intensely and loved everyone —every native one—I met, except a rich lady in the train for Milan and the woman in the office of our hotel in Florence. She had a bony smile, and was aridly efficient, and didn't lay herself out to be loved, anyway.

I do; & send mine.

To Norah Smallwood 27:x:1963

Darling Norah,
Can the kind arms of your dining room bed enclose me for the night of November 13th—or 14th? But DON'T put yourself out in any way. I have to record exactly four minutes speaking for the B.B.C.—and by the time they have arranged all their machinery and put me through their sieve it will take some hours, no doubt.

Back from Italy—and O God how COLD it is. And how DARK.

. . . My waking moments are confused with cats and foxes. There is a pair of amatory foxes who serenade us every night; and as love always makes people hungry, we daren't let either of the cats out after dark. Quiddity is too young to defend himself, and Kit too stout. So from sundown onwards they both rage up and down the house exclaiming Liberty! Liberty!, and trying by every means in their power to wear down my resistance till the moment when I shall open the door and say, Get out, both of you! It is very mortifying for them that so far they have not succeeded. During the day, when they could go out in safety, nothing will induce them to leave the kitchen hearthrug.

To Marchette & Joy Chute *26:xii:1963*

Dearest Marchette, dearest Joy,

You must bear with a handwritten letter: I have a kitten who is learning to type. In the end no doubt he will type much better than I do, but we can't both do it at once; and his will is younger and stronger than mine. His name is Quiddity, he is four months, his eyes are like gentians, his voice is like a foghorn, he is good and intelligent and unbiddable as an angel; and Valentine gave him to me to heal the gash in my heart left by the death of my dearest and wisest Niou, who died last summer, in the midst of all our calamities and anxieties over Valentine's health. Thank heaven, she seems really better now, since our holiday in Tuscany two months ago: though I don't think she will ever be entirely well and strong.[1] Too many waters have passed over her head, that hasn't more than three grey hairs in it.

1. She wasn't; and the letters are more and more filled with accounts of her illnesses and operations.

1964

To William Maxwell *5 : iii : 1964*

To William, with my love—and no equivocation as to what William.

Her ghost[1] appeared in Peterborough, her flesh appeared in London. I don't suppose there would have been much difference to the eye. She was made of dew and silver and the filigree of autumn-worn leaves. She was as much in earnest as a child, and as instantaneously. We met at some party or other, and with no more ado she began to talk about water, its quality and behaviour, and about Shelley's assignations with it, in his life, in his poetry, in his death. As you know, she believed she was his reincarnation. Maybe she was right. He never stayed long in any one place.

To Michael Howard[2] *17 : iii : 1964*

Dear Mr Howard,

I feel profoundly honoured by your suggestion that I should undertake T. H. White's biography. Alas, we neither met nor corresponded, though since *Loved Helen*[3] I have had no doubt I admired him and thought of him congenially.

But if there is this body of material—letters and diaries and the memories of his friends—for me to draw on, the fact that I did not know him should not be too much of an obstacle. The essential in a biography, so I believe, is that the subject of the biography should have known himself; and this T. H. White certainly did. If I do the book, it will be my aim and intention to make it, as far as possible, his self-portrait.

As you see, I very much incline to the project. I would not hesitate at all if it were not for the thought that David Garnett would be a better choice. But perhaps you have already asked him?

1. Six years after Elinor Wylie's death the composer David Diamond, then a young man, saw, for a few seconds only, through the window as he was approaching his studio at the MacDowell Colony in Peterborough, New Hampshire, a red-headed woman sitting at his desk with her face buried in her hands. E.W. had occupied this same studio before him, and the help said they had often seen her in this attitude.
2. One time Chairman of Jonathan Cape Ltd; died in 1974.
3. A volume of poetry published in 1929.

To Leonard Woolf *23:v:1964*

Dear Leonard,

Sowing and *Growing* in turn launched me into a sense of dialogue. As I read, I was talking to you in my mind, breaking off to follow a train of thought, recalling something that contributed. With *Beginning Again* I felt such concern, such an anguish of unavailing sympathy, that I could only sit in silence. That is why I have not written before. I have been sitting in silence for a fortnight.

There is so much else to say about the book; and not to acknowledge this would be to slight your total purpose and achievement. But I can't say it yet. Already I am writing like a printed book, and falsifying my heart.

To Alyse Gregory *12:vi:1964*

Dearest Alyse,

Yes, I do remember, I can't fail to, since time has only strengthened the truth of it. But the words have escaped me, as they have you. Roughly, that my critical intelligence is what I most value in myself because it keeps a sort of compass-like integrity, and supplies me with interest enough (rather than courage, I think) to want to go on living. In other words, curiosity to find out *what I think* about adverse circumstances carries me through them.

I would have answered sooner but your letter came just after I had been carried off to visit Alderney. Which I liked very much, and admired for its noble savagery. I don't mean so much the savagery of its coast-line and tide races as the indifference to its picturesque. Not for a long time have I seen an untrammelled landscape. It's not even wild—just careless.

And in the middle of this is a very small, compact, plain-faced, pale-faced town, where the children have black-currant eyes, and men hail each other in English on a French intonation.

To William Maxwell [undated, probably June 1964]

. . . My room is full of the smell of roses and new cut hay and of elder blossom; and coiled up in all this like the snake in Eden, is the smell of long wet winters in Ireland; Tim White's Irish diaries, written twenty years ago and more, but still exuding a smell of damp and melancholy and a very faint smell of paraffin. I see I shall be leading two lives at once, rather as I did when I was translating *Contre Sainte-Beuve*. It is half-past ten; but somewhere just within earshot a haycutter is still traversing a meadow. The light scythes ahead and the bales of hay fall one by one into the following darkness. I have watched it, so I know. It is a far more fatalistic process than any daylight cutting, the grass and the flowers in the grass have a vividness, an intensity of life as the light seizes on them.

To William Maxwell *8:viii:1964*

. . . White has fastened on me. I get up at 6.30 and work till 8.30, drinking black coffee and from time to time eating a little more bread & honey; and it is delightful. Not a bell, not a bore, not a telephone; and a sense of virtue that keeps me in a good temper all day. There is about five hundred weight of him disposed about the house. It is like trying to write the biography of a large and animated octopus—if octopuses are those things that writhe and thrash in every direction at once. I am getting involved in the queerest correspondences. There is a correspondence still *in petto* with a gentleman 'in the Persian Gulf' as Siegfried Sassoon expresses it, whose address has to be got from a nun in a convent in Worcestershire. And beside me is a letter from the man who stage-managed *Camelot* . . . But in spite of the five hundred-weight, there are the most agonising gaps and deficits. White dementedly left a quantity of his notebooks and files in a coalshed in bleakest Yorkshire; and the celebrated winter of 47 melted through the roof. Among the lost was a long run of letters from a man called L. J. Potts, who taught him at Cambridge. Potts is dead; the few of his letters to White that have survived show that he was one of the best English letter-writers. Potts, I discovered from one of these, knew, loved, had been taught by my father. I am inconsolable.

To Helen Thomas *23:ix:1964*

Dearest Helen,

I feel such deep sympathy for you. Every loss is unique, as every blade of grass is; but as one grows old the deaths of those younger than ourselves strikes on one with a particular clang of reproach—as though one should have been able to avert it, ward it off, gather it to oneself.

And, to lose a friend of Edward's . . . O poor Helen!

This is not a letter—just a sigh. I am working very hard just now on this biography—and seem only to live on the edge of my own existence.

And by the ending of the day I feel like the story of the conscientious Victorian who said, on waking and realising all he had to do, Dear me!—and did not speak again till the evening when he realised how little of it he had done, and said, Oh dear!

To Joy & Marchette Chute *4:x:1964*

Blest Pair,

Isn't it delightful that we are all having such blissful outdoor weather? Our nights are getting a trifle shrewish, but every morning the sun comes shining through the mists and approves of stubble fields so rosy and trees so green and Sylvia's zinnias blooming as gaudily as ever and Valentine and Fougère and Kit and Pericles[1] standing about on the lawn in their dressing gowns.

I have just come back from Cambridge, which was so lovely that it still hangs in my eyes: the willows weeping so contentedly, and young persons and swans and flotillas of ducks gently pursuing each other along Cambs. I thought once again that the young English were designed by providence to use a punt-pole; it is the perfect complement to their long legs and the national habit of leaning.

Marchette, bon voyage through those Pilgrim Fathers! I hope to be there, waving a flag and offering you a glass of champagne when you emerge. It is the Pilgrim Children who rivet my imagination, staring round them on the wilderness, hearing cats mewing in trees, seeing the swaying wild animal gait of red Indians and visited every night by a profusion of Northern Lights; and dying, strangled by cold and hunger in that first winter.

There is such a story there; but nobody writes it . . .

You have each sent me pictures of my dear Ben;[2] and I am very grateful. I loved him dearly, and still see him in this garden, drinking a vin rosé and completely foxed by the phenomenon of the Parish Magazine, which he read with bewildered attention. It was an aspect of English life he had never encountered.

To William Maxwell *11:xi:1964*

. . . Your Treasury Department is not so imbued in total confusion as our Inland Reserve; but it is of the same ilk.

1. Fougère was a French poodle, Kit and Pericles were cats.
2. Ben Huebsch, who had just died.

It is a variety of *style noble*. I have been studying a variant of it through the files of T. H. White's literary agents. White, like Mr Ross,[1] felt that authors should keep their gains, so he tried to sell the serial and film rights on new books before the book was published, so that the publisher shouldn't get any unearned 25% on these extras. He felt even more strongly that authors shouldn't pay state tax on earnings which by their nature are irregular and windfallen. This led him into a series of elaborate devices for tax-diddling. When this is being planned between him, his agent, and the cover-concern, it is as harmless as any rogue's parlour; but eventually a grand firm of solicitors had to be invoked, and their letters have a sanctimony and *style noble* which would make me vomit, if I didn't first laugh like a jay. In the end, he secured his riches so safely that he seldom had any money to call his own. I long to include all this in the book—but I would have to consult a solicitor first.

I find I am writing this book from the standpoint of an Aunt.

To Joy Chute *13:xi:1964*

Dearest Joy,

Yes, I can tell you with certainty of something I would very much like from Manhattan. Wash'n'Drys—which can't be found here. Considering the noble cargo you brought over in the spring it might seem exorbitant to be demanding more; but a considerable number have been lavished on a little boy in hospital. He is a *very* nice little boy who has survived clean as a shell, from a family background of poverty and scramble, and we are so much engaged with him that we are guaranteeing his schooling at a good small school, where during term-time he will be able to escape the scramble; and have proper school clothes. His rapture in a singularly hideous mulberry coloured blazer, with a gold badge like a screech, was one of the prettiest sights I've ever seen. But between the cup and the lip he developed meningitis and is still in hospital, though mending . . . Even a dab at *in loco parentis* lets one in for a great deal of anguish, and what with supporting his mother's and our own spirits, we feel rather tarnished, just now.

1. The editor of *The New Yorker* from its beginning until his death in 1954.

To Joy and Marchette Chute [Probably January] *1965*

. . . I dreamed that Arthur & Merlin had come out of the tumulus on Bodmin
Moor, and were living in a small manly sitting-room, with a coal fire, and
the kind of furniture that goes on from generation to generation in colleges:
creaking wicker arm-chairs, sagging bookshelves, and a black velvet glove
to put the coal on with. Arthur was writing his history of Britain, Merlin
was warming his toes. As I looked on, invisible as I usually am in my dreams,
I saw Arthur pause, scratch his head and put on the expression of those who
rack their brains. And Merlin instantly supplied the reference; and went on
warming his toes and Arthur went on writing his history.

To William Maxwell *7:ii:1965*

. . . My stepfather was one of my father's dearest pupils and possibly the
stupidest. He was nearer in age to me than to my mother, and when he came
to ask me for her hand I was perfectly delighted. His relations were not
delighted, and their side of the aisle at the wedding gave an impression that
they were gathered for a funeral, since his mothers and cousins and aunts
all wore black. Mr Saunter in *Lolly Willowes* has a certain likeness to him.
He died of angina, in his forties. I have never forgotten his large hardworking
dead hands folded on the shroud—like dirty lilies. He was one of the most
entirely good people I have ever known, and I was very fond of him.

To Alyse Gregory *10:ii:1965*

. . . if there is a sexual parentage in language, then I am sure the verb *to do*
was contributed by the she-half of creation. There is a fatalism in its industry
that is entirely feminine: faire la lessive, do the beds, do the onions: even *do
him in* suggests a wifely mixture of thoroughness and inattention.

To William Maxwell 21:ii:1965

... How did you like *The Cherry Orchard?* I saw them[1] when they came to London about three years ago. It was the second act which completely bowled me over—its easy-going desolation, ending in that anguished calling of Anya! Anya! And another unforgettable thing—the way that the people on the stage are all conscious of each other all the time, even when they are not particularly attending; and when they came in, they came into the group, not on to the stage.

It is beautiful, what you say about 'the power to turn gold into dust.' I too have known one person like that—you may have known her too, for she lived in New York till after the war—called Mungo Park. Countless people tried to feed her, clothe her, support her; she remained starving, in rags, and floating a couple of feet above the ground. I have known her eat a little peanut butter. Yet when she needed a place to live in and there wasn't an unoccupied attic in London she wrote to the Duke of Westminster and got a house. It was a derelict after bombing—but it was the house she wanted. Once at 2 A. M. she rang up Scotland Yard, explained that she was having a heart attack, needed a friend, and would they please send her a policeman? They did—and he stayed till morning, making her cups of tea and telling her about his childhood.

I feel for you in your sensible decision. I can tell you for your comfort that the only house I can never be dislodged from was our lovely Frankfort Manor, where we lived for two years and then were forced to be sensible about. I can still turn its door-handles and remember where the squeak came in the passage.

To Bea Howe 10:iv:1965

... Did you know that poor Jane Welsh Carlyle brought back *a nettle* from her mother's grave and cherished it in the Cheyne Walk garden—till a hireling gardener dug it up? Fascinating, melancholy, self-tormenting creature.

To Bea Howe 23:v:1965

... I came home to hear that my dear George Plank was dead. We were bequeathed to each other, so to speak, by Anne Parrish about ten years ago,

1. The Moscow Art Theatre.

and have been writing regularly to each other ever since: about everything and anything that came into our heads. He was the most modest of men, no shred of tuft-hunting, and knew everybody (my pen has died on me) from George Moore to Ada Lewis. When he was a young man he had a romantic friendship with Vita's remarkable mamma;[1] Lutyens built his little house for him. He began as a poor boy in a coalmining village in backward Pennsylvania; taught himself to draw and design, did *Vogue* covers during the great epoch of *Vogue*, came to England, fell in love with it—and lived alone as quiet, retired and neat as a badger. But I have to be glad he is dead. His heart was beginning to give out, he was going blind, he could not have gone on being a happy badger, and life in a nursing home would have been an ignominy for such a character.

We shall lie down together in Yale University Library. He bequeathed a great many letters to them, mine among them; and some of his to me are there already, and presently I shall have to part with the rest.

To William Maxwell *18:vi:1965*

. . . Our garden is being excessively romantic. It is full of rain and wind and the smell of syringa and sweet briar and the first roses. It has two hedgehogs to fetter it to earth. They came of their own accord so perhaps they will stay.

Our letter-box tits are flown. The house seems inordinately silent without their scissor-grinding, and I miss their mother a great deal. She had grown so accustomed to me that if we were both entering our homes at the same time she would practically shove me aside.

To Paul Nordoff *22:vi:1965*

. . . We are feeling distraught and melancholy. The local farmer has sold fields for building sites; we now have three houses two stone's throws away from ours, presently there will be others. Transistors will play, children will squabble on the river bank as to who is to throw the next stone at the moorhens's nest. And ultimately there will be a bypass road on the other side of the house. Valentine is right; we shall have to move. God knows where to, and whether it won't be fire after frying pan. I would like to move to the north; but I dread leaving Valentine's admirable doctor in Dorchester, who likes her, whom she likes, and who is the only doctor who has been able to help her thyroid condition.

1. Lady Sackville-West.

But no more river, no more garden; and, as Valentine said, farewell to so many ghosts who haunt here, to so many sorrows the river has flowed past and the trees taken into their shade.

To William Maxwell *23:xi:1965*

. . . I long to hear what you feel about *White in Ireland.* You will see that it is a narrative, not a biography. He was interesting enough for a narrative but not important enough for a biography. I realised this at first with alarm, then with delight, since it allowed me to use the narrator's devices of binds: references back and intimations forward. But at the same time I have enjoyed going back to the pursuits of my youth when I edited XVI cent. music and sat in committee debating whether to follow a manuscript which dotted a semibreve or a manuscript which didn't.

This scrupulosity gave me leave to force myself on his falconry friend, J. G. Mavrogordato, who lives in Wiltshire with two menservants, a goshawk, five falcons and two eagle owls. He didn't at all want to be visited on a fine afternoon when he might have been out on Salisbury Plain flying his peregrine. But he submitted—answered two questions, and then showed me round his birds. The manservant who had flown the peregrine came back while I was being shown round, getting out of the car with the bird on his wrist. A falcon is much more becoming to a man, even now, than an automobile.

But the strangest thing was the eagle owls. There was a fierce screeching while we were in the mews, coming from a shed next door. When he said he would show us an eagle owl too, and would we please stand back a little, and opened the door of a large shed, I expected to see the bird fly out. Not at all. It walked out, slowly, stumping, its feet spotted in beige feathers down to the talons, tall ears standing up on its head, enormous round fire-coloured eyes—and was exactly like a court dwarf in Velasquez: Just about as tall, as erect, as burly, as intimidating. But the stare glowed like a furnace. He fed the furnace with a (dead) day-old chick.

To William Maxwell *14:xii:1965*

. . . It was an endearing trait of Valentine's mother's that when she heard *The Blue Danube* on the radio, she would get up from her armchair and waltz round the room with an imaginary beau. She always got up for God Save whichever it happened to be, king then I think, and stood in a noble attitude, but probably still clutching any cat who happened to be sitting on her lap at the time.

To Janet Machen *25: vi: 1966*

Darling Janet,

Hold on. This is not as bad as you think.

Valentine had a car-crash on Tuesday. She is still in bed, and can't answer letters, so she has told me to write instead.

It was a head-on collision in a narrow lane near Mappowder. She was going slowly as she had just slowed for a squirrel. The approaching car seemed to her to be coming slowly too. It came round a bend. She had hooted. She drew into the side to let it pass. The next thing she knew was a violent crash and the nose of her car imbedded in the nose of the other.

She threw herself to one side, to shield Fougère. This probably saved her sight, as her head did not strike the windscreen (unbroken still) but apparently some part of the fascia board.

She was stunned, and remembers very little except bleeding violently, and the driver of the other car walking up and down the road saying 'I've got a witness, I've got a witness' to a man. Nothing was done for Valentine till a farm-hand came up and asked her if she was all right (!). She asked him to telephone to Mr King, and to Lucy Penny, whom she was going to, and gave him the numbers. Apparently, he did neither; but had the sense to ring up for an ambulance. Meanwhile a doctor had appeared, who was also Lucy's doctor, and said he would give the message. He did nothing for her. The ambulance took *an hour* to get there. All that time she was bleeding and collapsed, and trying to keep her senses. Then she was driven to Dorchester Hospital. I got a very confused telephone from Lucy, breaking it to me so anxiously that I supposed Valentine was dead; then assured she was only suffering from shock. When I got to Dorch. Hosp. she was just being brought in from the ambulance: streaming with blood, unable to walk, with the most appalling black eye, swelled like a soufflé, and a lump on her temple.

They washed her. They gave her neither pain killer nor stimulant—not even the proverbial cup of tea. Then she was taken off for X-rays, while I conveyed poor trembling but unharmed Fougère to the friendly hairdresser. The X-ray showed a broken nose, but no skull damage. They also found a splinter imbedded in her knee. She was then—still unfed except for a biscuit I produced—taken down to Weymouth to have her nose and eyes examined. She had been assured they would keep her for a night, probably two nights. In Weymouth by the grace of heaven she found an oculist she knows, a sensible man. He peered into her eyes, and found the sight was still there, though very wobbly; and said nothing could be done till the swelling went down, and that the best place for her was *her own bed in her own home*. So Mr King & I brought her back.

She is still in bed: her nose—her lovely nose—must be left for the present. Her eyes are black and blue, but the swelling has gone down, and she can use them again. She has a continual headache from the blow on her temple, all her bones are jarred, she is covered with bruises, and her left knee is too painful to be touched. (They did *not* X-ray it. I'm afraid it may have a crack) Hollins, dear Hollins, came next day, and observed grimly 'Well, it might be worse.' Which is true: but meanwhile it is damned bad.

The front of the car is in tatters. But can be remade. The engine all right. The steering wheel broken right off. She remembers wrenching it violently to the left, trying to avoid the other car; if it broke then, the rebound might have carried the car to the right, and so into the bonnet of the other car.

The passenger in the other car was hurt. She was in hospital, being X-rayed after Valentine—so I hope it was not too bad. Now, this morning, comes a solicitor's letter from the driver of t'other car, saying they intend to proceed on grounds of negligent driving.

This, for the moment, is our tale of woe. I have written it illegibly, I'm afraid; but I now am feeling retarded shock, and all of a tremble.

It is an immense solace to be able to pour out to you.

However—she is alive, and recovering, and didn't have to stay in Dorchester Hospital; thus, as she said, escaping death twice in one day.

TO WILLIAM MAXWELL *1:viii:1966*

Dear William,

Tonight is a happy holiday from conscience. I discover I am so well advanced in poor White's decline and fall that I can take an evening out and write to say I hope you are all well home and over those first ghastly days when everything is put away one can't remember where and 200,000 letters are cascading from every piece of furniture. This is the 200,001. You can read it with a calm mind, it needs no answer.

I am living in two tenses, and very agreeably. White's late diaries are so agonisedly personal that he bequeathed them to his publisher with a proviso that they must remain in the publisher's hands. I needed to read them, and with leisure, so we have made a solemn compromise. The diaries, in a solid yellow tin trunk, c. 1890 I should say, are deposited in the Dorchester Museum:[1] and every other day or so I am let in to the Hardy room, where

1. Properly, the Dorset County Museum.

they repose, unlock the trunk, and take relays of them to the library. It is a charming library, very large, with very solid smooth tables and chairs, and singularly unvisited. A few old gentlemen or old ladies come in to read periodicals; a young woman is doing some research on such a large book that she spreads it on the floor. One day the curator had a conversation with an old gentleman in a white raincoat about a portrait of Hardy which represented him with a broken nose. It was debated as to whether or no Hardy had a broken nose. I intervened in a godlike manner, & said Sir Sydney Cockerell spoke of it as broken and that he could be trusted as a careful observer. We all decided with pleasure that S. S. C. could not be wrong. The statue of Hardy in the town by Kennington shows him with a straight nose (it is the work that Augustus John called the statue of a frustrated market-gardener (it has some bocage round the feet) and nobody likes it except visitors.

TO WILLIAM MAXWELL *11:ix:1966*

Dear William,

It is very kind of you to sit on A BRIEF OWNERSHIP and give me a chance to do better with it. Here are amplifications

1 is a new opening and joins the text on p. 1 line 3.

2 is on p. 4, and substitutes for 'Fatal words! The next moment,'.

3 is a new ending, and follows on the solitary 'No.'

And here are amplifications of another kind: the notes of Warner's Works[1] which I promised you when we were in the shed along with White's Remains. Two only, but others shall follow, when I get my head out from remaining White and Daily Living. When I am tired, as I am now, it takes me half an hour to decide whether I shall make a herb or an onion omelette, and another half hour to recognise the omelette pan which is hanging in its usual place in front of my nose . . .

Alas, Valentine's trial went against her. She had no witness, so there was nothing but her word and her record of 41 years of unfaulted driving to go against the lie of the blue-eyed farmer's daughter who was driving t'other car. The fine was small, but because she lost, her license was automatically endorsed. It was painful to be told by the cross-examining police sergeant (it was a police prosecution) that she wasn't telling the truth; he did it twice; as he couldn't trap her, it was all he could do. It is still painful to be assured by every club-footed acquaintance she meets that it was a shocking decision, and that they can't think how it went that way, and that they really feel it quite dreadfully. It was a week ago. I am still clawing the air.

1. Accounts of how she came to write *Mr Fortune's Maggot* and *The True Heart*.

Dear William,

Your letter with the gay news of *Dull see Weem* accepted came just as we were setting out; and I hope I wrote to say how pleased I was, but I fell into our holiday with such a splash of abandon that I can't remember anything before it. If I didn't write, please forgive me . . .

We went in a car ferry train by night to Newcastle, and at Newcastle the first thing that caught my eye in the station was a notice saying: Baths. Gentlemen. How can people complain that British Railways are unenterprising? Almost from leaving Newcastle we began to go uphill, and the Cheviots passed us on to the Roxburgh hills, and they to the hill of Stirling and from Stirling one sees the Grampians, and the Grampians passed us on to the Cairngorms. By then, the higher mountains had a hackle of snow on their crests.

It was at Aberfeldy that Valentine paused to buy a morning paper & I, idling in the car, noticed a signpost saying Weem. So when she came back I said firmly our route was down that narrow road: and in a flash we had crossed the Tay on a bridge trimmed with obelisks and succeeded by an avenue of Lombardy poplars, and there was Weem. It is an amiable little place with a charmingly ornate ruined chapel in the best 15th cent. gimcrack manner, and a plainheaded hotel called The WEEM HOTEL; and from there, naturally we went on to see Dull. Dull is negligible; a scrabble of cottages and one large farm, all higgledy-piggledy as if spilt out of a basket. So we spent no time in Dull but drove up a long curly hill and came out on a moor with several small lakes on it and a view of the real Highlands beyond. It was one of the pleasures of our holiday that we were constantly driving long and steeply uphill and finding small lakes at the top. Gravity is powerless against granite. The lakes have got there and there they must stay, and this is very composing to the mind.

Yes, we went by the Drummochter Pass, and the Drummochter Pass is very fine indeed, miles and miles and miles of it, in a completely taciturn landscape. And when at last the road descends, and you come to a village and a butcher's van is drawn up in front of the Post-office and a dog is galloping off with a bone you look at it as if you had come back from the dead.

For the first time in my life I have realised Macbeth. So now I am left to ask myself how the Swan knew: for I think it improbable that he got to Sutherland, and equally improbable that he should have heard about it from an inhabitant; for one thing, the inhabitant wouldn't have got to Shakespeare & for another he would have been talking in Gaelic. Just his luck, I suppose. But it is very odd, because Macbeth is localised, every scene of it; and none of the others are, except when they get to London or back to the Cotswolds: just a general Illyria.

I got so well there, so cleaned and shaken-out and renewed that I have come back in a state of dreamlike incompetence. So, by dint of me driving her to bed at 9 p.m. every night and being in a technical rapture at driving on single-track roads along precipices, did Valentine. But I'm afraid she is not so well insured against duty. I hear her doing up a parcel at this moment, alas!

To William Maxwell *20:x:1966*

... DULL see WEEM.

This is awful. I supposed all was now clear, that my additions and your inspired sentence about 'Dull—as I seemed to know as if I had actually been there' had established that my Dull owed no allegiance to the gazetteer's Dull, and was entirely my own invention; and my stay there a brief idyll with a seaside resort in Bohemia, a castle in Spain, a Dull that never was.

Sit down, William. Lay a wet handkerchief across your forehead. Clear your mind of fact. Read Gal. 4. Is it not plain and manifest that there is an actual Dull (in Perthshire, 70 miles from the sea, etc.). And that having negligently learned this from the Gazetteer I had to submit to geography and leave the Dull I had conjured up from a name on a page and supplied with that idealistic dumb gardener?

I don't know how to make all this any clearer. I can't go on adding more explanatory postscript sentences like Mrs Finch writing about an arrival by train. Je sois au bout de mon Latin—at any rate for the moment.

1967

To William Maxwell 2:v:1967

... Did I tell you ... that I have been invited to become a Fellow of the Royal Society of Literature? I suppose they go by alphabetical order. It is the first public acknowledgement I have received since I was expelled from my Kindergarten for being a disruptive influence.

To William Maxwell 5:v:1967

Dear William,

What a present to make me on the 1ᵉʳ Mai. 'Prematurely anti-Fascist.' ... It soars above all other mortal distinctions. Oh, the inexhaustible solemn fatuity of the official mind. Stamped, too, not just endorsed. They had a stamp for it. Spanish Medical aid was /36 or /37. For at least four years you were a Communist Sympathiser, if not worse. Then, aliter visum, they saw it was just a youthful error: wrong, but rescindable. Prematurely anti-Fascist. Not in step with us, but we will overlook that. Thank God you told me. I might have died in the night and never known.

To Alyse Gregory 9:v:1967

... A young man—perhaps not even young: to me all creatures are classifiable as young—called Pouillard wrote to me a little while ago to say he is making a study of T. F. Powys, and can I tell him, etc, etc. ....

... On the whole M. Pouillard's questions are sensible—so far. Except that he enquires if I would call T. F. P. a mystic. Would I? Would you? I never feel at all sure as to what I would call a mystic; and my approach to the word is conditioned slightly by the remembrance of my father's habit of remarking: Il y a de la mystique là-dedans; a pejorative, whether it was applied to religious statements or patent corkscrews.

Dear William,

You say everything my heart wished you to say—and one thing which illuminates a motive I had in writing the book[1] though I had not formulated it to myself: of course you are right. He was an animal: 'one of them.' I must have admitted this subconsciously, else why should I have felt such particular *consent* to the passage about trying on the gasmask?[2] I can remember feeling that here, at any rate, was something I needn't reconsider.

One has a dozen motives, hasn't one? I did partly undertake it as a dare; seventy is rather an advanced age to begin an entirely different technique. Partly as a rescue operation; because his literary agent was doing all he could to persuade the trustee-executors to give the job to a very inferior flashy protégé of his and Michael Howard and John Verney & Harry Griffiths[3] were frantic to avert this. Partly because I wanted to do something that would take a long time and involve some sort of research (a Bestiary, in fact). But from the day I went to Alderney I knew I was to do it because it was a human obligation. He had been dead less than four months. His suitcases were at the foot of the stairs, as though he had just come back. The grander furniture had gone to the sale room, but the part of the house he mainly inhabited he still inhabited. His clothes were on hangers. His sewing basket with an unfinished hawk-hood; his litter of fishing-flies, his books, his *awful* ornaments presented by his hoi polloi friends, his vulgar toys bought at the Cherbourg Fairs, his neat rows of books about flagellation—everything was there, defenceless as a corpse. And so was he; morose, suspicious, intensely watchful and determined to despair. I have never felt such an *imminent* haunt. I said I would like to stay on and poke in the books; and Pat[4] & Michael Howard and kind Harry tactfully left me. I poked in the books—and immediately found an unposted letter to David Garnett & took charge of it. I sniffed at the coats, took one down, was almost felled by its weight and massiveness. I looked out of the windows at his views. I had been left so tactfully that no one had shown me where the light switches were. And when I left, it was dark and I had to grope my way in darkness down two flights of twisting stairs and out by a back door. It was all I could do, to lock that door, to lock up that haunt and go off swinging the iron key. I went back to the hotel and drank a brandy and told Michael I expected I'd do the book.

If this were a ghost story I could tell you that when I was there, alone,

1. *T. H. White.*
2. See *T. H. White*, pp. 108-9.
3. Friends of White.
4. Michael Howard's wife.

the next evening, it felt quite different. It didn't. It was unchanged. The only difference was in me. I felt more at home in it.

Even so, it was like feeling at home in hell when last summer I read through those diaries he bequeathed to Michael. Michael was tied by the bequest not to let them out of his keeping; but we compromised by a transfer to the keeping of the Dorchester Museum. They were lodged there, locked in a yellow tin trunk which in turn was locked in the Hardy Room. To the reverent delight of the Museum's janitor I used to have the Hardy Room unlocked, and unlock the yellow tin trunk, and carry off one volume at a time and sit reading it in the Museum's Library. I can't tell you how eldrich it was to sit in that calm Victorian saloon, with perhaps two or three local ladies gently gossiping in a corner or a regular visitor puffing at *The Times*, with White's raving, despairing soliloquy whispering on and on in my ear. It was that I ran into at 3 Connaught Square,[1] and locked up in the empty house.

To Martha Bacon Ballinger 26:viii:1967

Dearest Marnie,

Your mother was real to me because of two loves—your father's and yours. This, and the grey cloak, and a letter from her after your father's death about letters of his, are the indications: enough to make me be sorry for you and glad for her. A long decline brings a feeling of constraint; almost like farewelling some one who has got into a train and the train doesn't start. Everything is packed, settled, said: when the train begins to move and the face looking out of the window glides past one there is a sense of relief because something that seemed to have gone wrong has gone right. And with drugs and sedatives, even when one is thankful for them, there is always this gnaw of mistrust: will they hold out, how much longer can one rely on them? In this sense, I am glad for you too. Your part in her dying is over, you step back into life.

And then comes this 'Who is to have the soup-tureen?' The solemnest of industries, forsooth . . .

When my mother died I inherited a house I didn't like, yet esteemed enough to have a certain piety about selling it to someone who would make hay of it—the more so, since her ashes were buried in the garden. Then I discovered that two middle-aged school teachers, who had caravanned in its paddock for holidays, longed for it as for something unobtainable and a fairy-story. So I sold it to them, so cheap that my lawyer co-executor could not speak for fury: and have been happy ever after, flying home on my broomstick.

1. White's three-storied house in the town of St Anne, Alderney.

I am glad that the soup-tureen settlement is happening in a house in its senses. Valentine's mother, constitutionally unable to throw anything away, spent the last two years of her life staying with a niece in Sussex, while her house in Norfolk mouldered under the care of a gardener and factotum . . . When we went there to clear the house before selling it . . . we found waste-paper baskets still over-flowing, her coffee-cup still unwashed, her departing flurries of packing strewn everywhere. Over all this he had cast a last-minute tribute of D.D.T. It took us a fortnight of choking and cursing to do away with the moths and the rust and the maggots. But once a light surprised. I had got as far as the spareroom, and in the spareroom had made my way into the cupboard of a Victorian washstand. There I surprised a fox stole, complete with head, tail, maggots, etc, coiled inside a chamberpot. Beneath it was a miscellany of papers about the local Mothers' Union, and at the bottom was a framed photograph (glass broken, of course) of three nuns having tea in a garden.

. . . Our summer has been exceptionally fine and serene: and I have constantly felt a traitor: traitor to the roses when I listened to the news, traitor to the news when I looked at the roses. An American friend of ours who spent a day here on her way to Sweden said that the race riots were part of Viet Nam because the negroes consider that they have a disproportionate amount of military service and casualties and anyway are fighting a white man's war. Is she right? Or is it just another example of that fatal law of gravity: if you are down, everything falls on you. Race problem is building up here, too; fast in the industrial Midlands; and will be worse with the winter un-employment. The new unemployed will have no idea of what unemployment was like in the thirties: that is just the trouble. They will have no idea. Meanwhile the Opposition sits and smiles like the Indian Ocean and bets on the day when they will come back, and capital will flow out of pockets again (back into them, naturally, too) and the nation will be expected to thank God for their return to office.

To William Maxwell 12:ix:1967

. . . We go to Scotland on Monday: and by train to Newcastle if there isn't a railway strike by then. The car travels with us, rattling in a bleak conveyor while we loll in our sleeper. I am so tired, I am determined to do the thing in style. Last week I was blissfully tired after taking up a great deal of the garden. Now it is an indoor tiredness, and not blissful at all. Our usual dear caretaker has to go off to a sick mother and her substitute doesn't know the house and has a high standard of neatness in her own. So I have to write directions as to where everything is and then remember to put everything there, and sweep and polish much more than I care to. And bring in the geraniums and give them new pots. And send back the London Library books. And remove tea from the tin called Sugar (Valentine's personal arrangement) and put sugar instead. And . . . And . . . And. How I hate a house where everything is in order. It is so lifeless, so Almanach de Gotha.

To WILLIAM MAXWELL *14:ix:1967*

. . . There is a sort of half-baked railway strike going on, and I may have to revise my boast to you about taking the car northwards by train. The sensible thing to do, of course, would be to go a lesser distance. But we both feel we want quantities of sea air and salt water, and on this island one has to go a long way to get these in their native prime condition—and Valentine is intolerant of anything other. Ships and waves and ceaseless motion And men rejoicing on the shore did nicely for Coleridge, but men rejoicing have no charm for her. So it must be ultima Thule. How enchanting Coleridge is from the moment one gives up expecting to admire him! ON REVISITING THE SEA-SHORE AFTER LONG ABSENCE UNDER STRONG MEDICAL RECOMMENDATION NOT TO BATHE. Do you remember the third stanza of that, with its dazzling last line?[1] A friend of mine, much under his influence, once spoke of his birthplace as Mary St Ottery. When I hear good men who have never known a moment's emancipation in their lives saying how dreadful it is that the young smoke marihuana and take LSD I think of Coleridge and say nothing.

Valentine has now come back from the garage. New brake-pads had to be fitted to the car. They grunt implacably, nothing Mr King can do will stop them grunting. She can and will not drive to Scotland, she can and will not drive to Dorchester even, in a car that disgraces her by grunting like a pigstye. So there we are! Voyez le prochain numéro.

To WILLIAM MAXWELL *31:x:1967*

. . . At the moment I have five different calamities all needing support and counsel from me: a hysterectomy with where-to-put-the-dog trouble, two nervous breakdowns, a runaway wife and a funeral which will inevitably

1. 'Fashion's pining sons and daughters,
    That seek the crowd they seem to fly,
 Trembling they approach thy waters;
    And what cares Nature, if they die?'

be involved in the flood which now rises round us. The grave will be full of water, the coffin will bob on top of it unless some large stones are lashed on: but this must be left to the undertaker, I can foresee but not manage, beyond putting up a mourner or two and supplying sandwich fillings. And I hope I may have solved the dog. On the whole, the runaway wife is shaping best. She is a member of one of England's most stiff-necked high-minded and priggish families and the object of her middle-aged passion is a flimsy mauvais sujet. They are very happy, and I hope their incompatibilities will hold them together. This hope is sincerely felt by her injured husband. It is he who is getting my support and counsel and I have just assured him that he will soon feel very happy with the divorce he has served seven years for, like Jacob the Patriarch. But I *do* wish I could have her account too. Unfortunately we have little in common except a mutual knowledge of a story by Charlotte Yonge in which the hero is an albino curate with eyes like rubies: this is cordial, but not enough.

To George Painter *19:xii:1967*

Dear George,

Your letter[1] has given me infinite pleasure. You know how profoundly I admire your Proust, you must have guessed how I had your example before my eyes as I wrote my White—though the *tone* had to be totally different; for White was a single talent inattentively employed; I could not pretend he had a purpose or a star to steer by. I had to keep my head and a little to lose my heart. Choses de métier . . . Dear George, it is such a satisfaction to be able to discuss these distinctions of difficulty and know one is understood. And strictly between ourselves, out of earshot of all critics,

1. George Painter to STW: 'What a man! I had no idea. You have seen him as he might have seen himself in a moment of lucidity & self-forgiveness. Apparently the good Lord agrees with the value we set upon talent, since He exacted for his the price of such anguish. I have read your book very slowly for a month & feel as if I had lived another life & then died—it knocked me for six & will stay with me like an implanted second conscience. As a biography which is an imperishable work of art it stands with *Queen Victoria* or *Orlando* or Dr Johnson's *Savage* or the best *Lives of the Poets*, but it seems to me unique in its unerring moral sense. That is where it struck me deepest. What a *chose du métier!*—what courage—for only an *âme bien née* would notice its absence, if you had been content with truth, life, understanding & style, & yet without its presence everywhere a biography is hollow.

   It is the most difficult thing of all to weigh every action & feeling of a writer's soul, imperceptibly & accurately, & it is the most important. You have accomplished it . . .'

230

all clerics, we can agree that moral sense is the THING. And how sternly one must apply it to oneself as one works, examining one's own motives, merits, failings as much as one examines those of one's subjects. And then to fill the sentence in the right direction, to fill a form, not merely pages, to know when to press the tempo, when to relax it . . .

Your letter must have preceded you into my dreams, for last night I was in Paris in /92 and witnessed something I had never suspected: the excitement of a market flooded with the possessions of the rich. Not jewels or precious metals: the Republic had held on to these. But personal and cultural possessions, books, little boxes, china figures, dressing-table toys, silver saucepans, luxury articles. They were all for sale, the salesrooms overflowed into the streets and buyers of the metropolitan bourgeoisie, with the blood already rising round their ankles, and bread already in short supply, were handling, comparing, buying, thieving, running to and fro with stories of even better auctions in the next street, all with the greed of the peasant and the knowingness of the Parisian. Darting through these scenes like a hornet was a most horrible figure: an old lady, thin as death, elegant, dressed in the clothes of a proscribed modishness, her hair powdered, her bodice long and tightlaced, diamonds in her ears and on her bare neck. And with her fan she rapped on the back of any handsome young man who had taken her nymphomaniac fancy, and willy-nilly he went off with her. For everyone believed she was the mistress of someone influential, so that if you did not comply with her, the guillotine would get you.

Now isn't that a strange dream? It seems absolutely authentic to me because, as when I saw Chateaubriand & Lucille,[1] I had no art in or part in it, was a depersonalised witness. But as it preceded your letter's arrival, obviously you must have art and part in it, so I recount it to show it was duly received. And you know how well I wish you through the woods of Combourg and all the subsequent woods, forests primaeval, bosquets . . . Oh, I must live long enough to read this book.

1. Another dream.

1968

To Janet Machen *5:iii:1968*

My darling Janet,

I will write now, since tomorrow Valentine goes to see a surgeon about her breast. I didn't want to write before—we have known this since last week—because ill news when it is muffled in such uncertainties is not a thing to impart. Yet not to write at all would be to slight your love and faithfulness.

Last week the pain in her breast changed its character & became worse & darting, more like a neuralgia. Hollins says this kind of pain could be caused by pressure on a nerve, and that he feels that he must have a second opinion. He is still not at all convinced that it is cancer—only that it could be. I imagine the next thing may be an exploratory operation. I will let you know as soon as we know ourselves.

It is strange to go on living as usual yet with these earthquake shocks through one's foundations. She swears she is not perturbed. I believe this is true. For myself, I have no courage whatever, merely a queer sense of habit, and beneath habit, unreality.

Two operations, Janet; that Brompton Hospital fortnight; & the car accident, all within the last eight years.

To Marchette & Joy Chute *15:iii:1968*

. . . So here we are, neither coming nor going, and with that strange feeling of desertion which misfortune always brings—though friends are being very kind & some of them positively helpful. Valentine is composed & courageous. I can be neither; merely a copy cat. My imagination spends all its time in walking up to the brink, then shutting its eyes & being sick. I haul it back, shut it up in some practical occupation: then it escapes me & *da capo*. No words can convey my resentment that none of these calamities ever fall on me but always on her.

To Janet Machen *21:iii:1968*

My darling Janet,

It is cancer. On Tuesday she saw the breast expert at Guys. He is called

Sir Hedley Atkins, very well reported on by other similar patients. She liked him. He will do the operation himself on April 2nd; and she will be in the Nuffield Ward of Guys. He says the cancer is very conveniently sited & thinks it can be removed without involving the lymphatic glands in the armpit, so that there should be little or no swelling afterwards. He took a calm & cheerful view; no false hilarity or slap-you-on-the back, but re-assuring as to the results.

We spent a night at Farnham, on our way. During the night I added to the joy of nations by being violently sick & developing a temperature. So my plan of going with her fell to bits. Fortunately the kind and sensible Peg Manisty—cousin—turned up instead.

Practical people incline to say what a good plan I was ill since it was a distraction. It was a bit too much of a distraction, as later I went on to 103 & *raved*. But quite affably. And then by yesterday I was normal & we came back. I have never felt so *drenched* in ignominy.

I have a great many letters to write, this is the first.

To Marchette & Joy Chute *15: iv: 1968*   *c/o Miss Manisty.*
                                            Morleys. Mayfield.
                                            Sussex.

My dear darlings,

Valentine had her operation on the 10th & came through the anaesthetic well—*much* better than she usually does. She is still strapped round as tight as a leaky pipe, which *is* uncomfortable; but the house doctor & the nurses say she is going on nicely now, though she gave them a small alarm by running a temperature & looking as if she might be in for pneumonia. All that is at an end. Her temperature has been steady for two days and she no longer has to clasp an inhalation bottle in her arms and breathe up some modern equivalent of Friar's Balsam through gauze wrappings. Sir Hedley, who is her surgeon, sees her tomorrow when the wrappings & dressings come away. She is much easier, can get in and out of bed & walk to the loo looking like Charles 1st going to execution.

As for Mr Guy, my dear Marchette, I won't hear a word against him. His hospital is more like a college or a cathedral close: so quiet that one can hear every hoot from the boats on the river . . . It appears to be a custom of the house that everyone is gentle & leisurely. There are two fine Cockney cats and T. Guy's statue by Bacon has 32 marble buttons & an epitaph saying that after he had 'generously administered to the claims of consanguinity he founded this asylum'. Really an asylum: for down & outs, the destitute old & lunatics. The inmates have gone but the intention seems to have remained, for it is a quite remarkably merciful & unstarched institution.

Darling Joy,

I can scarcely believe the address as I write it. We are home! Only for a month, but home. Valentine's radiologist, who has been treating her with extreme caution because her skin is so fine, gave her a month's holiday before he finishes with her. We were in Sussex for a fortnight after she left Guys, we go back there in June. Strange semi-suburban landscape, yet in some ways more rural than here. For instance, a nightingale sang to us in the evenings. It is a wooded landscape, scarcely be-bungalowed at all. Going up & down to London daily, I watched the woods greening, the stitchwort and the milkmaids coming into bloom, then the first bluebells and the misty bird-cherries before London encompassed ;& had the strangest impression that the few rows of old two storied houses with curly chimney-stacks remaining among the tall trim post-war buildings were a sort of oppressed *fauna*: akin to badgers & foxes.

To William Maxwell *29:vii:1968*

Dear William,

This is still grapevine and must not be mentioned; but I must tell you at once as it will please you. I heard this morning that *A Love Match*[1] will be awarded the Katherine Mansfield Menton prize for 1968. I look on this as a triumph for incest and sanity.

A house smelling of turf and geraniums in a sea-girt bower almost sends me straight off to Miss Fitzgerald, and the map you so kindly enclosed transports me, just to look at it. We shall certainly go there before long. But not I'm afraid just yet. Valentine isn't yet in a state to enjoy intense enjoyment. We shall begin with the more moderate excitements of Wales, and keep a cushion of hotel staff between us and the realities of wild life.

Edward Ardizzone[2] & I met at a wedding last week. With champagne glasses in our hands and our best clothes girded about our loins we stared at each other with ashen faces as we recalled what we had severally endured at Healion's Hotel, Belmullet. At the end of three days of tea, stale baker's bread, metallic bacon and hard-fried eggs at every unremitting meal, I went out and ate grass. It was a wonderful wedding, high & low. It began

1. A short story included in the collection that was printed in England under the title of *A Stranger with a Bag* and in the United States under the title of *Swans on an Autumn River*. The lovers in question were siblings.
2. Writer and illustrator of books for children.

with the March from *Figaro*, played by the bridegroom's band of personal friends on wind instruments. The operation was done by a bishop from Australia, wearing a light summer cape, and the Dean of Windsor, who had the Blessing smitten from his mouth by a resonant amen from the band which he hadn't expected. Susannah Wesley, the family donkey, tied up in blue satin bows, came on as a dessert for the village children to go rides on. The bridegroom and his bevy of best men were dressed by Carnaby Street. The bride looked like a swan in a morning mist. I wore my hat. Valentine enjoyed it all very much and looked like the Empress Theodora. We are both much the better for it. Oh yes, and a detail I musn't forget. The long tables under the awning were trimmed with vases of peacock feathers, gently twiddling in the light breeze. (Sacred to Juno, patroness of marriage.)

To WILLIAM MAXWELL *14:xii:1968*

Dear William,

Unless the customs have been there before you, if you look between the spine and the spine's cover of *The Corner that Held Them* you will find a packet of Mr Unwin's Old Fashioned Sweet-Pea seeds: also, no doubt, some spores of anthrax, broomrape, rabies and Communism.

I recommend a good layer of damp—or dampened—moss-peat—in the trench where you sow them. If they germinate in a moist soil they will stand a hot summer better.

My address till over the New Year will be The GORING HOTEL, EBURY ST. S.W. 1. This is because Valentine has to have a further operation and will be at Guy's Hospital once more. I looked queerly at Waterloo where I had met you so gaily and where we had departed in September with a report of All Clear.

To JOY & MARCHETTE CHUTE *24:xii:1968*   *Goring Hotel.*
                                                  London.
                                                  S.W.1.

Dearest Both,

I have not written to thank you for the Christmas parcel. It arrived after we had left home. I did not want to overcast your Christmas, so I did not tell you why we had to come to London. On the 11th Valentine saw her surgeon about a pain near the old wound. He found another cancer.

So on the 19th he did a further operation, and this time took away all her left breast. She is slowly recovering—very steadfastly, very barely; but this second operation so soon after the first has been extremely taxing, and discouraging.

She has a room to herself at Nuffield House (Guy's Hospital S.E.1) and a balcony and two pigeons who sidle along the rail waiting to be fed and a bevy of London sparrows; and a kind sister and a sweet dutiful young nurse. And I go there every morning and stay till sundown; sometimes talking, sometimes just eying, and grunting. I am staying at this kind stately old hotel where the staff are like old family servants and where my young Italian waiter murmurs whenever he meets me, 'very kind-a'—by which he means not that he is kind to me or I to him, but expresses the kind relationship between us.

I seem to use this word 'kind' very frequently. When one is unhappy or anxious it is a quality one dwells on.

We don't know yet how long it will be before we go home. There can be no X-ray therapy this time—too soon after the last go. But they will keep her for another ten days at least, because of the dressings needing skilled care and also because they have designs of recruiting her strength with a blood transfusion.

TO WILLIAM MAXWELL *6:i:1969*   *The Goring Hotel.*

. . . I am only now beginning to admit how uncomfortably I have gone to my nice hotel bed & how bereftly I have lain awake in it. Though lying awake in London is a greatly entertaining renewal of my youth, and I have taken myself for many imaginary walks through streets & squares, looked in on my grandmother,[1] leant my elbows on the parapet of the embankment overlooking Chelsea Reach, remembered what would have seemed totally irrecoverable things: even my hats of the period.

TO WILLIAM MAXWELL *15:i:1969*   *Maiden Newton.*
                                    Dorchester.

. . . As for the further future, I don't intend to look at it till I have to; but the immediate future has brightened since we took the risk of the journey and came home. It is the libertine disorder & fallibility of one's own den after the correctitude of hotel & hospital which is so healing: the clock which is always a trifle late, the armchair heaped with books, the summer hat which hangs through all seasons just above the hatchet on the hall-chair, the cracks and creaks, the patches, the rivets.

C'est l'amitié qui règne entre cette pelote et le vieux chien . . . Do you remember that paragraph towards the end of Proust's CHARDIN—and which, I may remark, I translated so sympathetically[2]—about the bonds of friendship between rather shabby household objects?

TO ELLING AANESTAD[3] *23:i:1969*

. . . I read Holroyd[4] last year, with a general sensation that I was a fly reading

1. 'My darling grandmother ended her days in London—to the point of being killed by a poor taxi in Sloane Square. She said it was infinitely the best thing to do. (London: but she was all for sudden death, too.)' STW to Beatrice Howe, 15:xi:1968.
2. *By Way of Sainte-Beuve*, Chatto & Windus edition, p. 249.
3. At the time of his first meeting with STW, on shipboard, he was an editor with the American publishing firm of W. W. Norton and Company. When these letters were written he had retired and was living in Maine.
4. *Lytton Strachey* (1967-8), by Michael Holroyd.

treacle, but sustained by private amusement. For those soul-wracked characters, dear Elling, those tormented spirits, were by no means so tormented as Our Holroyd assumes. Most of the time they were delighting in their lot, drawing much natural amusement from the misfortunes of others and knowing themselves to be superior & sought-after beings—besides, in the intervals, distinguishing themselves by writing and painting rather well. And if bored, they had another reviving quarrel, or went to the Continent.

To Joy Finzi 5:ii:1969

Darling Joy—Not Catholic, Presbyterian, Quaker, Buddhist or agnostic —just an observer. What a *convincing* faith, though taxing. When I consider my own faith I can match it to nothing but seaweed with one end in sea & t'other fastened to sea's rock. The sea's moods shape its being. There it floats, twists, swirls, entangles, disentangles, rooted to a sea's rock identity.

To William Maxwell 6:ii:1969

. . . Another thing which made me badly wish for you was the big Constable canvas in the Burlington House exhibition. In the middle distance is Waterloo Bridge, being opened, with some puffs of cannon-smoke; and the river is alive with boats and barges decked with pennons and trappings, and as it is a choppy day the surface of the water is sending off darts of light. It raised me from the dead just to look at it. It is as though Constable had taken a long steady appraising stare at Canaletto and then charged straight through him. And that is not all. The owner of this glory is anonymous in the catalogue. There he sits, somewhere in the Midlands, I daresay, keeping his treasure to himself. Un vrai Milord. I wonder what else he has.

To William Maxwell 7:ii:1969

. . . Valentine now tears round the country: she can drive as well as ever, the same swallow-flights. Her brio is unchanged; but she has not the same reserves as she had and tires easily. This is inevitable: and when I can sit on her head and make her rest she does pretty well.

Today the weather is doing it for me. The northern blizzard has pounced down on us. It began like the Comédie Française with three blows, and snow whirling past, blown too hard to settle—snow like a swarm of bees. The wind sounds as if the air were on fire.

To Arnold Rattenbury[1] *14:ii:1969*

Dear Arnold,

You know any mention of Nancy dives into my heart. This is the cold time of year when she often visited us, keeping her ears warm under that leopard-skin bonnet, with her eyes whetted to a sharper aquamarine and her heron-legs strutting on the ice. Down she would sit in front of the fire, pull out a silk handkerchief & begin polishing her bangles. She had a cat's cleanliness—ardent, scrupulous & practical.

I despair of everything contemporary except the young. I think they are all right. I wish their nerves were in better condition, that's all . . . But as they face worse dangers than our lot did, maybe they are strong to the true pitch. And they are so persistently deplored by tradespeople and fogey foxhunters and arouse even fury in cold hearts, I think they must be all right.

To Joy Finzi *8:viii:1969*

. . . This miraculous summer still embraces us: the river flows gently and the moorhens converse and the enormous trout rise like explosions; we have never had such roses and the raspberries went on and on like Schubert and the figs are ripening. We have not slighted it, but we have been held back from it. Valentine's stiffened shoulder (now slightly unstiffening) was incessantly painful, made it almost impossible for her to type and very hard to drive. We were felled, one after the other, by a detestable local virus infection, like an influenza that wouldn't let go and behaved much as if it were whooping-cough. And though she got an All Clear from Hedley Atkins when she went to him in May, her last visit was not so satisfactory. There are signs that there is a spread to the lungs. He has put her on a course of hormone pills which, he says, will *contain* any further developments and eventually make her feel stronger; but so far they have only made her feel dead tired and nauseated and mentally depressed. I don't despair; it is too soon to tell, and I have just heard from a friend that the same treatment raised Enid Starkie from among the dead. But no two physiques could be more dissimilar than Valentine's and Enid Starkie's. I think the virus infection has a good deal to do with the lassitude and depression, since I feel stupefied with fatigue myself.

1. Poet, exhibition designer, editor (*Our Time, Theatre Today*).

Dear Elling,

You incline to hermitry. I will tell you about a visit to a hermit in this part of the world.

The hermit is a Dr Charles Smith, aged ninety, maybe a little over. He was married once, has a daughter & grandchildren. For the last twenty years he has lived as a solitary.

Knowing that Valentine was ill, he decided that the wisest course for her would be to learn Greek. So he arrived on the doorstep with a lexicon, a primer and a copy of the Greek Testament and gave her a first lesson. Whether Greek is really sanative or whether it was the spice of unexpectedness I don't know; but a week later she was well enough to drive ten or twelve miles for the return visit.

He lives on the fringe of Hardy's *Egdon Heath*, still in parts (though the Winfrith Atomic Station sprawls over many acres of it) as near as anything in the island to the landscape of before history: a sandy waste, traversed by countless vague ditches; tufted with osiers, buckthorn, gnarled squat hawthorns in thickets; here & there an ash tree or a later pinetree; and heather and bracken and alas! the inevitable rhodendendron spread from landowners' plantations further away. It is a fine place for rare plants, such as asphodel & bog-myrtle. Fern-owls nest there, and larks. The thickets are laced with honeysuckle.

A rough road crosses it & Dr Smith's hermitage stands back from the road, with a footpath leading to it. There is a neat dustbin at the junction of the footpath; otherwise, no sign of a habitation further on. The habitation is wood-built. The traditional pattern called 'two up and two down'. A parlour, a kitchen, two bedrooms. There is also a lobby, in which he keeps a great number of books and a fair number of boots.

We sat in his parlour & while he and Valentine were talking I inventoried its contents. A fireplace, laid with wood and fir cones. In front of it, a kettle for one on a butane gas-heater. A range of bookshelves from floor to ceiling. A table with a vase of wild flowers on it. Three chairs. A small wooden cupboard. A mat on the floor. Nothing else, except a portrait (of himself) above the hearth & a photograph of his daughter as a fat little girl.

I have never seen such a luxurious sparsity.

In the cupboard was a wine glass & a bottle of burgundy. He took these out, saying we would have a little sacrament of friendship. Valentine drank a sacramental draught, then I. It was a superb burgundy—drawn from the wood, for its bottle was labelled Tawny Port, a dubious brand at that. I handed him the wineglass. Rising to his feet, erect on his short old legs like a rooster crowing, he gave us a toast 'To Courage!!' & tossed off what was left, remarking to Valentine, 'The Clergyman always finishes it off, you know.'

There he lives, winter & summer, with the heath around him. A tame wild rabbit was sitting near his door. Snakes, adders & grass snakes come in from the heath like country neighbours.

To Marchette & Joy Chute 25:x:1969

Dearest Marchette, dearest Joy,

You will have foreboded why I have not written for so long, why no spoken words have come to you. Valentine is now very ill. Ten days ago we were still going on in a narrowing pattern of our daily life. She could still drive, though only for short journeys; she could walk in the garden with me and pick figs, her eyes sharper than mine to see them; and though she could not be up for more than half a day we could talk and discuss and laugh together at the antics of the cats. And in the morning she still brought me my breakfast, the habit of over forty years, and we read our letters together.

But suddenly she began to fail. Only love and her invincible fortitude is left. *And the fact that we are together.* Our doctor is sensible and merciful. He has told me that he does not want her to be taken to a hospital nor fidgeted with . . .

She may rally from this prostration; but it could not be for long, I think.

I have always prayed that I might not die first, though my age made it probable that I should; she is too sensitive, too dutiful, too vulnerable to be left alone. I am unswervingly thankful to believe that prayer has been heard.

We talk of you often, bless you for your love to us, bless you for your happiness together.

To Margaret Manisty[1] 30:x:1969

. . . We have talked of your suggestion of a night at The White Horse. I'm afraid Valentine is against it. She dare not let her feelings brim over. She is already fully charged with emotions of sundown and farewell, and does not wish to turn back to even the dearest aspects of her life. If this should change, I will tell you. But I think it will not. One must go to death down one's chosen path.

1. MBE, civil servant. A very distant cousin of Valentine Ackland, living at Mayfield, in East Sussex. STW set great store by her distinguished career in the Family Division of the High Court of Justice in London and then in the Judicial Office of the House of Lords.

To Janet Machen 2:xi:1969

My darling Janet,

It wrung my heart to hear your voice as you rang off. To weep in a public call-box—there are few greater desolations . . . I wish with all my heart I could say to you, Come. But if I am to hold out, I must shun sympathy. One glance of compassion undoes me; and I must not be undone, while Valentine holds on in 'the high Roman fashion'. I dare not imperil her courage & her stoicism, nor her present mood of concentrating on practical considerations: setting things in order, labelling bequests, preparing to leave with a clean pair of heels.

We are well provided, practically. Sibyl comes down to wash her, put her on the bedpan, & so forth, and shares the night-watch with a local body. Dr Hollins, who holds out no hope, and can't commit himself as to how much longer she is likely to live, is mercifully categorical in saying that she is better here than in any nursing-home. So I shan't have to throw myself down in the path of an ambulance taking her away—as I would have done, & murdered the driver. For here, at any rate, she is in control of the situation and her proud self.

No morphia so far; it may not even be necessary, since she is so weak. She drowses a good deal; and the nausea which tormented her till last week is past. But, Janet, it is so very hard for her to farewell a life she so passionately lived, to hear the swans fly over and see the leaves colour and know it is for the last time.

To William Maxwell 4:xi:1969

. . . Brendan Gill's speech[1] . . . revived Valentine to the excitement of reality. It set fire to her; perhaps the last thing to do so. For she is dying, dear William —slowly, irrevocably. Every day a sad step downhill. There was a sudden worsening about a fortnight ago, when the disease clamped down on her. It will be a matter of weeks yet, and the worst is still to come.

Our doctor says she will do better here, with me, and the river, and her books and belongings and the familiar noises of the house, than she would be in any sort of nursing home. He is an obstinate unillusioned man but I trust his obstinacy to be merciful. What there is to be done I share with our dear Sibyl and an alternating hireling, hospital-trained but retired into a married woman. People are being kind. The postman *creeps* into the house & sets down parcels as if they were of spun-glass instead of his old hurried emphasis.

1. Delivered at an anti-Vietnam War rally in Columbus Circle.

Except when I am with her, I feel like a ghost, a ghost in a house that is known but unfamiliar. I rehearse the unimaginable *pas seule* I shall enact later on.

It is strange how one's mind *refuses* to believe that this thing happens to everyone—death and loss, and watching them approach.

To Margaret Manisty *8:xi:1969*

Dearest Peg,

She lies under morphia: This morning she came out of it, talked to me a little, remembered Fougère, but couldn't remember where she was. I told her how I had dreamed of ourselves on the road to Innerleithen, getting out of the car to look at Traquair. There was a look of distant pleasure on her face. But the look of death is settling down on it. Hollins came this morning, and has stepped up the morphia to 4-hourly injections. We have a very kind gentle retired nurse who comes to give them. Her pulse is still strong but Hollins doesn't expect a long duration now—or wish for it.

To Janet Machen *9:xi:1969*

My darling Janet,

She died this morning, about 10.15. She had been under morphia for two days. The wind raged round the house, her body raged round her, & she knew nothing of either.

To William Maxwell *11:xi:1969*

... This evening her coffin was carried out of the house and put in a forget-me-not blue van—which would have surprised her. I heard her spirit laughing beside me.

I am passionately thankful that she is out and away, and that in a fashion we are back where we were, able to love freely and uncompromised by anxiety and doubtful hopes and miseries of frustration. One thinks one has foreseen every detail of heart-break. I hadn't. I had not allowed for the anguished compassion and shock of hearing her viola voice changed to a pretty, childish treble, the voice of a sick child.

Death transfigured her. In a matter of minutes I saw the beauty of her young days reassert itself on her blurred careworn face. It was like something in music, the re-establishment of the original key, the return of the theme.

Don't think I am unhappy and alone, dear William. I am not. I am in a new country and she is the compass I travel by.

To Marchette and Joy Chute *27:xi:1969*

My dear Darlings,

Your kind hearts will want to know how I am getting on.

Well, not too badly for a one-winged partridge (did you know the partridge is the emblem of fidelity?). There is a great deal to do, which I am thankful for, but as I slog on doing it I am revived by coming on fragments by her, letters, passages copied from everyone you can think of, feathers (she loved all small feathers) deposits in pockets, always including a pencil & a pocket comb, but also including lumps of sugar in case of a deserving horse, chocolate drops for dogs, interesting pebbles, small notes from me on the lines of 'Remember to have coffee' 'Keep warm' 'Come back soon'.

Her love is everywhere. It follows me as I go about the house, meets me in the garden, sends swans into my dreams. In a strange, underwater or above-earth way I am very nearly happy.

To William Maxwell *16:xii:1969*

... With a heart as normal as a stone I went to spend this last weekend with friends in Berkshire because they wanted to change my air. Their telephone rang. It was a telephone on which Valentine had often rung me. With an idiot intensity I thought, She will never telephone me again. And for a moment the whole of my grief was comprised in that deprivation. There is no armour against irrationality.

To Elling Aanestad *22:xii:1969*

...I mean to live on here, alone. I have three cats, my wits and a kind neighbour who comes in every morning to see if I've died in the night; and who helps me with house & garden ...

A friend (the widow of Vaughan Williams the composer) wrote to me

'Even desolation is a world to be explored.' There are some very dull patches in its landscape. Nothing is as one expects. In all my forecastings of life without Valentine I had not reckoned on boredom as an enemy to be overcome. I don't appear to bore others, but my God, how I bore myself!

I hope to do better when Christmas with its imprint of other Christmases is over and I launch myself into the cold seas of the New Year.

I wish you a happy one, dear Elling.

To William Maxwell *13:ii:1970*

... Lead you down the garden path? I wouldn't lead you; but did I never tell you the story of how, when I was young and gay, I sat for a whole hot afternoon in a small tent telling fortunes for 2/6 for some worthy purpose, I can't remember what; and gave my clients a great deal of advice what to do, as for instance to buy three and threequarter yards of green ribbon at the nearest draper's and then leave the shop walking backwards; and how, twelvemonths later, a strange woman arrived on my London doorstep, saying thank God she had traced me at last, everything I had told her had come true and would I please, please, tell her some more?

To William Maxwell *13:iv:1970*

... I have begun to write again—No, not a story, not a novel, and nothing for now. An archive. I found that Valentine had kept quantities of my letters, as I had kept quantities of hers. Reading through them, and putting them into sequence I realised that it is a notable correspondence and the sort of thing that should be put away in a tin box for posterity. So now I am entirely absorbed in writing the narrative links and explanations and so forth. I am mid-way in the prologue. It is far the best thing I have ever written—and an engrossing agony. I am terrified that I should die before I have finished this. A month ago, it was the only thing I had the least inclination for.

It is comfortable to know you are back, and DELIGHTFUL to know that you had such a happy holiday and that Venice was sunlit, and Ravenna full of new characters to think about. I daresay they all reposed in the thought, no, the conviction, that Plato studied with the Prophet Jeremiah, in Egypt ... apparently it was common knowledge in their time. I learned it from Hampden's book on The Enlightenment, which I have been reading in an attempt to improve my mind. It is as good as Dido being Jezebel's aunt —an unfortunate family—though not quite so well authenticated.

I must go and talk to Mr Palmer. The foundations of the house are giving way, and he is repairing them, aided by such a very very old man that there is really nothing of him between his sharp chin and his large gothic feet—just a faint continuity.

... One very pleasant thing has happened to me. I was musing on what to do about our Craske pictures, where to dispose of them, and whether I could settle them at Aldeburgh, to hang in the foyer and be admired during the Festival, and Reynolds Stone said, Write to Peter Pears; he likes pictures. So I did. And last week he came down to see them, liked them immensely and accepted them as just what was wanted; for in the re-building of the theatre (burned down last year after its first performance of *Idomeneo*) they are going to be more ambitious and enlarge themselves into an Art Centre; and the Craskes will hang in its gallery. Not only that; there will be an Exhibition of them, with others loaned, for next year's season. It was she[1] who found Craske, going to his house because an aunt had heard he made model boats; finding it full of pictures painted on any surface he could lay hands on, tea-trays, door-panels, Mrs Craske's pastry-board, and instantly recognised his quality, was his first buyer, his first promoter. So this will be a lovely and living memorial to her.

To David Garnett[2] *2:ix:1970*

... I liked Lot (I think Montcuq is in Lot?). We were there when the tobacco crop was being gathered, and the gatherers walked with vast bunches of tobacco plants, stems upward, in each hand and looked as if they were walking in farthingales. There were affiches in two languages: French and a dialect rather like Catalan. And I remember a small stone manor-house, empty except for a quantity of poultry, who squawked, flustered, strutted in and out, coupled and kept up an incessant conversation: and as I was watching them I realised that this was the nearest I should ever get to the Versailles of Louis XIV.

How old we both are, my dear. Alike in that, if in nothing else. In a way, I am now like the Sylvia you first knew, for I have reverted to solitude. I live in a house too large for me, with three cats; and when the telephone rings and it is a wrong number I feel a rush of thankfulness. I was grateful to you for your letter after Valentine's death, for you were the sole person

1. Valentine Ackland.
2. After a hiatus of thirty-eight years (said to have been imposed by Valentine Ackland) STW wrote to him again, in August 1970; 'Dearest David. How are you, where are you, what has happened about Hilton Hall, who are you in love with now? I heard from Michael Howard that you had finished the Carrington letters. A curious picnic in the cemetery.—did you enjoy it?' And the correspondence was resumed. By that time he was living occasionally on a converted barge in the Thames but mostly in France at Montcuq (Lot).

who said that for pain and loneliness there is no cure. I suppose people have not the moral stamina to contemplate the idea of no cure; and to ease their uneasiness they trot out the most astonishing placebos. I was assured I would find consolation in writing, in gardening, in tortoises, in tapestry, in doing another book like the White biography, in keeping bees, in social service (the world is so full of misery); and many of these consolers were people whom I had previously found quite rational. Your only runner-up was Reynold Stone's wife, who said, whisky.

But when one has had one's head cut off—

Please, if only for my peace of mind, outlive Michael Holroyd. For my pleasure too, come to that.

To Joy Chute 7:ix:1970 (in case you didn't know!)

. . . I have been feeling peculiarly dispirited and careless—and uninterested in myself. Partly the weather, I daresay. It has been—still is—cold and stormy—and destroying. Boughs from trees, everything in the garden drooping and entangled and the grass plot like a cobbled yard with fallen apples. I have blessed you & Marchette, I can't tell you how often, for my woollen wrap. I live in it. I sit with it over my knees and the cats sit under its shelter.

And partly the time of year, with last year's farewelling to all joys. Sometimes I become convinced that the melancholy I feel is her melancholy. There was so much she loved and was loth to quit: birds and trees and her own skills, one by one being filched from her—and me. I think how I should have felt if I had been leaving her alone and it appals me.

But almost the last thing she said to me, with her hand on my head as I sat bowed at her bedside in a sudden assault of woe, was 'It will be all right.' And she meant it; perhaps she even knew it. She was convinced that she would survive, and keep me company. And I constantly feel that she does, that I am sheltered and cherished. But what I can find no remedy for is the thought of her grief, her frustrated courage and hope.

There! I must not go on being so like poor Queen Victoria . . .

This is the time of year when the pair of swans further down the valley bring their cygnets up the river in a family party. Three cygnets this year—still in their ash-coloured cloaks but their swan plumage beginning to show through. They are inexpressibly beautiful—and so well-brought-up, so graceful and demure. They all circle round under this house waiting to be fed: it is one of their picnicking places. The parents hiss warningly if they see the cats looking at them: the cygnets keep up a very soft chatter—not quite a rustle, not quite a murmur; but the very voice of the river they were hatched to.

To Martha Bacon Ballinger *22:ix:1970*

. . . I have been re-reading *Carlyle's Recollections*. It is embarrassing how he harps on his wife's dimensions: brave little heart, noble little creature, indomitable little soul—he only just stops short of wee cowering crimson-tippit Beastie. My great-grandfather knew him, even stayed with him in Dumfriesshire. I can't believe he liked him, for he seems to have been a man of considerable discrimination. But they had a bond: they both went to the same watch & clock maker. For that matter, I opine Carlyle didn't much like my great-grandfather. He wrote of him as 'a small clear man'—by *clear* I gather he meant lucid not transparent: but the same obsession with size: blathering great bubblejock.

To David Garnett *14:xii:1970*

I am as dark and sad as (I think) any Fate could require. But to see the assiduity with which I avoid falling downstairs, catching colds, suffering from malnutrition, insomnia, insolvency, you'd suppose I was bent on survival. It is not so; I am just bent on keeping away from doctors and the Welfare State. and preserving my existence as a Moping Owl, with my three loving sensual unregenerate cats about me.

I wish you had a cat, better still a brace of cats, dear David. They are worth a waggon-load of disinterested well-wishers.

To Joy Finzi *30:xii:1970*

. . . I came back yesterday from Sussex: the downs flattened under snow, and from my warm bedroom a fine view of icicles. When I walked in I was convinced that a ghost was in the kitchen making marmalade. Two separate people had given me pomanders, and they had been possessing the house like virtuous poltergeists.

To William Maxwell *28:ii:1971*

Dear William,

When, how this will reach you, God knows . . . but here is a story and this is the day I finished it. The scalp, the legend & the motto are authentic. They belong to my mother's family and I drank my soup down to the scalp when I was a child; for the Hudleston service centred the scalp and had a mazarin-blue border, not flowers. The theme, as you will see, is still my obsessive Innocent & the Guilty. Perhaps one day, I shall be pure-minded enough to write a story where the innocent are charming and the guilty nauseating.

If The *N. Y.* takes this, will you please substitute Ralph for Guy? I forgot that Guy rightly belonged to Mr Stoat in *The view of Rome*.[1]

I was so glad, dear William, that you persevered when I was only a voice which didn't hear you.[2] Once I heard you, it was as though you were in the room; and I had no sense of astonished beginning, imminent ending— just a sense of talking to you again and of being loved and understood.

And perhaps this makes me seem even more ungrateful that I don't think of coming over in May.[3] But I am tied to the letters, to her poems and MSS—*to her*. Here, I am still in her ambience. I spend most of my time in a strange straying conversation with her, not so much haunted as possessed. Even at the cost of days when I am nothing but a machine which feels the cold, I can't interrupt this conversation. And though I made various attempts at staying with people who were everything that is kind to me it didn't really work—it was a jolt into a life I had forgotten. Here I live and continually remember more, see with her eyes, consult her, depend on her. She knew for we discussed it before her death—that I should live on here, by myself—and she approved.

She herself was convinced she would survive. 'I will never leave you,' she said in a letter of farewell. In the light of this it would seem childish and materialistic of me to cling to this house. But as I am both childish & materialistic I half-believe that when I leave it, I leave her. And leave myself.

---

1. In the collection called *A Stranger with a Bag* in England and *Swans on an Autumn River* in the U.S.
2. A transatlantic call, with a poor connection.
3. She was invited to address the American Academy of Arts and Letters.

Dear William,

Nancy Hale was right.[1] My father died when I was twenty-two, and I was mutilated. He was fifty-one, and we were making plans of what we would do together when he retired. It was as though I had been crippled and at the same moment realized that I must make my journey alone. My mother exclaimed, Now you are all I've got left—a cry of angry desolation. What on earth did she want in a daughter that I didn't have, you ask. A son. For the first seven years of my life I interested her heart; and I was an amusing engaging child and she enjoyed her efficiency in rearing me. But nothing compensated for my sex and later on it turned into doing her duty by me, and doing one's duty by inevitably hardens the heart against. And later still, she was jealous, and I could do nothing right. Valentine said that what she felt about me was an inverted possessiveness.

The person to be sorry for was my stepfather. He was much younger than she, gentle, affectionate, rather dunderheaded, inexhaustibly kind. She scorned him in her heart, and had no kindness for him, and no respect for him, and he wasn't so dunderheaded that he didn't know it.

Dear William,

I shall post tomorrow another porridge-coloured envelope with the letters from 1940-47, and one piece of narrative. This is not quite all of that decade: about half a dozen more letters and two more bits of narrative, and this will bring you up to the letters of September & November 1949 which you already have.

I went to Chaldon about three weeks ago to spend a weekend with my cousin Janet, who rents part of the Chydyok house—Llewelyn & Alyse's half—on the downs near the sea.

On our way to Chydyok we stopped for me to plant some more snow-drops round Valentine's grave: there are some already but one can never have enough snowdrops. It was a brilliant afternoon, with a wind from the sea, whirling cloud-shadows across the very green churchyard grass; and the rookery was in full shout, with parent rooks flustering overhead feeding

1. The American novelist and short story writer, whose father also died when she was twenty-two. Thirty years later, staying in our house in the country, she walked past an open door and saw me with my older daughter on my lap, brushing her hair, and remarked dubiously, 'I suppose it's all right, but don't ever die.'

their newly hatched young. I planted the snowdrops, absorbed in industry, then, feeling I would like a rest, I looked round for somewhere to sit on. There, all ready to be sat on, was the stone slab, rather well-cut, with everything of names and dates on it, and Valentine's choice of non omnis moriar—everything except the date of my death.

And as I sat down on it, William, I felt the most amazing *righteous* joy; as if I were doing just what I should, par excellence what I should; and that here was my indisputable right place. It was the first time since her death that I have felt that slightly rowdy emotion of joy.

To Marchette & Joy Chute *9 : iii : 1971*

. . . As you must have gathered by now, I have nothing of interest to tell you, except that I have a chilblain—like the crocuses. Oh, yes, and I have written and sent off another story for the New Yorker—to the N. Y. I mean, one must not be too forward—about a heraldic dinner service with a scalp on each bit of it: so much is true, it belonged to my mother's family, who also owned the priest who converted Charles II, striking when the iron was hot after the battle of Worcester and poor Charles II was in hiding and yawning his head off, imbedded in a very pious family. My mother was proud of this ancestral exploit; but said she would have been better at entertaining royalty. I remember my father saying in an undertone that Charles II was easily entertained.

To Marchette Chute *27 : v : 1971*

. . . I am reading Nathaniel Hawthorne's *English Journal*. As far as I can judge I shall be reading it for years to come: it is as thick as a Bible. Not so interesting, but for an English reader it has a sort of parochial charm. But mortifying: he thinks the English very ugly (the only person he has admired so far is a young footman in his rich livery!); and without conversation; and not intellectual. But let loose in the remains of pre-Mayflower England, which he doesn't have to disapprove of from national pride, he shows a touching affection for village churches, pious foundations, nestling cottages —even at times the English climate. In fact, he is a little homesick for his lost native land. He is shrewd, observant, dutiful, censorious, tolerant, devoted to his children, with an eye for gothic and ankles, and a great piety for Dr Johnson: in short, he would have made a very good Englishman.

If you had as much time as Marvell regretted he hadn't, I would say, Do read him. Like a lady I know, he wanted to hear a lark; and was rewarded with a sky full of them.

The Bristol Zoo's orang-utan recently had a live baby. Her devoted keeper stood at a sympathetic distance, glorying in this rarity and supposing she was glorying too. She bit through the cord, gave the infant a sniff, took it up in both hands and handed it to him. So he is now being a foster-parent to it, & both are doing well. So is she.

TO MARTHA BACON BALLINGER *14:vii:1971*

... Peter Pears was here last week; we had iced sorrel soup, Prague ham with seven different salads, and a quite childish array of strawberries—on a quid pro quo for the Aldeburgh asparagus—and we spent a happy idealistic afternoon telling each other how *we* would produce *The Magic Flute*.

TO JOY FINZI *4:viii:1971*

... I was almost forced to think I had too many strawberries. There was an enormous crop, every truss with all its fruits ripe on it like a bunch of grapes. I wore out my wits thinking who to give them to—for they had to go by hand & I scorned to jam them—Then it suddenly occurred to me, Nobody gives fair baskets of fruit to van drivers, who get so hot and so thirsty in their cabs. So I lay in wait for all the vans when they came to the door. And they too thought it a splendid new idea—especially the old man who brings the laundry, who is so old and ugly with such a squint and a battered smile and who comes in snowfalls when no one else bothers to.

TO MARCHETTE & JOY CHUTE *15:ix:1971*

... *The Music at Long Verney* brought me several letters—no one, so far, seems to object to me *inventing* a whole Haydn quartet; among them, a most touching letter from a man in San Francisco, whose wife was killed in a car accident two summers ago, & who had been looking forward to the sort of old age I bestowed on my two Verneys. And of course, I know exactly how he feels—and the degree of loneliness which makes it possible to pour one's grief out to a complete stranger . . .

There has been such a to-do in *The Times* correspondence columns because a London Producer announced his intention of putting a naked Desdemona into bed. Millions are drowning & starving in Bengal, Ulster spits like salt herring in a frying-pan, no one buys our poor wretched

Concorde—but all this is forgotten, letters on letters on letters appear daily, from experts on W.S. to experts on dressing-gowns . . . I read the letters with passionate interest, I have almost joined in the shindy myself.

To William Maxwell *19:xi:1971*

. . . I came home after posting that last envelope—as though I had just committed a serene suicide; with an inexhaustible choice of times & places where I might haunt. I have kept, pretty consistently, the vow against remorse and against regret (it would be blasphemous ingratitude to admit regret into the span of so much happiness): but I must take your word for it about the letters of the last decade. I can't reconcile myself to that slow, grinding accumulation of ill-health, calamity and self-exile. (It is strange that only after she knew she had cancer did she allow herself to *trust* our love again). I feel a childish indignation, a child's outcry of 'It isn't fair.'

But she keeps her word. She does not leave me. And remembering that deep folk-belief that the dead are at the mercy of the surviving—(Do you know that Breton story of the mother who saw her dead child shivering in a pool of dirty water, and cried out, and the child answered, Your tears, Mother?) I try to match her.

To Joy Finzi *10:xii:1971*

. . . I must tell you of a strange dream I had a few nights ago. I dreamed I was dead—so newly dead that I could perfectly remember the sensation of living, and how, at the moment of death I was turned off, sharply, at a right-angled tangent, into a completely different kind of existence, where everything except my consciousness was inexperienced, unknown, unrelated. It was a quite unemotional dream and curiously positive; so that it still remains with me as something I couldn't have imagined yet knew. A Euclidean dream, since line, angle and direction persisted through it.

1972

... When family pews meant anything, they had fireplaces in them, and the eldest son of the family poked them up before the sermon. At that date you never saw a gentleman on his knees. He remained seated & prayed into his hat. My poor father couldn't, because if he went to church it was to the school chapel, dressed as such; and for some deep mystical reason you can't pray into a mortar-board.

One of the Winter's Nights Entertainments of old age is recalling customs that were commonplace in one's youth: they start up like wyverns and Demon Kings.

If I don't immediately respond to that copy of *Love*,[1] it will be because I'm in Denmark. Paul & Clive[2] are there, working on impaired children, and their hired house sounded so agreeable & they invited me so feelingly that I said *Done!* The truth is, I was growing rather alarmed by the way I was acceding to routine; compliance with it felt increasingly like madness. 'Now I hang up the teacup on the 3rd hook. Now I put the blue plate in the rack.'

But whether I shall get there with the coal strike is another matter. Part of my plan is the sea-voyage from Harwich to Esbjerg, and there may not be trains to take me to Harwich. Fly I will not. I detest flying.

I wish you knew Reynolds Stone. He has a soft voice like bees in a lime-tree, and I have never heard him exclaim or known him talk for nothing; and he will fight like a tiger to save a tree, a badger, an old printing-press.

He had a wonderful commission last year. A very rich man in the North with acres of woodland, asked him up to take portraits—no, not of the family —of particular trees. And all day Reynolds sat in the woods looking like an old tramp and in the evening dined with the very rich man on oysters and saddle of mutton.

He works at one end of a large long room, walled with books, corniced with stuffed birds in glass cases. He works at a massive table, matted with every variety of confusion & untidiness, graving minutely on a small block. The other end of the room is a turmoil of wife, children, distinguished visitors, people dropping in—Janet's roaring lion-house, for she is a bishop's

1. An anthology of poetry, edited by Walter de la Mare (1943).
2. Paul Nordoff and Clive Robbins. After 1959 Nordoff devoted himself to music as therapy for emotionally disturbed children, and lived mostly in Europe.

daughter & has lion-hunting in her blood. And there sits Reynolds not merely immune, but liking it. He likes to work amid a number of conversations he needn't attend to, he likes to feel people within touching distance of his glass case.

To Kate Maxwell[1] *21:ii:1972*

... I don't agree with what you say about happiness "coming in spite of who I am rather than because of it." It is the *who I am* which accepts or refuses it. Look at a row of people in a concert-room, and see where happiness is accepted, though the means of happiness sings in every ear.

You see I am most carefully not telling you what to do. I can only deal with *what to be*. You have a great deal more to be, yet. Give it room to grow; don't squash it into performance. The present civilization is riddled by the do-ers and the done-by. Do you know what George Sand said as she lay dying? *Laissez verdurer*. Idiots suppose that she was giving directions about her grave.

To Marchette & Joy Chute *13:iii:1972*

Dear Darlings,

A letter from William Maxwell this morning told me he had brought you the Valentine-Sylvia letters. I am so glad they are with you. You will read them with love—as they were written. For two people who were so seldom separated, they seem very numerous; but when we had to be apart, we usually wrote twice a day.

We had no agreement about keeping them. We kept them, I suppose, because we loved too much to throw them away—it would have seemed a slight. They were preserved, not hoarded.

Many of them were almost untranscribable: creased with being carried in pockets, kept under pillows, read & re-read.

And it so nearly might not have happened. I might so nearly have lived unblessed.

Even now my desolation is enriched by her.

To Marchette & Joy Chute *29:iii:1972*

My dear Dears,

I found your two letters when I came home from Denmark.

1. Daughter of William and Emily Maxwell, then aged 17.

I am so glad you have read those letters—for now you know us. As I grow old and cold, sometimes I feel as though she and I were being whirled away from each other like leaves on an autumn wind; it restores, it reassembles me to know that we still exist to you, in our exact truth, in our reality; and that reading her letters, you will know the phoenix that I loved in life and reality: that we were truly so . . . 'so well completed in each other's arms.' A strange thing is, that we took the miracle almost for granted; heaven was our daily wear, at times, hell, too, but never completely; there was always, even in our worst afflictions and perplexities, a lining of comfort in each other.

Denmark was a pleasant jaunt, and completely effortless. My first sight of it from the ship was so exactly like the flat, sand-duned coast of Norfolk that I felt the boat had turned back during the night. There was still some snow lying, but by the next day the weather had forgotten anything of that sort. The sun shone, the larks sang. The air is deliciously pure and uncontaminated. The postman came to the door wearing his uniform of a scarlet jacket, and I walked out to inspect the village church, and found it had a splendid carved wooden pulpit of the 17th century, white walls & blue pews. Whitewash is laid on with a lavish hand. Even so, the landscape could do with more of it, for the countryside is peppered with neat and boxlike new dwellings and their undissembled brick is a bad red (a puny red) or an assertive ochre.

Paul and Clive waited on me hand & foot. They are both over six foot high, and when they stalked in with my breakfast tray I felt as if I were a she-Frederick of Prussia with giant valets de chambre. They are writing (did I tell you?) a book about their method of therapy by music; and were at the stage of knots in it; and in the mornings we disentangled the knots & in the afternoons went out to play. It was very peaceful and congenial, and much more to my liking than if I had gone there merely to idle. But we took one whole day off, and went across the Sound to Sweden. Sweden seemed immeasurably older, further off, sterner: part of a continent, whereas Denmark is an adjunct to it. Now I have sent for histories of Denmark and Sweden to the London Library and they arrived this morning; so presently I shall be less ignorant, I hope. I was ashamed of my ignorance. *Hamlet*, Caroline Matilda, and The Lion of the North is not enough.

To WILLIAM MAXWELL *22:iv:1972*

. . . You aren't the only one to mislay. Objects have got so bold about it in this house that they mislay themselves in front of my eyes and remain in front of my eyes, mislaid. I put it down to pollution. Probably at this moment I am staring at the clean copy of *The Sea Change* which has been unfindable since Valentine died. It was the copy she made, it was among her papers, I I have been through them a great many times, I never come on it. So I will try to force it into the open by looking for the working copy. Same text, but scrabbled over with working alterations by Paul and me. Foi d'animal.

For some time I have been admiring a large black and white cat, a solid shapely cat with one eye in a black surround so he looks piratical, who promenades in the field across the river. I must have looked at him too warmly, for now he comes into the garden. He does no harm, he makes no offensive; but he *sits at* the rightful inhabitants; and they enlarge their tails and hackle up their backs; from embarrassment, I think. Not a paw is raised; but the effect is un-restful. It reminds me of a Peace Committee I attended in Brussels in 1938, when the only smooth tail was Krishna Menon's, who annoyed everybody so exhaustively that he went about filled to the brim with the milk of human kindness, the embodiment of suavity and tolerance; and handsome as the Destroying Angel. No. I think it was 1937 . . .

. . . It is strange to think that during that summer when I was feeling as hollow as a hemlock stalk you were there all the time; and that when I came to *The N. Y.* office I was so accomplished in dissimulation[1] that you thought I was the person who wrote so airily and securely. There was a Thurber drawing on the wall. I hope it is still there.

To David Garnett *24:iv:1972*

. . . I will risk being a dame, dear, rather than forsake you. Last month, I was momentarily singed by the honour, for the U.S. Ambassador's social secretary introduced me to him as Dame Rebecca (she & I were there to be made honorary partakers of the A.A.A.L.[2] and Mr Annenburg had to make a small party for it). Earlier partakers attended, and *quantities* of total strangers in long white beards remembered meeting me. As for me, I was much as if I had been on a peak in Darien. Can I really have forgotten them all?

I liked the Ambassador.

1. The love affair between Valentine Ackland and a young American woman which so troubled their relationship in the late 1950s started at this time. See letter to Paul Nordoff, 14:vii:1939, p. 54.
2. She had been made an honorary member of The American Academy of Arts and Letters.

To David Garnett 8:v:1972

. . . Have you read *Munby*?[1] It is enthralling. For one thing, he seems to be a perfectly honest diarist: for another, he has set me off on a speculation as to whether do-gooders are in fact pursuing an intuitive policy of being done good to—a fulfilment of that *drang* towards the dark, the threatening, the forbidden which they felt as children, those dark alleys they weren't allowed to explore. That raises a further speculation about class distinction in Victorian philanthropists. Children of the poor grew up in those alleys, felt no gentry *drang* to explore them, and if they grew into philanthropy, just plainly wanted to demolish them, as savagely as Florence Nightingale. Do read *Munby* and tell me what you think

Last week I met Christopher Sykes—whom I meet from time to time & always with pleasure: he is that rarity, a Man of the World. He told me how after the fall of Berlin he had to investigate post-Hitler high society—it was in good condition and radiant with whitewash. At a party of the whitewashed was a rapscallionly Rumanian, who had the effrontery to refer to his participation in the pre-1945 doings. There was an appalled silence. Then the whitewashed tried to restore the tone of the party, disclaimed all knowledge of, disbelieved rumours, wondered how on earth anyone could have been so misled, so misguided, etc.

'*Someone* had to join the Nazis' said he; as one might say 'Some one had to go to the Jones's garden-fête'.

I am glad I have you to share this with. Altogether, I am glad I have you.

To Joy Finzi 23:v:1972

. . . I have sailed through my last round of visitors, I was positively sorry to see them go; I have written a short story; and I have made my almost final selection of Valentine's poems. (It is never finality with me: she was so various, so multicolored, so definite in her varieties, I despair of composing her). I have tried to keep it in something like order of time—though that was no answer. Yet I had to resist my novelist's instinct to imply a story in it, a roman à clef. In the end I fell back on music, on key arrangement and modulation. Meanwhile, of course, keeping the totally different calculations of lines to a page, and so forth.

I have never known such a *taunting* spring. Blackthorn, daffodils, pear & apple & tulips, hawthorn in mountains, now roses & syringa: everything

1. *Munby, Man of Two Worlds*, The Life and Times of Arthur J. Munby, 1828-1910, edited by Derek Hudson (1972).

that could bloom has bloomed paradisally; and scarcely a day when I could go out without being flayed by wind and drenched by rain-storms. It was queer to see the field across the river brilliant with buttercups and children playing there in the bulk of their anoraks, as bulky as little Breughels.

Oh, one lovely adventure! I have looked down on a heron rising. It got up from the nearside of the river, just below where I was standing on the deck. The span of its back was like a barn.

To Hilary Machen[1] 8:vii:1972

Dearest Hilary,

I wants to make your flesh creep.

I also wants to be practical. Why should I wait till I am dead and gone to do what I can enjoy doing now, and what I hope you will also enjoy now?

So here, my dear, is a pre-dated legacy (No, I can quite well afford it. I have always made it a rule in life to afford pleasures).

And I hope it will enable you to start your retired days with a little sense of amplitude; or to give a little extra flourish to the first steps in life of those charming, tuneable, well-behaved children of yours; or to abandon them and go round the world with Marian. In any case, to be agreeably surprised.

Your loving Pumblechook

To William Maxwell 10:vii:1972

Dear William,

Your letter came this morning. I was still thinking about it, and washing my hair, when the telephone rang. My cousin Rachel, to tell me she had long suspected she was under a curse, and had now been assured by an expert that she was—and that it was a curse of long standing, extending through generations, and did I think it had come in from the Highland side of the family. She was perfectly convinced, and, like all the demented, perfectly convincing. Reason would have been heartless. On the principle of Feed a

1. Son of STW's Aunt Purefoy and Arthur Machen. He received a classical education at the Merchant Taylor's School. When the depression overtook the family he was apprenticed to the firm of J. W. Walker and Sons, Organ Builders. Perceiving that no organs were going to be built in the near future, he took to his heels and fulfilled his destiny, which was to become the hero of a picaresque novel.

Fever, I supplied some more instances of hereditary doom and recommended trying an exorcist. After her, my hair still dank about me, came the parson, to ask how I was keeping and could I let him have a large kettle for the Youth Club's canteen. I couldn't, but consoled him with strawberries. The next telephone call was to ask me if I could adopt two frogs—a nature conservationist, and frogs are a dying race because of farming poisons. Again I had to refuse, three cats made this garden unsuitable for frog conservation. All this before mid-day. This island is inflexibly lunatic.

To Martha Bacon Ballinger *11:x:1972*

... It is mid-day, and so dusky I can barely see to write: a bloom of mist over everything and not a leaf stirring and birds making apprehensive noises as if they felt the long-due equinoctial gales invisibly overhead like hawks.

Mrs. Kemble: Fitzgerald[1] loved her, that alone would ensure that I do. He had the most searching good taste in his loves—in everything except his marriage; and I can't hold him responsible for that, since I am sure he didn't intend it, but was caught & didn't know how to escape. It was on a day like this that I saw his grave. The churchyard is so water-logged that newly-dug graves have to be baled out before the coffin is lowered into them. No wonder his rose liked it not & died.

To William Maxwell *19:x:1972*

Dear William,

Witchcraft again. Or why should my letters from Great Eye Folly come to your hand while I am sending Donald Gillespie[2] there to die as he wished to die?

I bless the witchcraft. I had forgotten the assertion of the little bell on the kitten's collar. He was very young, very slender—& indomitable. He used to sit at the edge of the waves, staring them out of countenance, taut with excitement and perfectly composed. And when he'd done with that, he used to walk off to the shed where the fishermen kept their crab-pots & fall asleep in that heavenly, that paradisal smell.

Three years later, after the tidal wave, we went back to see what had happened to the house. The hinder part, which faced inland, was still stand-

1. Fanny Kemble and Edward Fitzgerald.
2. A character in a never finished story.

ing. We could scramble up the stairs. We pulled open the door of the room, Valentine's sitting, above where I wrote those letters. It was strange to look down into the blue summer sea, basking & undulating there.

The people in the village—those of them who were left—spoke of the inundation as 'the great surge'.

To Hilary Machen *11:xi:1972*

Dearest Hilary,

3:49. 1.xii. Reading. And how much I look forward to it.

But as to fatlings—though there are few people more exasperating than those who say: 'My tastes are very simple' say it I must. I like my sherry dry and I like coffee for breakfast—and the vicinity of a coffee-pot, all the time to put my lips to when I'm so disposed—and for the rest I most enjoy family food, because that is something I don't have at home—too lazy to make it—baked potatoes, apple tart, steak-and-kidney pudding, toad-in-the-hole—that sort of thing. And any kind of soup Marian feels inclined to make; or to de-tin.

Divertimenti: you guess right. The 'dozen or so' singers and drinkers would be beyond my means. But I would love to meet the Cecilians again, I would like to come to church; and Dom Anselm,[1] however deaf, however demanding, I would like to visit, out of respect and retrospect. It would renew my youth to meet a hoary crocodile so much more venerable than myself. And Janet, of course.

1. Hilary Machen to the editor, 22:2:1980: 'The meeting with Dom Anslem Hughes, an aged Benedictine Monk, and another international authority on mediaeval polyphony, went off very well, considering that in 1920 he and she and [R. R.] Terry had fought viciously and in the print of various learned journals about the Worcester Fragments, discovered by Anslem as 16th. c. book bindings.'

1973

To WILLIAM MAXWELL *10:i:1973*

Dear William,

Indeed I knew Flora Moir.[1] I loved her next to my father, and she loved me next to him. And her father loved her beyond all others. I can't say for his father, the wine merchant in Aberdeen. Ask your Scotch genes. The wine merchant may have fixed his heart on a pretty daughter, but fixed it would have been: there is a bull's-eye gravity about the way these people love. The wine-merchant's father had been sent down to the port to meet two girl cousins from The Orkneys. One of them came off the packet so deadly sea-sick she could hardly speak or stand. It was done in a flash. No, Flora didn't know Mrs Carlyle. The Carlyles were away to Ecclefechan before she was out of leading-strings. But I daresay the wine-strainer did.

Wine-strainers were more functional then. A lot got into the bottles beside the juice of the grape: lees, pips, an odd wasp or two, native soil. By my time, it was useful if a bit of the cork got in—so tedious to fish out of your glass with a spoon . . .

. . . One of the things which horrifies me is to find myself saying, Well, I shall be safe out of it before the worst happens. It is ignoble; it is also improbable—at least, one can't bet on it.

To DAVID GARNETT *21:ii:1973*

Dearest David,

The house is not my own. The kitchen floor was rotting away, two strong men are hacking it out and replacing it with gangplanks, everything is either mislaid or put somewhere else, the new acid-blue paint is not the colour I chose, I can't get at the larder, a Pit lies between me and the refrigerator, the herb-bed is covered with shavings; it will all be worse before it is better . . .

1. STW had sent me, at Christmas, a silver wine strainer, with a note saying that it had belonged to her grandmother, Flora Moir. I asked if she knew her.

That is all I have to say—except to exclaim and bewail about tigers. Did you see the Wild Life figures? When the last tiger is dead, nothing can ever re-illume that beauty and glory. Tiger will be over. Tiger will be extinguished.

And the global population increased last year by 74 millions.

To David Garnett *1:iii:1973*

. . . Here is a passage from a letter by a friend in Belfast—an unfortunate man who dislikes noise & flurry.

'Three weeks ago a massive bomb in the shape of a hijacked petrol tanker was parked at the back door of the office. I had to get out quickly, forgot my coat, and felt very cold walking the shabby streets.'

I asked him to send me some Belfast newspapers (There used to be one with the noble name, *The Northern Whig*: I'm afraid it is dead & gone). They were one-half riot & murder, the other half, football.

To William Maxwell *31:iii:1973*

. . . At the beginning of the week I tripped on the topmost stair (I have no idea how or why) and cascaded down them on my back, reflecting during an interminable interval on the inconvenience of broken pelvises, cooking from a wheel chair and the fill-ups in *The Times* about old solitary women found dead after months of no one having noticed their absence (the last seemed far the best). At the bottom of the stairs there was a pause for reality, and I made some discreet experiments and found I still had an unbroken neck and an uncracked pelvis—but two, as I thought, ruined feet. So I got back on my horse in the traditional way, and groaned along to the kitchen and gave myself an arnica and some left-over black coffee, and three hours later I had rung up the local taxi and kept my appointment with the woman who washes my hair. I had braked with them all the way down the stairs and put too much determination into it, and they were confounded and driven backward like those people in the *Psalms*; and that was all there was to it; except shock. The cats' shock was far worse than mine. So, you see . . . born to be hanged. I defy you to find where the crack is in this story between writing with both feet and with one.

Valentine thought well of *The Good Soldier*. I couldn't keep up with it. —partly because I knew I ought to. I hate books that excite my sense of duty. I think his[1] ideas of noblesse oblige came from some inflamed genes of

1. i.e. Ford Madox Ford's.

his German ancestry, didn't they? I saw him once when I was in New York in 1929. He had a red face, unanimously red; and was stout and upright.

To William Maxwell *3:iv:1973*

Dear William,

I was cooking to the radio (two days entertaining ahead and my mind was absorbed by the shrimp filling for a vol-au-vent) and the announcer said 'There will now be an orchestral programme of works by Schumann, Berlioz and Prokoviev' and I remarked to the sauce 'Genoveva,' and a moment later the announcer said, 'Schumann's Overture to Genoveva.' HOW did I know? I wasn't thinking of it, they scarcely ever do it; and I had been too positive for it to be coincidence. I hope it won't happen again, I don't want to become a container of uncontrollable powers: they are usually so flippant and derisive.

To Martha Bacon Ballinger *4:iv:1973*

... I am glad you liked Quentin Bell's book. I thought it a marvel of tactful truth—and considerably better than Holroyd on Lytton Strachey, stuffed out into two volumes, like the Tables of the Law. And even so he didn't put in what I remember as the salient impression I had of talking to L.S.: that his breath was as cold as the Erlking's.

To Marchette & Joy Chute *8:iv:1973*

... I have been back in Elfhame again (do you remember the story in *The N. Yorker* about the mortal boy stolen by the fairies and the elfin child who replaced him at the Baker's?) This one is about the death of Tiphaine, and establishes that it was she who beguiled Thomas of Ercildowne, though for the purposes of my story the beguiling is fifty-fifty. It is rather beautiful and has a great deal of information about Elfhame unknown till now as I have just invented it. Oh, how I long to give it learned footnotes, and references. There is such heartless happiness in scholarship.

Benjamin Britten has been carried off to hospital with lesion of the heart. I am torn with pity for Peter Pears in his anxiety. When he was here last, he was telling me about the small plain cottage, too small for visitors, they had bought and were planning to retire to. It is so dangerous to have plans of that kind, my ill-boding mind tells me they will never get there, or get there too late to live in it with easy minds. And I am haunted by the sight of Ben's rather shrewish features melting into love when we began to talk about Mozart. I only knew him slightly before then, and no more since; but that conversation made me know him for ever.

Tomorrow I entertain, briefly, the County Archivist. It would be pleasant if our sublimes amalgamated—but I'm afraid she is rather correct and conscientious, and that my notions of the archival won't march with hers. Part of the trouble with all these people is no cellarage. They daren't overflow. They are fastened to discrimination.

To Marchette Chute *15:iv:1973*

. . . three Day-Books kept by the local WVS through /43 to /45. I gave them to the County Archives, and the archivist found them so inexplicable that I undertook to write a summary. What, for instance, said she, were Agricultural Pies? (farm-workers, in the cold wintry winds, were glad of them). So I read the books through again and ghosts thronged back. 'Lady Jackson rang up and complained about the Admiralty.' 'Received one bundle of old stockings'—that was for the *Make & Mend* campaign, and welcomed for hooked rugs. 'A quantity of dirty theology'—not as gay as it sounds, just paper salvage. An alloying theory was put about that Bibles and Prayer-books were pulped in a separate vat. It is consoling in the last book to find that we sent our store of black-out material to France, for pinafores for school-children. They are authentic history, some future Marchette will enjoy them; if she has the patience to read them: they are all holograph. I gaze with regret and amazement at my own entries: at that date I was *perfectly* legible. But even so, I could not calm Lady Jackson.

To William Maxwell *4:v:1973*

Dear William,

Here you are. It is still so recent that I believe in it. I hope you may too, but not to the extent of dreaming you are pursued by the werewolves.[1]

I couldn't keep up Saint-Simon, for I hadn't the personal animus which made his ink so durable. Barring the Doctors of Divinity, I didn't want to

1. This letter accompanied the story *The Mortal Milk*, which was published in *Kingdoms of Elfin.*

scratch & bite any of them. It is systems I hate. I am convinced that any system, once it is found to work, traps people into fear, idiocy and cruelty. It is the *found to work* which is the operative.

I am feeling hangdog and apprehensive because next week I shall have a man from Belfast staying here. He is a man who hates noise; sensitive, not unduly opinionated—for an Irishman, a natural solitary; and since the beginning of this wretched rumpus, has been in the middle of it, for he works on *The Belfast Telegraph*. He has a cantankerous mouth and that cantankerous Ulster accent; and since most things in Ireland except explosives still belong to the 18th century, I suppose one might call him a Whig. I felt so sorry for his large sensitive ears that I asked him to come here for a rest if he ever got a holiday. He's got it, and he is coming. I can't think how to behave. If I talk about Belfast, it will throw him back into what he comes to get away from; if I don't, he will think me unsympathetic, and, in my English way, not giving a thought to Ireland: if I just listen I shall begin to dislike him for his Ulster accent. And more than that: I have a superstitious feeling that all the tedium & violence and terror will come here with him and infect the house.

To Martha Bacon Ballinger *6:vi:1973*

. . . I have just been listening to news of a section of the ideally varied world which is postally directed as London N. 16. It is in the extreme north-east of London, a closed district inhabited by Polish Jews & Negroes. The Polish Jews are all strictly rabbinical with ringlets. The Negroes are not strictly anything. They live cheek by jowl, the Polish Jews observing every Levitical etiquette, the Negroes observing nothing, painting every separate brick of their houses a separate bright color while the Polish Jews have lace curtains and aspidistras. The Jews walk to the Synagogue through foaming Negro litter. They are so totally disparate that there is no racial antagonism, any more than there is between the thistle & the dock.

To David Garnett *18:vi:1973*

. . . Tiber makes love to you for the good reason that he loves you, and loves making love. Cats are passionate and voluptuous, they get satisfaction from mating but no pleasure (the females dislike it and this is wounding to the male), no voluptuousness; *and no appreciation* . . .

We had a dark grey cat (Norfolk bred, very Norfolk in character) called Tom. He was reserved, domineering, voluptuous—much as I imagine Tiber to be. When he was middle-aged he gave up nocturnal prowlings and slept on my bed, against my feet. One evening I was reading in bed when I became aware that Tom was staring at me. I put down my book, said nothing, watched. Slowly, with a look of intense concentration, he got up and advanced on me, like Tarquin with ravishing strides, poised himself, put out a front paw, and stroked my cheek as I used to stroke his chops. A human caress from a cat. I felt very meagre and ill-educated that I could not purr. It had never occurred to me that their furry love develops from what was shown them as kittens.

Were your hailstones blue? We once had such a storm here, with lightning ripping hail from the sky; and the hailstones were hard as marbles, and blue as aquamarines. And there was another storm, after a long drought, when the lightning was green. It was strange to see the bleached fields, the rusty trees, momentarily sluiced with the look of Spring.

I have been spared acquaintances who might have explained to me about blue hailstones & green lightning, so I can enjoy them with simple pleasure.

> Earth, that grew with joyful ease
> Hemlock for Socrates—

The longer I live, the more my heart assents to that couplet.

To Marchette & Joy Chute *14:vi:1973* *Maiden Newton*
Dorchester.

Both my Darlings,

Imprimis, this village is now advanced to a postcode number. DT2 0DX. DT is injurious, but out of date. When the village was half its present population it had seven public-houses. It still has its 18th cent. skittle-alley, is to that extent a Sweet Auburn. It has just got three amiable new inhabitants: Juliet Verney, who figures in the White Biography, and is a Verney of the *Verney Letters*,[1] and her two small sons. Physiognomy is a strange thing. I look out of my window & see Edmund Verney's 17th cent. wife dressed in a smock, walking up the drive wheeling a pram. She walks up the drive because their cottage—next to the butcher—has no garden, so I have persuaded her to use this one. Today her elder son (Tom) aged three I suppose was clasping a cake of Pears soap: his idol and passion. Several sizes too large for his hand, but held in a grip of iron.

1. See *Memoirs of the Verney Family During the Seventeenth Century* and *The Verney Papers*.

To David Garnett 2:vii:1973

... I have been having letter-box trouble myself ... The newsagent's man is lame and cannot walk up to the house, so I have *The Times* put in a lidded wooden bottle-box at the end of the drive. But a blue tit incontinently laid eight eggs in it, it had to be respected till she had hatched them and sent the fledglings into the world. (She did, all eight). Meanwhile *The Times* had to be left in a *low cellophane carrier* dangling from a willow, and usually arrived damp. And I have not a butler to air it for me. All very inconvenient. On n'a jamais le dernier mot avec les animaux, as your Madame Pierrette observed.

All faiths are worldly: Do you agree?—means for getting on, rising in the world, social insurance.

To Joy Chute 6:ix:1973   *Maiden Newton. Dorchester.*

... And every time I turn on the radio or look at the paper I learn that N.Y.C. is keeping up its heat wave. Oh, how I feel for you all, and how I fidget to come and try out some good ideas. Ice water, for instance. When my mother was a child in Madras she was a bridesmaid (with a wreath of forget-me-nots and blue kid boots). The wedding was a British wedding, so of course it took place at two in the afternoon. My mother drove in a carriage with her ayah and a pitcher of cold water. At intervals the ayah ladled out some more cold water & poured it over her head. And sheets, did you know, soaked in cold water & hung in windows *do* cool the air till they have dried; when you begin again.

My yearly *Serenata*, when my cousin Hilary and his family & his singing friends come and give me a concert of unaccompanied voices, went very nicely. As it is the quadrilateral century of Byrd's birth—I doubt if quadrilateral is correct but it is all I can think of except quaternion—we had a great deal of Byrd: motets in the little church, madrigals & canzanets in the garden; and for the three children, a syllabub. They had not met a sillabub before (take your choice) and looked like angels by Piero della Francesca as they ate it. Jean Larson[1] came, looking elegant as a sylph. This time her dress was right way round. She came to dinner earlier in the year in a stately confection of black taffeta—given to me as a cast-off & later given as a cast-off to Jean; and looked like Congreve's Mourning Bride, with the diving

1. A friend who lived in Dorchester and shopped for her during the last years of STW's life.

décolletage showing off her pretty white back. She is like the proverb about Spain: nothing is right & nothing goes wrong.

To William Maxwell 7:ix:1973

... since you liked Beliard so much, I am brave enough to tell you that I shall presently be off on another. This time, a teutonic kingdom, called Wirre Gedanken. But I don't stay long in it, as the story is about five high-minded fairies who leave Wirre Gedanken in order to lead better lives & meditate. Their names are Ludo, Moor, Tinkel, Banion & Nimmerlein. Their intentions are hampered because of currency: fairy gold, as you know, is dead leaves by the morrow. They are forced to run up bills with country shopkeepers, pay, and move elsewhere.

I found Wirre Gedanken in a cook-book. It is a sort of fried bun. It seemed to me it would be sinful waste to find such a name & do nothing with it. It means, according to the cook-book, Troubled Thoughts.

I have still to invent the catastrophe, a catastrophe for five persons. But if I don't fuss about it, I expect it will come.

Last night I heard a screech-owl in the garden, taking her little owls for a moonlight flit. Her maternal voice was extraordinarily gentle and solicitous, and they expressed themselves in brief tinny exclamations, very much as if they were striking small cheap triangles.

To William Maxwell 19:x:1973

... Dear me about the buggery.[1] Surely, whatever Mr Shawn has to say about it he must have said many times already? I can't believe (I'd like to) that I in my extreme respectable old age am the first person to pose the problem. If I am, may I have a commemorative plaque in your office, please?

To Norah Smallwood 24:x:1973

Darling Norah,

Yesterday I had Ian's letter about Dec 5th, and in answering it, all pleasure & acceptance, I said I should be in your flat just as in the old days.

1. See letter to David Garnett, 31:v:1977, p. 296.

This morning I woke a sadder, more reasonable creature. Darling Norah, I remembered your *stairs*. I doubt if I can manage them; though I am still all right on the level, I am very shaky on stairs, even short flights. How tiresome of me to be so octogenarian! What are we to do. Can you find a room for me in a nearby hotel; is there anyone who would put me up for the night?

I am sorry to be such a nuisance—just when everything is so lovingly arranged and all.

To Ian Parsons *19:xii:1973*

... My darlings, I hope you will have a very happy Christmas, and a better New Year than can reasonably be expected. Reason is a poor hand at prophecies. I dreamed last night that I was in Paris, explaining the British situation to a taxi-driver. 'Inflation' said I to him 'is the senility of democracies.' For some minutes after waking I thought this rather impressive.

To David Garnett *27:xii:1973*

... Yesterday I went out to lunch, and on either hand I had a printer. The left-hand printer asked me if I had known Charles Prentice. I said I knew him very well, and in a moment they were off, praising him like Cherubim & Seraphim; and knowing what they praised.
'And I shall smile, though underground.'
It was you, dear David, who showed my poems to Charles, & established me in the kind receptacle. My birthday party seemed incomplete without the pair of you.

I still write poems from time to time. Here is one.

Learning to walk the child totters between embraces,
Admiring voices confirm its tentative syllables:
In the day of unlearning speech, mislaying balance,
We make our way to the grave, delighting nobody.
Thus the wheel turns in the bright implacable river.

To Marchette and Joy Chute *28:xii:1973*

My dear darlings,
If you read your Who's Who attentively you will know that at the beginning of this month I became (for the first time in my life) an OCTO-GENARIAN.

Pause for veneration.

And I had a very good time of it. I was met at Waterloo with roses & a hired car by my oldest she-friend, Bea Howe, who wrote *Childhood in Chile*;[1] and driven to Brown's nice hotel where a room was booked for me. There, after our tea together, I changed into my flowing robe de style, and was gathered by my dear publisher, Ian Parsons, and taken to the Garrick Club for a small celebratory dinner. The dinner was in the Hogarth Room, panelled with 18th cent. portraits looking on at our 12th[2] cent. selves; and at every place there were four wine-glasses. I never thought to drink such wines again—nor to eat a more superlative fish souffle with prawn sauce. There was no one there I had not known & liked for a long, long time; & by the end of the evening I felt that the waiter & waitress were also dear old friends, they looked on our decent mirth with such kindness.

After a happy night at Brown's Hotel I rose full of octogenarian energy & took myself to the Chinese exhibition . . .

1. The correct title is *A Child in Chile*.
2. The handwriting is quite clear; I assume she meant to write '20th'.

⟨⟨⟨⟨⟩⟩⟩⟩ 1974 ⟨⟨⟨⟨⟩⟩⟩⟩

To Joy Chute *21:i:* (The Shinto Shrine in the falling snow) *1974*
Maiden Newton. Dorchester.

. . . I am cultivating a new Vice for my old age. I go to bed early—10.30 or so, eat half an orange, read about the Tractarians and fall asleep. The cats flock to bed with me, & see how much of them can sleep on my face. By compression & involution they manage quite a high quota. There are not enough poems in praise of bed—and rather too many of them are taken up with epithalamiums.

To Ian Parsons *8:iii:1974*

. . . But festina lente. Please be wary and keep your leg up. And here, to help pin you down, are 3 stories of mine, to amuse you. All in Warner's late manner.[1] Keep them till I come to Juggs when I will retrieve them. I myself enjoy them passionately. It is such a relief to escape from the human heart, which I was growing rather too familiar with.

To Joy and Marchette Chute *6:vi:1974*

Dear Darlings,
    Today is all waving and growing, flying and showering, shining and darkening. There is a strong south-west wind, and brief rain-pelts. The swallows are romping in the wind, dare-devilling it to blow its worst, and the mallard duck in the river is having a busy time looking after her flotilla of eight ducklings, that go round & round like tops on the excited water. Just now I watched her disentangling one of her sooty brood from a tangle of weed where a sudden gust had blown it. You could not see a better mother! She was as deft as a mother-cat in the way she shoved it free of the weed, at the same time keeping a sharp eye on the remaining seven babies bobbling around her; in the confetti of petals blown from the may-trees.
    I have had a very pleasant visitor: Dame Peggy Ashcroft, spending a couple of nights to recover from a Hardy reading she gave in Dorchester.

1. i.e. about Elfhame.

273

'Now there is nothing left for me but Volumnia' she said. With distaste; she does not feel akin to Volumnia. A part she has never played, again for reasons of distaste, is Isabella in *M. for M*. But the other day, she said, she saw a young actress play Isabella with such passionate chastity—passion, no priggery—that when Angelo 'a buttoned-up little Civil Servant' stretched out his hand to touch her knee the offense rocked the whole theatre.

We talked our professions all day: a heaven-like variety of conversation. I have not had such a let-out for years.

Since then, I have bestirred myself & read Rowse's *Simon Forman*. The Dark Lady is the slightest element in the book, though it has been made so much of. The central character is Forman himself; who is entrancing. A diary on a level with Pepys, as self-centred and as unabashed; and a society twenty times as rich, rich in strife, lechery, ambition, superstition, wire-pulling, absurdity—a Bartholomew Fair society; and Forman casting horoscopes for them, & prescribing for their sicknesses, and getting them out of their scrapes & abetting them in their villainies. A worldly John Dee; but still hearing spirits from time to time, & having portents in dreams.

To Ben Hellman[1] *31:viii:1974*

. . . It rains & rains, and is as cold as winter, and I am haunted by thoughts of our good harvest being destroyed—an exceptionally good harvest, so exceptionally liable to be destroyed. And this leads me back to 1916 when so many exceptionally good pupils of my father's were being killed in France. He died, mainly of grief, that autumn; so, as Christian would say, he was mercifully spared the casualty lists of 1917 & 1918.

To William Maxwell *6:ix:1974*

. . . *The body is embarked* . . . do you remember my poem about Allegra in *Time Importuned*? When I first knew the tomb[2] under the tree with a spiked iron railing round it I supposed the poet had climbed the railing in order to lie on the stone slab of that altar tomb. So I must have been a small child when I first knew Byron. For a long time he was the only poet I knew as a poet *outside a book*. On the way up to the churchyard one passed the wall-tablet saying 'Near this spot Anthony Ashley Cooper witnessed with shame & indignation the pauper's funeral.' (The pauper's body was in an occasional coffin used for conveying bodies from the workhouse. The coffin was on a

1. Editor and publisher of American trade magazines and books.
2. The tomb of John Peachey, on which Byron used to sit composing poetry when a boy at Harrow.

litter carried by two men who were drunk. They dropped the litter, the coffin fell off, the pauper's body fell out, & the schoolboy Anthony Ashley went on and became Lord Shaftesbury.[1]) You can't be *so* isolated from the early 19th cent. when you know me. And the view Byron looked at was the view, not much changed, from my nursery window.

. . . Above all other women I envy Lady Melbourne. Think of having that young leopard rolling in one's boudoir, extending & retracting its shining young claws, offering its white stomach to be tickled, trusting one with its wildness. Have you noticed how everyone who comes into contact with Byron is made real by it? Caroline Lamb's idiot son, Mrs Mule,[2] his menagerie, those Gambas. And the real hatefulness he bestows on those he hated?

I suppose it was because he was so completely truthful.

A. L. Rouse had an article the other day, saying we have not paid enough attention to his Cornish ancestry. Even allowing for Rouse's own Cornish ancestry, there may be something in it: a less trammelled, self-conscious variety of Celt than those inland Gordons.

I can't go on wearing out your eyes, talking about Byron. If you were here, I would talk about him all night and about the century which contained us both; and about his astonishing memory and wealth of information and wide reading; and about; and about . . .

To Bea Howe *31:ix:1974*

. . . I now think of arranging for a flat in the Dorchester museum, where I could be on exhibition for two hours a day, along with the Roman pavement, the ploughman's smock, Thomas Hardy's father's cello, & such-like interesting remains of other days.

To Ursula Vaughan Williams[3] *17:xii:1974*

Dear Ursula,
    Thank you very much for your article on R.V.W. and his choice of

1. Who changed the condition of the English working class by introducing legislation prohibiting employment of women and children in coal mines, providing for care for the insane, establishing a ten-hour day for factory workers, and promoting model tenements and schools for homeless children.
2. 'Mrs Mule, my firelighter,—the most ancient and withered of her kind,—and (except to myself) not the best-tempered . . .' Byron's *Journal*, February 27, 1814.
3. Poet. Widow of the English composer Ralph Vaughan Williams, whose biography she has written.

words. I imagine that marrying a poet may have had something to do with his sensitivity to them. And as you say, his work with folksongs. The words & tunes of folksongs are part of the same thing. Long acquaintance has made them so; they fit into each other like the blade and the handle of a scythe swung through many summer hayfields.

Dear Ralph! He'd rise like a fish to a tune. I remember long ago meeting him after a concert at the Queen's Hall, meeting on the staircase crowded with departers, & saying that one of the folksongs which Cecil Sharp found surviving in the Appalachians also survived in Mr Ironsides, the butcher at Wool. 'Which one?' said he. 'Sing it.' And standing in that jostle and shuffle of concert-goers, I sang it obediently.

1975

To William Maxwell *14:i:1975*

. . . Ever since the Dept. of Fidgets renamed the English Counties we have been so rearranged, divided up, added bits to, codified that our Maker wouldn't know us. Churches are shot into new dioceses and given whole new Bishops to fall out with; men in Yorkshire grind their sturdy teeth because they are now in Humberside—Humber being mud to the Ridings; total abstainers in Dorchester dislike being classified as D. T. 1. (I am a second-class drinker); Frome Vauchurch has been lowered, etc.

I think the best plan for the present is to ignore that DT2 oDY and address me with Lower F. V. Dorchester . . .

. . . I have been listening to Rasumovsky no. 3, with those glorious reeling drunks in the Finale. There is a delicious warm, wet, Southerly gale . . . I can't put much heart into my complaints.

And I am in the last lap of another story. Elfhame, this time. A party of high-minded Elfins secede from it in order to do a Walden; and devastate a manse without lifting a finger to accomplish it. It reminds me of Swift, she said modestly.

If the C.I.A. is opening our letters, I will remark helpfully that steaming is now thought tedious and old fashioned. The doggy way to do it is to use a dissolvent. Pass the brush over the top of the envelope, take out the letter, photograph it, replace it, pass a brush of solvent over the top of the envelope and leave to cool. DO NOT CONFUSE THE BRUSHES.

To Marchette Chute *5:ii:1975*

Dearest Marchette,

The B.B.C. does better things than read *Lolly Willowes*. Three nights ago they played *Timon of Athens*. I am still echoing it in my blood & bones. It is—heard—a magnificent piece; and, it seems to me, *personal*, an outburst of Shakespeare's feelings about the times, the turncoat times of new James after old Elizabeth. Where Alcibiades says to the Senators 'My wounds ache at you' is *crucial*. It might be Raleigh speaking. Surely, it is *observation* that portrayed those time-servers, particularly when they only half-knew that Timon had impoverished himself. They are not imagined as dramatic characters, they are scarcely characters at all; they are as arbitrary as representative vices in a morality play: except for Alcibiades and the Steward, who are recognisable persons, because Shakespeare could endure the sight of them. Alcibiades is particularly interesting because he implements his anger. He is—by his warlike lights—as honestly furious as Timon himself. He is an honourable bad character, like Churchill. Indeed, the Senators reminded me of Chamberlain's government at the time of Munich, the same shoddy ineptness and doting sauve-qui-peut.

Do, if you can distract yourself from Sydney, re-read *Timon*. I was quite bowled over by it. The final banquet, with the address to the Gods, is brilliantly dramatic—even *heard*. What must it have been like when it was seen, with the covered dishes of hot water—and the grimaces of the parasites!

I longed for you to be listening with me.

I suppose Shakespeare didn't finish because, having shot his bolt, he realised he hadn't written a likely play. No heroine, for one thing (the whores were brilliantly played, by the way); and too topical.

This is all I have to say this morning, except that it is suddenly sharp, bright winter; and that I love you.

To Emily Maxwell[1] *11:ii:1975*

... This is the time of year when we used to see gipsies. They had a regular pitch near by, which they used in their regular yearly round between wintering in the New Forest & summering on Sedgemoor. But the bushes have been grubbed up & a bungalow built, and they come no longer. I miss them—their grave brown faces & their low voices and their stately attitudes as they sat down on the doorstep. There was the grandmother with her grizzled hair in six tight pigtails, and Georgina with a new baby every year, the image of Madonna-like motherhood, who knocked out a policeman with one blow.

The strangest and loveliest sight I ever had of them was in Dorchester: a young girl, an imported bride (if you make a grand match, the bride is imported from the Balkans, where the stock is exceptionally pure and pedigreed). She was being taken shopping by a crone of a duenna who was instructing her, in Romany. I suppose she was about sixteen, very slender, very modest. She wore a full skirt of the brightest circus-pink gingham and a scarlet bodice, & her smooth thin arms wore heavy silver bracelets, and her narrow feet were in plimsoles. Then they went into the grocery-shop (one of the few first-rate shops in Dorchester). Later, I asked my friend across the counter what they had bought. Tea, he said. All the gipsies buy their tea

1. Wife of William Maxwell.

from us. They are very particular, they buy our best tea. The thing that made the deepest impression on me, even deeper than the girl's beauty, was her aristocratic aloofness. The circus-pink & scarlet & the bracelets naturally aroused attention: people stopped to stare at her. She was as unconcerned, as remote, as though she came from another world.

If you could lend me *The New Yorker* with the piece on the King of the Gipsies,[1] I would be very grateful. I miss our dear doorstep visitors; and it is one of my greatest prides that on a freezing March morning two of them were persuaded to come indoors and drink tea with me.

To Paul Nordoff *11:ii:1975*

Dearest Paul,

May you visit me in May? Indeed you may, & with all my heart. And the river shall sing you asleep, & the cats will sing you awake, and everything shall be easy & sloppy & unpunctual, and you shall have my newly invented dish of chicken in orange sauce and we will talk of our wicked pasts and be glad we had them.

And, my blue-shielded, blue-nosed, blue-behinded, blue-crossed, blue-Persianed Paul, you have made me very much happier by saying you will lean on me if you need to. This very morning I got a fine fat cheque from *The N.Y.* & said to myself, This will come in handy for Paul.

I am rather baffled by music programmes for deaf children. To me it sounds like picture exhibitions for the blind. But if you approve there must be something in it. Perhaps the children are only hard of hearing and can listen with appliances?

I wish I knew some place where you could go to recuperate. If only I knew someone in Wyoming—or Nova Scotia! I'm sure it should be a different scenery, change of atmosphere as well as change of air. If only one could hire a new self as one can hire a Moss Bros suit, become a painter, an inventor, a market gardener, a missionary, a professional Sufi person. I had a letter from a young Sufi person, telling me she was going to leave N. Y. C. and earn a living by selling bread and necklaces. It would probably be very good for you to swim in the sea.

I had a letter from Soo Pinney,[2] who is very concerned about you. You don't realise how many people love you, dearest Paul. One doesn't, in those black periods when one doesn't love oneself. But the loving goes on.

1. By Joseph Mitchell, published in *McSorley's Wonderful Saloon* (1943).
2. Susanna Pinney, her typist, who became her friend and later on her literary executor, and made a posthumous collection of STW's autobiographical stories, published in 1981 under the title of *Scenes of Childhood*.

... we[1] went to Ashley Chase, and I have my two Helleborii viridis.

It was the kind of afternoon only the maniac English ... would undertake. It began (after a drive along a very narrow lane that got worse & worse) by walking across a sloping field where a few hardy, long-standing tufts of grass floated on a morass. And the rains of 1975 must have fallen on it. I also fell on it—slipped, & fell tidily on my back.[2] This was worse for Roger & Antonia than me. For while they chivalrously hauled me to my feet they also began to slip. Then we came to a fence & a gate opening directly into a splendid gorse thicket, about eight foot deep, in brilliant blossom & brilliant bristle. After that, was the wood. Full of primroses, and spotted orchis leaves, and a different kind of mud, horizontal mud, so to speak, instead of the perpendicular kind of the field. It is a very old and neglected wood. We went increasingly down hill, sliding most of the way and hearing water running in a gulley. In the middle of all this is the arched west wall of an old chapel: if you look in your copy of BOXWOOD[3] you will see its picture. Here the ground was briefly flat, with two slab tombstones, and a stone-built altar. After that was a precipice & the green hellebore, and the brook. Antonia disappeared down the precipice and washed a little mud off in the brook. Roger & I applied ourselves to theft. Digging into a pavement of tree roots at a slope of 1 in 4 is quite a tussle. Exhausted, we returned to the chapel & had cigarettes, I on the altar, Roger & Antonia on the grass on either side, cantoris e decani.[4] We returned, uphill; at one place I felt that Roger & Antonia must have grown tired of hauling me, so I showed my majestic mind by going on all fours.

At the end of this delicious excursion we were all breathless, wet-footed to the knee, muddy to the eyebrow and much the better for it.

To Bea Howe *18:iv:1975*

Dear Bea,
    It is raining. I thought you might like to know.

1. Roger Peers, curator of the Dorset County Museum, and Gräfin Antonia von und zu Trauttmansdorff, a young Englishwoman who lived nearby in the village of Litton Cheney.
2. She was, at this point, 83.
3. A book of sixteen wood engravings by Reynolds Stone, each of which was accompanied by a poem by STW, published in 1957.
4 'Normally as second only to the dean, in choir, he (the chanter) had the first return stall, on the north side of the choir, facing the altar; for which reason the north side is called *Cantoris*, or the chanter's side, as contrasted with *Decani*, the dean's side.' *Grove's Dictionary of Music and Musicians.*

And the Cambridge (England) astronomers have discovered not only a new star, but a new type of star; so they are in all the raptures & contortions of being thrown out. If I could return to the world & choose my lot in life, I think I would choose to be an astronomer. Writing about Elfins is the nearest I can get to the abstract, but astronomy would be abstracteder. It would be a form of thinking, with intensity, about nothing. I try, often and earnestly, to think about nothing, but when I am on the brink of nihilism, I smell the soup boiling over, or I sneeze, or the cats charge in saying The soup—etc. Or I fall asleep, and instantly begin to dream of some concrete object, like an alligator.

It is very satisfactory, isn't it, about Cambodia. All those snub-nosed opponents embracing each other. I can't look on it as a full recompense for the dead, the desolate, the ruined; but it is a great deal better than nothing.

To Joy Chute *20:iv:1975*

. . . My cousin Janet was telling me about a quiet middle-aged man, who teaches at Westminster School, and lives with a boa constrictor called Josephine & a python called Edith. Both are very loving embracing animals, though rather inconstant, for they embrace for warmth rather than from abstract devotion. They coil round his neck, they also coil round the necks of his young pupils. If you think how deliciously hot children [are], you can imagine the delight of Josephine & Edith.

To William Maxwell *22:iv:1975*

. . . To remember every detail of a street, a house, a garden; *once well known*: What tree it was that rustled over what wall; where the breaks in the sidewalk came, where the post-office was—or the garden shed with the bunch of hose hanging on what accustomed nail. If one can remember things, without emotion, conscientiously in their order, one can *bore oneself to sleep*.

To David Garnett *8:v:1975*

Dearest David,

If you come to England in October it would be very good & kind of you to visit me. Or I might hoist myself up to London to see you. I was there briefly last month, and watched a very fine blizzard *terrifying* Whitehall, dwarfing & bleaching it. I had been visiting Ian & Trekkie Parsons, where I met Quentin Bell & his very handsome & stately wife. She sat upright, well back into her chair—not a fidget in her. I think she is descended from one of those Oliviers you played with as a child. I liked her very much, and felt she had been composed by Gluck.

Are your woods full of nightingales? The best orchestras of nightingales I ever heard were in the woods round Aubeterre. They sang in rivalry, but the rivals were massed choirs. Another pleasant thing I remember at Aubeterre was an old man who had moored a shallow boat to the riverbank (Drôme) filled it with earth and grew salads in it. My deep-sea-diving, *cum* naturalist, *cum* stone-mason friend,[1] who long ago was our garden boy took me for a drive last Sunday. His car was full of rattles & squeaks, & he remarked thoughtfully that it was like a wood at night.

To Ben Hellman *15:vii:1975*

... I am making a curry. It is cooking very slowly, as curries should, and the house is gently filling with a delicious smell of spices, chicken, shallots & green gooseberries, all coming to love each other, and waiting for the moment of nuptial blessing when I shall add the tomato.

Do you know that I am a gifted cook, & excel in curries? They are, so to speak, in my blood. One side of my inheritance is a long line of those wicked exploiting John Company Anglo-Indians, like my grandfather Josiah Hudleston. His garden was full of irremoveable holy men, his porch was ornamented by beggars slowly winding worms (on sticks, one twirl an hour) out of their sores, tailors with sewing-machines, scholars with grievances, and friends & relations of the house-servants who had dropped in for conversation. Oh, & people with a dog for sale, or a durian,[2] or a dried fish. He hated nothing that God had made; except missionaries. If there had been more wicked exploiting, etc. people like him there would have been no Indian Mutiny. (I have inherited the abhorrence of missionaries as well as the curries.)

To Bea Howe *16:x:1975*

... David came last week, & I gave him brandy with his coffee, and some admirable fillet steak. I watched his start of delighted surprise when he sank his teeth into the first mouthful.

1. Colin House, who helped to take care of her in her last illness and in whose arms she died at daybreak on 1 May 1978, in her house by the River Frome.
2. An evil-smelling, delicious-tasting tropical fruit.

After the first mutual shock of seeing ourselves so much changed for the worst, we found we had not changed so much after all, and it was a happy visit. Nerissa[1] was with him. She had been driving him all over England, visiting William[2] in Grisedale, & a cousin in Wales, & a cousin's widow in Somerset—& so on. I asked after Hilton. Hilton he gave to Richard,[3] Richard has let it to a model tenant. The model tenant is devoted to lawns. The lawn is like an advertisement, smooth grass paths have been cut through the orchard, there is not a nettle left. Bunny seemed pleased. I listened in woe. I detest the thought of lovely sombre untidy Hilton turned into a stockbroker's bijou.

Nerissa was charming, & *extremely* beautiful, & very like Vanessa. She wore *large* scarlet boots, and lives in Bethnal Green, in a house divided into flats for the new generation by the L.C.C. I suppose the indigenous inhabitants are put away in some High-Rise horror, or transferred to the new outskirts.

I have been through a devastating interval of no impulse to write: I think (I say it in a cautious whisper) I may be getting out of it. It was worse than hell while it lasted. It was Limbo, peppered with visitors.

To William Maxwell 7:xii:1975

... My table is a welter of little bits of paper saying: Remember Mrs Hodges, 11, 11, post Tomkins, more string, bird-seed, order crumpets for Saturday, cats' sprats, rector's bottle. The little bits of paper are mislaid, & others, conjectural, are added to them. The kitchen is a riot of feeding friends, droppers-in, cats, and birds. In my dementia I do Christmas with my little hatchet. Yesterday I addressed a letter to Mrs Casserole.

How are you? Have you properly got over that operation? Will you keep the New York apartment, or fold yourself inside the garden fence of Baptist Church Road? What is the name of that unfortunate man whose fate it is to deal with me after you leave *The N. Y.*?

What is man's chief end? Death, I would suppose, since we practise for it every night of our lives. I understand your resentment at the death of people you love. I feel even angrier at the death of those who are cut short; or their frustration; like Ben Britten, who cannot write the flute part at the top of an orchestral score without having his arm lifted for him, or Solomon with his technique and interpretation imprisoned in his palsied arms; even

1. His youngest daughter.
2. His second son.
3. His eldest son, now a director of the publishing house, Macmillan London Ltd.

more for the young who go down into the pit in battles of the Somme. *That* is intolerable. I was brought up to think it a sin to waste bread, and I have lived all my life in a world that wastes life. When you shall hear the sudden surly bell, don't, I beg you, be angry on my behalf. Remember all the nets that didn't catch me, all the lies that didn't trap me, all the tarbabies I didn't get stuck on.

━━◆◆◆◆◆◆ 1976 ◆◆◆◆◆━━

To Joy Chute *9:i:1976*

Darling Joy,

This is to announce how February is to be inaugurated in Wessex. Antonia & I will tie on our deerstalker caps, grasp our alpenstocks, pull on our galoshes, and set out from Dorchester South Station (familiar to you) on a journey of artistic discovery. And at Brockenhurst we shall get out of the train and discover Mrs Cameron's Ex Voto.

Mrs Cameron[1] had a son who came back from India (by train from Southampton, we believe) and met his mother on the platform of Brockenhurst Station. And she commemorated this reunion by presenting the Gr. Western Railway (as it was at that date) with a collection of her portrait photographs of Eminent Men of the time.

Everyone knows so much. When conversation lags at a dinner-party, guests ask each other if they know about the Cameron photographs. Everyone does. But as far as Antonia & I know, no one has ever seen them.[2]

That is because trains don't stop at Brockenhurst. Mrs Cameron's son must have pulled the communication cord, or tipped the engine driver. Let us, I said to Antonia, go to Brockenhurst, even if it means spending a night there; and *see* those photographs. Antonia studied catalogues of trains, & discovered not only an east-bound train which stops at B. but a west-bound train that leaves it about an hour later; and added that she had bought a dear little picnic-basket.

Every difficulty can be overcome by having an Antonia. So there we shall be, pilgrims to Mrs C's Ex Voto, looking at all those eminent men, all as eminent-looking as can be: Darwin with a furrowed brow, Tennyson in a wide-brimmed hat, Carlyle in a shawl, Ruskin with a rug.

To Susanna Pinney *20:1:1976*

Darling Soo,

Here is the proposed order of the elfin stories—And WHAT am I to call them?

1. Julia Cameron, the great Victorian photographer.
2. As it turned out, they didn't either. The pilgrimage was postponed, and never took place.

Chatto & the Viking want the text in March: Viking to publish in /76, Chatto early in /77. Viking promise an early paperback, but say that reviewers only attend to hardback; so they want to do a small hardback edition first.

How are you? Are you properly well again, and not being got down by overwork? If I don't ring you up to ask it is not because I am not concerned, but from a feeling that if, by some strange chance, you are sitting with your feet up, it would be no kindness to get you on to them.

[P.S.] There has been a notable fox-hunting here. There were so many foxes that the hounds didn't know which to chase. Whenever they got on a line, another fox started up and led a hound-schism astray: across the river, into gardens & graveyards, uphill and down dale.
Result. No kill: Hounds exhausted and breathless. Foxes grinning.

To Ben Hellman 29:i:1976

. . . Can you suggest any suitable aspersions to spread abroad about Mrs Thatcher? It is idle to suggest she has unnatural relations with Mrs Barbara Castle; what is needed is something socially lower: that she eats asparagus with knife & fork, or serves Instant Mash potatoes. One would think her voice would be enough to damn her; but it hasn't done so. I never thought I would live to regret the suppression of Edward Heath, but now I pine to see his honest British teeth in the public press again.

To Joy Finzi 1:iv:1976

. . . The daffodils are more punctual than I. The first pages of the foreword to Valentine's poems are done—done with effort, for I found it melancholy to go through letters & diaries & see hope stiffening into patience & patience putting on the weeds of resignation.

Then I gave way to a variety of difficulties. I was not so banal as to have influenza, but I had an extremely tedious chill; then I had to find a gardener, Sibyl having decided to retire; then I had to read every word of an enormous book to check if the cuts broke the flow of the whole; they didn't; but it is still an enormous book and the expense of publishing it will be the death of Chatto & Windus; then I had to attend to my own book, making sure that the final text had its stays properly laced; then I broke loose from duty and wrote a long short story; and now I have to think forward to a series of

286

loving visitors covering this month and part of next. I wish I had a house to do them all justice, *all at once*. Blenheim, for instance . . . .

I went to Chaldon one afternoon last week. The snowdrops we planted have grown into a grove; and the air was black with rooks & loud with their general conversation. I suppose it was general; it may have been about politics, with opinions.

To David Garnett *30:v:1976*

. . . I went for a strange drive last evening. There was a thick mist, and through the mist scampered innumerable rabbits, visible & invisible. I was being taken to a party where I heard of an American who was complaining to a Hebrew Jew about the wickedness and treachery of the Russians. 'They haven't even a *word* for détente.' The Hebrew Jew said musingly 'What is détente in French?'

Do you ever feel the childishness of old age? I don't mean second-childhood, but the particular childish excitement at being able to do things dexterously?—to pour out milk without spilling it, to put things back in their proper places, to be capable and responsible? It is a pure pride, as it was then. I only get it occasionally, and it lasts like morning dew.

To Emily Maxwell *15:vi:1976*

Darling Emmy,

My Friend Degas[1] came last Saturday, & ever since then I have been in and out of Halévy's home, with the feeling that I knew or knew of every one who was mentioned.

It is extraordinary how Paris of that date is such a familiar milieu. A book about people in London of the same period would be full of unknowns to me: even Hampstead or Chelsea would be a clatter of strange names to me.

But I did not know that Degas was an anti-Dreyfusard. Another of his misfortunes.

It is all comprised, foretold, in the Nadar photograph of him: his long sad nose, his long sad self, his crepe-banded hat. When I study the various pictures of him, I feel as though I were listening to the sea.

1. By Daniel Halévy, translated and edited by Mina Curtiss (1964).

To Marchette & Joy Chute *4:vii:1976*

. . . My hand shakes with heat & watering-cans. When I am not carrying a four gallon watering can, I am holding a large fan. Yesterday I rescued a bumble-bee with it. The bumble-B. was tangled in a cobweb behind the fridge—which amplified its buzz to the Dead March in *Saul*. When I had disentangled it and pulled its cobwebs off the foolish insect went back & back to chains & slavery. It was only by fanning it violently that I drove it out of the outer door. It went off into the bay tree saying that only by the greatest courage & dexterity had it got the better of a hurricane.

In this dreamlike heat I have been sorting the original Valentine & Sylvia letters for you. She so life-like, so authentic, that she seems to be in the room with me. It is myself I cannot believe in. Was I ever like that, I think: so free, so spirited, so weathercock to every small wind. What has become of the woman? She must have been overlooked when they ended the story, when the last letters were written.

To William Maxwell *13:vii:1976*

Dear William,

You will find Shelley's lake in *Prometheus Unbound*. It is a lyric, & begins 'On a poet's lip I slept.'

I am glad you approve of a collection of letters. I will make out a list of possibles, and meanwhile here is an early one, kept by my father.

S.T.W. to G.T.W. Aug. 1903 Strete. Devon. 'There are a lot of cats, a yellow & a grey one and a little tabby kitten and a tabby cat (I think it is the kitten's mother) and a thin stripy one that belongs to the grocer, and a white one with yellow and black spots, which belongs to Mrs Wallis, and I think there are more.

Your loving Sylvia.'

aet.9—and much the

same preoccupations as now.

Your story. I know that trouble with too many characters. I went out of my mind with *The Flint Anchor*, trying to make them all grow older simultaneously; and I had to kill off two bishops in *The Corner*. It sometimes helps to be lifelike: to make their first appearance a name or a comment, and build them up later. Proust's device. I have never had to tackle *invention & memory*; but I would rely on invention of the two; memory is the vinegar of the pair, and you remember the Spanish recipe for salad dressing: a profligate with the oil, a miser with the vinegar, a counsellor with the salt & a madman to beat it all together.

No, one never learns: it would stultify learning. Robert Bridges, finishing a poem: 'Casting thee forth, my child, I rise above thee'.

But if you leave it all to come together, like a stew, it will come together. And meanwhile, you are writing it, & in heaven.

I have been enjoying the Bicentennial. There is a lovely picture of Signing the Declaration, a crowded yet orderly canvas, with all the signatories with two legs apiece. Besides, I am much attached to Jefferson & like being reminded of him . . .

Antonia took me for a drive yesterday. We could have thought ourselves in Umbria, the landscape was so bleached and bare: and curiously ennobled, by its misfortunes. Higgledy-piggledy little collections of sheds & cottages on the distant hillsides looked compact and timeless, like mountain villages, as though they were fortified, and expected wolves next winter. All the usual smoothness & slight fubsiness was gone, instead the timelessness of a skeleton. And instead of flowers, hordes of butterflies, basking on the hot earth, drifting through the hot air.

To Mavis Gallant[1] *1:viii:1976*

Dear Mavis Gallant,

My copy of *Poèmes à la France* was long ago irreparably borrowed. I am most grateful to you for offering me a replacement.

As you say, it is of its period, and hard to reconcile with today. But it is true of its period. Love of France was part of English education, as it was in the 17th and 18th centuries, and the 19th too, except for an ill-guided moral affection for Germany. It was a kind of satelisée affinity: France, the planet, did not reciprocate, felt no impulse to.

I doubt if it still exists. I suspect that air-travel has put a stop to this sort of thing. People can get themselves carried anywhere, 'eat fish and chips in Spain', as Leavis numbered among the charms of a Welfare State; and *go nowhere*.

I was bequeathed to Daniel Menaker, who seems most anxious to please and befriend, but so far has had to exert himself to gloss over the fact that Mr. Shawn doesn't like me (as a contributor: I have never met him)[2] Vieux singe ne plaît à personne.

1. Canadian novelist, short story writer, and journalist. Like STW, she has been a frequent contributor to *The New Yorker*.
2. In the years after William Shawn became the editor, *The New Yorker* published 95 stories by STW.

Dear William,

You tantalise me. I wish I could sit with bats in a cave with crystals and look at a snow-capped mountain. Snow: Antonia said to me. Do you remember that cold spell in January when everything froze & I washed my face with snow?

It is like some complicated sentence on the damned to have day after day, week after week, of flawless hot weather and to wish it away. Trekkie in Sussex wrote, 'our lawns are like loofahs.' Last week the New Forest was on fire: I could smell the burning here, carried on a brisk east wind. One of the firemen engaged in the fighting said that it was carried from the centre of the fire by escaping rabbits with their fur blazing. Nothing can stem the wild poetry of the race. You can judge the state of my garden when I tell you that even *weeds* don't spring from it.

The only creatures that thrive are moths & butterflies, but they prefer it indoors, and flit about the house as though it were woodland.

To William Maxwell *14:ix:1976*

The cats & I are so healthy & so hungry that we snatch the food from each others' mouths and filch the blanket from each others' shoulders. We sit before the fire and listen to the owls, and leave wet footmarks all over the house. At any moment there will be snow on the Grampians. It is very odd being kicked into winter while the leaves are still on the trees.

. . . Have you ever known a murderer? It appears that I have done so. He was a particularly amiable, generous, sensitive man, and I was much attached to him, and grieved when he killed himself. A good project of his had folded up for lack of support, and I supposed he killed himself from frustration. Now his widow has told me it was from remorse because, many years back, he had killed his first wife. I wish I could think she lied or fancied, but she told me sincerely, to unbosom herself. The longer one lives, the more one has to pity. He was totally unsuited to be a murderer. I am haunted by the thought of his long memory of a frightful, incompatible deed. So much so that, as you see, I too have to unbosom myself. One has to be Sophocles to take this kind of thing calmly—if Sophocles did.

To David Garnett *26:ix:1976*

. . . I hear a leisurely splashing from the river. It is the aquatic cow, who morning and evening goes for a walk in it. The river runs full and fast.

The last time I saw a copy of *Figaro* it was full of how les bobbies ran for their lives in Notting Hill. By now you may have read how our drought has been followed by torrential rains. According to Londoners, this was caused by powerful Ugandan Asians performing a rain ceremony in Hyde Park. In Devonshire, on the other hand, it is attributed to Local Government. Local Government put stand-pipes in every town street, and since then it has rained every day.

Is *Up She Rises* the ancestral book you told me about?—I shall make a point of living through the winter so as to read it. *Kingdoms of Elfin* should be out early next year. What a pair we are!

   Madam, how does my gay goshawk?
   Madam, how does my doo?[1]

If you hadn't intervened, dear David, I should have gone on writing poems & hiding them in hatboxes, & being an ornament to the Plainsong & Medieval Music Society, and publishing such learned treatises on the Hoquet in the 14th cent. at long intervals. How glad I am you intervened. And how grateful.

TO JOY CHUTE *21:x:1976*

Darling Joy,

I think you should know about our Remarkable Cow.

She is a black & white Holstein, one of a herd that grazes in the opposite field. During the drought, when there was nothing to graze on, she took to wading in what was left of the river, & grazing on brooklime; and developed this into long solitary walks up the river.

The weather changed; the river rose; she went on walking. When the river was in spate she went on imperturbably walking, with the water over her back. It is her daily routine: she sets out in the morning, climbs the other bank, grazes in a field she has no right to graze in—cf. the solitary Highland lass[2]—comes back about an hour before sundown—looking ineffably calm and righteous.

I have grown very fond of her—and use her as a river-gauge. I used to know the river's level by how far it rose up a stake. I now go by how far it goes up the cow.

TO MARCHETTE AND JOY CHUTE *22:xi:1976*

... *The New Yorker*, whom I had come to despair of, have taken a story:

1. Scottish form of *dove*.
2. In Wordsworth's *The Solitary Reaper*.

mortal, this time, but about an adolescent girl-child, as near Elfin as mortal can be. Viking Press will deliver you a copy of *Kingdoms of Elfin* as soon as it is published: January, I hope, but maybe February. They cannot possibly deliver it *with my love*: they would need a jewelled truck and a retinue of cherubs to do that; or a barge burning upon the East River.

I have hung up my winter curtains and got out another blanket and am generally woolling myself up; for though it isn't really cold yet, there is a feeling in the still night-air that it soon will be. Winter, whetting its knife. I have also got out, with deep appreciation, your mother's black stole, in which I feel at once comfortable and dignified—qualities not often simultaneous. It is dignity I can't often manage. I am usually comfortable.

I have lost my remarkable cow, who was so dear and so mysterious to me. The herd of which she was the intellectual ornament has been moved to a different pasture with no access to her chosen field (unless she can undo two gates and cross the lane). I miss her a great deal. She has been replaced by four brown cows, comfortably warm and russet, but prosaic—no sense of an au-delà.

To William Maxwell *22:i:1977*

Dear William,

When you last wrote you were reading the letters of Anne Thackeray Ritchie. I hope you have fallen in love for life, and will make her a habit. It is as though a small bird came & settled on one's hand with no particular consciousness of doing it, but sure of being well received. Do you know her *Blackstick Papers?* She knew all the notabilities, alighted on them—her father's hostess—remembered with an easy affection, had gazed with veneration on George Sand, listened to Joachim. She was the perfection of dilettante, because she took delight; and her easy transparent English has inherited her father's button-holing without making a special thing of it. Another reason why I love her is that she exasperated Leslie Stephen. Think of the knotted emotions in his bosom when the unpunctual, mislaying, imperturbable lady of his house made that scandalous marriage with a young man half her age.

This has been a dark week for me. Paul Nordoff died on Monday— of cancer in a hospital in the Ruhr. He was a bi-lingual, so he didn't have to die in a foreign language; and the man in charge was a friend of his. I rang him up twice a week or so—strange loving & lively conversations over the Pit. At the news he was dead I was thankful for his sake: he had dreaded losing his patience & gaiety: but I was appalled by the realisation of the *total* discrepancy between the quick & the dead.

To William Maxwell *7:ii:1977*

Dear William,

Those farmers of yours seem (to judge by your recital of labour pangs) to be getting along very nicely, and to have the novella well in hand. Their indifference to the shape of sentences and varieties of construction is true to life: it is how they build barns and mend fences; if they have seized on a memory that has turned out to be impossible that, dear William, is how they have always made their legends. I daresay you find them disconcerting, but I am sure you can rely on them.

I have spent today with Peter Pears: that is to say, he came to lunch, and as he came in his sister's car where she had not attended to the battery, at five p.m. on a beautiful spring evening we were still walking about in the garden waiting for a mechanic to set him going.

We discussed the problem of going on living after one has been cut in half. He has found his solution in the harp. There can never be another accompanist like Ben; and pianist after pianist has played beautifully in his pianist's compartment, and nothing came of it; but Ossian Ellis the harpist & he get along very nicely, and Ravel's songs, especially *Sainte*, bloom on harpstrings. I suggested they might try Moore's Irish melodies. It was one of my good ideas. He looks so gaunt, so solitary, that except for his height and his speaking voice I think I could not have recognized him. As I have been having influenza I daresay he felt equally at a loss. But the soup (J. artichoke, *Palestine soup, a palpable misnomer*) re-established me as me.

By this time tomorrow I shall have shed the dregs of that influenza, for Antonia is coming in the morning to keep me in bed all day. The weather forecast is showers and gales from the southwest: the perfect lullaby.

And if you should get a fit of worrying how I am, if I have been snowed up, bitten by a corgi, chased by a cow, fallen into the river, etc., then INSTANTLY REMEMBER Antonia, who keeps a loving eye on me, knows by intuition where I keep the cloves & the bay leaves, puts back books where they belong, mulls me cider, takes me for drives, entertains me at Baglake where I sink, as if heaven ordained it, into the most comfortable chair by the fire, lights my cigarettes, refills my glass—and likes my company. And has a low voice, & is a quiet mover. As quiet and comfortable as Lady Anne Conway's Quakers—Did you know that story? She was one of the learned ladies of the 17th cent and Dr Henry More, the Theo-philosopher of St Johns Coll. Cambridge wrote to her as one theo-philosopher to another. But she suffered from migraine, was obliterated by loud voices & sudden clamours; so she had Quakeresses as her attendants. And when the pious platonical Henry More learned this, he told her to get rid of them, they were as anti-Anglican as the Devil himself. And she explained she could not, would not, And he cast her off & never wrote to her again.

I beat my breast when I remember that when I was young I was narrow-minded as he. Different stumbling-block; but the same idiocy. Oh dear!

To William Maxwell *28 : ii : 1977*

. . . My memory decays, Did I send you a copy of Valentine's 1949 auto-biography?—about her tormented youth, and trying not to become an alcoholic. If I didn't, a carbon shall come to you . . .

One reason why my memory decays is that I have three cats, all so loving and insistent that they play cat's-cradle with every train of thought.

They drove me distracted while I was having influenza, gazing at me with large eyes & saying: O Sylvia, you are so ill, you'll soon be dead. And who will feed us then? FEED US NOW!

To David Garnett 5:iii:1977

Dearest David,

Up She Rises came two days ago. I am no further than Portsmouth, but I must now and at once write to tell you that I love Clementina with as much reality as if she had come to life in a story by Defoe, & that I followed her every mile of that journey. It is a triumph of narrative: *you tell it as she would remember it*: the mutton cutlet and mashed turnip, the very small teapot, the hot bath before the fire, the carnation in the conservatory, and her mind always ahead of her feet, even the places where she rested, or slept dry, things she would put behind her. Oh! that villainous Yorkshire laundress: the cheese on the other hand was better than Scotch cheese. Borrow would have hugged you.

You set me thinking. The journey is the artery of fiction from the *Aeneid* on. Stationary stories are as special as orchids. Jane Austen, H. James, are an order of enclosed contemplatives. Stendhal—I never cease to bless you for telling me to read Stendhal, as you did at the end of that long walk in the Essex flats—is always on the move, if only dodging the police.

To William Maxwell 20:v:1977

Dear William,

Today is Valentine's birthday. A day with lilies of the valley coming into bloom, and the thrush singing in the height of the tall aspen poplar she planted, and worthy to be her birthday—except that the wind is in the north-east and belies the sunshine. And those kind Chutes rang up after their breakfast to remember her with love.

This day a month Antonia will be driving me to Aldeburgh, where I am to sit cocked up in the limelight, listening to Peter Pears reading some of my poems; and trying not to look too pleased with them. Me trying, that is. He is reading the long dream poem about following the burial procession of the cross to its grave in the desert, crossing the Mediterranean on air and meeting a shooting star going off on its own errand. He wants some more of the later ones to go with it, & this led to sorting through a vast stack of them. One would think I had never done anything else but write poems.

When I consider how my days are spent I am at a loss to know how it all got packed in, & I still preserving an air of leisure; and reading the leaders in *The Times*. And drinking coffee all day, as befits the great-great granddaughter of a Mevrow, if that's how she spelled it—it seems odd. Her married name was Reijnette.—if that's how it's spelled; and her husband founded a town in South Africa.

But it was a great-great uncle, though also on the distaff side, who displayed such self-control and aplomb. He was on his way back from India, sitting on deck with his slippered feet resting on the rail, when one of the slippers fell off and sank into the ocean. So he kicked off the other. Now that *would* be an inheritance worth having.

Meanwhile, I have you, dear William, all the more endeared by not being a relation.

To DAVID GARNETT *31 : v : 1977*

Dearest David,

From the start I have hung on your approval, waited for your verdict—even when I flouted it. You can imagine how pleased I am with your praise of *Elfin*,[1] and with your analogy of the child 'quite certain of the facts of its imagination' . . .

No, I don't mention homosexuality. Even if I had known that Irish fairies are pederasts, I doubt if I would have gone to the Kingdom of Nephin to explore for it—though in the first version of 'The Blameless Triangle' Mustafa buggered the lot, with no ill-feeling on any one's part. But elfins, as I saw them, seldom love, unless they are very young, like the girl at Blokula, or love a mortal, like Tiphaine. Perhaps their longevity keeps them cool-blooded, or their extreme self-consciousness. Un amour de convenance is more their line. I am still finding out more about them. If I am spared, I may do another volume. There are three stories already—and a heavenly amount of research involved. Oberon, for instance, was a hermeticist, and had a Lullian Wheel,[2] and a bowl of prophetic goldfish.

I shall be here all July, please come to lunch—to stay, if that would be

1. *Kingdoms of Elfin.*
2. Raimón Lull, the 13th-century Catalan visionary and philosopher, annoyed the Moors in North Africa by preaching Christianity to them and they stoned him to death at the age of eighty. His scholasticism was so bizarre that oddities he was not guilty of attached themselves to his name, and the Lullian Wheel may have been one of them. However, in spite of considerable research, I have not as yet found evidence that any contrivance used for occult purposes and known by that name ever existed, except in Elfindom.

more restful for you, at any rate, to stay long enough for an after lunch siesta. I am deplorably the worse for this last year's wear and tear, and a prey to vain regrets—that I shall never see the Aurora Borealis again, or listen to larks—too deaf; or walk up hills, too lame, or re-read *Clarissa* in small type—too lazy to get her in a later edition than my sharp-eyed great-grandfather's.

To Joy Chute *15 : vi : 1977*

. . . Everything is damp. It rains incessantly . . . The garden is full of roses that are too damp to open, and mown hay that will never be fit to feed any animal short of a whale—I don't know if whales eat hay—and strawberries rotting under nets; and rejoicing birds who sing such cheerful notes that I can only suppose they are full of malice; it can't be only slugs—another thing the garden is full of.

But we jubilated bravely last week, aided by the national scheme of bonfires. It was heartening to see them catch alight—helped by copious libations of paraffin—and burn with such conviction, here, there, & every-where. I visited the Litton Cheney bonfire, & sat wrapped in a sheepskin jacket in a weatherproof car. The strong & brave stood round, spell-bound as every right-minded person is by a bonfire, black worshipping silent silhouettes while the fire crackled and shouted. A very pagan spectacle, so it was surprising to hear these prehistoric worshippers of the fire-god end the ancient rite with the national anthem.

And at that moment, the bell rang, and there on the doorstep was Colin . . . with a bass (shad, I think, to you). He in his diver's suit and the bass both straight out of the sea.

To William Maxwell *13 : vii : 1977*

Dear William,

Your shaving-brush sits in my bathroom cabinet, and from time to time, unobtrusively catches my eye with a mute enquiry when it will see you again. I tell it to be patient; that you are busy with a novel. Il reviendra à Pâques, ou à la Trinité, I say. We would like, meanwhile, to know how the novel is getting on, & you.

I think I told you I was going to Aldeburgh, as part of the Festival programme. It all passed off very painlessly. Peter Pears read a number of my poems, ancient and modern, so beautifully that I forgot to be con-strained and sat enjoying them. And I am posting by sea, because there's no hurry for them, two copies, one for you, one for Kate, of the booklet he had made for the occasion of the most recent of them, some of which were read. The finest part of the programme was when he & t'other tenor (who was there to sing various settings of me) leaped back over six centuries & sang two *a cappella* pieces by Machaut. You remember what I said about Machaut in *The Corner That Held Them*.[1]

But the best part of that excursion was being driven to Aldeburgh by Antonia, who did not know that East Suffolk landscape, & back via Ely because she did not know Ely—a mere circumbendibus of about 100 miles in our homeward journey. That was so satisfactory, and we lunched so happily on the edge of a cornfield where the corn was so tall & regular that it paralleled the pillars of the cathedral's nave, that we plan a circumbendibus from the romanesque apostles at Malmesbury into Wales to admire St David's. It is pleasant for me that Antonia, who as a child grew up in the East Indies, has since explored the Sahara & Turkey, doesn't know much about England. So I display the fens round Ely while she tells me about remotest Turkey. Our minds grow broader & broader, while we compete, like Shelley's nightingales, with experimental soups.

I spent yesterday morning admiring a most eloquent thunderstorm. The sky twitched with lightning, the crashes came so immediately after the flashes that there was no time to judge the distance by counting five between them, it was as much as I could do to say *Klopstock*.

The dragging river rushed into spate, in an hour the garden was paved with rose-petals. It shows what a summer it has been, & is being, for roses that this morning there are as many roses as ever; and their scent is unlocked in the watered air. Till now I had to interrogate them for it.

To David Garnett *13:vii:1977*

Dearest David,

Will the 29th July suit you? It is a good date for me: though I could manage the 30th, if that would be better for you. I hope you will trust my cooking enough to come to lunch. And who will come with you, for I hope you won't be driving yourself: Dorset is a thick soup of caravans & traffic blocks percolating to the beautiful sea. Hot Cross soup.

1. '"Now, John! The Machaut Kyrie." The three voices sprang into the air. If *Triste loysir* had seemed a foretaste of paradise, the Kyrie was paradise itself. This was how the blessed might sing, singing in a duple measure that ran as nimbly on its four feet as a weasel running through a meadow, with each voice in turn enkindling the others, so that the music flowed on and was continually renewed.' See p. 203, Chatto & Windus edition; p. 237, Viking Press edition.

I shall think of you on Friday, being made a Doc. of Lit. I hope there will be a great deal of ceremony, that you will be robed and hooded, and given a bouquet & an illuminated scroll, and that Birmingham will be at its brightest. And that Richard won't mislay you in those environs. I would like to picture arriving by canal in a state barge; but that is too much even for my wilder hopes.

And I shall address this letter to Hilton Hall behind its grand gates. I hope it doesn't look too sleek. I recall it in its apples on the floor, coffee-pot on the hob days—gaunt and hospitable.

To Joy Chute *13 : vii : 1977*

. . . She laid six beautiful eggs and sat on them as a mother should, and I was proud as a grandmother; one day she was gone. She could not have deserted, some tragedy must have taken place: a scolding magpie, some wretched child with a catapult, a hawk, a cat *not one of mine*. I grieved, & felt so badly that I had to ask Peg Manisty who was staying here to take the nest out of the letter-box; I had not the heart to do it. She did, & together we mourned over all that patience and skill, and the six eggs that would never be six small tits. And left it in a basket on the hall table and went for a drive to forget our sorrows. When we came back, the six eggs were gone. My practical cats had eaten them.

To Jean Larson *21 : ix : 1977*

. . . Last night when I was being driven along the Powerstock Road I saw glittering through the darkness two emerald-green stars . . . the reflecting eyes of a fox. This reminded my driver that she had once heard a family of young foxes talking among themselves. Their voices were gentle and lady-like.

To Trekkie Parsons[1] *30 : ix : 1977*

I have always regretted the impetuosity with which I have given books and letters away to institutions. I gave my grand *Tudor Church Music* volumes, and my *Madrigal School* set to Morley College, and they were

1. Painter. Wife of Ian Parsons.

destroyed in an air-raid. If I had not been so damned public-spirited, they would be alive still. Bequeath your Leonard letters if you feel you should let Sussex have them. But let Sussex wait.

To William Maxwell *7:x:1977*   *Cequatia*[1]

Dear William,

It is a rainy Saturday afternoon, yesterday it was a rainy Friday afternoon, tomorrow it will be a rainy Sunday afternoon. With no Verdi Requiem (by far his grandest opera) to listen to, I will write to you and get my pleasure that way.

I did not know the details of Stevenson's death.[2] It must have been just what he would have approved of—that assumption of responsibility. Do you know that at the time when the Boycott household in Ireland were being boycotted he wanted to go and live with them? . . .

My nose *se retrousse* over those Thames & Hudson books,[3] but for all that I like them, because I am incarnately a tripper, a reader of house plaques. I like to see what the place was like; though it would often be more to the purpose to show what X & Y saw from their windows. When Valentine and I visited Grasmere, and saw William's garden hat and Dorothy's favourite teacup—gawdy—Valentine opened the oven door in their kitchen. *It grated.* And in a flash I was there, watching Dorothy put in another of those mutton pies, after which William was so often indisposed.

To Margaret Manisty *1:xii:1977*

. . . It has been detestably cold, and I did somewhat wilt beneath it, but am now spry & recovered, thank you. Antonia gave me a divine day in bed. And you have now given me those persons by V. Eyck, with a great deal of explanation attached. It seems to me that the explainer protests too much. The centre of the picture is the hands, in their ritual clasp, and the lady is certainly great with child—her straight back redressing the frontal bulge shows as much—and the gentleman in the hat is demonstrating that the child is his, parented but not legitimised. And the dog may be an emblem

1. An invented address because she was tired of writing 'Frome Vauchurch'.
2. Robert Louis Stevenson's, in Samoa. As he was crossing the room he turned to his wife and asked, 'Do I look strange?' and lapsed from consciousness.
3. *R. L. Stevenson and his World; Conrad and his World*, etc.

of fidelity, but, I think, it is just an expression of dog's (lady's dog) habit for being in the foreground. Just such a dog walks past on the opposite bank every morning, taking its gentleman for a constitutional. The *gentleman* is an expression of fidelity. His sneezes ring out over the drenched meadow.

You don't say how you are.

To William Maxwell *6:i:1978*

... It is no time of year. It is certainly not Jan 6, 1978. The grass is as green as grass, the skies are high and fathomless. The birds are singing. This morning the first aconite bloomed in the path. I do not feel as graceful as the landscape. My legs are like ancient monuments, they ache and give way, and my cats look at me deploringly, and say privately to each other that I am a shadow of my old self, a shadow even of what I was before Christmas. Belatedly, old age has clawed me in its clutch. But I am almost as good as ever in bed, they say; and if there is a cold spell later on, there we shall be; and Antonia will bring her little porringer and nourish us.

But I shall not re-read Colette. I have looked forward to doing this, & find to my grief that I have outlived her.

To William Maxwell *29:i:1978*

... About a month ago I had a sudden collapse. Antonia kept me in bed for a while, & for a while it was debated whether or no I had had a very small stroke. It wasn't; merely old age had laid a rather sudden grasp on me, especially my legs. I can only walk very slowly, & cling to whatever is near for a support. I have a doctor, who is the image of death, & prescribes so many different pills that if I took them all I should be incapable of taking anything else. Unfortunately, he cannot prescribe better weather. You have had blizzards, we have had floods, & now for the last two days the wind has blown like an ancient curse. But do not worry about me. When the weather improves, so will I; and meanwhile the worst of my sufferings is the amount of care, solicitude, visiting that I provoke among my friends. I have almost forgotten what silence sounds like.

How lovely to hear the whole of the *Winterreise*. Long ago I heard it sung by Peter & Ben—at the original pitch, which makes the soloist sound much younger & his sentiments those of youth, genuinely self-pitying & rodomontade. And I shall never forget how Ben made the crow's wings flop, how heavy, remorseless & pursuing they were... The cycle has become the prey of baritones, out for a melancholy constitutional. It has lost its vagrancy. If I could have my way I would keep it in a box with a lid, & only allow it to be sung by young tenors, not vocalizers, either. I have never heard what type of voice Schubert had, have you?

To Joy Chute 3:ii:1978

. . . I am sorry to write to you by such a poor weak paw. For some reason two bad legs make it impossible to type, & not all that easy to write.

I have been given a young Cape Jessamine, about two foot high, and on the advice of its grower it stands in a dark corner of the room—where it looks unearthly & like Valentine's ghost. Like Valentine's ghost, it scents the whole room. Do you grow one in your window bay? Its wants are simple—much like mine. It wants to be kept warm.

The oil strike near Corfe Castle is no great surprise. All that stretch of the coast is so full of oil it *smells* of it, and at intervals small scientific men used to drill here and there. Since this find, there will be more of them, larger, with more machinery.

To David Garnett 3:ii:1978

. . . *After the Death of Don Juan* is to be re-issued. It is a good book, & was swamped by 1938-39 events. It may well be swamped this time too, but at any rate it has got its head up.

I am pleased with your doctor's good opinion on you, though they give with one hand & take away with the other. You are very much better than you were two years ago—& have cataract. I was yesterday assured by my doctor that there was nothing wrong about me, and that my heart might sweep me off at any moment. Let us disregard these crows, & look forward to meeting in July. By then you will have discovered the charm of kangaroos and wattle. A call to Gräfin Antonia von Trauttmansdorff (9923 222) will tell you if I am here to have my hand held or among the glorious dead.

To William Maxwell 17:ii:1978

I wish you could come in, and make a fuss of me. It is one of the ironies of old age—that one longs to be made a fuss of, when [one] has built up a reputation that one doesn't care for fuss. I am grown very old, dear William. I hobble on two baddish legs, and cling to anything within reach. And I have grown so small, I scarcely know myself. And so slow. But really I should congratulate myself that my wits are still about me. When my mother was my age, she was senile. And I am not that, and I can still see to read, & hear to talk; and if the weather were not so biting & blighting I might not feel so like a dead leaf . . . de ça, de là, comme le vent n'emporte.

To Trekkie Parsons 24:ii:1978

. . . now that it is all over I begin to realize how *terrifying* it was. The worst was the wind. It *yelled* like a catfight, and never left off blowing the snow horizontally across the landscape. Drifts everywhere; and hard-packed snow, like a thick layer of mutton-fat. 5 or 6 inches, where it wasn't 5 or 6 feet in drifts. It was ugly, because the sun never came out. Yesterday it began to thaw. There are dead ewes, dead calves, emerging from the drifts. I suppose they will be collected & burned; for the ground is hard as iron, beneath a thin skin of slush.

And what did I do? Stayed in bed for warmth as long as I could, and read Byron. He is a good companion for such times; and listened for that maniac wind to begin again, but so far it hasn't. The people here were so intimidated that they have become devoutly superstitious, & believe that tomorrow all this will begin again.

To Joy Chute 28:ii:1978

. . . My, Joy, what has been going on since I last wrote to you. Not a patch on Boston,[1] of course. There was a picture in *The Times* of a Bostonian in a pitchblack sky staggering for his balance & not finding it, that we all looked at at [sic] reverence. We were still thinking of the sorrows of Boston when our own wind rose, and rose, & ROSE! And for two days it blew incessantly & yelled inflexibly and froze more and more. And on the 3rd morning I noticed it was blowing, & looked out and saw why. The garden, the fields beyond, the hills beyond the field were all made of snow in the most extraordinary shapes—shapes the wind had blown them & frozen them into, so that nothing looked like itself. And there was Mrs Cleall's son, snow up to the waist, helping his mamma over the fence on her way to dig me out. The lane was solid snow drift, so they had walked here on top of a hedge.

It was far too cold to break or flaw. It changed from time to time for the wind roused up again, & blew the snow across the landscape making deeper drifts, smoother & more perilous slopes. When it blew the snow it blew it in straight horizontal bars across the landscape. Trains couldn't run. Dorchester, Bridport, Weymouth, Yeovil were isolated. There was no post, no food vans, no milk-collection.

One morning the sky was full of sea-gulls, hunting for something to eat—and not finding it. Their Chesil Beach, with salt water on either side of it, was covered with ice. On the fifth morning there was a faint thaw.

1. Where the snow was eight feet deep on the sidewalks.

304

Antonia was in the kitchen, cooking lunch. On Saturday the first mail got to the village, and on Sunday I fell asleep, listening to the tale of our sufferings, & how well we had behaved on the wireless.

There are still snowdrifts under the hedges, & lying in the garden. But I walked out this evening, and heard chaffinches clinking their spring songs and at last felt that we had won through. The look is at last more green than white.

While it lasted as a mysterious emergency, it was tonic. But now everyone is dead tired, and never wants to be heroic again . . . Antonia has been a marvel—She was alone—Robin was in sunny Bahia. She had one thing after another to see to; carrying round the milk, getting bales of hay to sheep, pouring hot sweet drinks into children, walking over (6 miles on frozen slush) to nourish me.

Goodnight, my darlings. I must go to bed. I am at least 10 years older than I was before this. Love, love.

To William Maxwell *5:iii:1978*

. . . it is warm, even when I am not expecting William with bronchitis,[1] even when other houses are cold. I have 3 storage heaters, electric fires full on, a coal-burning kitchen stove: people come in from the cold world and exclaim how hot it is. Central heating by oil could not make it warmer; & I am afraid of oil.

. . . But I expect you and Emmi in May. I wish I could be sure of expecting you here, but at the moment I am not fit to be a hostess, I crawl about the house, inclining to fall over, and even when firm on my feet, I crawl. I may be a better creature in May—with a hot April I could almost be sure of it.

I have talked it over with Antonia, & she hopes you will spend a night at Baglake,[2] which is a memorably tall, plain, mid-Georgian stone house, and she would drive you over here. But here in Maiden Newton, two steps from here, is Rainbow Villa, a memorably plain-headed contemporary 'guest-house', which has comfortable beds & good breakfasts, & you have never been in a finer example of British bourgeoisie. You could come on here, sit in the garden, read in the house, visit Toller Fratrem (unchanged) be given lunch & supper by me.

1. I had contracted bronchitis in Egypt and when we arrived at her house in the early spring of 1976, her study and one bedroom had been warmed for me. The temperature of the rest of the house was the same as outdoors, and the front door stood wide open.
2. A farm on the outskirts of Litton Cheney, where she was living at the time.

And for the remainder of your visit, it occurs to me that you have never been to the part of Scotland you were fetched from: I suppose Maxwells have been there for much longer than they have been away from it. Familiar Great-aunts & slightly removed Cousins would survey you as you approached your Castle of the larks—wasn't it called Caerlaverock Castle?

... Today I have sat in the sun without an attempt of bravery. It *shone*, & crocuses came into bloom all round, exploded into bloom.

I am sorry about Emmi's nonagenarian father. I hope this will not interrupt all our plans.

But meet we will.

To Ian Parsons *30:iii:1978*

Darling Ian,

I doubt if I shall send any more letters marked 'do not destroy'.[1] What a comfort it is to think you are at the office looking after the business that was begun so long ago by dear Charles; and have never wavered from following him.

[*P.S. in her handwriting*] I have asked Soo Pinney, who typed this, to look after my unpublished writings, etc.

To Norah Smallwood [early] April [*1978*]

Darling Norah,

Thank you very much for your copy of *Contre Sainte-Beuve*. I have just been reading it to myself with great admiration.

If Proust were not now under a cloud, I would say, reprint it it. [sic] But bear in in [sic] mind for USA.

Lovely to hear you. Lovely that you animate Ch. & W.

My love
Sylvia

Is there still a copy of my *Opus 7*—poem, you published, about 1931 ... These racks of time!

1. Meaning by him, before they went into the office file.

Index

Index of recipients (in Roman type)
and a partial index of persons referred to (in italics).

Aanestad, Elling, 237, 240, 244
Ackland, Ruth, *63 et passim*
Ackland, Valentine, *19 et passim*
Albaret, Celeste, *207*
Albert of Saxe-Coburg-Gotha, *27*
Aragon, Luis, *89*
Ardizzone, Edward, *234*
Ashcroft, Peggy, *273*
Austen, Jane, *295*

Bacon, Leonard, 135, 138, 143, *146*
Baldwin, Stanley, *43*
Ballinger, Martha Bacon, 195, 198,
   206, 207, 227, 249, 253, 261, 265,
   267
Balzac, Honoré de, *91, 162, 186*
Beauvoir, Simone de, *207*
Bell, Anne Olivier, *282*
Bell, Quentin, *265, 282*
Bevin, Ernest, *106*
Boswell, James, *144*
Bourbon, Marie Amélie de, Note on
   Summer Will Show, 39
Brenan, Gamel, *20*
Brenan, Gerald, *20*
Brewer, Franklin, *56, 101, 159, 190,
   191*
Bridges, Robert, *289*
Britten, Benjamin (Lord Britten of
   Aldeburgh), *150, 265, 302*
Brontë, Anne, *35*

Brooke, Rupert, *136*
Butler, Victor, *9, 11*
Byrd, William, *188, 269*
Byron, Lord, *205, 274, 304*

Cameron, Julia, *285*
Carlyle, Jane Welsh, *179, 217*
Carlyle, Thomas, *179, 249*
Castle, Barbara, *286*
Cecil, Lord David, *13, 139*
Chamberlain, Neville, *55, 278*
Charles II, *194, 252*
Chateaubriand, Francois René de,
   187, 231
Chaucer, Geoffrey, *110*
Chute, Joy, 207, 210, 214, 215, 216,
   232, 233, 235, 241, 244, 247, 248,
   252, 253, 256, 265, 266, 268, 269,
   271, 273, 280, 281, 285, 288, 291,
   295, 297, 299, 303, 304
Chute, Marchette, 109, 120, 121,
   123, 137, 139, 143, 170, 171, 175,
   201, 207, 210, 214, 216, 232, 233,
   235, 241, 244, 247, 253, 256, 265,
   266, 268, 271, 273, 277, 288, 291,
   295
Clare, John, *78*
Clark, Steven, 44, 49, 51, 58, 98, 104,
   114, *141*
Clough, Arthur Hugh, *201*
Cockerell, Sir Sidney, *222*

Coleridge, S. T., *180, 229*
Colette, *302*
Constable, John, *238*
Cooper, Anthony Ashley, *274*
Cowper, William, *21, 78, 138*
Craske, Peter, *21, 247*
Cunard, Nancy, 83, 85, 86, 89, 90,
    92, 98, 102, 106, 108, 117, 119,
    126, 131, 183, *198, 239*
Curtiss, Mina, *124, 287* note

Dante, *25*
Deffand, Mme du, *114*
Degas, Edgar, *287*
de Gaulle, Charles, *106*
Diamond, David, *211n*
Dickinson, Emily, *141*
Dolin, Anton, *94*
Donne, John, 6, *149*

Eckermann, Johann Peter, *7, 183*
Edgeworth, Maria, *12*
Eiloart, Nora, *45, 98, 99, 102, 104,*
    118, 180, 192, 207, 216, 227,
    251
Eiloart, Ronald, *3, 192, 216, 251*
Eisenhower, Dwight, *137*
Eliot, T. S., *176*

Finzi, Joy (Mrs. Gerald), *167,* 177,
    234, 238, 239, 249, 253, 254, 259,
    286
Fitzgerald, Edward, *261*
Ford, Ford Madox, *264*
Forman, Simon, *274*
Fry, Roger, *73*

Gallant, Mavis, 289
Garnett, David, 2, 3, 4, 5, 6, 7, 8, 11,
    14, 20, *93, 226, 240, 247, 249,*

258, 259, 263, 264, 267, 269, 271,
    281, 287, 290, 295, 296, 298, 303
Garnett, Nerissa, *283*
Garnett, Ray, *7, 8, 15*
Garnett, Richard, 20, *283, 299*
Gaskell, Elizabeth, *130, 144*
Genlis, Mme de, *186*
George VI, *43, 132*
Gide, André, *90*
Gilbert, Morris, 85
Gill, Brendan, *199, 242*
Gladstone, W. E., *201*
Glasgow, Ellen, *21*
Gluck, Christoph, *31*
Goethe, *7, 180, 183, 189*
Goncourt, Edmond and Jules de,
    142, 171
Grant, Duncan, Note on *Mr
    Fortune's Maggot*, 10
Gregory, Alyse (Mrs L. Powys), 25,
    27, 56, 81, 82, 85, 94, 96, 99, 114,
    116, 122, 130, 140, 146, 151, 153,
    154, 158, 159, 164, 208, 212, 216,
    225
Grignon, Mme de, *144*

Hale, Nancy, *251*
Halévy, Daniel, *287*
Hardy, Thomas, *34, 148, 222*
Hare, Augustus, *177*
Hawthorne, Nathaniel, *252*
Heath, Edward, *286*
Hellman, Ben, 274, 282, 286
Herrick, Robert, *170*
Hogarth, William, *192*
Holroyd, Michael, *237, 247, 265*
Hoskins, Dorothy, 150
Hoskins, Dorothy (?), 145
House, Colin, *282, 297*
Howard, Michael, 211, 220

Howe, Bea, 1, _11_, _12_, 74, 217, _272_, 275, 280, 282

Hudleston, Dorothie Purefoy (Mrs Arthur Machen), _181_

Hudleston, Father John, _194_

Hudleston, Josiah, _282_

Huebsch, Ben, 12, 71, 80, 87, 92, 115, 159, 214

Hughes, Dom Anselm, _262_

Ionesco, Eugène, _163_

Kemble, Fanny, _261_

Knopf, Alfred, _12_

Larson, Jean, _269_, 299

Lipton, Julius, 35, 36, 38, 40

Lipton, Queenie (Mrs Julius), _35_, 38, _41_

Lobrano, G. S., _117_

Louis Philippe, Note on _Summer Will Show_, 40

Lowell, Amy, _144_

Machaut, Guillaume de, _298 and note_

Machen, Arthur, 20, _48_, _64_

Machen, Hilary, _87_, 260 and note, 262, 269

Machen, Janet, 59, 188, 220, 232, 242, 243, _255_

Macpherson, Aimée Semple, _14_

Manisty, Margaret, _233_, 241, 243, 300

Mante-Proust, Mme, _151_

Markova, Alicia, _94_

Martello, Aldo, _107_, _115_

Mathilde, Princesse, _162_

Maxwell, Emily (Mrs William), 278, 287

Maxwell, Kate, _163_, 256

Maxwell, William, 55, 96, _104_, 117, 123, 127, 130, 131, 132, 133, 136, 137, 140, 141, 142, 145, 148, 156, 157, 161, 162, 163, 166, 171, 173, 174, 177, 178, 186, 189, 194, 195, 196, 199, 200, 201, 203, 204, 205, 206, 208, 209, 210, 211, 212, 213, 214, 216, 217, 218, 219, 221, 222, 223, 224, 225, 226, 228, 229, 234, 235, 237, 238, 242, 243, 244, 246, 250, 251, 254, 255, _256_, 257, 260, _261_, _263_, _264_, _265_, _266_, _270_, _271_, 277, 281, 283, 288, 290, 293, 294, 295, 297, 300, 302, 303, 305

Mayne, Ethel Colborn, _144_

Mayor, Andreas, _182_, _183_, _187_

Melbourne, Lady, _275_

Menaker, Daniel, _289_

Milton, John, _120_

Mitchison, Naomi, 46

Mitford, Nancy, _164_

Moir, Flora, 263

Moir, George, _179_

Neville, Henry, _22_

Newman, John Henry, _200_

Nordoff, Paul, 44, 48, 53, 54, 56, 60, 61, 62, 63, 64, 66, 67, 70, 71, 72, 73, 75, 78, 87, 91, 92, 94, 97, 101, 102, 103, 111, 113, 116, 120, 125, 127, 129, 146, 149, 150, 159, 167, 175, 191, 218, _255_, _257_, 279, _293_

Nordoff, Sabina, _105_, _113_

Norton, Charles Eliot, _130_

Owen, Harold, _208_

Painter, George D., 162, _179_, 186, 230

Park, Mungo, _217_

Parrish, Anne, *168*, *217*
Parsons, Ian, *45*, 98, 107, 124, 156, 169, 186, 187, 271, 272, 273, *281*, 306
Parsons, Trekkie, *281*, 290, 299, 304
Pears, Sir Peter, *253*, 265, *293*, *295*
Peers, Roger, *280*
Peyrefitte, Roger, *96*
Pinney, Susanna, *279*, 285, *306*
Plank, George, 168, 170, 172, 174, 177, 179, 180, 182, 183, 184, 185, 189, 190, 191, 192, 193, 194, 198, 200, 202, 203, *217*
Potts, L. J., *213*
Powys, Gertrude, *131*
Powys, Llewelyn, 19, 25, 27, 28, 29, 30, 31, 33, *56*, *85*
Powys, Philippa, *24*
Powys, T. F., *3*, *4*, *6*, *12*, *13*, *142*, *145*, 225
Powys, Violet, *24*
Prentice, Charles, 3, *5*, *6*, *17*, 18, 20, 30, *32*, *115*, 271
Proust, Marcel, *115*, 124, *151*, *154*, *156*, *160*, *161*, *181*, *183*, *186*, *187*, 207, 230, 288, *306*
Prude, Walter, *109*
Pusey, Edward Bouverie, *201*

Rattenbury, Arnold, 239
Raymond, Harold, *14*, 16, 17, 19, 23, 29, 81, 84, 142
Raymond, Vera, *14*
Rembrandt, *172*
Remizov, Aleksey Michailovich, *14*
Rickword, Edgell, 50
Rimbaud, Arthur, *99*
Ritchie, Anne Thackeray, *293*
Robbins, Clive, *255*, 257
Ross, Harold, *104*, *215*
Rossini, Gioacchino Antonio, *71*

Rowse, A. L., *274*, *275*
Rousseau, Douanier, *21*

Saint-Simon, Duc de, *60*, *164*
Sand, George, *256*, *293*
Schubert, Franz, *146*, *302*
Schumann, Clara, *168*
Scott Moncrieff, C. K., *186*
Scott Moncrieff, George and Joanna, *186*, *187*
Shakespeare, *170*, 277
Shawn, William, *203*, 289
Shelley, Mary, *111*
Shelley, Percy Bysshe, *111*, *113*, *130*, *180*, 211, 288
Simpson, Wallis Warfield, *43*
Sitwell, Edith, *143*
Smallwood, Norah, *168*, *179*, 181, 183, *184*, *186*, 187, 209, 270, 306
Smith, Dr Charles, *240*
Sophocles, *290*
Spencer Smith, Lady, *153*
Spender, Stephen, *49*
Starkie, Enid, *99*, *239*
Stendhal, *295*
Stephen, Sir Leslie, *293*
Stevenson, Adlai, *137*
Stevenson, Robert Louis, *300*
Stone, Janet, 165, *166*, *170*, *172*, 255
Stone, Phillida, *163*
Stone, Reynolds, *166*, *170*, *172*, *185*, *247*, 255
Strachey, Lytton, *265*
Sykes, Christopher, *259*

Thatcher, Margaret, *286*
Thomas, Edward, *70*, *204*
Thomas, Helen, 204, *207*, 208, 213
Thoreau, Henry David, *148*
Tomlin, Garrow, 27
Townsend Warner, George, *251*, *288*

Trauttmansdorff, Gräfin Antonia von und zu, *280*, *285*, *290*, *295*, *300*, *302*, *303*, *305*
Trelawney, Edward, *111*
Truman, Harry, 101, *137*

Untermeyer, Jean Starr, 31, *35* note, *198*

Vaughan Williams, Ralph, *167*, *275*
Vaughan Williams, Ursula, 167, 244, *275*
Verlaine, Paul, *99*
Verney, Sir John, *226*
Verney, Juliet, *268*
Victoria, Queen, *27*, *248*

Wagner, Richard, *112*
Wang, Shelley, *50*

Warburg, Frederic, *32*
Warburg, Mrs Frederic, *32*
Warner, Elizabeth, 78
Warner, Oliver, 23, 28, 29, 32, 34, 35, 39, 42, 45, 46, 51, 53, 55, 77, *193*
Webster, John, *6*
West, Rebecca, *258*
White, Elizabeth Wade, 41
White, T. H., *211*, *215*, *221*, *226*, *222*, *230*
Wilson, Edmund, *104*
Woodforde, Parson, *140*
Woolf, Leonard, *169*, 172, 212, *300*
Woolf, Virginia, *7*, *73*, *186*
Wordsworth, Dorothy, *300*
Wordsworth, Mary, *171*
Wordsworth, William, *175*, *300*
Wylie, Elinor, *211*